NEW FACES IN NEW PLACES

NEW FACES IN NEW PLACES

THE CHANGING GEOGRAPHY
OF AMERICAN IMMIGRATION

DOUGLAS S. MASSEY
EDITOR

RUSSELL SAGE FOUNDATION • NEW YORK

The Russell Sage Foundation

The Russell Sage Foundation, one of the oldest of America's general purpose founda-
tions, was established in 1907 by Mrs. Margaret Olivia Sage for "the improvement of
social and living conditions in the United States." The Foundation seeks to fulfill this
mandate by fostering the development and dissemination of knowledge about the country's political, social, and economic problems. While the Foundation endeavors to
assure the accuracy and objectivity of each book it publishes, the conclusions and interpretations in Russell Sage Foundation publications are those of the authors and not of
the Foundation, its Trustees, or its staff. Publication by Russell Sage, therefore, does
not imply Foundation endorsement

Library of Congress Cataloging-in-Publication Data

New faces in new places : the changing geography of American immigration / Douglas S.
Massey, editor.
    p. cm.
    ISBN 978-0-87154-586-2 (cloth) ISBN 978-0-87154-568-8 (paper)
    1. United States—Emigration and immigration. 2. Small cities—United States. I. Massey,
Douglas S.
    JV6465.N484 2008
    304.8′73—dc22

                                                                            2007031271

The paper used in this publication meets the minimum requirements of American National
Standard for Information Sciences—Permanence of Paper for Printed Library Materials.
ANSI Z39.48-1992.

Text design by Suzanne Nichols.

RUSSELL SAGE FOUNDATION
112 East 64th Street, New York, New York 10021
10 9 8 7 6 5 4 3 2

TABLE OF CONTENTS

About the Authors

◇

Douglas S. Massey is Henry G. Bryant Professor of Sociology and Public Affairs at the Woodrow Wilson School and president of the American Academy of Political and Social Science.

Carl L. Bankston, III is professor and chair in sociology and co-director of the Asian Studies Program at Tulane University and president of the Mid-South Sociological Association.

Frank D. Bean is Chancellor's Professor of Sociology and Economics and director of the Center for Research on Immigration, Population, and Public Policy at the University of California, Irvine.

Chiara Capoferro is the manager emeritus of the Mexican Migration Project and lives in London, where she continues to serve as a consultant to the project.

Katharine M. Donato is professor of sociology at Vanderbilt University, and fellow at the Vanderbilt Centers for the Americas and for Nashville Studies.

Katherine Fennelly is professor of public affairs at the Hubert H. Humphrey Institute, University of Minnesota, and the 2006–2007 Fesler-Lampert Chair in Urban and Regional Affairs.

David Griffith is professor of anthropology at East Carolina University and author of the recent book, *American Guestworkers: Jamaicans and Mexicans in the U.S. Labor Market.*

Charles Hirschman is Boeing International Professor of Sociology and Public Affairs at the University of Washington.

Michael Jones-Correa is professor of government and director of American Studies at Cornell University

WILLIAM KANDEL is a sociologist in the Resource and Rural Economics Division of the U.S. Department of Agriculture's Economic Research Service.

YUKIO KAWANO is associate professor in the department of economics at Daito University in Tokyo.

MARK A. LEACH is assistant professor of sociology at Southern Illinois University, Carbondale.

HELEN B. MARROW is lecturer in the Committee on Degrees in Social Studies at Harvard University.

ALFRED NUCCI is a consultant on research projects using U.S. Census Bureau household and business micro-data, and is a former researcher at the U.S. Census Bureau's Center for Economic Studies.

EMILIO A. PARRADO is associate professor of sociology at Duke University.

DEBRA LATTANZI SHUTIKA is associate professor of English and cultural studies at George Mason University, and directs the Mason Project on Immigration.

CHARLES TOLBERT is professor and chair of the Department of Sociology at Baylor University and holds Special Sworn Status at the Center for Economic Studies, U.S. Census Bureau.

JAMIE WINDERS is assistant professor of geography in the Maxwell School of Citizenship and Public Affairs at Syracuse University.

*Dedicado a la memoria de los migrantes
muertos en la frontera
por el sueño de mejorar sus vidas*

*Dedicated to the memory of the migrants
killed on the border
for the dream of improving their lives*

CHAPTER 1

PLACES AND PEOPLES:
THE NEW AMERICAN MOSAIC

CHARLES HIRSCHMAN AND DOUGLAS S. MASSEY

The magnitude and character of recent immigration to the United States, popularly known as the post-1965 wave of immigration, continue to surprise policymakers and many experts. The first surprise was that it happened at all. The 1965 amendments to the Immigration and Nationality Act, also known as the Hart-Celler Law, were a product of the civil rights era of the 1960s. Ending the infamous national-origin quotas enacted in the 1920s—the central objective of the 1965 amendments—was a high priority for members of Congress, many of whom were the children and grandchildren of Southern and Eastern European immigrants who had been excluded early in the twentieth century. The expectation was that there would be a small blip in arrivals from Italy, Greece, and a few other European countries as families divided by the immigration restrictions of the 1920s were allowed to be reunited, but that no long-term increase would result (Reimers 1998, chapter 3).

This expectation was not borne out, however. Almost 5 million immigrants came to the United States during the 1970s—the highest level of immigration, in both absolute and relative terms, since the early decades of the twentieth century (U.S. Department of Homeland Security 2003, 11). The 1970s were only the tip of the iceberg, however. The number of immigrants who arrived in the 1980s exceeded that of the 1970s, and both numbers were surpassed by arrivals in the 1990s. Not only were the numbers far higher than anyone expected, but the new immigrants came not so much from Europe but mainly from Latin America and Asia—regions that were not on the national agenda as sources for a major wave of immigration.

1

The new criteria for admission under the 1965 act were family reunification and scarce occupational skills (Keely 1979). The new preference system allowed highly skilled professionals—primarily doctors, nurses, and engineers from Asian countries—to immigrate and eventually to sponsor the entry of their family members. About the same time, and largely independent of the 1965 Immigration Act, immigration from Latin America began to rise. Legal and undocumented migration from Mexico surged after a temporary-farm-worker program known as the Bracero Program was shut down in 1964 (Massey, Durand, and Malone 2002). Migration from Cuba arose from the tumult of Fidel Castro's revolution, as first elites and then professional, middle-class, and, finally, working class families fled persecution and the imposition of socialism in the 1960s and 1970s. During the 1980s, the Cubans were joined by refugees from Central American nations such as Nicaragua, El Salvador, and Guatemala (Lundquist and Massey 2005); and the collapse of the United States-backed government in South Vietnam after 1975 sent successive waves into the United States from Indochina (Massey 1995).

In recent years, the "immigration problem," as it has been widely labeled, has been the subject of repeated national commissions, investigative reports, and congressional legislation (Smith and Edmonston 1997, chapter 2). Although the apparent goal of American policy has been to cap or reduce immigration, the opposite has occurred. By 2000, there were over 30 million foreign-born persons in the United States, almost one third of whom arrived in the prior decade. Adding together these immigrants and their children (the second generation), more than 60 million people—or one in five Americans—have recent roots in other countries (U.S. Census Bureau 2005).[1]

In the middle decades of the twentieth century, the era of mass immigration was a distant memory for most Americans, but by the end of the century, immigration had become a major population trend shaping American society. Immigrants and the children of immigrants are a visible presence in American educational institutions, from kindergartens to graduate schools. Many businesses, including food processing, taxi driving, custodial services, construction, and, of course, agriculture and domestic service, are dependent on immigrant labor. All political parties are wooing Hispanic and Asian voters, many of whom are newly naturalized immigrants. Immigration is very likely to be a continuing influence on the size, shape, and composition of the American population for the foreseeable future.

The latest surprise has been the shift in the geography of the new immigration (Singer 2004). One of the standard findings of research on the post-1965 immigration wave during the 1970s and 1980s was its concentration in the states of New York, California, Texas, Florida, and Illinois, generally within a handful of "gateway" metropolitan areas such as New York, Los Angeles, Houston, Miami, and Chicago (Portes and Rumbaut 1996, chapter 2). Although different nationalities may have been concentrated in different areas (Puerto Ricans in New York, Cubans in Miami, Mexicans in Los Angeles, etc.) there was a common pattern and interpretation. Once immigrant pioneers had established a beachhead with ethnic neighborhoods and economic niches in certain industries, later immigrants flowed to the same places (Waldinger 1996; Waldinger and Lichter 2003). Migrants were drawn to immigrant-ethnic communities that could offer assistance to newcomers seeking housing, jobs, and the warmth of familiarity (Massey 1985).

The majority of new immigrants still settle in the traditional gateway cities; but as Douglas Massey and Chiara Capoferro show in chapter 2 of this volume, California and New York became much less dominant in the 1990s and during the early years of the new century than they were during the 1970s and 1980s. Immigrants now settle in small towns as well as large cities and in the interior as well as on the coasts. Immigrants have discovered the Middle West (see chapters 7 and 8 of this volume, by Katherine Fennelly and David Griffith, respectively) and the South (see chapter 6, by Katherine Donato and Carl L. Bankston III; chapter 9, by Helen B. Morrow; and chapter 10, by Jamie Winders) as well as traditional gateways in the East and West (see chapter 11, by Debra Lattanzi Shutika, and chapter 12, by Michael Jones-Correa). Given the virtual absence of immigrants in many regions of the United States up to 1990, even a small shift away from traditional gateways implied huge relative increases at new destinations. The absolute numbers of new immigrants arriving in Georgia, North Carolina, and Nevada may number only in the hundreds of thousands, but in relative terms the growth of immigrant communities in these areas is frequently off the charts.

The increasing diversity of immigrant settlements is inextricably bound up with the growing volume of immigration. Even if there had been no proportional shift in destination patterns, there would have been sizable increases in the absolute numbers of immigrants going to new destinations. The doubling of immigration from the 1970s to the 1990s remains a fundamental reason why the presence of immigrants is evident in so many places with little history of recent immigration. However, the growing volume of immigration has also had additional indirect effects on the destination choices of new and secondary migrants, as immigrant niches in gateway cities become saturated, making labor-market opportunities in other areas seem more attractive (Light 2006).

This volume offers new analyses and interpretations of the growth and settlement of immigrants in new destination areas. Drawing upon the empirical analyses assembled here, we can begin to see why immigration has become a national phenomenon and why immigrants are increasingly drawn to small and medium size towns throughout the United States. The studies reported here also offer tentative conclusions about the economic, social, political, and cultural responses to immigrant communities in new destinations. With their distinctive languages, appearances, and cultures, the new immigrants, along with their American-born children, at times encounter indifference and even hostility on occasion, but the dominant response still appears to be incorporation within the larger American "nation of immigrants."

IMMIGRATION IN AN AGE OF INDUSTRIAL RESTRUCTURING

At the individual level, potential migrants are affected by incentives and information. Potential migrants are pushed by hard times, a lack of jobs, or by a shortage of "good jobs" that provide desired social and economic rewards. Just as potential migrants differ in their skills and needs, what constitutes a sufficient push will vary between communities and between individuals in the same community. Landless and small-scale farmers may be pushed off their lands as commercial markets replace traditional norms of tenancy. At the other end of the spectrum, college graduates may take flight if they see only dead-end careers with few rewards and opportunities in the local labor market. People of all classes may depart in the absence of viable markets for capital and credit, seeking to self-finance home acquisition with earnings from international migration.

Economic pulls attract migrants in ways that complement the variety of push factors. The promise of wages, even at the lowest levels of compensation, may be very attractive for poor foreign workers with few choices locally. In professional and high-tech circles, scholarships, prestige, and opportunities for challenging careers lure workers to relocate internationally. Sometimes, however, the mere existence of labor demand is not enough, and migratory processes must be jump-started through deliberate recruitment, as during the Bracero Program from 1942 to 1964 and with the various visa programs for temporary workers today.

People can only respond to the various pushes and pulls if they are aware of them, of course; and individuals are not wholly independent actors, but are constrained by information about opportunities in distant locations. Social ties embedded within migrant networks can provide this information and lower the costs of migration. Brave and resourceful pioneers may be willing to migrate in the face of limited knowledge and to bear the costs of the journey and settlement on their own, but pioneers are, by definition, a rare species. Most migrants follow in the footsteps of friends and family members who have already made the journey and can offer advice, encouragement, and funds to subsidize the costs of transportation and settlement. Migration streams from a specific place of origin to a specific place of destination reflect the inherent tendency of earlier migrants to assist their relatives and neighbors with temporary housing and the search for employment. The hypothesis of "cumulative causation" posits that social networks of friends and family broaden the base of migration so much that other factors—those that originally caused the migration—become less important over time (see Massey et al. 1993, 448–50).

The enumeration of micro-level pushes and pulls and the measurement of their effects together constitute only the first step in explaining why people move from place to place. A larger task is to account for the structural conditions that give rise to microeconomic incentives in places of origin and destination. In general, neither absolute poverty nor the poorest places are associated with high levels of migration (Portes and Rumbaut 1996, 272). Most peasants and laborers, however poor and destitute they may appear to denizens of developed nations, have a place in traditional societies that provides them with subsistence and reciprocal ties of obligation to friends and family within their social class. Catastrophic natural disasters, wars and civil violence, political crises, and other social transformations are among the "shocks" that upset traditional societies and provide the impetus to migrate.

In modern times, however, "economic development" has generally been most forceful in promoting long-distance migration, embracing such diverse processes as the commercialization of agriculture, the development of wage labor markets, the creation of modern consumer tastes, and the loss of traditional forms of social insurance. Once migration develops for these structural reasons, the self-reinforcing nature of social networks and cumulative causation take hold and flows increase and broaden to include other groups far removed from the initial pioneers (Massey and Zenteno 1999).

Immigrants, of course, are drawn by the same economic and social currents that affect domestic migrants, though there are critical differences. Most important, international migrants are constrained by political factors, including state policies designed to minimize, control, and regulate flows across borders (Massey 1999). These regulations inevitably raise the costs of migration in financial terms and in other ways that affect liberties and even life itself (Eschbach et al. 1999). For those who qualify for legal entry, immigration typically requires the payment of fees, long waits in bureaucratic queues, repeated visits to consulates or embassies, and innumerable indignities and delays before final approval (Jasso and Rosenzweig 1990; see also chapter 2, this volume). For others with fewer resources or family connections in the United States, illicit or undocumented migration may be the only means of entry, but clandestine migration comes with additional risks of apprehension, criminal prosecution, imprisonment, and even death during the crossing of treacherous borders (see Singer and Massey 1998).

In contrast to the relatively well developed body of theory and research on the forces that promote international migration, less theoretical attention has been paid to those influencing the selection of destinations within the United States. In part, this gap occurs because the reasons seem almost too obvious to many observers. Although there is some variation by nationality, the majority of immigrants have traditionally settled in a handful of large metropolitan cities on the West and East coasts characterized by expanding wealth, dynamic labor markets, and already well-established immigrant communities (Portes and Rumbaut 1996, chapter 2). Even when the federal authorities have established programs of spatial dispersion, as was the case with Cuban and Vietnamese refugees, secondary migration revealed a seemingly iron law of spatial concentration. New immigrants tend to settle in the largest cities where earlier immigrants of the same national origins have previously settled. In addition to the social and economic support provided by earlier arrivals, large global cities also generate a high demand for informal-sector service jobs that attracted new international migrants (Sassen 1991).

The chapters in the first part of this volume offer glimpses into the emerging pattern of settlement in new destinations for immigrants to the United States. The big five destination states (New York, California, Illinois, Texas, and Florida) were still attracting most immigrants in the late 1990s, but the proportion of Mexican immigrants going to them has dropped to 60 percent, and less than half of other immigrant streams are now settling in traditional destinations (see chapter 2, this volume). The shift in the geography of immigration has been especially dramatic for Mexicans, who from 1965 to 1990 focused overwhelmingly on destinations in California, and to a lesser extent Chicago and selected cities in Texas. Because of the dramatic escalation of border enforcement efforts in El Paso and San Diego, historically the two busiest border crossings, long-established flows were deflected to new crossing points and new destination regions (Orrenius 2004; Massey, Durand, and Malone 2002).

Because the volume of immigration has increased dramatically, these shifts do not necessarily imply a lessening of the absolute numbers of immigrants going to traditional destination cities and states. For example, the number of recent immigrants who arrived over the prior decade in metropolitan areas jumped from 8.3 million in 1990 to 12.4 million in 2000 (see chapter 4, this volume, by Katharine Donato, Charles Tolbert, Alfred Nucci, and Yukio Kawano). This shift represents a dramatic increase, to be sure, but since it builds on past trends, it is not wholly unexpected and the largest metropolitan areas are long accustomed to the arrival of foreigners. In new destination areas, however, the sudden upturn of immigration is front-page news.

Although smaller in absolute terms than in established areas, the growing number of foreigners is a new phenomenon—at least in the memories of those alive today. Immigrant laborers are creating ethnic niches in local labor markets and schools and churches are struggling to adapt to an upsurge in Spanish-speaking newcomers, as day-laborer sites have created a political storm in some areas. Which immigrants are going to these new destination areas and why? The classical theories of cumulative causation and global cities predict continuity, not change, in the traditional patterns of immigrant settlements; the border enforcement trends highlighted by Massey and Capoferro (see chapter 2) account for some of the changes, but they don't explain everything.

Through a variety of empirical approaches, the chapters in this volume suggest several potential explanations. Mark Leach and Frank Bean (chapter 3) find that immigrants to new destinations are generally heterogeneous in terms of individual traits and characteristics, but the places they go have basic economic facts in common: they tend to be places with well-developed and growing low-skill service sectors, thus pointing toward industrial restructuring as a driving force behind geographic diversification. They also show, once again, that once a new destination has attracted a critical mass of new immigrants, others are relatively more likely to follow them. Thus, industrial restructuring creates an initial demand for immigrants in new locations and then processes of cumulative causation take over to channel subsequent cohorts of migrants to these new destinations.

Likewise, in their study of immigrants to new destinations in 1990 and 2000, Donato, Tolbert, Nucci, and Kawano (chapter 4) find that the characteristics of immigrants to nonmetropolitan destinations in the South and Midwest were quite different from those going to traditional areas of destination. Especially within counties where the native white population was declining, the new immigrants tended to be younger, more poorly educated, more recently arrived, and more Mexican; Donato and colleagues also find, like Leach and Bean, that the new immigrants were moving in response to growth in particular low-wage industries.

Thus immigrants appear to be overrepresented in secondary-labor-market jobs that are typically shunned by native-born workers. The presence and expansion of poorly paid jobs that are difficult, dirty, and sometimes dangerous in small towns and rural areas is a common thread in many "new destination" areas. Leach and Bean report that Mexican migrants to new destinations are likely to be employed in construction and services whereas Donato and colleagues find that new immigrants to nonmetropolitan areas are increasingly employed in manufacturing. Where the proportion of immigrants employed in manufacturing declined in metropolitan areas from 1990 to 2000, in nonmetropolitan areas it significantly increased. The native-born, meanwhile, were less likely to work in manufacturing in 2000 than in 1990, regardless of location.

These patterns are most salient in what Donato and colleagues call "offset counties"—those in which immigrant growth offsets a population decline among natives. In these areas, immigrants in general and Mexican immigrants in particular were overrepresented in meatpacking, leather processing, and carpet and rug manufacture. Although these industries were present in 1990, they expanded over the ensuing decade and immigrants appear to have played a major role in their growth in the face of stiff global competition.

It thus appears that the increasing geographic diversity of immigration to the United States is related to broader structural changes in the American economy and to the decreasing attractiveness of certain jobs to native-born workers. This volume offers two detailed studies of industrial restructuring to buttress this interpretation. Emilio Parrado and William Kandel, in chapter 5, analyze the changing structure of the meatpacking and construction industries and Donato and Bankston in chapter 6 study changes in southern Louisiana firms that provide services to oil extraction and refining industries along the Gulf Coast.

"Industrial restructuring" is a generic term used by these authors to describe shifts in the American economy away from large-scale capital-intensive production and a relatively well-paid, unionized, and mostly native workforce toward labor-intensive production and low-paid, non-unionized, foreign workforces. International competition and technological innovation have cut the profit margins of older companies that held virtual monopolies on the manufacture, distribution, and marketing of goods within many industrial sectors. Some American manufacturers were unable to compete with cheaper imports and they shifted production to plants overseas in low-wage countries; but in other cases foreign firms opened more efficient, non-unionized manufacturing plants in the United States, often in rural or small towns with lower prevailing wages.

One of the common features of industrial restructuring is the prevalence of labor subcontracting and the overall informalization of labor relations (Portes and Sassen 1987). Subcontracts to smaller firms allow larger companies to achieve greater flexibility and minimize employment costs, but smaller firms have lower profit margins and are much less likely to offer fringe benefits such as health insurance or retirement programs. Donato and Bankston (chapter 6) provide a classic description of the operation of the informal economy and the emergence of a segmented labor market in their account of changes in the industrial organization of the oil and gas industry in southern Louisiana.

Over the last few decades, the oil industry has experienced recurrent booms and busts. Labor needs during periods of expansion are supplied by hundreds of small and medium-size firms that compete for contacts to build and repair ships and equipment and to supply services needed for offshore oil rigs, ports for supertankers, refineries, and natural gas pipelines. Although most of these workers (such as welders and pipe fitters) are skilled and their wages are well above the minimum, the industry's boom-and-bust cycle has led to increasing levels of contract employment and high worker turnover. With declining job security, native-born workers, and especially their children, have tended to look for alternative careers. Some seek to become small-business owners or managers; others have found more secure jobs in the formal sector. As a result, shortages of labor during periods of rapid expansion have increasingly been met by immigrant workers who are available, flexible, and willing to accept unstable conditions of employment that native-born workers find intolerable.

Trends in the construction and meatpacking industries, as presented by Parrado and Kandel, are quite different both from each other and from the southern Louisiana petroleum economy, though one feature is consistent: the need for a plentiful and flexible workforce to occupy disagreeable jobs. During the 1980s and 1990s, meatpacking and other food-processing industries were largely deskilled and increasingly dominated by vertically integrated firms that sought to remain competitive by decentralizing production to rural areas of the South and Midwest. Fennelly, in chapter 7, cites the case of a meatpacking firm in Minnesota that closed its unionized plant and then reopened the same plant as a non-union shop hiring only immigrant workers.

The construction sector has grown most rapidly in America's "exurbs"—small towns on the periphery of expanding metropolitan areas. As shopping centers, strip malls, and housing developments have developed apace while central cities have declined, small companies and competitive labor markets have kept wages in the construction sector low. Although immigrants do not dominate the construction sector, they provide an important source of labor in an economic arena that has become less attractive to native-born workers.

Taken collectively, the chapters in the first half of this volume clarify the major cause for the decentralization of immigrant labor away from gateway cities on the East and West Coast to medium-size and small communities in the Midwest and South. American industries and employers, facing greater international competition and declining profit margins, have sought to cut costs through subcontracting, deskilling, and decentralizing production to areas with lower wage rates. Although not all industries restructure in the same fashion, they all seek to achieve common outcomes that affect workers—lower wages, fewer unions, reduced fringe benefits, and easier layoffs. These "new jobs" are not attractive to American-born workers, especially younger workers with the credentials or connections to find formal-sector employment. Because immigrants have fewer options and are generally more tolerant of difficult working conditions and job instability, especially if they lack documents, they fill the gap in an increasingly segmented domestic labor market.

The transformation of meatpacking from a skilled trade of unionized craft workers in large cities to an industrial production line of unskilled, non-unionized workers in rural and small towns may be the most obvious case of industrial restructuring, but similar processes are reported in almost every chapter in this volume, from welders in southern Louisiana, to construction workers in North Carolina, to domestic service workers in Nashville, to mushroom workers in Kennett Square, Pennsylvania. But settlement patterns are also shaped by geographic considerations. Donato and colleagues show that many of the new nonmetropolitan immigrant destinations are closely connected to Interstate 35, which winds its way north from Texas to the Midwest and provides an accessible pathway by which products can reach urban markets.

Finally, social mechanisms allow immigrant workers to respond to changes in economic demand. Just as social networks and institutions of mutual support have led to the concentration of immigrants in traditional gateway cities, immigrant entrepreneurs and middlemen quickly recruit friends, families, and co-ethnics to new destination areas. Each pioneer immigrant community creates the potential for additional immigration through network-driven processes of cumulative causation, and eventually for the creation of satellite settlements in nearby towns where immigrant niches can be reproduced.

RESPONSES TO THE NEW IMMIGRANTS

During the first few decades after the post-1965 wave of immigration began, most native-born Americans had relatively little personal contact with immigrants. The concentration of immigrant families in Los Angeles, New York, Miami, Chicago, and a few other places meant that most Americans, especially those in the South, had only fleeting experiences with foreigners. There was, of course, an intense national debate in the 1970s and 1980s over immigration policy, immigrant adjustment, and a widespread perception that America's borders were "broken," but during this period these conditions were generally distant from the day-to-day lives of most Americans. Although immigration may have been viewed as a "crisis," for many citizens it was a crisis in the abstract.

As the chapters in this volume make clear, the situation in the early twenty-first century is quite different. With immigrant communities popping up in many new places and the growing presence of monolingual Spanish speakers in schools and hospitals, new questions about ethnic diversity and assimilation are confronting American communities that have not experienced them in recent memory—in some cases in over two hundred years. Although solutions to some issues may be relatively painless, such as hiring translators or bilingual staff in public offices providing health care, police, and other services, other issues raise more fundamental questions about access to opportunity, social justice, inter-group relations, and, of course, identity.

With their keen analytic eyes focused on these social problems, the authors of the last six chapters address the potential for xenophobic responses to immigration in new destination areas. They offer clear evidence that many new immigrants are not being completely welcomed nor even accepted in new destination communities. The United States has a long and sordid history of intolerance and organized discrimination against African Americans, American Indians, Mexican Americans, and other minorities (Alba and Nee 2003; Lieberson 1980; Massey and Denton 1994; Montejano 1987); and social scientists in recent years have been among the leading truth tellers who have documented racial and ethnic disparities and the yawning gap between the noble words of America's founding documents and the reality of injustice and segregation.

In vivid accounts drawn from Fennelly's focus group interviews (chapter 7), working class Minnesotans voice their fears that Hispanics, Somalis, and other newcomers bring crime, economic competition, and a tax burden to their communities. These people are also concerned that immigrants do not seem to be committed to learning English and assimilating to American society. Minnesota survey data show that perceptions of the "Hispanic burden" are strongest among whites with the least education who are living in nonmetropolitan areas. Many of these people have neither the substantive knowledge nor the practical experience to deal with unfamiliar languages and cultures, especially in a context where the newcomers are perceived as competitive threats.

In his overview of immigrants to four small-town "new destination" communities in chapter 8, David Griffith finds little overt hostility but does report a variety of responses ranging from indifference to paternalism to exploitation that are linked to class relations between immigrants and natives and among the immigrants themselves. Jamie Winders (chapter 10) finds that both black and white natives in Nashville are quite uncertain about where Hispanics are supposed to fit into the American mosaic of race and ethnicity. She reports that residents of this city do not have a clear conceptual map of how to categorize the new immigrants within a social context that has historically been dominated by a white-black color line. Especially in the South, Americans are used to thinking in black and white racial terms—literally and figuratively—and are still unsure about what to make of the new brown-skinned arrivals. In this region, race relations are colored with the history of state-sanctioned discrimination and segregation, and the wounds from this long history are undercurrents in almost every political and social discussion about persisting inequality and injustice in the United States (see Fredrickson 2003).

Like Winders, Marrow, in chapter 9, reports on incipient tensions between African Americans and Hispanic newcomers in the South. Since many new immigrants fill jobs at the bottom of the occupational ladder and therefore seek low-cost housing, there is a high likelihood that blacks and Hispanics will come to see themselves as competitors in labor and housing markets. Some African Americans also resent that Hispanic immigrants receive the benefits of affirmative action even if they have just arrived in the United States. In North Carolina, Morrow reports more competition and tension between African Americans and Hispanics in rural areas with a larger African American population than those with a smaller African American population, though the relative amount of tension is quite different in the political and economic realms. In areas with large black populations, the demographic weight of African Americans combined with the lack of political voice among Hispanics mitigate the political threat of the new immigrants, underscoring the importance of the demographic as well as economic and social context of reception.

In her social history of immigration and community festivals in Kennett Square, Pennsylvania, Debra Lattanzi Shutika, in chapter 11, documents how local whites first ignored the presence of the local Mexican community and then attempted to incorporate them but also to control the expression of Mexican culture to conform to their preferences and preconceptions. When the Mexican community wanted to create a more authentic festival, the local authorities intervened to marginalize their efforts, forcing them to celebrate a minor Mexican holiday rather that was increasingly being used by the alcohol industry as a sales vehicle than acknowledging their own national independence day, which was of little commercial interest in the United States.

These accounts, perhaps structured by prior assumptions, might be interpreted as evidence of the persistence of American hostility to new immigrants and a continuation of the xenophobia that characterized responses to immigration early in the twentieth century. As noted earlier, there is a long history of prejudice and discrimination against native and foreign minorities by old-stock white Americans (Higham 1988). With a muddled picture and conflicting evidence, it is easier to see a pattern of continuity than to search through the inconsistencies. Nonetheless, there is sufficient evidence to indicate that history is not repeating itself entirely, and a new paradigm of immigrant inclusion may be emerging.

In her Minnesota telephone survey, Fennelly recounts that native whites generally report positive feelings toward Hispanics, with two thirds agreeing that Hispanics make a contribution to the economy. Amazingly, two thirds of whites report that they like having Hispanics as coworkers, friends, next-door neighbors, and even as family members. Not all Minnesotans feel this way, of course, and many people have decidedly mixed or even negative feelings about the Hispanic newcomers in their midst. In focus-group discussions, white Minnesotans expressed positive and empathetic sentiments about Hispanics as well as concerns about the effects of immigrants on public safety, the quality of schools, property values, and employment opportunities. Now, as in the past, perhaps the most characteristic reaction to new immigrants is one of ambivalence.

Such ambivalence is probably a more accurate barometer of the feelings of small-town residents, who tend to fear social change, especially when it comes in the form of strangers who are viewed as being in direct competition for jobs. The closure of a unionized meatpacking plant and the replacement of local workers with immigrants quite understandably shake the economic confidence of local workers and leave them vulnerable to anti-immigrant rhetoric promulgated by political demagogues. It is entirely understandable that there are negative sentiments toward immigrants, but the overall picture still shows a significant degree of acceptance and even of a positive reception.

Griffith's study of community responses to Hispanic immigrants in four rural communities in the Midwest and South (chapter 8) suggests they have been met by growing acceptance. Initially Hispanic men were recruited to work in agriculture and food processing, but over time they have moved into a wider variety of occupations and industries and some have become very successful entrepreneurs. Hispanic families with children have also arrived, and there is much greater participation in schools, churches, and other local institutions as well as greater geographic dispersion into nearby communities. These changes have made it more difficult to stereotype or pigeonhole Hispanics as a monolithic community separate from native-born Americans, thus confirming yet again Gordon Allport's (1954) contact hypothesis.

According to Griffith, Hispanics are often viewed positively because they have given economic and social vitality to declining industries and communities. Their presence has also helped to keep some local schools open and has given a new mission to local churches. Some employers have shifted from an acceptance of immigrant workers to active efforts to hire more. Another indication of an emerging positive response is that many public institutions, especially in health care, are seeking Spanish-speaking staff and volunteers to provide better services to those who cannot speak English. These changes do not mean that inter-ethnic relations are always harmonious or that stereotypes have disappeared—simply that Hispanics are increasingly being considered part of the local communities with needs that should be addressed by public authorities.

Given that Hispanics and African Americans are often competing for jobs, the potential for black-brown antagonism is real. Nonetheless, public opinion polls generally show that blacks remain favorably disposed toward immigrants (Smith and Edmonston 1997, 392), and Marrow (chapter 9, this volume) reports incipient signs of a new "black-brown" political coalition in one county where both groups were in the minority. The ambiguity of where Hispanics "fit" in the American race and ethnic mosaic (see chapter 10, this volume, by Jamie Winders) suggests that immigration could function as a social force to stimulate a reconceptualization of race and ethnicity away from the traditional black-white dichotomy toward a more nuanced conceptualization of race as a continuum intertwined with social class, as it is in Latin America.

The historical race relations model of "us versus them" is a paradigm inherited from an era when a difference in skin color meant destiny. Hispanic origin, like some European-origin categories, combines elements of physical appearance, language, and culture. Most Hispanics are of mixed European-Amerindian or European-African origins. Changes in status, mother tongue, and culture sometimes allow for ethnic identity to be a matter of choice, especially for the children and grandchildren of immigrants (Smith and Edmonston 1997, 113–22). Another important force is intermarriage, which is creating blended populations of European, Hispanic, and Asian ancestry (Bean and Stevens 2003, Chapter 9). To the extent that immigration is changing the popular American understanding of race and ethnicity from fixed and unchangeable categories to a conceptual framework that emphasizes diversity and overlapping ancestries, it might be possible to transcend the traditional racial dichotomy.

In chapter 12, Michael Jones-Correa reports that the growth of the population of minority and immigrant students in two wealthy suburbs of Washington, D.C., could have been the source of major political struggles as middle-class whites tried to protect their "quality schools" from immigrant children—but this generally did not happen. Although conflict did occur in a few instances, in the institutional context of public schools as a common resource and with leadership from school administrators guided by professional ethics instead of a desire to hoard scarce goods, there was actually a massive redistribution of local funds to support the schools with the most-disadvantaged students.

A look backward to the nineteenth and the early twentieth centuries reveals how different and much more tolerant contemporary American society is when compared to the past. In the decades prior to the American Civil War, the Know-Nothing movement directed vitriolic hatred at Catholic immigrants, particularly from Ireland. Although the political success of the Know-Nothing Party eroded with the outbreak of the Civil War, the Know-Nothings were merely the first in a long series of American organizations that mobilized hatred and violence against perceived outsiders well into the middle decades of the twentieth century (Higham 1988).

Anti-immigrant sentiments resumed in the second half of the nineteenth century, primarily directed at Chinese. By 1882, the anti-Chinese coalition had become so strong that Congress enacted the so-called "Chinese Exclusion Act" (Hutchinson 1981, 77–84; Lee 2003); when employers responded by recruiting Japanese workers instead, the government responded by negotiating a "Gentlemen's Agreement" with Japan wherein Japanese authorities agreed to prevent the emigration of its citizens to the United States.

With immigration from Asia effectively closed off, during the first decades of the twentieth century the anti-immigration movement concentrated its attention on Catholics and Jews from Eastern and Southern Europe—the "new immigrants" of their day. The hysteria against foreigners came to a head after the First World War, culminating in 1921 and 1924 with the inclusion of "national origins quotas" in American immigration law, which barred admission to immigrants from anywhere except northwestern Europe (Bernard 1981, 492–93). The enactment of the quotas, along with the onset of the Great Depression in 1929 and the outbreak of the Second World War in 1939, succeeded in curtailing immigration to the United States for several decades (Massey 1985).

Perhaps the most important force moving the United States toward limits on immigration in the past was the rising tide of nativism—a fear of foreigners that gradually became intertwined with racial ideology in the first two decades of the twentieth century. American nativism had deep roots in anti-Catholicism, anti-Semitism, and a fear of foreign radicals, but by the late nineteenth century (Higham 1988, chapter 1) the belief in the inherent superiority of the Anglo-Saxon "race" had become the dominant element of American racial ideology. These beliefs and the link to immigration restriction had widespread support not only among threatened working class natives, but also among many well-educated elites (Baltzell 1964).

Expressions of intolerance in American society, including indifference and a widespread lack of sympathy for the problems of immigrants, continue to characterize contemporary American society, but early-twenty-first-century American society is a far cry from what it was before the 1960s, when bigotry was explicitly built into immigration law. President Truman, in the message accompanying his veto of the 1952 McCarran-Walter Immigration Act, which reaffirmed the 1920s national origins quotas (and was subsequently passed by Congress anyway), explained the discriminatory character of American immigration policy as follows (quoted in Keely 1979, 17–18):

> The quota system—always based upon assumptions at variance with our American ideals—is long since out of date. . . . The greatest vice of the present system, however, is it discriminates, deliberately and intentionally, against many of the peoples of the world. . . . It is incredible to me that, in this year of 1952, we should be enacting into law such a slur on the patriotism, the capacity, and the decency of a large part of our citizenry.

In overriding Truman's veto, members of the House and Senate simply reflected the popular opinion of most Americans that foreigners were not wanted.

These sentiments appear to have changed in the last few decades of the twentieth century. Although there have been persistent efforts to slow down the pace of immigration since 1965 and the passage of the Hart-Celler law, none have been successful; and although there are still voices of nativism in the anti-immigrant community, immigrants appear to have been tolerated and even accepted by increasing proportions of the native-born American population. As more immigrants and their children become part of the American mainstream and ultimately voters, there is even less likelihood that new barriers to immigration will be enacted.

CONCLUSIONS

The increasing geographic dispersion of immigrants throughout American society reflects the rising volume of contemporary immigration and the growing dependence of the American economy on immigrant labor. With more than a million immigrants entering the United States annually, their presence has become increasingly visible throughout the country. But there are other factors besides mere numbers drawing immigrants and their families away from Los Angeles, New York and other gateway cities and toward small towns in Iowa, Georgia, and North Carolina. Competition in the increasingly globalized world economy has lowered the relative earnings of American industrial workers. As American consumers have benefited from cheaper, and often better, products and services from abroad, many workers have seen the promise of reliable lifetime employment, fringe benefits, social insurance, and adequate pensions disappear.

Not all workers and industries have been affected similarly by global competition, but the pressure to cut costs has encouraged many employers to look for employees who are willing to work harder for less compensation. Perhaps the supply of immigrant workers has emboldened more employers to increase their demand for such workers; whatever the precise sequence of cause and effect, there is clearly a reciprocal dynamic between globalization, industrial restructuring, and immigration, especially from Mexico. Coming to fill jobs that are no longer attractive to native-born workers and that would not even exist were it not for immigrants' taking them, Mexicans are not only the most numerous immigrants but also the most overrepresented among those taking jobs requiring the least education.

The increasing availability of immigrant workers and their geographic dispersion throughout the country are not simply the product of large corporations trying to lower labor costs. Many individual American families, too, are purchasing more "immigrant labor" to replace traditional home-produced goods and services, including child care, lawn care, gardening, and food preparation (in restaurants, in grocery stores, or at home). The lower wages of immigrants have kept consumer prices lower in the United States than in other industrial countries, and smaller communities, including the "exurbs" on the periphery of large cities, have become more attractive to the native-born as the cost of living, and housing in particular, has risen to record heights in metropolitan areas on the East and West coasts. These same economic forces create economic demand that "pulls" increasing numbers of immigrants to many of the new destination areas.

Although most immigrants still live and work in large metropolitan areas, including the suburbs of gateway cities, there was a real shift in patterns of immigrant settlement during the 1990s and this has continued unabated into the early years of the current century. The new geography has made immigration a national rather than a regional phenomenon, and immigrant entrepreneurs as well as labor recruiters and employers have been critical links in the process.

Immigrants typically enter new destination areas as strangers with a cultural outlook shaped by their country of origin and limited English fluency. Competition over jobs, especially in an age of downsizing and outsourcing, clearly exacerbates tensions. With little experience in cross-cultural communications and few institutions in existence to integrate strangers, it is not surprising that small-town America has been indifferent, insensitive, and sometimes even hostile to newcomers. The popular image of small towns as parochial and suspicious of outsiders has some validity.

Nonetheless, immigrants and their families seem to have found a place in many new destination communities. One simple reason is that immigrants often create their own communities through kinship networks, mutual aid associations, religious institutions, and even sports clubs. Moreover, in many communities there are native-born Americans who, because of religious convictions, moral principles, or memories of their own immigrant forebears, reach out and assist the strangers. Perhaps the major reason for the acceptance of immigrants in many areas, however, is functional interdependence. Immigrant workers fill economic niches that keep some industries in business; immigrants are willing to provide low-cost services that might not otherwise be available; immigrants create economic demand for housing and local enterprises; and immigrant families also provide a clientele for schools, churches, and other organizations, many of which include natives. Although social interactions might begin with stereotypes, over the long term, the culture of the new immigrants, including their work ethic and familial commitments, can also become the basis of mutual respect.

We do not wish to paint over or minimize the frequent problems experienced by immigrants in the contemporary United States. Immigration is not a smooth process. Long-distance migration often begins with economic dislocation at places of origin and destinations. Dislocation, adjustment, and adaptation are often euphemisms for the painful process of separation and loss for immigrants as well as the costs of change endured by immigrant-receiving communities. Yet there are also positive benefits from immigration—the economic gains for individuals and the communities in which they settle, as well as the broadening of minds that comes with new experiences and associations. The balancing of these losses and gains are likely to be major challenges for more American communities, large and small, in all parts of the country for the foreseeable future, as the United States continues to elaborate its historical destination as a nation of immigrants.

NOTES

1. The formal definition of an immigrant is a foreign-born person who receives an immigrant visa ("green card"). However, about one half of persons acquiring immigrant visas are already present in the United States. In this volume, the foreign-born population, as counted in censuses and surveys, is considered to be equivalent to the immigrant population, although many of the foreign-born do not intend to become permanent residents. The general patterns reported here are similar regardless of the definition of the immigrant population.

REFERENCES

Alba, Richard and Victor Nee. 2003. *Remaking the American Mainstream: Assimilation and Contemporary Immigration.* Cambridge, Mass.: Harvard University Press.

Allport, Gordon W. 1954. *The Nature of Prejudice.* Cambridge, Mass.: Addison-Wesley.

Baltzell, E. Digby. 1964. *The Protestant Establishment: Aristocracy and Caste in America.* New York: Vintage Books.

Bean, Frank D., and Gillian Stevens. 2003. *America's Newcomers and the Dynamics of Diversity.* New York: Russell Sage Foundation.

Bernard, William S. 1981. "Immigration: History of U.S. Policy." In *Harvard Encyclopedia of American Ethnic Groups,* edited by Stephen Thernstrom. Cambridge, Mass.: Harvard University Press.

Eschbach, Karl, Jacqueline Hagan, Nestor Rodriguez, Ruben Hernandez-Leon, and Stanley Bailey. 1999. "Death at the Border." *International Migration Review* 33(2): 430–54.

Fredrickson, George M. 2003. *Racism: A Short History.* Princeton, N.J.: Princeton University Press.

Higham, John. 1988. *Strangers in the Land: Patterns of American Nativism, 1860–1925.* 2nd edition. New Brunswick, N.J.: Rutgers University Press.

Hutchinson, Edward P. 1981. *Legislative History of American Immigration Policy, 1798–1965.* Philadelphia, Penn.: University of Pennsylvania Press.

Jasso, Guillermina, and Mark R. Rosenzweig. 1990. *The New Chosen People: Immigrants in the United States.* New York: Russell Sage Foundation.

Keely, Charles B. 1979. *U.S. Immigration: A Policy Analysis.* New York: Population Council.

Lee, Erika. 2003. *At America's Gates: Chinese Immigration During the Exclusion Era, 1882–1943.* Chapel Hill, N.C.: University of North Carolina Press.

Lieberson, Stanley. 1980. *A Piece of the Pie: Blacks and White Immigrants Since 1880.* Berkeley, Calif.: University of California Press.

Light, Ivan. 2006. *Deflecting Immigration: Networks, Markets, and Regulation in Los Angeles.* New York: Russell Sage Foundation.

Lundquist, Jennifer H., and Douglas S. Massey. 2005. "The Contra War and Nicaraguan Migration to the United States." *Journal of Latin American Studies* 37(1): 29–53.

Massey, Douglas S. 1985. "Ethnic Residential Segregation: A Theoretical Synthesis and Empirical Review." *Sociology and Social Research* 69(3): 315–50.

———. 1995. "The New Immigration and the Meaning of Ethnicity in the United States." *Population and Development Review* 21(3): 631–52.

———. 1999. "International Migration at the Dawn of the Twenty-First Century: The Role of the State." *Population and Development Review* 25(2): 303–23.

Massey, Douglas, and Nancy Denton. 1994. *American Apartheid: Segregation and the Making of the Underclass.* Cambridge, Mass.: Harvard University Press.

Massey, Douglas S., and Rene Zenteno. 1999. "The Dynamics of Mass Migration." *Proceedings of the National Academy of Sciences* 96(8): 5328–35.

Massey, Douglas, Jorge Durand, and Nolan J. Malone. 2002. *Beyond Smoke and Mirrors: Mexican Immigration in an Era of Economic Integration.* New York: Russell Sage Foundation.

Massey, Douglas S., Joaquin Arango, Graeme Hugo, Ali Kouaouci, Adela Pellegrino, and J. Edward Taylor. 1993. "Theories of International Migration: A Review and Appraisal." *Population and Development Review* 19(3): 431–66.

Montejano, David. 1987. *Anglos and Mexicans in the Making of Texas, 1836–1986.* Austin, Tex.: University of Texas Press.

Orrenius, Pia M. 2004. "The Effect of U.S. Border Enforcement on the Crossing Behavior of Mexican Migrants." In *Crossing the Border: Research from the Mexican Migration Project,* edited by Jorge Durand and Douglas S. Massey. New York: Russell Sage Foundation.

Portes, Alejandro, and Rubén G. Rumbaut. 1996. *Immigrant America: A Portrait.* Berkeley, Calif.: University of California Press.

Portes, Alejandro, and Saskia Sassen. 1987. "Making It Underground: Comparative Materials on the Informal Sector in Western Market Economies." *American Journal of Sociology* 93(1): 30–61.

Reimers, David M. 1998. *Unwelcome Strangers: American Identity and the Turn Against Immigration.* New York: Columbia University Press.

Sassen, Saskia. 1991. *The Global City: New York, London, Tokyo.* Princeton: Princeton University Press.

Singer, Audrey. 2004. *The Rise of New Immigrant Gateways.* Washington: Center on Urban and Metropolitan Policy, Brookings Institution.

Singer, Audrey, and Douglas S. Massey. 1998. "The Social Process of Undocumented Border Crossing." *International Migration Review* 32(3): 561–92.

Smith, James P., and Barry Edmonston, editors. 1997. *The New Americans: Economic, Demographic, and Fiscal Impacts of Immigration.* Washington: National Academy Press.

U.S. Census Bureau. 2005. "The Foreign-Born Population of the United States." *Current Population Survey, March 2004.* Detailed tables (PPL-176). Accessed at http://www.census.gov/population/www/socdemo/foreign/ppl-176.html.

U.S. Department of Homeland Security. 2003. *Yearbook of Immigration Statistics, 2002.* Washington: U.S. Government Printing Office.

Waldinger, Roger. 1996. *Still the Promised City? African Americans and New Immigrants in Post-Industrial New York.* Cambridge, Mass.: Harvard University Press.

Waldinger, Roger, and Michael I. Lichter. 2003. *How the Other Half Works: Immigration and the Social Organization of Labor.* Berkeley, Calif.: University of California Press.

PART I

☒

EMERGING PATTERNS OF IMMIGRANT SETTLEMENT

CHAPTER 2

⤨

THE GEOGRAPHIC DIVERSIFICATION OF AMERICAN IMMIGRATION

DOUGLAS S. MASSEY AND CHIARA CAPOFERRO

A salient characteristic of immigration throughout the world is its geographic concentration. Immigrants tend not to disperse randomly throughout destination nations, but to move disproportionately to places where people of the same nationality have already settled. To a large extent, this selective channeling of immigrants to specific destination areas reflects the influence of migrant networks (Massey 1985). Because international migration is costly in both monetary and psychic terms, migrants display a strong tendency to draw upon social ties they have with current or former migrants in order to reduce the costs and risks of international movement (Massey et al. 1998). For someone contemplating a trip to the United States without documents, knowing someone with prior migratory experience can dramatically increase the odds of crossing the border successfully, finding food and lodging, and securing a good, steady job (Massey et al. 1987).

Migrant networks have long functioned to channel migrants to specific places of reception. Their operation was noted early in the twentieth century by William I. Thomas and Florian Znaniecki (1927) and they have been rediscovered in the post-1965 era (Tilly and Brown 1967; Choldin 1973; MacDonald and MacDonald 1974). In both eras, migrants drew upon networks to migrate in response to structural transformations arising from the creation and extension of markets in the course of economic development (Massey and Taylor 2004). The recent period of globalization is no exception. Unlike the earlier era of globalization, however, the present one is characterized by the emergence of a select set of "global cities" that serve as centers of command and control for world markets (Sassen 1991).

These urban centers house corporations that manage global capital flows and coordinate the international division of labor, attracting skilled and unskilled workers from throughout the world. As a result, a very few cities (New York, Los Angeles, Chicago, Houston, Miami) and a very few states (New York, New Jersey, California, Illinois, Texas, and Florida) receive a disproportionate share of America's immigrants, much larger than the shares received by leading cities during the classic period of immigration early in the twentieth century. Whereas, between 1901 and 1930, 36 percent of all immigrants went to the five most important urban destinations and 54 percent when to the top five destination states, from 1971 to 1993 nearly half of all immigrants (48 percent) went to the top five urban areas and 78 percent went to the five most important states, leading Douglas S. Massey (1995) to conclude in 1995 that geographic concentration was a quintessential and distinctive feature of the new immigration compared with the old.

During the 1990s, however, something dramatic happened—there was a marked shift of immigrants away from global cities and the states or regions where they are located toward new places of destination throughout the United States. Not only did immigrants flow into states that hadn't received immigrants in any number since the 1920s such as Pennsylvania (see Shutika 2005); in many cases they entered states that had never before experienced any significant immigration of any sort, such as North Carolina (Bailey 2005; Griffith 2005), Georgia (Hansen 2005; Hernández-León and Zúñiga 2005), Virginia (Bump 2005), Arkansas (Schoenholtz 2005), and Louisiana (Donato, Stainback, and Bankston 2005), Kentucky (Rich and Miranda 2005), and Delaware, Maryland, and Virginia (Dunn, Aragonés, and Shivers 2005).

To date, most of the scholarly work has focused on the geographic deconcentration of Latin American immigration (Zúñiga and Hernández-León 2005), although some investigators have considered the integration of Asians and other non-Hispanic groups in new areas of reception (Bump, Lowell, and Pettersen 2005; Fennelly 2005). For the most part, however, the literature consists of case studies of interactions between Latin Americans and non-Hispanic black and white natives, typically within places heretofore bereft of a significant Hispanic presence (Bailey 2005; Bump 2005; Solórzano 2005; Schoenholtz 2005; Gouveia, Carranza, and Cogua 2005; Shutika 2005; Grey and Woodrick 2005; Dunn, Aragonés, and Shivers 2005; Rich and Miranda 2005). Studies suggest the geographic transformation has been particularly dramatic in the case of Mexicans, the nation's largest immigrant group (Massey, Durand, and Malone 2002).

Prior to the Great Depression, Mexican immigrants concentrated heavily in the Southwest, with 86 percent of all migrants going to just three states: Texas, California, and Arizona. Some 55 percent of Mexican immigrants between 1900 and 1929 went to Texas alone (Durand, Parrado, and Massey 1999). After the Second World War, California surpassed Texas as the leading destination and Illinois eclipsed Arizona to yield a new rank ordering of destinations. By 1970, 53 percent of Mexican immigrants in the United States lived in California, 27 percent resided in Texas, 6 percent were in Illinois, and 5 percent lived in Arizona (Durand, Massey, and Capoferro 2005).

As the new immigration gathered steam after the implementation of the 1965 amendments to the Immigration and Nationality Act, Mexican immigration grew even more concentrated geographically, focusing increasingly on California. Among those Mexicans who arrived in the United States between 1975 and 1980, for example, 59 percent went to California, 21 percent went to Texas, and 9 percent went to Illinois, together accounting for nine of ten newly arriving Mexicans (Durand, Massey, and Capoferro 2005).

This pattern of regional concentration persisted through the 1980s. Among Mexican immigrants who arrived in 1985–1990, nearly two thirds (63 percent) went to California, with another 20 percent going either to Illinois or Texas (Durand, Massey, and Capoferro 2005). Sometime after 1990, however, there was a dramatic shift in migration patterns. California fell sharply in popularity as a destination for Mexican immigrants, and though the decline was less severe for Texas and Illinois, they too fell in importance. Among Mexicans who arrived in the United States between 1995 and 2000, only 28 percent went to California, 15 percent to Texas, and 6 percent to Illinois. Rather than accounting for 90 percent of the inflow, these three states suddenly accounted for less than half (Durand, Massey, and Capoferro 2005).

Despite the research done to date, we still lack a clear description of the changing geography of American immigration. Jorge Durand, Emilio A. Parrado, and Massey (1999) and Durand, Massey, and Chiara Capoferro (2005) focused exclusively on the Mexican case. Micah N. Bump, B. Lindsay Lowell, and Silje Pettersen (2005) only examined the period from 1990 to 2000 and only contrasted Latin American and Asian immigrants in the year 2000. Here we focus on foreigners who entered the United States in the five years prior to the census or survey to measure trends in immigrant destinations during the late 1970s, late 1980s, the late 1990s, and during the first five years of the new century, comparing patterns for Mexicans, other Latin Americans, Asians, and immigrants who were neither Asian nor Latino. We seek to understand the degree to which geographic diversification characterizes other national-origin groups besides Mexicans, whether the beginnings of the geographic transformation can be detected prior to 1990, and whether the pattern of diversification is being sustained into the new century.

POSSIBLE CAUSES OF THE NEW GEOGRAPHY

From the evidence adduced to date, it is apparent that something quite dramatic happened toward the end of the twentieth century to reconfigure the geography of the "new" immigration to the United States. What that something was and how it affected different nationalities is far from clear. Several historical developments have been mentioned as possible causes for the geographic diversification of immigration to the United States. They could have operated alone or in some combination to bring about the change. In the remainder of this section, we review the leading candidates that have been put forward to explain the shift of immigration destinations, thus setting the stage for the analyses that follow in this chapter and later chapters.

The Immigration Reform and Control Act and the Saturation of Labor Markets

The arrival of a new era of American migration was foreshadowed by the passage, in October of 1986, of the Immigration Reform and Control Act (IRCA). The legislation sought to combat undocumented migration to the United States in three ways. First, to eliminate the attraction of American jobs for immigrants, it imposed sanctions on employers who knowingly hired undocumented workers. Second, to deter people from trying to enter the United States illegally in the first place, it allocated new resources to expand the Border Patrol. Finally, to wipe the slate clean and begin afresh, it authorized an amnesty for undocumented migrants who could prove continuous residence in the United States after January 1, 1982, which was combined with a special legalization program for undocumented farmworkers that was added to appease agricultural growers.

IRCA had many important effects on patterns and processes of immigration, but of greatest relevance here is the massive wave of legalization it authorized, ultimately providing residence documents to more than 3 million persons. Of these, 2.3 million were Mexicans, about three quarters of the total. Given the increasing focus of Mexican immigration on California over the prior decades, these newly legalized immigrants were heavily concentrated in that state, which accounted for roughly 54 percent of the total. In Los Angeles County alone the number of legalizations reached 800,000 and it exceeded 100,000 persons each in Anaheim, Riverside, and San Diego. In smaller communities located in California's agricultural zones—in counties surrounding cities such as Bakersfield, Fresno, Salinas, Stockton, and Visalia—the number of legalizations ranged from 20,000 to 50,000 (U.S. Immigration and Naturalization Service 1992).

As a result of IRCA, local labor markets throughout California were suddenly inundated with a wave of newly legalized workers. Legalization did not simply bring workers out of the shadows. Because the eligibility criteria for farmworker legalization were so loose and ill defined, the program was plagued with massive fraud and actually served to attract many new immigrants into the state in addition to the settled undocumented residents and seasonal laborers who were legitimately legalized. The sudden increase in local labor supply, coming on top of a severe economic recession, made California much less attractive as a potential destination. At the same time, the acquisition of legal documents suddenly gave former undocumented workers new freedom of mobility to try their luck elsewhere. Thus, unusually high levels of joblessness in California during the 1990s at once served to discourage new immigrants from arriving and to encourage those already present to look for opportunities in other states.

Proposition 187

The decade of the 1990s started with a severe recession in California, as the Berlin Wall crumbled, the Soviet Union disintegrated, and the Cold War came to an abrupt and unexpected end. The ensuing cutbacks in military spending led to a rather deep and prolonged economic downturn in southern California, home to numerous defense contractors. With his state mired in economic turmoil, Governor Pete Wilson's 1994 reelection campaign was foundering. He could do little about the economy and was slipping badly in the polls when he hit upon a winning campaign strategy. Taking advantage of public anxieties about immigration, he blamed the state's economic troubles on immigrants. Using footage taken from a Border Patrol video, he produced a television commercial that featured immigrants dashing across the border and into traffic at the state's principal port of entry from Mexico. Against this backdrop, a narrator intoned, "They keep coming. Two million illegal immigrants in California. The federal government won't stop them at the border, yet requires us to pay billions to take care of them" (Dunn 1996; Andreas 2000; Massey, Durand, and Malone 2002).

To symbolize his determination to "stop the invasion" of immigrants, he called up California's National Guard and as the TV cameras rolled, he dispatched them to patrol the border near San Diego. The anti-immigrant hysteria stirred up by the governor also led to the circulation and passage of a referendum to take concrete actions against immigrants. Proposition 187 sought to prohibit undocumented migrants from using publicly provided social services, including the public schools. It required state and local agencies to report suspected illegal aliens to the California attorney general and federal immigration authorities, and it made the manufacture, distribution, sale, or use of false citizenship or residence documents a felony under the law.

After its lopsided passage by voters, the terms of the proposition were immediately challenged in court by the American Civil Liberties Union and other groups. Although most of its provisions were ultimately declared unconstitutional and never went into effect, the proposition provided an important rallying point for mobilization against immigrants and sent a strong signal to immigrants in California that the state's welcome mat had definitely been removed and they were no longer wanted. With the passage of Proposition 187, California citizens sent a strong symbolic message to potential migrants that they were most unwelcome and could expect a decidedly chilly reception upon arrival. In a rather explicit way, they sought to discourage potential immigrants from entering their state, especially from Mexico.

Selective Hardening of the Border

During 1993 to 1994, the Immigration and Nationalization Service developed a new border enforcement strategy that came to be known as "prevention through deterrence." The basic idea was to prevent Mexicans from crossing the border illegally in order to avoid having to arrest them later (Andreas 2000). The strategy had is origins in September 1993, when the Border Patrol chief in El Paso, Silvestre Reyes, on his own initiative launched Operation Blockade as an all-out effort to prevent illegal border crossing within El Paso, Texas. Within a few months, immigrants had been obliged to go around Silvestre's imposing wall of enforcement resources, and the immigrant traffic through El Paso itself was dramatically reduced.

The policy was extremely popular with the city's residents, 85 percent of whom were of Mexican origin but who had grown weary of unwelcome visitors. A survey carried out by a local nonprofit organization revealed that what bothered El Paso residents was not undocumented migrants per se, but the fact that they frequently stopped in yards to drink water and rest. It was thus the invasion of private space that people didn't like; if the migrants had been invisible or had remained in public areas, few would have cared.

As a result of the operation, Reyes was lauded as a local hero and ultimately went on to be elected to Congress. Naturally, his superiors in Washington, D.C., took note of the favorable publicity and the apparent success of Operation Blockade. After renaming it Operation Hold-the-Line to assuage Mexican sensibilities, its strategy and tactics were incorporated into the Border Patrol's strategic plan for 1994. In October of that year, the INS launched a second operation using the approach pioneered by Reyes in El Paso, this time along the busiest stretch of border in San Diego.

For Operation Gatekeeper, officials installed high-intensity floodlights to illuminate the border day and night, as well as an eight-foot steel fence along fourteen miles of border from the Pacific Ocean to the foothills of the Coastal Range. Border Patrol officers were stationed every few hundred yards behind this formidable wall (which came to be known as the "tortilla curtain"), and a new array of sophisticated hardware—motion detectors, infrared scopes, trip wires—was deployed in the no man's land it fronted (see Dunn 1996). As in El Paso, the operation was a huge success. From being the busiest point on the entire border, San Diego became positively tranquil, even boring for Border Patrol Officers, who were forced to sit in their vehicles staring at a blank wall for hours on end. Operation Gatekeeper put an end to the chaotic images of migrants running through traffic en masse to cross the border without papers that had so troubled California's voters. Once again, the border appeared to be "under control."

Of course, throwing up blockades in El Paso and San Diego did not really stop undocumented migrants from entering the United States, it simply channeled them to other, less visible, locations along the two-thousand-mile border. Passage through remote mountains, high deserts, and raging rivers was too costly and risky to undertake as long as easier routes through San Diego and El Paso remained relatively open, but once Operation Hold-the-Line and Operation Gatekeeper had made these sectors difficult to traverse, the prospect of crossing in more distant and dangerous areas did not look so bad.

One immediate result of the Border Patrol crackdowns, therefore, was to deflect undocumented migrants to new crossing points in the deserts of Arizona and the wilder parts of the lower Rio Grande Valley (Orrenius 2005). Because these sectors were more lightly patrolled than urbanized segments of the border, the probability of apprehension actually fell quite sharply (Massey, Durand, and Malone 2002). Once they were across the border in relatively open territory, undocumented migrants were free to travel anywhere in the United States and they were much less likely to just proceed directly to San Diego or Los Angeles. Not surprisingly, therefore, the shift in border-crossing traffic away from El Paso and San Diego was accompanied by a sharp reduction in migrants going to Texas and, especially, California (Massey, Durand, and Malone 2002).

At the same time, the increased costs and risks of border crossing prompted migrants to remain in the United States rather than returning home to face the gauntlet at the border on a return trip. As a result, trip durations lengthened and rates of return migration plummeted among the undocumented (Reyes 2004; Riosmena 2004). As migrants gave up circulating and stayed longer, they sent for spouses and children and the composition shifted increasingly from male workers to dependent women and children. Thus United States border policy had the effect of simultaneously deflecting migratory flows away from California while accelerating the rate of net population growth among undocumented migrants, perhaps accounting for the rapidity of the geographic transformation.

Changing Geography of Labor Demand

One final factor potentially influencing the distribution of immigrant destinations was the changing geography of labor demand. Data from the U.S. Bureau of Labor Statistics reveal that employment growth in southern and mountain states far outpaced that in California and Illinois, historically two of the top immigrant-receiving states. Whereas the number of jobs in California and Illinois increased by 15 percent between 1988 and 1998, employment grew by 59 percent in Nevada, 42 percent in Utah, 40 percent in Arizona, 38 percent in Idaho, 35 percent in Colorado, 30 percent in Georgia, 24 percent in Oregon, 20 percent in Tennessee, and 19 percent in South Carolina (U.S. Bureau of Labor Statistics 2000). Not only was the recession of the early 1990s sharper and deeper in California than in other states, but it ended earlier and more completely in southern and mountain states than in California. In 1999 the unemployment rate averaged 5.3 percent in California, but stood at 4.3 percent in Nevada, 3.6 percent in Utah, 4.5 percent in Arizona, 4.9 percent in Idaho, 3 percent in Colorado, 3.8 percent in Georgia, and 4.1 percent in both Tennessee and South Carolina (U.S. Bureau of Labor Statistics 2005).

These geographic patterns of job growth and unemployment are strongly associated with rates of internal migration between states. California lost a net of 756,000 residents to other states from 1995 to 2000, and the big gainers were Georgia at 341,000, North Carolina at 338,000, Arizona at 316,000, Nevada at 234,000, Colorado at 162,000, and Tennessee at 146,000 (Perry

2003). It would be surprising if high-employment states attracting such large numbers of domestic migrants were not also attracting significant numbers of international migrants as well.

COMPARING POTENTIAL EXPLANATIONS

We have outlined four possible explanations for the diversification of immigrant destinations during the 1990s:

- The flooding of labor markets in California and other traditional immigrant-receiving states with newly legalized workers during the early 1990s, reducing their attractiveness to new immigrants and giving the newly mobile legalized immigrants strong incentives to look for opportunities elsewhere

- The chilling effect of California's Proposition 187, which explicitly signaled to immigrants that they were no longer welcome in that state

- The selective hardening of the border in San Diego and El Paso, which channeled undocumented migrants away from California and Texas and toward new crossing points and final destinations

- The surge of labor demand in southern and western states, combined with a weakening of demand in California

These explanations are by no means mutually exclusive. But not all of them would be expected to affect all immigrant groups equally. Specifically, changes whose effect are concentrated on the southern border would be expected to influence the behavior of Mexicans primarily, and to a lesser extent migrants from elsewhere in Latin America who traverse Mexico to enter the United States by land, but not immigrants from Europe, Africa, Asia, and the Pacific, who typically enter through other gateways. Moreover, whereas Proposition 187 and IRCA's flooding of local labor markets made California less attractive for all immigrants and the surge in labor demand in the southern and mountain states made new destinations more attractive for everyone, the selective hardening of the border would only influence the behavior of people who heretofore had crossed in El Paso and San Diego—Mexicans and to a much more limited extent Central and South Americans. Thus, to the extent we find a pronounced shift in destinations for Mexicans but not other groups, we may conclude that the emergence of a new geography of immigration in the 1990s had more to do with changes in United States border policy than with the other factors we have mentioned.

DATA

Building on the foregoing observation, we undertake a descriptive analysis of changing destinations for four broad groups of immigrants: Mexicans, other Latin Americans, Asians, and all other immigrants. In order to bracket the crucial decade of the 1990s, we focus on immigrants who arrived in the United States during four periods: 1975 to 1980, 1985 to 1990, 1995 to 2000, and 2000 to 2005. Contrasting arrivals during the period 1995 to 2000 with those from 1975 to 1980 and 1985 to 1990 will reveal the uniqueness of the 1990s compared to earlier periods, and the comparison with 2000 to 2005 will indicate the degree to which the new geography has been sustained to the present. Likewise, comparisons across the four immigrant groups will reveal the degree to which geographic diversification was a general trend affecting all immigrants or whether it was largely confined to Mexicans.

Our analysis relies on answers to a question included on the decennial census and the annual Current Population Survey on place of residence five years ago. Foreign-born persons who reported that they resided outside the United States five years earlier are presumed to have immigrated to the United States at some point during the interval between then and the date of the census or survey. These data are tabulated from the Public Use Microdata Samples (PUMS) prepared by the U.S. Bureau of the Census for the 1980, 1990, and 2000 censuses of population, and from the March 2005 demographic supplement to the Current Population Survey. We focus interpretation on changes in distribution of recently arrived immigrants by state of destination from 1975 to 1980 to 2000 to 2005.

THE NEW GEOGRAPHY OF IMMIGRATION

During the period from 1965 to 1990, immigration flowed overwhelmingly to five key states: California, New York, Texas, Florida, and Illinois. At a considerable distance behind this "big five" was a second tier of states that received significant numbers of immigrants, within which foreigners constituted a visible presence: New Jersey, Massachusetts, Washington, Virginia, and Maryland. Until the 1990s, upward of 80 percent of all immigrants went to these ten states. In order to document the emergence of new immigrant-receiving states, we selected for detailed scrutiny any state that accounted for more than 1 percent of the inflow of any group during the period of observation, which yielded a list of twenty potential "new destinations."

Table 2.1 shows the distribution of recently arrived immigrants by state in the five years prior to 1980, 1990, 2000, and 2005. States are

TABLE 2.1   Distribution of Recent Immigrants to the United States in 1980, 1990, and 2000

State	Thousands of Persons Arriving in U.S. During Previous Five Years				Distribution (Percentage)			
	1980	1990	2000	2005	1980	1990	2000	2005
Big five								
California	426.3	1,353.7	1,211.7	1,055.4	31.1	35.3	21.1	22.7
New York	176.6	515.8	569.5	275.6	12.9	13.4	9.9	5.9
Texas	116.5	258.7	584.0	438.6	8.5	6.7	10.2	9.4
Florida	79.2	276.8	469.0	405.8	5.8	7.2	8.2	8.7
Illinois	75.9	171.2	300.9	237.9	5.5	4.5	5.2	5.1
Second tier								
New Jersey	50.7	166.1	267.1	149.4	3.7	4.3	4.6	3.2
Massachusetts	35.2	107.6	151.8	74.5	2.6	2.8	2.6	1.6
Washington	29.0	61.2	135.4	121.5	2.1	1.6	2.4	2.6
Virginia	25.6	87.5	145.2	142.0	1.9	2.3	2.5	3.1
Maryland	24.7	83.0	108.7	116.4	1.8	2.2	1.9	1.6
New destinations								
Arizona	14.7	56.4	114.1	161.8	1.1	1.5	2.5	3.5
Colorado	17.5	29.0	105.7	68.3	1.3	0.8	1.8	1.5
Connecticut	13.6	46.3	70.7	45.0	1.0	1.2	1.2	1.0
Georgia	10.2	44.3	172.3	140.7	0.7	1.2	3.0	3.0
Hawaii	18.8	32.6	35.1	14.7	1.4	0.8	0.6	0.3
Indiana	8.7	12.3	58.7	49.7	0.6	0.3	1.0	1.1
Kansas	8.3	17.7	36.2	24.3	0.6	0.5	0.6	0.5
Louisiana	14.6	14.0	20.5	15.6	1.1	0.4	0.4	0.3
Michigan	25.4	48.2	116.1	127.5	1.9	1.3	2.0	2.7
Minnesota	7.2	22.5	67.7	66.3	0.5	0.6	1.2	1.4
Missouri	9.5	15.3	45.9	29.3	0.7	0.4	0.8	0.6
Nevada	6.5	18.5	60.4	68.7	0.5	0.5	1.0	1.5
North Carolina	11.5	30.4	140.7	130.6	0.8	0.8	2.4	2.8
Ohio	19.5	40.2	84.3	74.1	1.4	1.0	1.5	1.6
Oregon	13.9	33.0	65.9	35.4	1.0	0.9	1.1	0.8
Pennsylvania	25.2	71.2	97.2	116.7	1.8	1.9	1.7	2.5
Rhode Island	6.3	17.8	18.7	12.1	0.5	0.5	0.3	0.3
Tennessee	5.7	12.2	52.0	73.0	0.4	0.3	0.9	1.6
Utah	5.5	14.6	49.1	24.3	0.4	0.4	0.9	0.5
Wisconsin	10.6	21.1	46.6	58.9	0.8	0.5	0.8	1.3
Other states	76.8	149.7	327.8	478.6	5.6	3.9	5.7	10.3
Diversity index	n.a.	n.a.	n.a.	n.a.	70.4	66.2	77.4	77.8
Total	1,371.5	3,838.4	5,750.8	4,646.8	100.0	100.0	100.0	100.0

Source: Authors' compilation of Public Use Microdata Samples and Current Population Survey, 2005.

grouped under three headings: the big five, the second tier, and new destinations. There is just one figure for immigrants going to the remaining twenty states.

The emergence of a new geography of immigration during the 1990s is at once apparent with a quick glance at the numbers and percentages going to the big five. Between 1980 and 1990 geographic concentration was increasing among newly arrived immigrants. The share going to California rose from 31.1 percent among those who arrived 1975 to 1980 to 35.3 percent among those entering 1985 to 1990. Over the same period, the share going to New York increased slightly, from 12.9 percent to 13.4 percent, while the percentage going to Florida rose from 5.8 percent to 7.2 percent. Although the proportion going to Illinois and Texas fell somewhat, the share of immigrants flowing into the big five nonetheless grew from 63.8 percent to 67.1 percent. The relative number going to second-tier states increased very slightly, from 12.1 percent to 12.2 percent, and the proportion going to the twenty new destinations fell from 18.5 percent to 15.8 percent.

During the 1990s the growing concentration of immigration to the big-five states in general, and California in particular, was reversed. The share of immigrants going to California fell sharply, from 35.3 percent among those arriving from 1985 to 1990 to just 21.1 percent among those who entered 1995 to 2000, a shift that was sustained during the first five years of the new century, in which 22.7 percent of arrivals went to California. The share going to New York also fell from 13.4 percent, to 9.9 percent, whereas Texas, Florida, and Illinois increased their relative shares by modest amounts. Where two thirds of all immigrants had gone to the big-five states in 1985 to 1990, by 1995 to 2000 the figure had dropped to just 55 percent and it fell to 52 percent over the ensuing five years.

For the most part, immigrants diverted away from the big-five states were not going to second-tier states, either. Indeed, the share going to New Jersey, Massachusetts, Washington, Virginia, and Maryland fell slightly, from 14 percent to 12.1 percent. Instead, there was a pronounced diversification of the geography of immigration toward entirely new states of destination. Notable increases are observed in Arizona, which moved from 1.1 percent of all recently arrived immigrants in 1980 to 3.5 percent in 2005. Likewise, Georgia went from 0.7 percent to 3.0 percent; Indiana from 0.6 percent to 1.1 percent; Michigan from 1.9 percent to 2.7 percent; North Carolina from 0.8 percent to 2.8 percent; and Pennsylvania from 1.8 percent to 2.5 percent.

Although these percentages may seem quite modest, they conceal very rapid shifts in the absolute size of flows into states that heretofore had received very few migrants from abroad. In Arizona, for example, the number arriving during the previous five years went from 15,000 in 1980 to 162,000 in 2005. The flow into Georgia likewise grew from 10,000 to 141,000 while Michigan went from 25,000 to 128,000, North Carolina from 12,000 to 131,000, and Pennsylvania from 25,000 to 117,000.

The data thus reveal a sharp geographic diversification of immigration during the 1990s that continued into the period 2000 to 2005. In order to measure changes in diversity we computed Henri Theil's (1972) entropy index, henceforth simply called the diversity index:

$$E = \frac{-\sum_{i=1}^{n} p_i * \log(p_i)}{\log(n)} \times 100, \tag{2.1}$$

where n is the number of categories (for example, states) and p_i is the proportion of people in category i (for example, state i). The index varies between 0 and 100. Minimum diversity occurs when all people are concentrated in one category and maximum diversity occurs when each category contains exactly the same number of people (see White 1986). Thus, the higher the index number, the greater the diversity.

In table 2.1, the diversity index is shown at the bottom of the columns under "Percentage Distribution." It can be seen that diversity fell during the 1980s—the index went down from 70.4 among immigrants arriving 1975 to 1980 to 66.2 among those entering 1985 to 1990. Thereafter the index jumps sharply upward, reaching 77.4 among immigrants arriving between 1995 and 2000 and inching up to 77.8 among those entering between 2000 and 2005. Something clearly happened during the 1990s to diversify the destinations of immigrants to the United States, shifting the nation from one geographic equilibrium before 1990 to a new equilibrium by 2000. A comparison of the geography of immigration across major groups might shed light on what that something was.

MEXICANS AND OTHER LATIN AMERICANS

Table 2.2 shows percentage distributions of recently arrived immigrants by state of destination for Mexicans and other Latin Americans. The trend of geographic concentration and then rapid diversification was particularly pronounced for Mexicans. Between 1980 and 1990, the concentration of immigrants in California accelerated. Whereas in 1980, 57 percent of recent arrivals from Mexico went to California, by 1990 the figure had reached 63 percent. By the end of the 1980s, in other words, nearly two thirds of all Mexican immigrants were entering just one state, and much of this

TABLE 2.2   Distribution of Recent Mexican and Other Latin American
             Immigrants to the United States in 1980, 1990, and 2000
             (Percentages Except as Noted)

State	Mexicans				Other Latin Americans			
	1980	1990	2000	2005	1980	1990	2000	2005
Big five								
California	56.6	62.7	28.2	33.4	23.2	24.7	11.8	9.1
New York	0.6	1.9	2.4	0.5	24.3	20.0	14.9	7.3
Texas	21.4	14.2	19.7	14.8	5.1	5.1	5.8	8.0
Florida	0.6	1.9	3.1	6.0	18.8	21.8	8.2	24.9
Illinois	9.2	6.0	6.6	5.1	1.8	1.4	1.8	0.6
Second tier								
New Jersey	0.1	0.5	1.2	1.6	8.3	6.6	9.3	8.0
Massachusetts	0.1	0.1	0.2	0.0	2.3	3.8	4.9	4.0
Washington	0.6	1.0	2.0	0.5	0.6	0.3	0.5	0.9
Virginia	0.0	0.3	0.7	0.8	1.6	3.1	3.5	3.9
Maryland	0.1	0.1	0.3	0.6	1.9	2.9	2.3	1.9
New destinations								
Arizona	2.5	3.2	5.5	7.5	0.4	0.6	0.5	1.2
Colorado	1.0	0.9	3.5	2.0	0.6	0.2	0.7	1.3
Connecticut	0.0	0.1	0.3	0.6	0.7	0.9	2.1	2.0
Georgia	0.0	0.8	4.4	2.1	0.2	0.8	2.1	3.4
Hawaii	0.2	0.1	0.0	0.0	0.4	0.0	0.0	0.3
Indiana	0.1	0.1	1.3	1.0	0.8	0.1	0.5	1.3
Kansas	0.4	0.3	1.0	0.5	0.2	0.1	0.4	0.3
Louisiana	0.0	0.0	0.1	0.0	1.5	0.5	0.4	0.6
Michigan	0.1	0.2	1.1	0.4	0.9	0.5	0.8	2.4
Minnesota	0.0	0.1	0.8	1.1	0.0	0.1	0.6	0.2
Missouri	0.0	0.2	0.7	0.3	0.4	0.3	0.3	0.1
Nevada	0.9	1.0	1.6	2.5	0.2	0.3	0.8	1.1
North Carolina	0.3	0.4	4.0	3.1	0.5	0.4	2.0	6.8
Ohio	0.1	0.0	0.5	1.5	0.4	0.4	0.5	0.7
Oregon	0.8	1.2	1.6	1.3	0.0	0.3	0.3	0.0
Pennsylvania	0.3	0.2	0.4	2.0	0.8	1.0	1.0	2.1
Rhode Island	0.0	0.2	0.0	0.0	0.8	0.8	1.2	1.1
Tennessee	0.0	0.0	1.3	1.4	0.4	0.1	0.4	2.2
Utah	0.2	0.3	1.2	0.3	0.0	0.3	0.7	1.7
Wisconsin	0.2	0.3	1.1	1.7	0.5	0.1	0.2	0.0
Remaining states	3.6	1.7	6.2	7.4	2.5	2.5	21.5	2.6
Diversity index	38.2	39.2	67.7	66.5	58.7	58.7	67.6	71.2
N (thousands)	233	831	180	1,625	171	641	925	707

Source: Authors' compilation from Public Use Microdata Samples, 1980, 1990, 2000, and Current Population Survey, 2005.

concentration was at the expense of the two other historical destination states for Mexicans, Texas and Illinois. The share of recent immigrants going to the former state dropped from 21.4 percent to 14.2 percent between 1980 and 1990, while the proportion going to the latter went from 9.2 percent to 6 percent. New York and Florida, in contrast, registered small increases. Overall, diversity remained fairly stable at a relatively low level, with an index of 38.2 in 1980 and 39.2 in 1990.

The change in the geography of Mexican immigration after 1990 was truly dramatic. The share of recent immigrants going to California fell precipitously, from 63 percent in 1990 to 28 percent in 2000, and the diversity index correspondingly rose from 39.2 to 67.7, a huge change for a single decade. Figure 2.1 captures the extent of the change by showing pie charts of immigrant destinations 1985 to 1990 and 1995 to 2000. In the earlier period, 86 percent of all Mexican immigrants went to the big-five states, just 2 percent went to second-tier states, and 10 percent flowed into potential new destinations, leaving a remainder of just 2 percent of the total inflow. Ten years later, the big five accounted for just 61 percent of the total and new destinations had expanded to 30 percent, with 3 percent going to the second tier and 6 percent going to the remaining states.

Although the percentage going to Texas between 1990 and 2000 increased initially, from 14.2 percent to 19.7 percent, by 2005 the share had gone back down to 14.8 percent. Instead of going to California and Texas, at the beginning of the new millennium Mexican immigrants were moving in large numbers to a host of new locations throughout the country. The percentage of recent arrivals going to Florida went from 0.6 percent in 1980 to 6 percent in 2005, and in Arizona the increase was from 2.5 to 7.5 percent. Several states that had received virtually no Mexican immigrants in 1980 had become major destinations by 2005. Georgia increased its share of Mexican immigration from 0.0 percent in 1980 to 4.4 percent in 2000 before falling back to 2.1 percent in 2005. Between 1980 and 2005 the share of immigrants going to Indiana went from 0.1 to 1 percent, while the share grew from 0.0 percent to 1.1 percent in Minnesota; 0.9 percent to 2.5 percent in Nevada, 0.3 percent to 3.1 percent in North Carolina; 0.3 percent to 2.0 percent in Pennsylvania, 0.0 percent to 1.4 percent in Tennessee, and 0.2 percent to 1.7 percent in Wisconsin. Mexican migration had been transformed from a regional phenomenon affecting three states into a national movement to a wide variety of states scattered throughout the country.

The right-hand columns of table 2.2 reveal that while the trend toward geographic diversification was shared by other immigrants from Latin America, it was not nearly as pronounced as that observed for Mexicans. For other Latino migrants, the diversity of destinations was much greater

FIGURE 2.1   Destinations of Recent Mexican Immigrants, 1990 and 2000

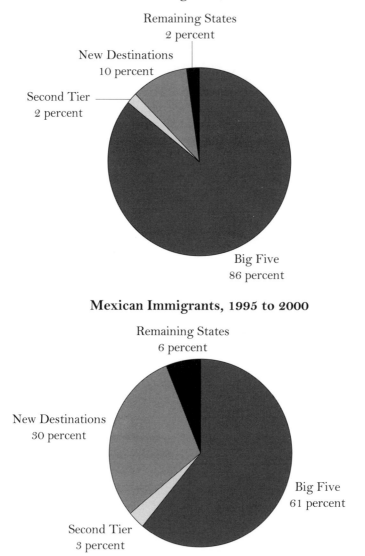

Mexican Immigrants, 1985 to 1990

Remaining States
2 percent

New Destinations
10 percent

Second Tier
2 percent

Big Five
86 percent

Mexican Immigrants, 1995 to 2000

Remaining States
6 percent

New Destinations
30 percent

Second Tier
3 percent

Big Five
61 percent

Source: Authors' calculations from Public Use Microdata Samples, 1990 and 2000.

to begin with and didn't change that radically during the 1990s. The diversity index for Mexicans went from 39.2 to 67.7 between 1990 and 2000, and the index for other Latin American immigrants went from 58.7 to 67.6. Thus, the geography of Mexican and other Latin American immigration was equally diverse by 2000, but Mexicans had transformed more radically from a much more homogeneous baseline.

From 1980 to 2005, California and New York experienced steady declines in their importance as destinations for other Latin American migrants. The share of recent Latin American immigrants going to California fell from 23 percent in 1980 to just 9 percent in 2005, and in New York the percentage dropped from 24.3 percent to 7.3 percent. Among the big-five states, Florida and Texas generally increased their share of Latin American immigrants while the proportion going to Illinois fell. Notable gains were experienced in Massachusetts (where the share went from 2.3 percent to 4.0 percent), Virginia (1.6 percent to 3.9 percent), Arizona (0.4 percent to 1.2 percent), Colorado (0.6 percent to 1.3 percent), Connecticut (0.7 percent to 2.0 percent), Georgia (0.2 percent to 3.4 percent), Michigan (0.9 percent to 2.4 percent), North Carolina (0.5 percent to 6.8 percent), Pennsylvania (0.8 percent to 2.1 percent), Tennessee (0.4 percent to 2.2 percent), and Utah (0.0 percent to 1.7 percent).

By 2005 the diversity index had surged ahead to reach a value of 71.2, exceeding that of Mexicans (66.5) by a significant margin. The move toward evenness in the distribution of destinations for Latin American immigrants is indicated by the pie chart in Figure 2.2. Whereas among those arriving in 1985–1990, 72 percent went to the big-five states, 17 percent went to second tier states, and just 8 percent and 3 percent went to new destinations and remaining states, respectively, by the 1995-to-2000 period only 42 percent went to the big five, while 21 percent went to the second tier, 16 percent to new destinations, and 21 percent to the remaining twenty states.

ASIANS AND OTHERS

Table 2.3 shows the distribution of destinations for recent Asian and other non-Asian, non-Latino immigrants. These two sets of immigrants also experienced a general move toward diversity after 1990, but the shift was even more modest than that observed among Latin American migrants. Among Asians, the diversity index for recently arrived immigrants fell from 71.1 to 68.1 between 1980 and 1990, and then increased to 75.2 in 2000, where it held fairly steady, reaching 75.9 in 2005. The share of recent Asian immigrants going to California fell from 34.9 percent in 1980 to 23.2 percent in 2005, but the share going to New York, Texas, Florida, or Illinois showed little systematic change. Among second-tier states, the share going

FIGURE 2.2   Destinations of Recent Other Latin American
Immigrants, 1990 and 2000

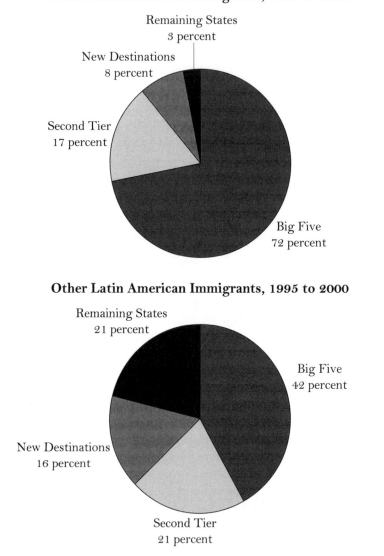

Other Latin American Immigrants, 1985 to 1990

Remaining States
3 percent

New Destinations
8 percent

Second Tier
17 percent

Big Five
72 percent

Other Latin American Immigrants, 1995 to 2000

Remaining States
21 percent

Big Five
42 percent

New Destinations
16 percent

Second Tier
21 percent

Source: Authors' calculations from Public Use Microdata Samples, 1990 and 2000.

TABLE 2.3   Distribution of Recent Asian and Other Immigrants to the United States in 1980, 1990, and 2000 (Percentages Except as Noted)

State	Asians				Non-Asian and Non-Latino			
	1980	1900	2000	2005	1980	1990	2000	2005
Big five								
California	34.9	36.8	27.8	24.2	15.8	18.1	11.1	13.7
New York	8.8	11.8	10.8	8.6	20.0	20.6	15.1	10.2
Texas	6.2	4.9	6.0	6.3	5.7	4.2	5.6	5.8
Florida	2.2	1.9	2.6	3.4	7.9	9.1	9.2	8.4
Illinois	5.8	4.7	4.8	6.3	4.7	4.8	6.2	6.7
Second tier								
New Jersey	2.8	4.6	5.4	3.8	5.0	5.7	5.2	1.8
Massachusetts	2.0	2.7	2.7	2.3	4.7	4.5	4.1	1.7
Washington	3.2	2.4	2.9	3.5	2.2	1.9	3.3	5.9
Virginia	2.5	2.8	3.5	6.7	2.2	2.7	3.1	1.8
Maryland	1.7	2.4	2.3	1.1	2.8	3.0	3.1	7.3
New destinations								
Arizona	0.6	0.9	1.1	1.3	1.1	1.3	1.5	1.5
Colorado	1.4	0.8	0.9	0.9	1.5	0.9	1.5	1.5
Connecticut	0.8	0.8	1.2	0.4	1.9	2.8	1.9	1.0
Georgia	0.9	1.5	2.0	3.9	1.2	1.2	2.9	3.3
Hawaii	3.2	2.0	1.9	1.0	0.2	0.6	0.3	2.0
Indiana	1.0	0.5	0.9	1.0	0.4	0.4	1.2	1.1
Kansas	0.8	0.7	0.6	0.6	0.6	0.5	0.4	0.6
Louisiana	1.8	0.4	0.5	0.9	0.6	0.5	0.6	0.0
Michigan	2.6	2.0	3.2	5.0	2.3	1.6	2.6	3.9
Minnesota	0.9	0.9	1.2	1.9	0.6	0.8	1.9	2.3
Missouri	0.8	0.6	0.9	1.7	1.0	0.4	1.1	0.4
Nevada	0.5	0.4	1.0	1.0	0.3	0.3	0.5	0.7
North Carolina	1.0	0.9	1.2	1.4	1.1	1.3	2.1	1.3
Ohio	2.0	1.8	2.3	0.8	1.9	1.4	2.4	3.3
Oregon	1.5	1.1	1.2	0.5	0.9	0.6	1.1	0.8
Pennsylvania	2.2	2.5	2.6	2.6	2.7	2.9	2.7	3.4
Rhode Island	0.2	0.4	0.2	0.1	0.9	0.6	0.3	0.3
Tennessee	0.5	0.5	0.8	0.5	0.5	0.5	0.8	2.7
Utah	0.4	0.4	0.7	0.2	0.7	0.5	0.7	0.5
Wisconsin	0.9	1.0	0.9	1.8	1.0	0.5	0.6	0.8
Remaining states	6.0	4.9	5.9	6.3	7.6	5.7	6.9	5.3
Diversity index	71.0	68.1	75.2	75.9	76.7	73.8	81.2	80.0
N (thousands)	534	1,313	1,550	1,238	433	1,054	1,475	1,077

Source: Authors' compilation from Public Use Microdata Samples, 1980, 1990, 2000, and Current Population Survey, 2005.

to New Jersey rose from 2.8 percent in 1980 to 3.8 percent in 2005, whereas the share going to Virginia climbed from 2.5 percent to 6.7 percent. Significant gains were also registered in Arizona (0.6 percent to 1.3 percent), Georgia (0.9 percent to 3.9 percent), Michigan (2.6 percent to 5.0 percent), Minnesota (0.9 percent to 1.9 percent), and Wisconsin (0.9 percent to 1.8 percent).

The pie chart in figure 2.3 shows how the distribution among major destination states changed for Asian immigrants between 1985 and 1990 and between 1995 and 2000. As can be seen, the share going to the big five fell from 60 percent to 52 percent, while the second tier grew from 15 percent to 17 percent and new destinations rose from 20 percent to 25 percent; the remaining states held fairly steady at 5 percent to 6 percent.

The residual category of non-Asian and non-Latino immigrants displayed a similar trend of high initial diversity (index value of 76.7) that decreased slightly between 1980 and 1990 (to 73.8) before increasing in 2000 (to 81.2) and stabilizing thereafter (index value of 80 in 2005). The major trend was a shift away from New York, as the percentage of recent immigrants going to that state was halved, from 20.0 percent in 1980 to 10.2 percent in 2005. Likewise, the share going to neighboring New Jersey dropped from 5.0 percent to 1.8 percent and the percentage going to Connecticut fell from 1.9 percent to 1.0 percent. The number going to Massachusetts likewise fell from 4.7 percent in 1980 to 1.7 percent in 2005.

In short, we observe a systematic geographic diversification away from the Northeast among non-Asian, non-Latino immigrants. Corresponding to losses in the Northeast were substantial gains in Washington State (2.2 percent in 1980 to 5.9 percent in 2005), Georgia (1.2 percent to 3.3 percent), Michigan (2.3 percent to 3.9 percent), Minnesota (0.6 percent to 3.3 percent), Ohio (1.9 percent to 3.3 percent), Pennsylvania (2.7 percent to 3.4 percent), and Tennessee (0.5 percent to 2.7 percent). The shift toward greater evenness is indicated by the pie charts in figure 2.4, which shows that the share going to the big five fell from 56 percent to 47 percent between 1985 and 1990 and 2000 and 2005 while the percentage going to new destination states rose from 20 to 27 percent.

THE BIG PICTURE

The changing geography of immigration is summarized in figure 2.5, which plots trends in the diversity index for Mexicans, other Latin Americans, Asians, and non-Asian, non-Latino groups from 1980 to 2000. Although all groups shifted toward a greater diversity of destinations between 1990 and 2000, the biggest change was obviously for Mexicans, who evinced a relative homogeneity in destinations before 1990 but a very high diversity after

FIGURE 2.3   Destinations of Recent Asian Immigrants, 1990 and 2000

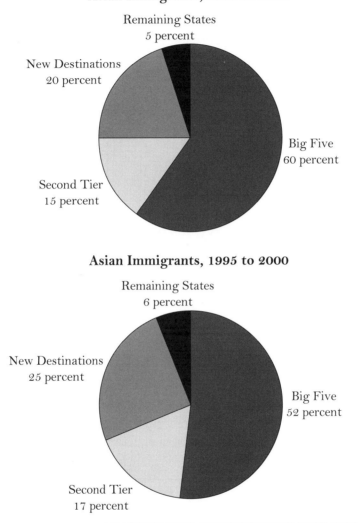

Asian Immigrants, 1985 to 1990

Remaining States
5 percent

New Destinations
20 percent

Big Five
60 percent

Second Tier
15 percent

Asian Immigrants, 1995 to 2000

Remaining States
6 percent

New Destinations
25 percent

Big Five
52 percent

Second Tier
17 percent

Source: Authors' calculations from Public Use Microdata Samples, 1990 and 2000.

2000. The geographic diversity of Mexican destinations was substantially lower than that of other immigrant groups in 1980 and 1990, but by 2000 and 2005 it had risen to levels roughly comparable with the diversity observed for non-Mexican immigrants.

From these data we conclude that to some extent Proposition 187 and IRCA's legalizations made California less attractive; at the same time,

FIGURE 2.4   Destinations of Recent Non-Asian, Non-Latino
Immigrants, 1990 and 2000

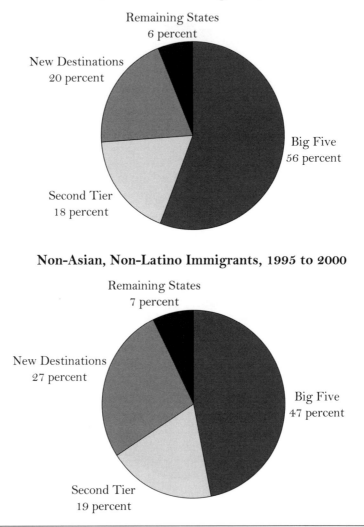

Non-Asian, Non-Latino Immigrants, 1985 to 1990

Remaining States
6 percent

New Destinations
20 percent

Big Five
56 percent

Second Tier
18 percent

Non-Asian, Non-Latino Immigrants, 1995 to 2000

Remaining States
7 percent

New Destinations
27 percent

Big Five
47 percent

Second Tier
19 percent

Source: Authors' calculations from Public Use Microdata Samples, 1990 and 2000.

surging labor demand elsewhere made other states more attractive, and in response to these forces, Asians, other Latin Americans, and non-Asian, non-Latino immigrants shifted to new destinations in the United States. But these factors do not explain the massive character of the shift in immigrant destinations during the 1990s, which occurred only among Mexicans

FIGURE 2.5   Diversity of Destination States for Immigrants to the
United States, 1980 to 2005

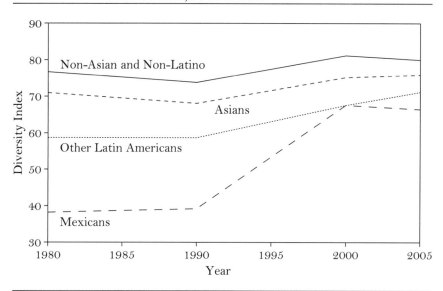

Source: Authors' calculations from Public Use Microdata Samples, 1980, 1990, and 2000, and Current Population Survey, 2005.

and which therefore points to changing United States border policies as a clear contributing cause of the new immigration pattern. Although immigration would have diversified steadily during the 1990s as result of changing labor demand and changing social climates in California and elsewhere, absent the selective hardening of the border the inflow of Mexican immigrants would not have been deflected away from California toward new states of reception throughout the country in such a dramatic and massive fashion. The transformation of immigration from a regional to a national phenomenon, then, owes much to the enforcement strategy of "prevention through deterrence" adopted after 1993.

REFERENCES

Andreas, Peter. 2000. *Border Games: Policing the US-Mexico Divide.* Ithaca, N.Y.: Cornell University Press.

Bailey, Raleigh. 2005. "New Immigrant Communities in the North Carolina Piedmont Triad: Integration Issues and Challenges." In *Beyond the Gateway: Immigrants in a Changing America*, edited by Elzbieta M. Gozdziak and Susan F. Martin. Lanham, Md.: Lexington Books.

Bump, Micah N. 2005. "From Temporary Picking to Permanent Plucking: Hispanic Newcomers, Integration, and Change in the Shenandoah Valley."

In *Beyond the Gateway: Immigrants in a Changing America*, edited by Elzbieta M. Gozdziak and Susan F. Martin. Lanham, Md.: Lexington Books.

Bump, Micah N., B. Lindsay Lowell, and Silje Pettersen. 2005. "The Growth and Population Characteristics of Immigrants and Minorities in America's New Settlement Areas." In *Beyond the Gateway: Immigrants in a Changing America*, edited by Elzbieta M. Gozdziak and Susan F. Martin. Lanham, Md.: Lexington Books.

Choldin, Harvey M. 1973. "Kinship Networks in the Migration Process." *International Migration Review* 7(2): 163–76.

Donato, Katharine M., Melissa Stainback, and Carl L. Bankston III. 2005. "The Economic Incorporation of Mexican Immigrants in Southern Louisiana: A Tale of Two Cities." In *New Destinations: Mexican Immigration in the United States*, edited by Víctor Zúñiga and Rubén Hernández-León. New York: Russell Sage Foundation.

Dunn, Timothy J. 1996. *The Militarization of the U.S.-Mexico Border, 1978–1992: Low-Intensity Conflict Doctrine Comes Home*. Austin, Tex.: University of Texas, Center for Mexican American Studies.

Dunn, Timothy J., Ana María Aragonés, and George Shivers. 2005. "Recent Mexican Migration in the Rural Delmarva Peninsula: Human Rights Versus Citizenship Rights in a Local Context." In *New Destinations: Mexican Immigration in the United States*, edited by Víctor Zúñiga and Rubén Hernández-León. New York: Russell Sage Foundation.

Durand, Jorge, Douglas S. Massey, and Chiara Capoferro. 2005. "The New Geography of Mexican Immigration." In *New Destinations: Mexican Immigration in the United States*, edited by Víctor Zúñiga and Rubén Hernández-León. New York: Russell Sage Foundation.

Durand, Jorge, Emilio A. Parrado, and Douglas S. Massey. 1999. "The New Era of Mexican Migration to the United States." *Journal of American History* 86(2): 518–36.

Fennelly, Katherine. 2005. "Latinos, Africans, and Asians in the North Star State: Immigrant Communities in Minnesota." In *Beyond the Gateway: Immigrants in a Changing America*, edited by Elzbieta M. Gozdziak and Susan F. Martin. Lanham, Md.: Lexington Books.

Gouveia, Lourdes, Miguel A. Carranza, and Jasney Cogua. 2005. "The Great Plains Migration: Mexicanos and Latinos in Nebraska." In *New Destinations: Mexican Immigration in the United States*, edited by Víctor Zúñiga and Rubén Hernández-León. New York: Russell Sage Foundation.

Grey, Mark A., and Anne C. Woodrick. 2005. "'Latinos Have Revitalized Our Community': Mexican Migration and Anglo Responses in Marshalltown, Iowa." In *New Destinations: Mexican Immigration in the United States*, edited by Víctor Zúñiga and Rubén Hernández-León. New York: Russell Sage Foundation.

Griffith, David C. 2005. "Rural Industry and Mexican Immigration and Settlement in North Carolina." In *New Destinations: Mexican Immigration in the United States*, edited by Víctor Zúñiga and Rubén Hernández-León. New York: Russell Sage Foundation.

Hansen, Art. 2005. "Black and White and the Other: International Immigration and Change in Metropolitan Atlanta." In *Beyond the Gateway: Immigrants in a Changing America*, edited by Elzbieta M. Gozdziak and Susan F. Martin. Lanham, Md.: Lexington Books.

Hernández-León, Rubén, and Víctor Zúñiga. 2005. "Appalachia Meets Aztlán: Mexican Immigration and Intergroup Relations in Dalton, Georgia." In *New Destinations: Mexican Immigration in the United States*, edited by Víctor Zúñiga and Rubén Hernández-León. New York: Russell Sage Foundation.

MacDonald, John S., and Leatrice D. MacDonald. 1974. "Chain Migration, Ethnic Neighborhood Formation, and Social Networks." In *An Urban World*, edited by Charles Tilly. Boston, Mass.: Little, Brown.

Massey, Douglas S. 1985. "Ethnic Residential Segregation: A Theoretical Synthesis and Empirical Review." *Sociology and Social Research* 69(2): 315–50.

———. 1995. "The New Immigration and the Meaning of Ethnicity in the United States." *Population and Development Review* 21(3): 631–52.

Massey, Douglas S., and J. Edward Taylor. 2004. "Back to the Future: Immigration Research, Immigration Policy, and Globalization in the Twenty-First Century." In *International Migration: Prospects and Policies in a Global Market*, edited by Douglas S. Massey and J. Edward Taylor. Oxford: Oxford University Press.

Massey, Douglas S., Jorge Durand, and Nolan J. Malone. 2002. *Beyond Smoke and Mirrors: Mexican Immigration in an Age of Economic Integration*. New York: Russell Sage Foundation.

Massey, Douglas S., Rafael Alarcon, Jorge Durand, and Humberto Gonzalez. 1987. *Return to Aztlan: The Social Process of International Migration in Western Mexico*. Berkeley, Calif.: University of California Press.

Massey, Douglas S., Joaquín Arango, Graeme Hugo, Ali Kouaouci, Adela Pellegrino, and J. Edward Taylor. 1998. *Worlds in Motion: International Migration at the End of the Millennium*. Oxford: Oxford University Press.

Orrenius, Pia M. 2005. "The Effect of U.S. Border Enforcement on the Crossing Behavior of Mexican Migrants." In *Crossing the Border: Research from the Mexican Migration Project*, edited by Jorge Durand and Douglas S. Massey. New York: Russell Sage Foundation.

Perry, Marc J. 2003. "State-to-State Migration Flows: 1995–2000." Census 2000 Special Reports CENSR-8. Washington: U.S. Government Printing Office.

Reyes, Belinda. 2004. "U.S. Immigration Policy and the Duration of Undocumented Trips." In *Crossing the Border: Research from the Mexican Migration Project*, edited by Jorge Durand and Douglas S. Massey. New York: Russell Sage Foundation.

Rich, Brian L., and Marta Miranda. 2005. "The Sociopolitical Dynamics of Mexican Immigration in Lexington, Kentucky, 1997 to 2002: An Ambivalent Community Responds." In *New Destinations: Mexican Immigration in the United States*, edited by Víctor Zúñiga and Rubén Hernández-León. New York: Russell Sage Foundation.

Riosmena, Fernando. 2004. "Return Versus Settlement Among Undocumented Mexican Migrants, 1980–1996." In *Crossing the Border: Research from the Mexican Migration Project*, edited by Jorge Durand and Douglas S. Massey. New York: Russell Sage Foundation.

Sassen, Saskia. 1991. *The Global City: New York, London, Tokyo*. Princeton, N.J.: Princeton University Press.

Schoenholtz, Andrew I. 2005. "Newcomers in Rural America: Hispanic Immigrants in Rogers, Arkansas." In *Beyond the Gateway: Immigrants in a Changing America*, edited by Elzbieta M. Gozdziak and Susan F. Martin. Lanham, Md.: Lexington Books.

Shutika, Debra Lattanzi. 2005. "Bridging the Community: Nativism, Activism, and the Politics of Inclusion in a Mexican Settlement in Pennsylvania." In *New Destinations: Mexican Immigration in the United States*, edited by Víctor Zúñiga and Rubén Hernández-León. New York: Russell Sage Foundation.

Solórzano, Armando. 2005. "At the Gates of the Kingdom: Latino Immigrants in Utah, 1900–2003." In *Beyond the Gateway: Immigrants in a Changing America*, edited by Elzbieta M. Gozdziak and Susan F. Martin. Lanham, Md.: Lexington Books.

Theil, Henri. 1972. *Statistical Decomposition Analysis*. Amsterdam: North Holland.

Thomas, William I., and Florian Znaniecki 1927. *The Polish Peasant in Europe and America*. New York: Knopf.

Tilly, Charles, and C. H. Brown. 1967. "On Uprooting, Kinship, and the Auspices of Migration." *International Journal of Comparative Sociology* 8: 139–64.

U.S. Bureau of Labor Statistics. 2000. "Employment Growth by State 1988–98." *Occupational Outlook Quarterly Online* 44. Accessed at http://www.bls.gov/opub/ooq/2000/spring/contents.htm.

———. 2005. "Local Area Unemployment Statistics." Bureau of Labor Statistics website. Accessed at http://www.bls.gov/lau/lastch00.htm.

U.S. Immigration and Naturalization Service. 1992. *1991 Statistical Yearbook of the Immigration and Naturalization Service*. Washington: U.S. Government Printing Office.

White, Michael J. 1986. "Segregation and Diversity: Measures in Population Distribution." *Population Index* 52(1): 198–221.

Zúñiga, Víctor, and Rubén Hernández-León. 2005. *New Destinations: Mexican Immigration in the United States*. New York: Russell Sage Foundation.

CHAPTER 3

⊁

THE STRUCTURE AND DYNAMICS OF MEXICAN MIGRATION TO NEW DESTINATIONS IN THE UNITED STATES

MARK A. LEACH AND FRANK D. BEAN

During the 1990s Mexican migrants to the United States increasingly spread throughout the country (Johnson 2000; Massey, Durand, and Malone 2002; Passel and Zimmerman 2001; Suro and Passel 2003). Nourished both by international migrants from Mexico and by Mexican-born internal migrants who had previously arrived in the country but had moved away from traditional destinations, communities of Mexican-born persons became increasingly visible, not only in large urban metropolises such as New York and Atlanta but also in small towns throughout the Midwest and South.

The Mexican-born were no longer concentrating nearly as much as before in the traditional receiving states, the four border states of the Southwest—Arizona, California, New Mexico, Texas, and Illinois, mostly Chicago—but rather were dispersing elsewhere, which illustrated that such migration had become a national rather than a regional phenomenon. The magnitude of the shift was dramatic. The percentage of the country's Mexican-born persons living in new destination states rose from a mere 10 percent in 1990 to 25 percent by 2000 (Ruggles and Sobek 2003), substantially more than doubling in a single decade.

Such enormous increases, even from relatively small bases, generate important consequences for new destinations, repercussions that depend substantially on how well the recent arrivals fare economically in their new locations (Bean and Stevens 2003).[1] Because many of the new migrants come as unauthorized entrants with very low education levels, observers often think the Mexican immigrant group will not join the economic mainstream within a reasonable period of time (for example, Huntington 2004; but for an alternative view, see Bean, Brown, and Rumbaut 2006). If for no other reason, such pessimistic views are belied by the substantial heterogeneity that exists among the migrants and the places they settle.

At this juncture research on the migration of Mexicans to new destinations has largely focused on describing the size and geography of the flows. It has yet to explore the extent to which different types of migrants go to certain kinds of locales. Developing a portrait of the kinds of migrants and destinations that feature most prominently in the new Mexican dispersal is critical both for understanding the forces driving such migration and for guiding future work seeking to clarify the implications of the new migration for successful immigrant incorporation.

This chapter examines factors associated with the spread of Mexican-born persons across the United States. We focus on Mexicans not only because their spread has been so extensive but also because other recent national-origin groups are not yet sizable enough to achieve national distributions in sufficient numbers to make analyses meaningful. First, we ask to what extent do large numbers of Mexican-origin persons moving to new destinations increase the numbers of later arrivals who move after migration networks have become more established and ethnic communities, more developed? In other words, who are the Mexican migrants who have settled in the new destinations and when did they settle there? Second, are there different types of migrant streams? And if so, how do they vary in terms of such factors as age, U.S. experience, household living arrangements, education, country of origin, and marriage and family patterns? Third, how much heterogeneity is there among new migrant destinations? Are there various kinds of settlement areas? Answers to the foregoing questions hold theoretical importance both for understanding processes of international and domestic migration and for deciphering the roles new destinations may play in affecting Mexican origin incorporation outcomes.

THEORETICAL BACKGROUND

In discussing the underlying forces that drive geographic dispersal among Mexican-born persons in the United States, scholars usually focus on "push" and "pull" factors, often discussing only a few variables within each category to explain migration, despite theoretical arguments that migration is due to multiple factors across various analytical levels that operate at both origin and destination (Lee 1966; Massey 1999). We approach Mexican migrant dispersal to new destinations with this in mind, seeking to reveal whether multiple factors operate at both the individual and aggregate levels to influence increased movement among Mexican-origin persons. On the "push" side, we note that Mexican migration to the United States historically has predominantly involved labor migration or persons moving primarily to work (Portes and Bach 1985). Such movements are governed substantially in their structure and dynamics by processes of cumulative causation (Massey et al. 1987; Massey, Goldring, and Durand 1994). This means that migration flows derive not only from demographic and economic factors at origin (Bean et al. 1990), but also from self-perpetuating social phenomena that cumulatively build upon previous migration through the existence and functioning of social networks (Massey 1999; Massey, Goldring, and Durand 1994).

We expect to find here evidence that such processes operate similarly among new-destination migrants, meaning that both internal and international migrants may be more likely to settle in places in which Mexican migration has previously occurred. Migration under processes of cumulative causation would thus build upon previous flows and gain momentum from larger numbers of earlier migrants. Prior research, however, is not explicit about which of three different groups of co-ethnic persons might be most involved in the social networks that foster such migration—recently-arrived other migrants, earlier-arrived other migrants, or native-born co-ethnic members of the immigrant group, or all three to some degree. In the research reported here, we assess the effects of all of these.

If we accept the argument that cumulative causation may be involved in driving Mexican migration to new states, we would also expect the relative size of each of these three groups to relate positively to increases in migration, with whichever group is most important in this regard showing the strongest relationship. Moreover, the dynamics of cumulative causation lead us to expect this increase to be relatively larger at higher levels of increase, but only up to a point. Processes of cumulative causation, because they involve the operation of social ties at the destination, function relatively independently of economic and demographic factors (Light 2003). This means, however, that the flows deriving from them may also continue even after the demand for immigrant labor has largely been filled, generating labor-market saturation. As such effects kick in, processes of cumulative causation may be expected to exert their influence to diminished degrees, thus causing the relationships between the relative size of some destination groups (such as recently arrived other migrants) and the magnitude of current migration to reveal a concave, curvilinear pattern.

Also, cumulative causation suggests that different types of migrants may engage in migration at different points in the process because the costs of migration are reduced for those migrating later rather than earlier. For example, in international flows, the first migrants to leave a Mexican community typically are male heads of households, who are then followed by younger sons and nephews (Massey, Goldring, and Durand 1994). Subsequently, the process becomes less gender selective as women and children become more involved in it. Similar dynamics might be expected in the case of migration flows to new American destinations. According to previous research on internal migration among Mexican-born persons, the earliest migrants to new destinations, called "seed" migrants, are likely to have considerable prior U.S. experience, which would make them less dependent on ethnic communities and more familiar with a wider range of jobs and housing options (Bartel 1989; Kritz and Nogle 1994; Neuman and Tienda 1994; Saenz 1991). Such migrants may be less likely to be involved in industries that recruit immigrants, since they may have broader economic opportunities as a result of previous work experience in the United States.

Prior research about emigration from sending communities in Mexico and patterns of migrant selectivity are also relevant for processes of internal migration to new locales in the United States. When the costs of migrating to a destination are relatively high because of the presence of few other migrants, earlier migrants who move there should be more strongly selected. As more migrants settle in the destination and an ethnic community grows, social support networks develop that facilitate the flow of information and resources back to other potential migrants, both about the availability of jobs and the provision of housing upon arrival, information that lowers the costs of migration (Massey et al. 1987). Once migrations into new destinations build momentum, places may become increasingly attractive to additional migrants and the flows increasingly self-sustaining. Thus, we would expect the characteristics of the most recent migrants to change with reductions in the costs of migration as the momentum of flows builds.

Also on the "push" side, Douglas S. Massey, Jorge Durand, and Nolan J. Malone (2002) cite a series of immigration-related legislation in the late 1980s and 1990s as factors also driving geographic dispersion and increased settlement among Mexican-born persons around the country. They argue that a combination of national and local policy changes, such as strengthened economic ties between the United States and Mexico through the North American Free Trade Agreement (NAFTA), operated to increase migration flows across the United States-Mexico border. Others, such as legalization through the Immigration Reform and Control Act (IRCA), beefed-up border controls, and such seemingly immigrant-antagonistic political campaigns as the one for Proposition 187 in California, either encouraged long-term settlement in the United States or, partly through increased labor-market competition in traditional destinations, led to dispersal of migrants to new geographic regions (Massey, Durand, and Malone 2002).

Finally, Ivan Light (2003) argues that competition for housing in immigrant communities has helped to generate local antigrowth policies, at least in the case of Los Angeles, that create spill-over effects out of traditional destinations and channel international migration to new destinations. Such policies and trends imply that, in addition to cumulative causation, local, state, and national policies may affect the dynamics of international migration flows and patterns of settlement, redirecting immigration from Mexico and creating conditions that encourage internal migration among Mexican-born persons already in the United States.

On the "pull" side of the equation, demand-side factors may also influence the growth of Mexican communities in new destinations. New economic dynamics and industrial restructuring create attractive conditions in new destinations for Mexican immigrants. Such processes in the past two decades have generated new structures in global metropolitan areas, recasting cities as centers of high-end services involving information and financial management, while at the same time fostering place-specific demand for low-skilled services as well (Sassen 2000). Immigrants, particularly Mexican-born persons, play a vital role in these places by filling such demand for inexpensive, flexible labor (Bean and Lowell 2003), as the growth of Mexican communities in Raleigh-Durham, Atlanta, and Minneapolis illustrates. The widespread boom in construction during the latter half of the 1990s also generated demand for low-skilled Mexican labor in many locales.

The ongoing restructuring of specific industries during the 1980s and 1990s created still additional demand for low-skilled and unskilled labor, at least in some locations. For example, beginning in the 1960s, food-processing industries began to consolidate from regional operations into export-oriented conglomerates. In response to increased global demand and competition, the industry reduced production costs by relocating to rural areas and deskilling production processes while simultaneously working to weaken labor unions, thus increasing the need to recruit immigrant labor to reduce labor costs (Broadway 1995; Gouveia and Saenz 2000; Griffith, Broadway, and Stull 1995). In addition to such economic dynamics and industrial restructuring, decreasing birth rates and higher levels of education among the native-born in the United States over the past thirty years have reduced the relative size of the unskilled native population (Farley 1995) available and willing to fill low-end and unskilled jobs.

Not unrelated to factors mentioned above, other indications, primarily in media reports (Steven Greenhouse, "Crossing the Border into the Middle Class," *New York Times*, June 6, 2004; Daryl Kelley and Carlos Chavez, "California Dreaming No More," *Los Angeles Times*, February 16, 2004) and research (Hernández-León and Zúñiga 2000, 2003), suggest Mexican-born persons are settling in new destinations for life-style reasons similar to those among native-born persons. Migrants appear to be leaving over-crowded and expensive traditional destinations and seeking out new settlement areas where it may be feasible to purchase homes and take advantage of expanding local economies. Migrants' personal reasons for moving to new destinations are not, of course, directly discernible from census data, but the presence of families in certain kinds of places may indicate this kind of migration, as opposed to the presence of labor migration, which is typically dominated by young single males.

The work of Rubén Hernández-León and Víctor Zúñiga (2000, 2003) in the migrant community of Dalton, Georgia, found that the growth of the Mexican community there evolved over several decades and generally followed a series of stages of migrant selectivity. Married couples were among the first to settle after living elsewhere in the United States. Their motivations were often to leave impoverished urban neighborhoods in traditional destinations such as Los Angeles and Houston in search of safer small-town environments and better schools for their children. Spurred on by growth in the carpet-manufacturing plants and poultry industry, the community swelled in the 1990s as more recent settlers with little U.S. experience arrived directly from Mexico.

In sum, multiple factors may contribute to the dynamics of Mexican settlement, and we expect to find that Mexican-born persons who migrated to new destinations are diverse both in their own characteristics and in the kinds of places in which they settled. We break our analyses into three sections in order to begin to answer the questions posed above. We first provide a graphical overview of the growth of Mexican-born migration flows into new destination states over the past twenty-five years. This illustrates the variation in timing and rates of growth occurring in Mexican communities throughout the country. We provide a profile of average characteristics for both individual migrants and the places in which they settled. These provide a foundation for our multivariate analyses and enable us to assess what characteristics of Mexican-born persons are most strongly related to migration to new destinations as well as to assess the relative importance of the destination characteristics that are most strongly related to the volume of migrant flows.

Second, we employ principal-components analysis (PCA) to show that migrants to new destinations over the past twenty-five years are diverse in terms of individual characteristics, household structures, and the economic and industrial specializations of the states into which they moved. (principal components are unique dimensions of information.)

Third, we use the resulting principal-component scores, along with cumulative causation variables, in ordinary least squares (OLS) regression models to assess multivariate relationships between kinds of migrants and destination structures on the one hand and the relative size of migration flows on the other.

DATA

Our data come from the Integrated Public Use Microdata Series (IPUMS) for the 1980, 1990 and 2000 censuses (Ruggles and Sobek 2003). The sample consists of recent Mexican-born male migrants, ages eighteen to sixty-four, who settled in new destinations. The sample members were identified by responses to questions regarding their ethnicity, citizenship, and residence five years prior to the census. We focus only on recent migrants in order better to capture data about those who migrated and the particular conditions at the time they did so rather than about all migrants residing in a destination at a particular point in time. Also, the recent Mexican-born migrants in our sample had moved to new destinations either from other states or directly from Mexico. Their place of previous residence is an important variable in our analyses. We construct individual- and household-level and state-level variables that enable us to analyze the attributes of the migrants as individuals, of their living arrangements, and of the places in which they settled. These make up our set of independent variables.

In hypothesizing that multiple factors influence the relative size of migration flows, our dependent variable is the relative number of recent Mexican migrants in the state in which the migrant settled. We calculate this by dividing the total number of recent Mexican-born migrants by the total population of the state and multiplying by 1,000 to obtain the number of migrants per 1,000 population. Measuring flows at the community level would be a more appropriate research approach since social support and cumulative effects of migration might be thought to operate most strongly within communities. However, this level of detail is not available in census microdata.[2] We thus use state-level data and match the relative size of the

FIGURE 3.1   Average Recent Mexican-Born Migrant Percentage of Population in Low- and High-Growth States, 1980 to 2000

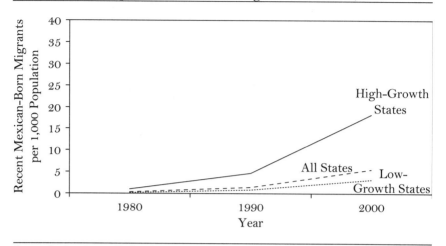

Source: Authors' compilation from IPUMS data.

migration flow for the state to which they migrated to each migrant in our sample for either the decade of the 1980s or the 1990s.

Figures 3.1 and 3.2 illustrate the change in our dependent variable— the relative size of the migration flow—over the past two decades. Figure 3.1 depicts the average size of the migration flow into new destination states, which on average grew from 0.3 migrants per thousand population in 1980 to more than 5 migrants per 1,000 in 2000. We also break out the average size of state flows into averages for high- and low-growth states to illustrate variation in both timing and rates of growth among the flows. This observation validates, at least in part, theoretical perspectives suggesting the growth of migration flows to new destinations did not occur solely as a result of certain policy changes in the late 1980s and 1990s. Rather, larger social and economic processes operating over the past few decades also facilitated growth in migration flows and affected states to different degrees at various times.

This line of reasoning is reinforced by figure 3.2, which shows that the share of recent migrants in several states grew from below one migrant per thousand in 1980 to between two and five migrants per thousand in 1990.[3] Such changes are similar to those occurring in other states with low growth of recently arrived migrant population, whose average growth line is at the bottom of figure 3.1.[4] Thus, a cross-sectional analysis of only one decennial census may be insufficient to fully capture structures and changes that in reality have been operating to some extent for over two decades, if

FIGURE 3.2   Average Recent Mexican-Born Migrant Percentage of Population in High-Growth New Destination States, 1980 to 2000

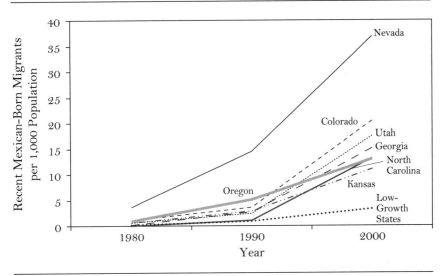

Source: Authors' compilation from IPUMS data.

not longer. Therefore, we pool 1990 and 2000 census data to construct our sample of recent Mexican-born migrants. Although we present results for the pooled data, we also performed our analyses separately for each decade, and observed no large differences (these results are available upon request from the authors).

We do not consider migration flows in the 1960s or 1970s in our analyses because of limited numbers of data points in 1970 census data, a circumstance that precludes an analysis of the 1960s. We calculate several independent variables using data from the previous decade relative to the timing of our dependent variable (using 1980 data to predict 1990 flows, for example), and this, similarly, prevents an analysis of the latter half of the 1970s. Thus, we use 1980 census data here only in conjunction with 1990 data to analyze the decade of the 1980s, and we use 1990 data in conjunction with 2000 data to analyze the decade of the 1990s.

INDIVIDUAL, HOUSEHOLD, AND STATE CHARACTERISTICS

Descriptive statistics for our independent variables in each decade and for the pooled decades are provided in table 3.1. Evidence of some diversity among the migrants and the destinations across the two decades emerges from the means. Mexican-born persons who migrated into new destination

TABLE 3.1   Individual and Household Characteristics of Recent
Mexican-Born Migrants and Characteristics of the
Places They Settled, 1990 and 2000
(Percentage Except as Noted)

Attribute	1990	2000	Combined
Number of cases in sample	5,221	24,693	29,914
Migrants' individual attributes			
Age	29.3	29.3	29.3
U.S. experience			
Percentage naturalized	16.4	8.8	10.0
Percentage with U.S. origins	43.8	32.1	34.1
Average years in U.S.	7.0	6.3	6.4
Marriage and family			
Percentage married	29.3	28.4	28.5
Percentage householder or			
spouse of householder	41.7	39.2	39.6
Percentage living with own children	26.5	26.0	26.1
Migrants' household attributes			
Percentage living with nonfamily			
household members	42.8	50.8	49.5
Percentage living in vertically			
extended household	7.5	11.0	10.4
Percentage living in horizontally			
extended household	35.3	46.3	44.4
New destination state attributes			
State industries			
Percentage agricultural industries	3.0	2.3	2.4
Percentage food manufacturing	1.3	1.2	1.2
Percentage retail trade	16.1	16.2	16.2
Percentage construction	6.9	8.0	7.8
Percentage durable manufacturing	9.6	9.1	9.2
Percentage low-skill service industries	7.8	7.2	7.3
Percentage wholesale trade	4.3	3.5	3.6
Percentage of Mexican			
self-employed migrants	5.4	5.4	5.4
Economic indicators			
Average earnings	$24,159	$25,230	$25,051
Unemployment rate	5.3	4.8	4.9

(Continued)

TABLE 3.1   Individual and Household Characteristics of Recent
             Mexican-Born Migrants and Characteristics of the
             Places They Settled, 1990 and 2000
             (Percentage Except as Noted) (*Continued*)

Attribute	1990	2000	Combined
Migration flow in previous decade			
Recent Mexican-born per 1,000			
in state for previous decade	0.6	2.6	2.3
Not recent Mexican-born per 1,000			
in state for previous decade	2.3	3.3	3.2
U.S.-born Mexican origin per 1,000			
in state for previous decade	8.7	10.8	10.4

Source: Authors' compilation from IPUMS data.

states in the 1980s are much more likely to be naturalized (16.4 percent) than those migrating into such states in the 1990s (8.8 percent). A similar difference exists for the percentage arriving in new destinations from elsewhere in the United States as opposed to directly from Mexico (two fifths are internal migrants during the 1980s but only one third during the 1990s).

The latter finding may indicate that those with more U.S. experience are less dependent on established ethnic communities and thus able to move to places where few other Mexican-origin persons already reside when the migration flows were generally smaller in the 1980s. They may also have accumulated savings and other resources in their time in the United States which would provide valuable resources in the absence of such support networks. Alternatively, the phenomenal growth of immigration flows in the 1990s may have simply been driven by industry sectors that rely heavily on unauthorized migrants. In any case, important questions are raised as to who the original seed migrants were as compared to the pioneer and settler migrants who arrived later—important questions for future research.

We also note that the percentage of migrants that live in horizontally extended families—in which uncles, aunts, cousins, or adult siblings live with the householder—increases over the course of the decade, from 35.3 percent to 46.3 percent. This result, too, could derive from a greater presence of unauthorized migrants during the 1990s. Recent international immigrants, legal or unauthorized, may often rely on extended-family members for initial housing, particularly labor migrants whose wages are too low to support independent housing. Increased reliance on extended-family members may be evidence of the operation of one mechanism that lowers the costs of migration, which in turn causes more migration, according to the theory of cumulative causation.

Turning to the characteristics of the states in which the migrants settled, the trends over the two decades reflect changes in the structure of the American economy in general. The number of jobs in agricultural and manufacturing sectors declined notably in the course of the decade while those in the construction and retail trade industries increased. It is also notable that Mexican migrants, possessing the lowest skill levels among all immigrant groups in the United States, settled in states where the low-skill service sector declined slightly in size over the decade. This may reflect some restructuring and outsourcing of jobs that were traditionally held by native-born whites but are now shifting to immigrant labor, as discussed, but it also may reflect demographic changes in the native-born community, such as aging due to out-migration of young people and low fertility, that make for diminished supplies of low-skilled natives.

Finally, we consider three cumulative causation variables that describe the Mexican-origin population in the state in the decade prior to the migrants' move to the state: the relative size of recent Mexican-born migrants (those migrating five years before the census), the relative size of the Mexican-born population not migrating in the previous five years, and the relative size of the American-born Mexican-origin population. Both of these figures increased from the 1980s to the 1990s, but the number of recent prior migrants increased the most by far, more than quadrupling, whereas earlier migrants increased by less than half, and the native-born Mexican group increased by only about one eighth. Other things equal, therefore, the stock of social capital accessible to new migrants was increasing rapidly in destination areas.

PRINCIPAL-COMPONENTS ANALYSIS

For two reasons, we employ principal-components analysis (PCA) to analyze variables that the literature suggests might affect migration. We do so first for theoretical and second for methodological reasons. PCA enables us to identify independent dimensions of information that explain substantial portions of variance among a group of variables, which in this case includes most of our independent variables (Kim and Mueller 1978; Rummel 1970). PCA thus allows us to test the supposition that migrants who settled in new destinations may be described in terms of multiple individual and destination attributes, which may indicate various influences and explanations for the migration flows to new destinations as distinct from explanations that emphasize only one kind of influence.

Methodologically, PCA also provides a way to simplify our OLS (ordinary least squares) regression analyses by reducing multi-colinearity due to correlations among independent variables through its grouping of such variables into single dimensions. Typically, multi-colinearity is minimized through data reduction, which eliminates variables that are highly correlated with others that remain in the regression model. This may, however, remove explanatory information if the correlations are not extremely high. Although there is overlap in the variance explained between two correlated variables by definition, if they are not perfectly colinear then they each have explanatory power that is mutually exclusive of the other variable (in PCA this is referred to as uniqueness). So removing one variable or another may reduce overall explained variance. For example, we found marital status and presence of own children in the household to be correlated (and thus a source of multi-colinearity) in preliminary regression models. Conducting the principal-components analysis helps to eliminate such multi-colinearity problems.

Our general objective is to delineate the dimensions of migrant destination factors that might relate to the relative size of migration flows. The output of PCA is a set of new variables, derived from the principal components, which are simply linear combinations of the original variables. One of the main advantages of using PCA, other than retaining all our variables, is that the component scores are constructed in such a way that they are orthogonal to one another, or completely uncorrelated. Because of differences in variance across the individual-level and state-level variables, we conducted the PCA on each set separately to obtain two sets of factor scores. So the scores across the two levels of analysis will not necessarily be uncorrelated in our regression analyses, although they will be within levels. Table 3.2 shows the results of our analysis.

Our first inference from table 3.2 is that Mexican-born migrants to new destinations in the 1980s and 1990s were diverse in terms of both what kinds of individual attributes affected migration and what kinds of places they settled in, just as the theory predicts. At the individual level, two principal components show eigenvalues above 1^5 with multiple variables having high loadings on each, indicating that patterns of characteristics vary among migrants settling in new destinations. The fact that only certain variables were grouped together in a couple of factors and that other variables were not correlated enough to merit inclusion in these factors indicates that the migrants were heterogeneous across multiple dimensions. The same is true for the kinds of places in which they settled. The migrants did not all go to the same kinds of places, indicating that multiple kinds of flows are involved in settlement in various kinds of new destinations.

TABLE 3.2   Principal Components for Recent Mexican Migrants to New Destinations, United States, 1990 and 2000

	IPC1[a]	IPC2[b]	
Individual-level analysis			
Traditional family			
Married	88*	8[f]	
Householder or spouse of householder	78*	13	
Lives with own children	85*	10	
Lives with non-family household member	−58*	−8	
U.S. experience			
Migration origin within United States	25	72*	
Years in United States	23	84*	
Arrived in U.S. at fourteen or younger	−12	77*	

	SPC1[c]	SPC2[d]	SPC3[e]
State-level analysis			
Agriculture and food processing			
Average wages	−85*	−14	−8
Percentage in agricultural industries	85*	−16	6
Percentage in food manufacturing	76*	−39	−13
Construction and low-skill service			
Percentage in low-skill service industries	−16	76*	−37
Percentage in construction	15	86*	−5
Percentage in durable manufacturing	29	−66*	−9
Trade			
Percentage in retail trade	46	31	66*
Percentage in wholesale trade	2	−31	72*
Percentage of self-employed Mexican migrants	−11	−2	71*

Source: Authors' compilation from IPUMS, data.
[a] IPC1 = Individual-level component 1.
[b] IPC2 = Individual-level component 2.
[c] SPC1 = State-level component 1.
[d] SPC2 = State-level component 2.
[e] SPC3 = State-level component 3.
[f] Factor loadings are multiplied by 100 and rounded to the nearest integer.
*Absolute values of 50 or greater, indicating high loadings.

One can interpret the dimensions in terms of the variables that have high absolute loadings on each principal component. The first individual-level principal component loads positively on being married and other variables that indicate the migrant lives in a nuclear-family household. So this dimension indicates that migrants who settled in new destinations can be described in terms of their marital status and family-formation patterns. Many migrants to new destinations likely moved with their families while others went as single males. These two groups might move for different reasons: families may hint at more permanent settlement and migration resulting from more usual motivations such as seeking out better lifestyles, neighborhoods, and schools, whereas single migrants may indicate labor-specific migration motivations.

We summarize descriptions of the principal components for the individual, household, and state levels in table 3.2. The first individual-level component, IPC1, is the "family" structure; the second individual-level component, IPC2, describes migrants in terms of U.S. experience—whether they migrated from within the United States, the number of years they have been in the United States, and their age upon initial arrival in the country. Intuitively one would expect these variables to be correlated, and this is confirmed in the principal components analysis. State-level principal component 1 (SPC1) distinguishes states with relatively higher concentrations of both food-processing and agricultural industries. Interestingly, the average earnings for those in the labor force in these kinds of states tend to be low. State-level principal component 2 (SPC2) describes states in terms of relatively large construction and low-skill service sectors and relatively small durable manufacturing sectors. State-level principal component 3 (SPC3) reflects higher concentrations of trade industries and rates of migrant self-employment.

Again, the most important finding from the PCA is that neither recent Mexican migrants nor destinations can be described in terms of just one kind of flow, indicating that multiple factors are involved in processes of migration to new destinations. Mexican-born migrants are not a homogeneous group in terms of individual attributes nor in terms of the economic activity occurring in the places in which they settled: they form nuclear- and extended-family households, are single and married, have both more and less U.S. experience, and have settled in diverse places with different kinds of economic activities.[6]

REGRESSION MODELS

With the results of the principal-components analyses in hand, we now turn to multivariate analyses to understand how the degree of previous migration and what kinds of flows most relate to growth in the relative size of the recent-Mexican-migrant population in destination states. Migration theories imply that different factors influence migration processes under different circumstances. For example, we expect that migrants with more U.S. experience will migrate to places in which the flows are smaller and less developed (Neuman and Tienda 1994; Saenz 1991). Also, strong construction and low-skill service sectors typically create demand for low-wage immigrant labor, so we also expect migrants into such places to arrive in larger numbers. To assess these kinds of ideas, we regress the relative size of the migration flow on the five principal component scores, the cumulative causation indicators, and seven other variables. The seven other variables are indicators of sources of influence that prior research and theory suggest may affect the extent of Mexican migration.

We also include in our models the relative sizes of different segments of the Mexican-origin population in the decade prior to the migrants' arrival. These variables allow us to test for the effects of cumulative causation (including decreasing costs of migration) on the relative size of migration flows. Theory would suggest that recent migrants in the prior decade may have the greatest effect, since they are likely to have the closest ties to additional potential migrants (Massey et al. 1987). American-born Mexican-origin persons may also have some effect because they often function as primary recruiters, owing to their greater U.S. experience, which enables them to serve as middle-men between American companies and potential co-ethnic migrants.

Including the cumulative causation indicators in the models along with principal-component-factor scores also enables the examination of the effects of the different kinds of migration (as represented by the principal components) controlling for differences in growth due to cumulative causation processes. Also, when we include the relative size of the state's recent Mexican-migrant population in the model as an independent variable, the coefficients on the factor variables may be interpreted as representing decade change in the relative number of recent Mexican migrants to the states.

The series of nested regression models in table 3.3 shows the relationships between the various individual and household and destination-state attributes on the one hand and the relative size of migration flows on the other. We first focus on the effects of previously existing Mexican-origin populations. As expected, the results show that cumulative causation plays a major role in migration to new destinations. For each migrant per 1,000 population who settled in new destination states in the previous decade, there were more than 4 more migrants per 1,000 population in the subsequent decade. Also, American-born Mexican-origin persons exert a relatively small contribution to the growth of migration flows and only the squared term for recently arrived migrants is significant, indicating support for the theoretically expected pattern of smaller increases due to cumulative causation the larger the prior flows.

TABLE 3.3   OLS Models of Recent Foreign–Born Mexican Share of State Population in Current Decade, New Destination States, 1990 and 2000

Parameters	Model 1	Model 2	Model 3	Model 4	Model 5
Intercept	3.3***	3.5***	3.8***	3.6***	3.3***
Recent foreign-born Mexican share of state population, last decade (1)	4.2***	5.7***	5.2***	5.2***	5.5***
Not recent foreign-born share of state population, last decade (2)	−2.2***	−3.5***	−2.9***	−2.9***	−2.9***
U.S.-born Mexican share of state population, last decade (3)	0.4***	0.3***	0.3***	0.3***	0.3***
(1), Squared		−0.2**	−0.2*	−0.2**	−0.2**
(2), Squared		0.2	0.1	0.1	0.1
IPC1: Traditional family forms			−0.3**	−0.2*	−0.2*
IPC2: U.S. experience			−0.6***	−0.6**	−0.6**
SPC1: Agriculture and food processing			2.5**	2.3*	2.2
SPC2: Construction and low-skill service			6.1*	5.9*	6.2*
SPC3: Retail and wholesale trade			−6.2**	−6.0**	−6.4**

(Continued)

TABLE 3.3   OLS Models of Recent Foreign-Born Mexican Share of State Population in Current Decade, New Destination States, 1990 and 2000 (*Continued*)

Parameters	Model 1	Model 2	Model 3	Model 4	Model 5
Age				−0.2	−0.1
Age squared				0.2	0.2
Naturalized[a]				0.0	−0.1
Less than high school education[b]				0.2**	0.2**
State unemployment rate				−0.6	−0.8
1990 census[c]					0.9
N	29,914	29,914	29,914	29,914	29,914
F	249.8***	479.8***	756.4***	695.9***	734.3***
R^2	0.87	0.89	0.91	0.91	0.91

Source: Authors' compilation from IPUMS data.

*p < .10; ** p < .05; *** p < .01; tests of significance based on the estimation of robust standard errors adjusted for degrees of freedom due to the inclusion of both individual and aggregate levels in the models.

[a] Reference category: not naturalized.
[b] Reference category: high school or higher education.
[c] Reference category: 2000 census.

Thus, prior migration begets more current migration, as theory suggests, at an increasing rate in the beginning and at a decreasing rate later. More specifically, recently arrived prior migrants have the greatest impact on future migration. Earlier-arriving prior migrants, by contrast, show a negative effect, net of recently arrived migrants. In interpreting this, we must note that these two prior Mexican-migrant-share variables show a strong positive correlation ($r = 0.90$), meaning that earlier-arrived prior migration exerts an indirect positive effect on current migration even though its direct effect is negative. The latter negative relationship may represent something of a "ceiling" effect. That is, although in general, "old" migration begets "recent" migration, which begets "current" migration, unusually high old migration also begets a less current migration at the highest levels.

Consistent with the idea that multiple factors contribute to the dispersion of the Mexican-born population, almost all the principal-component-factor scores show strong relationships with current migration flows. In other words, cumulative causation is not the only dynamic involved in the growth of migration flows. We can now begin to understand how various kinds of migrants contribute to the migration process (see table 3.3). The negative coefficient (from model 4; see table 3.3) on the principal component that describes U.S. experience, −0.6, indicates that those with more time in the United States migrate to states with relatively smaller migration increases, or conversely, those with the least experience are more involved in migration to places experiencing larger relative increases in Mexican migration. Many of these are undoubtedly young unauthorized male migrants, the kind for whom the costs of migration are the lowest. Not coincidentally, U.S. experience suggests the prior accumulation of general American cultural resources for coping with life in new destinations and thus would allow Mexican-born persons to go to places with relatively fewer co-ethnics.

Younger migrants are also associated with relatively smaller flows. At first this seems counterintuitive to relatively more U.S. experience. But the earliest migrants to new destinations may in fact be among the 1.5 generation, who were born in Mexico and arrived in the United States at an early age. This would provide them with more American education, which likely translates into a broader range of options, including migration to new destinations where they might hope for better opportunities relative to traditional destinations (Light 2003).

Relatively small coefficients on the principal components and variables that describe individual attributes indicate that personal characteristics are not the primary drivers of migration to new destinations. Rather, the models are dominated by principal-components-factor scores indicating larger concentrations of certain kinds of industries in the states to which migrants moved, along with the cumulative causation variables. As predicted by theory, higher concentrations of state workers in construction and low-skill service sectors, indicating perhaps a greater presence of larger high-end service sectors, which in turn create demand for low-end services, are strongly positively related to larger flows of migration. More jobs in the food-processing industry and agriculture are also related to larger migration flows, although not to the extent that low-skill service and construction densities are.

The underlying reasons for these labor flows may have to do with the demographic changes outlined previously. Fewer native-born persons are available and willing to do low-end service jobs, which creates higher demand for immigrant labor. A predominance of persons with less than high school education in states with more migration is consistent with this hypothesis, given that such a result undoubtedly derives from the presence of low-skilled unauthorized migrants.

Similarly, the small but statistically significant coefficient for the "non-traditional-family" factor (−0.2) indicates that living with non–family members or with other relatives is related to larger flows, whereas living with a spouse and children is related to smaller increases in flows. Interestingly, being married and living in a nuclear family is not strongly related to the relative size of migration flows. If the migrants are moving more for the usual reasons for migration—lifestyle choices and better job opportunities—this makes sense, because families may in general respond more to conditions at migration origin, such as school overcrowding or high crime rates, than to conditions at destination, which our models emphasize. Or they may tend to become more involved in the more mature stages of migration as the flows start to subside somewhat because of saturation effects. We also tested for effects of compositional change across the decade (model 5) but this is not significant in the model.

CONCLUSIONS

Migration between Mexico and the United States has a long history and the dynamics of the flows have been extensively studied and well documented. Even through the mid-1990s, many scholars of immigration did not expect Mexican-born persons to migrate and settle in destinations outside the traditional regions in the Southwest in significant numbers. Thus, many observers were caught by surprise when dramatic growth occurred in the Mexican-born population in new destination states during the 1990s. It also underscored that little was known about the structure and dynamics of this significant population shift. This chapter has sought to fill this gap by pursuing three goals: to gauge the extent to which cumulative causation mechanisms drive growth in current Mexican migration to new destinations; to chart who the migrants were and how their characteristics related to growth in new destination migration; and to assess the larger economic and demographic forces that shape the extent of Mexican migration to new destinations across the United States.

One of the most important findings of the present research is that cumulative causation processes drove the dispersal of the Mexican-born population throughout the country during the 1990s to a considerable degree. Places with more migration before the 1990s begot further migration later on, although, within this overall tendency, variations occurred that were related to place and flow characteristics. Regarding our second objective, we also observe that Mexican migrants to new destinations are a heterogeneous group. They vary across several demographic and socioeconomic factors and variables. This is an important finding in and of itself. Popular public perceptions and even academic scholarship sometimes assume that Mexican-born immigrants constitute a large homogeneous group of low-wage, unauthorized laborers (Huntington 2004). Our findings run contrary to this assumption. Certainly many of the migrants who settled in new destinations likely arrived there directly from Mexico, without documents, but others, who possess much more U.S. experience and who even had naturalized, also engaged in the process, providing insights into how Mexican migrants change the longer they are here (Bean, Brown, and Rumbaut 2006).

Regarding our third objective, we also find evidence that various demand-related factors played important roles in migration to new destinations. The states with larger service and construction industries experienced larger inflows of Mexican-born persons, undoubtedly as a result of global economic changes in which the concentration of capital and business and financial services creates locales with high growth rates in both high- and low-end service jobs, as well as jobs in commercial and residential construction. We also surmise that demographic changes contribute to the demand for immigrant labor, since in many states there are few native-born persons willing to do low-end service work. The evidence noted of cumulative causation suggests that such processes are likely to work in combination with economic and demographic factors but are not solely dependent on them as a major driver of growth in Mexican-born populations in new destinations.

We believe our findings hold important implications for the incorporation of immigrants into American society and for immigration policy debates. Regarding the former, indications that the Mexican-born persons settling in new destinations are not solely young male target earners arriving directly from Mexico leads us to think that settlement in new destinations may be a new pathway or strategy for some to achieve socioeconomic mobility. Other research in which we are currently engaged suggests that although Mexican migrants in new destinations may earn less than they might have in traditional destination states, their earnings gaps with natives in the new locales are smaller than they would have been with the natives in the traditional destination states (Leach and Bean 2006). Further work on such topics is certainly warranted. Also, we note that the current policy proposals for "guest-worker" programs offered as "solutions" to unauthorized migration do not appear to take into account that many Mexican-born persons are involved in patterns of settlement throughout the United States, not just patterns suggesting that they primarily come to work for a short time and then return home. A "guest-worker" program that does not deal with these realities may not succeed, at least not as a means for checking unauthorized immigrant flows.

NOTES

1. Throughout this chapter we refer to Arizona, California, New Mexico, Texas, and Illinois as "traditional destinations" of Mexican immigration. "New destinations" include all other states within the United States.
2. We considered an analysis of only metropolitan areas, but this would exclude migrants living in smaller towns and rural areas, which are expected to be an important component of new destinations
3. Colorado, from 1.0 in 1980 to 3.6 in 1990; Utah, 0.6 to 2.5; Georgia, 0.1 to 2.71; Oregon, 1.0 to 5.1; Kansas, 0.6 to 2.8.
4. Iowa: 0.7 in 1990 to 5.32 in 2000; Michigan, from 0.6 in 1990 to 3.29 in 2000; and Alabama, from 0.2 in 1990 to 3.13 in 2000 (not shown separately in graphic), among others.
5. We use this common rule of thumb to assess the explanatory power of each principal component. The eigenvalues for each principal component represent the amount of variance among our independent variables that each explains. They are ordered according to their explanatory power such that the first principal component always explains the most variance. The last two components at the individual level only contained one variable with high loading so we included the variable rather than the component score in our regression model.
6. We recognize that our data focus on migrant attributes and "pull"-side economic actors and give no information about migrant origins. These will be considered in future analyses.

REFERENCES

Bartel, Ann P. 1989. "Where Do the New U.S. Immigrants Live?" *Journal of Labor Economics* 7(4): 371–91.

Bean, Frank D., and Gillian Stevens. 2003. *America's Newcomers and the Dynamics of Diversity.* New York: Russell Sage Foundation.

Bean, Frank D., Susan K. Brown, and Rubén G. Rumbaut. 2006. "Mexican Immigrant Political and Economic Incorporation." *Perspectives on Politics* 4(2): 309–13.

Bean, Frank D., and B. Lindsay Lowell. 2003. "Immigrant Employment and Mobility Opportunities in California." *The State of California Labor* 3: 87–117.

Bean, Frank D., Thomas J. Espenshade, Michael J. White, and Robert F. Dymowski. 1990. "Post-IRCA Changes in the Volume and Composition of Undocumented Migration to the United States: An Assessment Based on Apprehensions Data." In *Undocumented Migration to the United States: IRCA and the Experience of the 1980s*, edited by Frank D. Bean, Barry Edmonston, and Jeffrey S. Passel. Washington: Urban Institute.

Broadway, Michael J. 1995. "From City to Countryside: Recent Changes in the Structure and Location of the Meat and Fish Processing Industries." In *Any Way You Cut It: Meat Processing and Small Town America*, edited by Donald D. Stull, Michael J. Broadway, and David Griffith. Lawrence, Kan.: University Press of Kansas.

Farley, Reynolds. 1995. "Introduction." In *State of the Union: America in the 1990s*, edited by Reynolds Farley. New York: Russell Sage Foundation.

Gouveia, Lourdes, and Rogelio Saenz. 2000. "Global Forces and Latino Population Growth in the Midwest: A Regional and Subregional Analysis." *Great Plains Research* 10(2): 305–28.

Griffith, David, Michael J. Broadway, and Donald D. Stull. 1995. "Introduction: Making Meat." In *Any Way You Cut It: Meat Processing and Small Town America*, edited by David Griffith, Michael J. Broadway, and Donald D. Stull. Lawrence, Kan.: University Press of Kansas.

Hernández-León, Rubén, and Víctor Zúñiga. 2000. "Making Carpet by the Mile: The Emergence of a Mexican Immigrant Community in an Industrial Region of the U.S. Historic South." *Social Science Quarterly* 81(1): 49–66.

———. 2003. "Mexican Immigrant Communities in the South and Social Capital: The Case of Dalton, Georgia." Unpublished manuscript.

Huntington, Samuel P. 2004. *Who Are We? The Challenges to America's National Identity*. New York: Simon & Schuster.

Johnson, Hans P. 2000. "Movin' Out: Domestic Migration to and from California in the 1990s." In *California Counts: Population Trends and Profile*. Report. San Francisco, Calif.: Public Policy Institute of California. Accessed at http://www.nationalcitynetwork.org/showdoc.html?id=32006&p=1.

Kim, Jae-On, and Charles W. Mueller. 1978. *Factor Analysis: Statistical Methods and Practical Issues*, edited by E. M. Uslaner. Newbury Park, Calif.: Sage Publications.

Kritz, Mary M., and June Marie Nogle. 1994. "Nativity Concentration and Internal Migration Among the Foreign-Born." *Demography* 31(3): 509–24.

Leach, Mark A., and Frank D. Bean. 2006. "Moving into Mobility? Internal Migration and the Incorporation of Mexican-born Persons." Unpublished paper, University of California, Irvine.

Lee, Everett S. 1966. "A Theory of Migration." *Demography* 3(1): 47–57.

Light, Ivan. 2003. "Immigration and Housing Shortage in Los Angeles, 1970–2000." In *Host Societies and the Reception of Immigrants,* edited by Jeffrey G. Reitz. La Jolla, Calif.: University of California, San Diego, Center for Comparative Immigration Studies.

Massey, Douglas S. 1999. "Why Does Immigration Occur? A Theoretical Synthesis." In *Handbook of International Migration,* edited by Charles Hirschman, Philip Kasinitz, and Joshua DeWind. New York: Russell Sage Foundation.

Massey, Douglas S., Jorge Durand, and Nolan J. Malone. 2002. *Beyond Smoke and Mirrors: Mexican Immigration in an Era of Economic Integration.* New York: Russell Sage Foundation.

Massey, Douglas S., Luin Goldring, and Jorge Durand. 1994. "Continuities in Transnational Migration: An Analysis of Nineteen Mexican Communities." *American Journal of Sociology* 99(6): 1492–533.

Massey, Douglas S., Rafael Alarcón, Jorge Durand, and Humberto Gonzalez. 1987. *Return to Aztlan: The Social Process of International Migration from Western Mexico.* Berkeley and Los Angeles, Calif.: University of California Press.

Neuman, Kristin E., and Marta Tienda. 1994. "The Settlement and Secondary Migration Patterns of Legalized Immigrants: Insights from Administrative Records." In *Immigration and Ethnicity: The Integration of America's Newest Arrivals.* Washington: Urban Institute Press.

Passel, Jeffrey S., and Wendy Zimmerman. 2001. "Are Immigrants Leaving California? Settlement Patterns of Immigrants in the Late 1990s." Paper. Urban Institute. Accessed at http://www.urban.org/UploadedPDF/are_immigrants_leaving_ca.pdf.

Portes, Alejandro, and Robert L. Bach. 1985. *Latin Journey: Cuban and Mexican Immigrants in the United States.* Berkeley, Calif.: University of California Press.

Ruggles, Steven, and Matthew Sobek, 2003. "Integrated Public Use Microdata Series, Version 3.0." Minneapolis, Minn.: Historical Census Projects, University of Minnesota.

Rummel, Rudolph J. 1970. *Applied Factor Analysis.* Evanston, Ill.: Northwestern University Press.

Saenz, Rogelio. 1991. "Interregional Migration Patterns of Chicanos: The Core, Periphery, and Frontier." *Social Science Quarterly* 72(1): 135–48.

Sassen, Saskia. 2000. *Cities in a World Economy.* Thousand Oaks, Calif.: Pine Forge Press.

Suro, Roberto, and Jeffrey S. Passel. 2003. "The Rise of the Second Generation: Changing Patterns in Hispanic Population Growth." Vol. 2003. Los Angeles: Pew Hispanic Research Center.

CHAPTER 4

✕

CHANGING FACES, CHANGING PLACES: THE EMERGENCE OF NEW NONMETROPOLITAN IMMIGRANT GATEWAYS

KATHARINE M. DONATO, CHARLES TOLBERT,
ALFRED NUCCI, AND YUKIO KAWANO

Since 1990, studies have documented the widespread growth of immigrant populations in American communities not known as common destinations in the past. One recent analysis of the changing geography of Mexican immigrants described shifts from traditional destinations in California and Texas to new states such as Colorado, Utah, and Nevada, and to new cities such as New York City, Phoenix, Las Vegas, and Denver (Durand, Massey, and Charvet 2000). Other studies illustrate the breadth of the foreign-born population's geographic dispersion over the past fifteen years, with new destinations as varied as Dalton, Georgia, a small town well known for its carpet production (Engstrom 2001; Hernández-León and Zúñiga 2000); Garden City, Kansas, and Storm Lake, Iowa, where meatpacking employers sought low-wage workers (Grey 1999; Stull, Broadway, and Erickson 1992); and Houma and Morgan City in southern Louisiana, where semiskilled employment opportunities in the oil and gas industry proliferated (Donato, Bankston, and Robinson 2001; Donato, Stainback, and Bankston 2005).

These migratory trends have been accompanied by the rapid growth of Hispanic populations nationwide (Suro and Singer 2002); by the year 2000, Latinos had become the nation's largest minority group, edging out African Americans for the first time in United States history. Approximately half of all nonmetropolitan Latinos now live outside the five southwestern states of Arizona, California, Colorado, New Mexico, and Texas (Kandel and Cromartie 2003). These trends underscore the complexity of immigration's new geography (Kandel and Cromartie 2004; Zúñiga and Hernández-León 2005).

These trends are provocative in part because of what they imply for nonmetropolitan areas that have begun attracting immigrants but that have little experience or infrastructure to assist newcomers (Griffith 1995; Guthey 2001; Singer 2004; Donato et al. 2007). Welcome or not, new immigrants constitute a key factor in the "rural rebound"—e.g., when rural population growth occurs following years of stagnation or decline—documented by demographers during the 1990s (Johnson 1998, 1999; Johnson and Beale 1998, 1999). Indeed, immigrants have offset native population decline in some nonmetropolitan areas and fueled growth in others. As a result, the face of rural America has an increasingly foreign face (Fix, Martin, and Taylor 1997).

In this chapter we move beyond qualitative evidence to evaluate empirically how the foreign-born presence has shifted geographically since 1990, including to nonmetropolitan areas. Specifically, we draw on confidential data specially tabulated from the 1990 and 2000 censuses of population to provide the geographic detail and analytic flexibility necessary not only to measure spatial shifts in the distribution of foreigners, but also their changing social and demographic characteristics. These data permit a richer, and more detailed analysis of the changing faces and places of nonmetropolitan America than heretofore available.

DATA AND METHODS

We base our analysis on tabulations of confidential data extracted from the 1990 and 2000 censuses of population, selecting foreign-born persons from each source to examine the changing geography of migration during the 1990s. The data files were produced internally within the U.S. Census Bureau and contain geographic detail down to the block group level, a level of detail not normally available in the public domain. Because these data are confidential and protected under title 13 of the United States Code, we conducted all analyses at the Census Bureau headquarters under controlled conditions, and they were approved by the bureau's Disclosure Review Board. Our willingness to comply with these restrictions meant that we were not confined to the large geographic areas (the Public Use Microdata Areas, or PUMAs) that other researchers have been forced to rely on in studying immigration.

In addition to a more detailed geography, internal Census Bureau data also offer greater flexibility to produce novel tabulations that take advantage of a larger sample size. The internal files we used contain the full set of long-form questionnaire responses, which was administered to approximately 17 percent of the United States population (compared with only a 5 percent sample for the largest publicly available file). We use these data to define and characterize a set of what we termed "offset counties," counties where the arrival of the foreign-born actually stemmed a population decline caused by a decrease of natives in the population, to yield a sustained, and in some cases an increased, population during the 1990s. Internal data also allow us to describe the attributes of people who live in these places, working upward from actual microdata to generate custom profiles of foreigners and natives.

CHANGING FACES, CHANGING PLACES

Our analysis proceeds in two stages. We begin by describing shifts in the native- and foreign-born populations of United States metropolitan and nonmetropolitan areas since 1990, focusing on recently arrived immigrants. These tabulations reveal the extent to which the foreign-born are present in new counties around the United States and to identify which counties experienced a decline in the native-born population that was offset by a rise in the foreign-born population—these are our "offset counties." In a second stage, we construct a profile of the foreign-born and native-born residents of these counties, describing shifts in key individual characteristics and household attributes, such as education, naturalization, place of birth, earnings, and income. These tabulations raise many questions about future population trends in nonmetropolitan areas, issues that we consider in the last section.

The Emergence of Offset Counties

Table 4.1 shows changes in the relative size of the native- and foreign-born populations of United States nonmetropolitan and metropolitan counties between 1990 and 2000.[1] As can be seen, some 3.2 percent of nonmetropolitan residents were born abroad in 2000, compared to only 1.9 percent in 1990. Likewise, the foreign-born percentage also increased in metropolitan areas, going from 9.5 percent to 13.1 percent over the period. Particularly striking are the last two rows of the table, which describe shifts in the share of foreign-born who are recently arrived (those who entered over the prior decade). In 1990, a little over one third (35.7 percent) of the foreign-born living in nonmetropolitan areas had arrived in the prior ten years, but by 2000 recent arrivals made up almost half (45 percent) of foreigners in nonmetropolitan counties.

TABLE 4.1   Foreign-Born and Total Population of U.S. Metropolitan and Nonmetropolitan Areas in 1990 and 2000

Place of Birth	Nonmetropolitan Areas		Metropolitan Areas	
	1990	2000	1990	2000
Percentage native-born	98.1	96.8	90.5	86.9
Percentage foreign-born	1.9	3.2	9.5	13.1
Total population (thousands)	50,897.9	56,159.3	197,812.0	225,262.6
Recent foreign-born (thousands)[a]	352.2	795.2	8,311.5	12,383.1
Percentage of all foreign-born	35.7	45.0	44.3	42.2

Source: Authors' compilation of U.S. Census Bureau Long-form Sample Data, 1990 and 2000.
[a] "Recent foreign-born" refers to those who entered United States within ten years prior to the census date.

These percentage shifts were the result of dramatic growth in the absolute number of foreigners in nonmetropolitan areas, with the total more than doubling from 352,000 in 1990 to 795,000 in 2000. Although considerably larger in metropolitan areas, the foreign-born population grew less dramatically in the 1990s, going from 8.3 to 12.4 million, a 56 percent increase, but not as great as the 78 percent increase recorded in nonmetropolitan areas, and the percentage of recently arrived foreigners in metropolitan areas actually fell slightly between 1990 and 2000, going from 44.3 percent to 42.2 percent. These patterns of change led us to consider two basic questions: First, within metropolitan and nonmetropolitan areas, did foreign-born populations grow evenly in the 1990s? And second, which counties would have lost population had it not been for growth among the foreign-born?

Table 4.2 summarizes patterns of population growth within metropolitan and nonmetropolitan counties during the 1990s, classifying them by whether native and foreign populations increased or decreased. The first column shows that of the 590 nonmetropolitan counties that lost population in the 1990s, about a third (33.9 percent, or 200 in total) lost native and foreign residents alike. Although the absolute number of metropolitan counties was smaller, about the same share (31.2 percent) of the 80 counties that declined in size also experienced losses in both populations.

TABLE 4.2   Metropolitan and Nonmetropolitan Counties Classified by Native-Born, Foreign-Born, and Total Population Increase or Decrease Between 1990 and 2000

| Change in Native and Foreign Populations | Change in Total Population 1990 to 2000 | | | |
| | Nonmetropolitan Areas | | Metropolitan Areas | |
	Decrease	Increase	Decrease	Increase
Foreign-born decrease				
Native-born decrease	33.9%	n.a.	31.2%	n.a.
Native-born increase	1.7	10.6%	5.0	2.7%
Foreign-born increase				
Native-born decrease	64.4	3.5[a]	62.5	4.1[a]
Native-born increase	n.a.	86.1	n.a.	93.2
Total counties	590	1,695	80	740

Source: Authors' compilation of U.S. Census Bureau Long-form Sample Data, 1990 and 2000.
[a] Native-born population decline offset by foreign-born population growth.

Particularly noteworthy, however, are the counties that grew in population only because of gains in the number of foreign-born. Among the 1,695 nonmetropolitan counties that experienced population growth, 3.5 percent (60 counties) were sustained only by an increase in the number of foreign-born, and among the 740 metropolitan counties that grew overall, 4.1 percent (or 30) were sustained by growth in the foreign-born population. This subset of "offset" counties includes places that avoided overall population decline because of growth in the foreign-born population.

To see where the newly growing nonmetropolitan counties were located, we selected offset counties that exceeded the national median for nonmetropolitan change in the foreign-born population, percentage foreign-born, and percentage change in foreign-born. Using GIS, we then superimposed major north–south transportation corridors on this subset of thirty-eight nonmetropolitan counties. As Figure 4.1 indicates, many counties are proximate to Interstate Highway 35 which stretches from Laredo TX to Duluth MN. This is a busy freight and passenger highway known as the "NAFTA Corridor" because buses filled with migrants use it daily, heading north and south. Many of the bus companies, such as Tornado, Conejo, and Mares, have acquired property along the highway to use as rest stations and restaurants or taquerias. The development of these transportation services is more than a convenience; it enables and influences

FIGURE 4.1   Location of Offset Countries Along Interstate 35 in the Midwestern United States

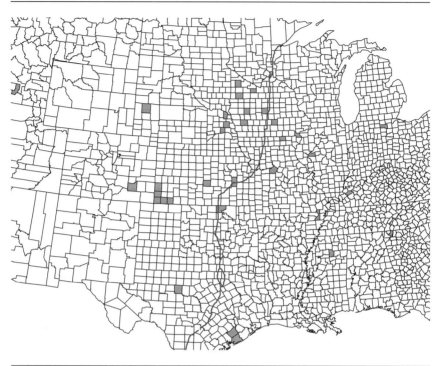

Source: Thematic map created by Charles Tolbert.

the emergence and maintenance of new immigrant destinations outside traditional urban destinations.

Changes in National Origins

We now turn to an analysis of changes in the characteristics of foreign-born persons living in metropolitan and nonmetropolitan areas of the United States during the 1990s, emphasizing the attributes of offset counties as compared to others, beginning with national and regional origins. Table 4.3 documents substantial differences in origins between metropolitan and nonmetropolitan areas over the decade, a pattern that characterizes both offset and all United States counties. In 1990, somewhat over one third of the foreign-born in nonmetropolitan offset areas (37.3 percent) were born in Mexico and another 15.2 percent came from other Latin American countries. Just ten years later, however, the origins had shifted

TABLE 4.3   Distribution of Immigrants by Country or Region of Birth in Offset and All Counties, 1990 and 2000

Country or Region of Birth	Nonmetropolitan Areas		Metropolitan Areas	
	1990	2000	1990	2000
Offset counties				
Mexico	37.3%	58.5%	8.9%	13.1%
Other Latin America	15.2	15.5	30.8	32.4
Asia	14.8	10.6	22.5	26.8
Europe	20.6	10.1	26.8	21.3
Middle East	0.5	0.5	2.4	2.1
Africa	0.6	1.2	1.9	2.8
North America	6.7	3.2	1.5	1.1
Other	4.2	0.3	5.3	0.3
Total (thousands)	38.6	90.7	4,243.4	6,092.7
All counties				
Mexico	32.6	48.9	21.2	28.3
Other Latin America	6.2	9.0	21.6	23.0
Asia	17.8	15.8	23.4	24.7
Europe	26.6	17.3	21.8	16.1
Middle East	1.0	0.8	2.1	1.9
Africa	1.2	1.4	1.9	2.9
North America	9.7	6.1	3.5	2.5
Other	4.9	0.8	4.6	0.5
Total (thousands)	987.9	2,767.0	18,779.4	29,340.9

Source: Authors' compilation of U.S. Census Bureau Long-form Sample Data.

dramatically, with Mexicans making up 59 percent of all foreigners in nonmetropolitan offset counties, while the share of other Latin Americans remained fairly stable at 15.5 percent.

Thus, over the decade, the regional origins of immigrants to offset counties grew far more concentrated in Mexico. An index of dissimilarity computed between the two distributions reveals that nearly a quarter (24 percent) of immigrants would have to be moved in 2000 to achieve the distribution of 1990. Although the shift is less extreme, much the same pattern prevailed among all counties between 1990 and 2000, with a greater concentration of origins in Mexico. Aside from Mexicans and Latin Americans, the relative share of other national origins either declined or stayed the same over the decade among nonmetropolitan counties.

Across offset counties, for example, Asians as a percentage of the population declined from 14.8 percent to 10.6 percent from 1990 to 2000, compared to a drop of 17.8 percent to 15.8 percent in all counties. The share of Europeans dropped from 20.6 percent to 10.1 percent among offset counties and from 27 percent to 17 percent in all counties.

Although metropolitan offset counties tell a similar story, the growth in the relative size of the Mexican population was generally more modest than in nonmetropolitan areas. Thus the share of Mexicans among foreigners in metropolitan offset counties rose from 8.9 percent in 1990 to 13.1 percent in 2000 (compared with 37 percent and 59 percent in nonmetropolitan offset counties) and from 21 percent to 28 percent in all metropolitan counties (compared with figures of 33 percent and 49 percent in nonmetropolitan areas). Thus, Mexican immigration appears to have driven growth in nonmetropolitan counties more than in metropolitan counties.

Census data on migration over the past five years also suggest greater mobility to nonmetropolitan than to metropolitan counties, but only among the foreign-born. As shown in table 4.4, native-born residents of nonmetropolitan offset counties displayed a relatively high degree of geographic stability, with upward of 60 percent not moving in the five years prior to the census at both points in time. In contrast, those born abroad were quite mobile. For example, among foreigners in nonmetropolitan offset counties in 1990, 17.7 percent were living outside the United States five years earlier, 25.8 percent lived in another nonmetropolitan area, and 16.2 percent lived in a United States metropolitan area. Only 41.3 percent of foreigners had not moved at all. Mexicans were the most mobile of all, with 21.1 percent moving from outside the United States between 1985 and 1990, 31.3 percent entering from another nonmetropolitan area, and 16.2 arriving from a metropolitan area.

By 2000, the geographic mobility of foreigners had grown even more marked. Among Mexicans living in the United States in 2000 who moved the previous year, 26.0 percent arrived from abroad, 29.8 percent arrived from another nonmetropolitan area in the United States, and 13.8 percent arrived from a United States metropolitan area. The rise in the percentage of Mexicans who had been abroad in the previous five years suggests more movement directly from Mexico into nonmetropolitan offset areas during the 1990s. Moreover, the relatively low rate of entry from metropolitan areas suggests a tendency for immigrants, especially Mexicans, to remain in a nonmetropolitan area once settled there, a pattern that was replicated across all counties.

As the column for metropolitan areas reveals, there was little movement of foreigners in general or Mexicans in particular from nonmetropolitan

TABLE 4.4 Internal Migration of Native-Born, Foreign-Born, and Mexican-Born Persons in Offset Counties and All Counties Between 1990 and 2000 (Percentage)

| | Nonmetropolitan Areas | | | | | | Metropolitan Areas | | | | | |
| | 1990 | | | 2000 | | | 1990 | | | 2000 | | |
Migration Status	Native-Born	Foreign-Born	Mexico-Born	Native-Born	Foreign-Born	Mexico-Born	Native-Born	Foreign-Born	Mexico-Born	Native-Born	Foreign-Born	Mexico-Born
Offset counties												
No move in last five years	60.9	41.3	36.6	62.1	34.2	30.4	64.6	48.4	37.1	65.4	49.5	42.0
In metro area five years ago	9.3	16.2	11.0	8.7	16.6	13.8	33.6	32.8	42.5	32.7	33.3	38.5
Nonmetro five years ago	29.3	25.8	31.3	28.6	26.4	29.8	1.4	0.5	0.6	1.2	0.4	0.6
Abroad five years ago	0.5	17.7	21.1	0.5	22.7	26.0	0.4	18.3	19.8	0.8	16.7	18.9
All counties												
No move in last five years	61.9	44.4	40.2	61.7	41.2	37.4	51.1	42.0	36.8	58.1	43.5	38.5
In metro area five years ago	10.0	15.9	12.1	10.7	15.2	11.6	39.2	38.4	42.7	38.3	37.8	41.6
Nonmetro years ago	27.7	23.0	30.4	27.2	23.2	28.5	3.2	1.0	1.0	3.0	1.1	0.9
Abroad five years ago	0.3	16.6	17.4	0.4	20.4	22.5	0.4	18.6	19.5	0.5	17.8	18.8

Source: Authors' compilation of U.S. Census Bureau Long-form Sample Data.

to metropolitan areas, and there was less of a tendency for immigrants to enter metropolitan areas directly from abroad. Furthermore, fewer than 0.6 percent of foreigners or Mexicans moved from a nonmetropolitan to a metropolitan area in the five years prior to either 1990 or 2000. These data suggest that many immigrants do not stop first in a major urban portal before moving to a nonmetropolitan area, and that once living in nonmetropolitan areas they are relatively unlikely to proceed to an urban destination.

Change in Socioeconomic Origins of Immigrants

Table 4.5 shows selected individual and household characteristics of those born in the United States, abroad, and in Mexico for metropolitan and non-metropolitan counties of the United States. Generally speaking, during the 1990s, as the American-born population grew older the foreign population became younger. In addition, those present in 2000 were more likely than the foreign-born in 1990 to report having fewer years of formal schooling and were less likely to graduate from high school. However, the trend of declining skill did not mimic the trend for poverty status. Among all groups in all areas, fewer persons lived in poverty in 1990 than in 2000.

Nationwide, nonmetropolitan counties in 2000 housed older, better-educated foreign-born and Mexican-born immigrants than offset counties. Offset counties also had foreign-born and Mexican-born populations that were younger than native-born populations, and both groups experienced declines in number of years of schooling, even though over the decade the poverty rate dropped for both groups as compared to natives. Although they were younger and less educated than natives, some 29 percent and 43 percent of the foreign-born and Mexican-born populations, respectively, lived in poverty within nonmetropolitan offset counties in 1990, compared with 23 percent and 28 percent in 2000. This improvement reflects robust economic growth in the 1990s.

Patterns of change differ somewhat among metropolitan offset counties. The average age of foreigners remained the same throughout the decade, approximately forty, but as in nonmetropolitan offset areas, immigrants came to have fewer years of schooling and were less likely to graduate from high school by 2000. But in contrast to nonmetropolitan offset areas, we observe relatively small declines in poverty among the foreign-born in metropolitan areas during the 1990s, and the contrasts between the native- and Mexican-born are especially stark. Compared to United States natives, Mexicans were, on average, much younger and had fewer years of schooling with fewer high school graduates but more persons

TABLE 4.5   Individual and Household Characteristics of Native-Born, Foreign-Born, and Mexican-Born Persons in Offset and All Counties in 1990 and 2000

| | Nonmetropolitan Areas | | | | | | Metropolitan Areas | | | | | |
| | 1990 | | | 2000 | | | 1990 | | | 2000 | | |
Migration Status	Native-Born	Foreign-Born	Mexico-Born	Native-Born	Foreign-Born	Mexico-Born	Native-Born	Foreign-Born	Mexico-Born	Native-Born	Foreign-Born	Mexico-Born
Offset counties												
Mean age	35.8	40.4	32.2	37.2	34.5	30.3	34.4	40.9	31.4	34.4	40.5	32.2
Mean years' schooling	9.7	9.2	6.4	8.7	6.4	4.4	10.5	10.8	7.8	9.1	9.8	6.1
Percentage high school or more	51.9	41.3	14.2	31.3	17.8	5.7	58.3	56.1	27.0	40.3	40.6	12.9
Poverty rate	16.7	29.3	42.7	13.8	23.2	27.8	14.0	15.7	20.4	12.5	15.3	19.4
Percentage naturalized	—	42.6	29.2	—	29.5	19.9	—	42.7	22.2	—	44.1	21.8
Mean years in U.S.	—	17.5	12.2	—	13.2	10.7	—	15.9	12.4	—	15.7	12.8
Percentage entered U.S. within last five years	—	7.2	10.9	—	31.7	37.0	—	9.0	11.0	—	22.9	28.8
Percentage speak English well	—	48.6	49.1	—	44.9	41.7	21.9	54.4	49.1	—	55.0	44.8
Percentage speak English at home	—	24.6	4.9	—	13.6	4.3	—	5.9	5.6	—	17.7	4.9
Mean household size	2.6	3.2	4.1	2.4	3.6	4.2	2.5	3.2	4.5	2.4	3.2	4.7
Mean years household residence	12.2	8.5	6.7	12.6	7.0	5.6	12.4	9.9	6.3	13.1	9.4	6.8
Percentage household with children under eighteen	38.1	46.5	67.1	35.1	58.4	73.1	31.5	44.3	72.2	31.0	46.8	73.4
Median household income (thousands)	24.0	23.0	17.0	25.0	23.0	20.0	35.0	24.0	29.0	25.0	33.0	30.0

(Continued)

TABLE 4.5   Individual and Household Characteristics of Native-Born, Foreign-Born, and Mexican-Born Persons in Offset and All Counties in 1990 and 2000 (*Continued*)

| | Nonmetropolitan Areas | | | | | | Metropolitan Areas | | | | | |
| | 1990 | | | 2000 | | | 1990 | | | 2000 | | |
Migration Status	Native-Born	Foreign-Born	Mexico-Born	Native-Born	Foreign-Born	Mexico-Born	Native-Born	Foreign-Born	Mexico-Born	Native-Born	Foreign-Born	Mexico-Born
All counties												
Mean age	36.0	42.7	33.8	37.7	38.1	32.3	34.9	39.4	31.9	36.4	39.2	32.9
Mean years' schooling	9.6	10.0	6.7	8.8	7.7	4.9	10.5	10.5	7.4	9.5	9.1	5.7
Percentage high school or more	51.2	48.9	18.1	31.1	27.6	8.9	59.9	52.7	22.5	41.6	37.6	11.9
Poverty rate	18.6	29.5	42.0	14.0	25.5	31.7	12.4	18.4	29.3	10.3	18.2	26.1
Percentage naturalized	—	46.6	28.7	—	36.9	23.6	—	40.1	22.1	—	40.5	22.3
Mean years in U.S.	—	19.5	14.2	—	16.2	12.5	—	15.9	12.8	—	15.7	13.4
Percentage entered U.S. within last five years	—	7.0	10.2	—	28.1	33.1	—	8.9	11.1	—	24.1	28.1
Percentage speak English well	—	48.6	48.9	—	46.5	43.4	—	53.1	46.4	—	53.5	43.7
Percentage speak English at home	—	30.7	6.2	—	21.6	5.5	—	21.5	6.2	—	16.5	5.5
Mean household size	2.6	3.1	4.1	2.5	3.3	4.2	2.5	3.3	4.5	2.5	3.4	4.5
Mean years household residence	12.1	9.7	7.5	12.0	8.5	6.7	10.7	8.7	6.8	11.0	8.2	6.6
Percentage household with children under eighteen	39.0	44.7	69.5	35.8	51.5	72.0	36.4	47.2	72.8	35.2	50.9	73.8
Median household income (thousands)	22.0	23.0	16.0	24.0	25.0	19.0	31.0	31.0	24.0	32.0	31.0	24.0

Source: Authors' compilation of U.S. Census Bureau Long-form Sample Data.

living in poverty. Moreover, trends across the ten-year period suggest that both foreign- and Mexican-born populations grew more disadvantaged with respect to skill. In contrast to the large declines in poverty observed in nonmetropolitan offset counties, Mexicans and foreigners experienced only tiny declines in metropolitan offset counties.

These differences are consistent with other attributes of the foreign-born and Mexican-born populations. In keeping with other researchers (Liang 1994; Woodrow-Lafield et al. 2004), we found that Mexicans had lower naturalization rates than foreigners as a whole, but trends in naturalization differed by metropolitan status. In nonmetropolitan offset counties in the 1990s, Mexicans became less likely to be naturalized: just 20 percent of Mexicans were naturalized in 2000, a decline from 29 percent in 1990. In metropolitan offset counties, in contrast, approximately 22 percent of those born in Mexico reported being naturalized, with little change over the decade. Mexicans were also different in terms of length of United States residence compared with foreigners in general. Among those in nonmetropolitan offset counties in 2000, Mexicans had spent the fewest years in the United States, around eleven, compared with approximately thirteen years for foreigners in general. These figures represent a decline from those prevailing in 1990, and in both census years they were lower than comparable figures in metropolitan offset counties.

Both foreign-born and Mexican-born persons in nonmetropolitan counties are distinguished by high rates of geographic mobility. In these counties in 2000, 31.7 percent of the foreign-born and 37 percent of the Mexican-born entered the United States over the last five years, considerably more than in 1990. The figures were also higher than rates of entry for foreigners and Mexicans in metropolitan offset counties. Not only were the foreign-born in nonmetropolitan offset counties relatively newer arrivals but in 2000 they were also less likely to speak English well and to speak English at home. Among metropolitan offset counties, only those born in Mexico were less likely to report speaking English well.

Less differentiation in household characteristics is seen between Mexicans in nonmetropolitan offset counties and those in other areas. Two types of differences appear. The first contrast is between households headed by someone born in Mexico as opposed to a foreigner in general, with the former households being larger, having fewer years of United States residence, more children under age eighteen, and less income in 2000. At least two thirds of Mexican households across all counties contained minor children. The second contrast is between nonmetropolitan foreign-born in offset counties and their metropolitan counterparts. Within offset counties, the nonmetropolitan foreign-born, especially those from Mexico, reported fewer years of residence and about one third less in income than in metropolitan areas.

Occupation and Employment

These tabulations reveal clear differences among Mexicans residing in off-set nonmetropolitan areas and those in other areas. The data in table 4.6 indicate whether similar variations exist in labor force characteristics. A key differential that is immediately evident refers to the percentage working in manufacturing. Among the foreign-born and Mexican-born populations of nonmetropolitan offset counties, one third to one half (38 percent of the foreign-born and 48 percent of the Mexican-born) were employed in manufacturing in 2000. These figures differ sharply from those in metropolitan offset counties, where just 17 percent of foreigners and 27 percent of Mexicans were employed in manufacturing. Moreover, the groups' concentrations in manufacturing in offset counties were substantially higher than in all counties. In general, this concentration reflects both demand and supply factors. Since the mid-1980s, as nondurable manufacturing activity has increased in nonmetropolitan areas, more semi- and unskilled jobs have appeared there (Galston and Baehler 1995; Gordon, Richardson, and Yu 1998; Drabenstott, Henry, and Mitchell 1999). But, as we have seen, it is also true that by 2000, the Mexican-born in offset nonmetropolitan areas were more likely to be younger, with less education, fewer years of United States experience, and less English-language competency than Mexicans in 1990. These shifts suggest that change in migrant selectivity is also related to the foreign-born, and especially the Mexican-born, concentration in manufacturing in the nonmetropolitan United States.

The Mexican experience itself, however, does not vary much between metropolitan and nonmetropolitan sectors. The wages of foreigners in metropolitan areas were uniformly higher than in nonmetropolitan areas, but the contrast for Mexicans was small in 1990 and trivial in 2000. This finding was not specific to offset counties but obtained in all counties, both in terms of median earnings and median wages (measured in constant 1989 U.S. dollars). The pattern suggests that the labor-market experience of Mexicans in the United States is distinct from that of natives and foreigners in general, irrespective of place of residence.

Concentration of Immigrants in Different Industries

Tables 4.7 and 4.8 present the top five industries in nonmetropolitan and metropolitan offset counties ranked according to the number of workers; the number of foreigners; the percentage of foreigners; and the percentage

TABLE 4.6 Occupational and Employment Characteristics of Native-Born, Foreign-Born, and Mexican-Born Persons in Offset and All Counties, 1990 and 2000

| | Nonmetropolitan Areas | | | | | | Metropolitan Areas | | | | | |
| | 1990 | | | 2000 | | | 1990 | | | 2000 | | |
Migration Status	Native-Born	Foreign-Born	Mexico-Born	Native-Born	Foreign-Born	Mexico-Born	Native-Born	Foreign-Born	Mexico-Born	Native-Born	Foreign-Born	Mexico-Born
Offset counties												
Unemployment rate	5.8	5.9	7.9	5.2	7.3	9.1	6.7	7.7	9.9	6.8	6.6	7.8
Self-employment rate	12.5	11.3	4.4	11.9	8.0	5.1	7.7	9.9	3.9	8.1	9.0	4.8
Percentage employed full-time	78.1	80.0	84.1	77.9	81.2	81.6	77.3	80.2	81.4	76.5	79.8	81.2
Percentage in agriculture	7.7	13.8	24.8	5.8	10.0	13.9	0.5	0.4	2.1	0.3	0.3	1.3
Percentage in construction	6.0	5.7	6.5	6.6	7.0	8.2	4.8	5.5	7.5	4.6	5.8	10.0
Percentage in manufacturing	20.5	25.4	35.3	18.6	38.8	48.1	12.6	20.9	34.0	9.9	16.9	26.7
Median yearly earnings[a]	15.0	12.0	11.0	15.0	13.0	12.0	22.0	18.0	12.0	23.0	18.0	12.0
Median hourly wages[a]	7.7	6.8	5.8	7.8	6.7	6.2	11.9	9.9	6.9	11.9	9.7	6.7

(Continued)

TABLE 4.6 Occupational and Employment Characteristics of Native-Born, Foreign-Born, and Mexican-Born Persons in Offset and All Counties, 1990 and 2000 (*Continued*)

| | Nonmetropolitan Areas | | | | | | Metropolitan Areas | | | | | |
| | 1990 | | | 2000 | | | 1990 | | | 2000 | | |
Migration Status	Native-Born	Foreign-Born	Mexico-Born	Native-Born	Foreign-Born	Mexico-Born	Native-Born	Foreign-Born	Mexico-Born	Native-Born	Foreign-Born	Mexico-Born
All counties												
Unemployment rate	6.9	8.3	12.6	5.8	7.5	9.7	5.8	7.7	11.2	5.2	6.7	9.4
Self-employment rate	12.0	11.0	5.7	11.7	9.2	5.5	8.5	9.7	5.6	8.9	9.7	6.7
Percentage employed full-time	77.0	75.5	79.9	77.2	77.4	80.2	78.1	78.3	78.6	78.1	78.9	79.1
Percentage in agriculture	7.4	15.9	32.9	5.2	12.7	21.3	1.4	2.7	8.9	0.9	2.0	6.0
Percentage in construction	7.2	5.5	7.1	8.0	7.5	10.4	6.3	6.6	10.7	6.5	7.9	15.2
Percentage in manufacturing	20.0	18.7	20.8	17.8	23.2	27.8	14.6	19.7	25.5	12.5	16.5	20.1
Median yearly earnings[a]	15.0	12.0	9.0	15.0	12.0	11.0	20.0	16.0	11.0	20.0	16.0	11.0
Median hourly wages[a]	7.7	6.9	5.4	7.9	6.6	5.6	10.0	8.7	6.3	10.2	8.6	6.2

Source: Authors' compilation of U.S. Census Bureau Long-form Sample Data.
[a] Earnings and wages (in thousands) are given in constant 1989 dollars.

TABLE 4.7   Ranking of Top Five Industries in Nonmetropolitan Offset Counties, 1990 and 2000

Kind of Ranking	1990 Industry	Percentage	2000 Industry	Percentage
By size of workforce				
1	Elementary and secondary schools	6.1	Construction	6.6
2	Construction	6.0	Elementary and secondary schools	6.6
3	Eating and drinking places	4.8	Restaurants and other food services	5.0
4	Agricultural production—crops	3.8	Hospitals	3.1
5	Hospitals	3.2	Animal slaughtering and processing	3.0
By size of foreign workforce				
1	Meat products	10.3	Animal slaughtering and processing	18.0
2	Agricultural production—crops	7.5	Carpet and rug manufacturing	7.1
3	Eating and drinking places	7.1	Construction	7.0
4	Construction	5.7	Restaurants and other food services	6.6
5	Hotels and motels	3.9	Crop production	5.1
By share of foreign-born				
1	Miscellaneous food preparation	28.7	Animal slaughtering and processing	45.9
2	Not specified metal industries	22.1	Seafood and other miscellaneous foods	41.1
3	Fishing, hunting, and trapping	19.0	Carpet and rug manufacturing	28.7
4	Meat products	17.1	Leather tanning and products	28.1
5	Leather products	16.9	Not specified food industries	27.5
By share of Mexican-born				
1	Meat products	12.3	Animal slaughtering and processing	34.0
2	Leather products	9.9	Leather tanning and processing	28.1
3	Groceries and related products	8.1	Resins, synthetic rubber, and filaments	27.2
4	Miscellaneous wholesale, nondurable goods	7.9	Carpet and rug manufacturing	25.2
5	Agricultural services	6.7	Not specified food industries	24.3

Source: Authors' compilation of U.S. Census Bureau Long-form Sample Data.

TABLE 4.8   Ranking of Top Five Industries in Metropolitan Offset Counties, 1990 and 2000

Kind of Ranking	1990 Industry	Percentage	2000 Industry	Percentage
By size of workforce				
1	Construction	5.0	Elementary and secondary schools	5.4
2	Hospitals	5.0	Construction	4.9
3	Elementary and secondary schools	4.8	Restaurants and other food services	4.5
4	Eating and drinking places	4.2	Hospitals	4.5
5	Banking	2.7	Colleges and universities	2.4
By size of foreign workforce				
1	Eating and drinking places	6.8	Restaurants and other food services	6.9
2	Hospitals	5.7	Construction	5.8
3	Construction	5.5	Hospitals	2.6
4	Apparel and accessories	3.0	Elementary and secondary schools	2.6
5	Banking	2.8	Electronic component manufacturing	2.3
By share foreign-born				
1	Taxicab service	61.6	Cut and sew apparel manufacturing	76.6
2	Shoe repair shops	60.9	Footwear and leather goods repair	75.4
3	Apparel and accessories	60.4	Knitting mills	72.0
4	Leather tanning and finishing	57.7	Taxi and limousine service	71.3
5	Dressmaking shops	57.4	Private households	68.3
By share Mexican-born				
1	Canned, frozen, preserved foods	19.5	Crop production	29.4
2	Agricultural production–crops	18.7	Landscaping services	27.6
3	Landscape and horticultural services	17.9	Fruit and vegetable preserving	27.0
4	Sugar and confectionery products	17.0	Animal slaughtering and processing	26.8
5	Meat products	13.7	Not specified metal industries	25.0

Source: Authors' compilation of Census Bureau Long-form Sample Data.

of Mexicans. Three patterns emerge from these tables. First, foreigners tend to work in different industries than natives and display a higher level of concentration in particular industries. Among nonmetropolitan offset counties in 2000, for example, the top five industries for total workers were construction, elementary and secondary education, restaurants and other food services, hospitals, and animal slaughtering and processing. In the same counties, however, only three of the five industries remained among the top five employers for foreigners, with the latter displaying high concentrations in two industries that contained relatively few natives: carpet and rug manufacturing and crop production. Summing across all industrial categories, we find that approximately 44 percent of the foreign-born in 2000 worked in the top five industries, compared to just 24 percent among workers in general.

Consistent with recent research on the meatpacking industry (Kandel and Parrado 2003, 2005; Stull, Broadway, and Griffith 1995), by 2000 the most popular industrial sector among foreigners in nonmetropolitan offset counties was animal slaughtering and processing, followed by carpet and rug manufacturing (see Hernández-Léon and Zúñiga 2000, 2003) and then construction, restaurants and food services, and crop production. Together these industries seem to offer an abundant supply of low-skill, low-wage jobs to foreign workers in nonmetropolitan offset counties.

Many of the same industries appear in the third panel of rankings by the percentage, rather than absolute number, of foreigners. Almost half (45.9 percent) of all employees in animal slaughtering and processing were born outside the United States in 2000, and 41 percent of those in seafood and other miscellaneous foods were likewise foreign-born. Slightly more than one quarter of the employees in the remaining three industries—carpet and rug manufacturing, leather tanning and products, and unspecified food industries—were foreign-born. These rankings were considerably different from those seen in 1990, when the industry containing the highest share of foreigners, miscellaneous food preparation and kindred products, employed just 29 percent of the foreign-born. Furthermore, among the industries found in the 1990 rankings, two—not-specified metal and fishing, hunting, and trapping—did not even appear in the 2000 rankings.

Differences with respect to ranking are most dramatic when we consider industries on the basis of the percentage Mexican-born working in them. In 2000, approximately one-third of workers in animal slaughtering and processing, and another 28 percent in leather tanning and products, were Mexican, compared with figures of just 12 percent and 10 percent in comparable industries in 1990. In 2000, one quarter of all employed workers within industries that manufacture resin and synthetic rubber products, carpets and rugs, and those described as not-specified food industries were also Mexican-born. A decade earlier, Mexican-born workers represented less than 10 percent of workers in three of the top five industry employers: groceries and related products, miscellaneous wholesale, and agricultural services.

Table 4.8 shows similar rankings for offset metropolitan counties. One key difference between nonmetropolitan and metropolitan counties was that in 2000, colleges and universities replaced animal slaughtering and processing as a top-five metropolitan employer. However, three of the top five employers of the foreign-born in metropolitan areas were different than in the nonmetropolitan areas: hospitals, elementary and secondary schools, and electronic component and manufacturing. The last two categories replaced apparel and accessories and banking–two industries that appeared in the top five rankings in 1990.

Particularly noteworthy are the rankings of metropolitan industries by their proportion of foreign-born workers. Among offset metropolitan counties, 77 percent of workers in the cut-and-sew apparel-manufacturing industry were foreign-born, compared with 75 percent in footwear and leather goods repair, 71 percent in knitting mills and taxi and limo services, and 68 percent in private households. In nonmetropolitan offset counties, proportionately fewer workers were concentrated in such a distinct set of industries. The same general finding holds for industry rankings by percentage of Mexican-born workers. With the exception of animal slaughtering and processing, the top industries for Mexican workers in offset metropolitan areas differed substantially from those prevailing in nonmetropolitan offset areas: approximately 30 percent of workers in crop production, 28 percent in landscaping, and 27 percent in fruit and vegetable preserving were born in Mexico.

On the whole, tables 4.7 and 4.8 document significant differences in the top employers in metropolitan and nonmetropolitan areas of the United States. Stark rural-urban differences also appear when industries are ranked by the number of foreign workers, by the percentage of foreign workers, and especially the percentage of Mexicans. Despite these differences, however, industries that contain the largest shares of foreign- and Mexican-born persons share an important feature: they offer low-wage, low-skill jobs that are presumably not attractive to United States natives.

CONCLUSIONS

This chapter examined geographic and compositional shifts in the foreign-born population of different areas of the United States during the 1990s. Using internal data from the U.S. Census Bureau, we documented the new demographic complexity that has accompanied the dispersion of immigrants into nontraditional, nonmetropolitan gateways of the United States. Our results reveal that the characteristics of immigrants in nonmetropolitan areas, especially those where population decline was prevented by the arrival of foreigners, are vastly different from those of foreigners in other areas. We also find that the population of immigrants in the 1990s contained a disproportionate percentage of recently arrived Mexicans who were attracted by employment opportunities within particular industries offering low-skill and low-wage jobs. The new settlement patterns were not restricted to the southern United States, as many new immigrants went to midwestern plains states as well as the South.

This new demographic complexity has important implications for successful immigrant incorporation. On the one hand, it may be the most recent step in a long-established pattern whereby people migrate to centers of economic development as industries disperse spatially. There are many examples of migration following labor opportunities in United States history, including the migration west created by the gold rush, and the west-to-east and south-to-north migration flows to construct the railroads and other infrastructure. The close ties that have now developed between American meat and agricultural processing and Mexican immigrants may just be a contemporary example of the same process, with similar implications for incorporation into United States society. On the other hand, the new immigration from Mexico may be a transitional circumstance in industries that subsequently will follow the path of many American industries: eventually they move abroad, first south to Mexico and later to China.

On the whole, there is reason for optimism. Mexican immigrants have made substantial gains, in socioeconomic terms, in the 1990s. By 2000, fewer Mexicans in nonmetropolitan areas lived in poverty, and the median incomes and wages were substantially higher than in 1990. Moreover, most worked in manufacturing jobs that offered higher pay and more stability than agricultural jobs in the past. Another reason for optimism regarding successful incorporation into American society of Mexican immigrants living in nonmetropolitan areas is that they live in larger households, most of which contain children. Such ties suggest that Mexicans are permanently settling in nonmetropolitan areas rather than live as transient, short-term residents.

Yet this optimism must be tempered by the relatively low levels of education observed among the Mexican-born in nonmetropolitan counties. Low education is a source of concern, given that fewer than 10 percent of all Mexicans born in these countries completed high school in

2000. Together with declines in naturalization and English competency rates, low rates of English use at home, and the growing presence of recently arrived migrants, Mexican immigration may not represent an opportunity for growth and development despite signs of economic success in the 1990s.

This research was made possible by the Population Division of the U.S. Census Bureau and by the U.S. Department of Agriculture's National Research Initiative. An earlier version of this paper was presented at the annual meeting of the Rural Sociological Society in August 2003, in Montreal.

NOTE

1. We used the Office of Management and Budget's (OMB) 1993 standard definition of metropolitan and nonmetropolitan statistical areas. See http://www.census. gov/population/www/estimates/aboutmetro.html.

REFERENCES

Donato, Katharine M., Carl L. Bankston III, and Dawn T. Robinson. 2001. "Immigration and the Organization of the Onshore Oil Industry: Southern Louisiana in the Late 1990s." In *Latino Workers in the Contemporary South*, edited by Arthur D. Murphy, Coleen Blanchard, and Jennifer A. Hill. Athens, Ga.: University of Georgia Press.

Donato, Katharine M., Melissa Stainback, and Carl L. Bankston III. 2005. "The Economic Incorporation of Mexican Immigrants in Southern Louisiana: A Tale of Two Cities." In *New Destinations of Mexican Immigration in the United States: Community Formation, Local Responses and Inter-Group Relations*, edited by Víctor Zúñiga and Rubén Hernández-León. New York: Russell Sage Foundation.

Donato, Katharine M., Charles Tolbert, Alfred Nucci, and Yukio Kawano. 2007. "Recent Immigrant Settlement in the Nonmetropolitan United States: Evidence from Internal Census Data." *Rural Sociology* 72(4): 537–59.

Drabenstott, Mark, Mark Henry, and Kristin Mitchell. 1999. "Where Have All the Packing Plants Gone? The New Meat Geography in Rural America." *Economic Review* 84(3): 65–82.

Durand, Jorge, Douglas S. Massey, and Fernando Charvet. 2000. "The Changing Geography of Mexican Immigration to the United States: 1910–1996." *Social Science Quarterly* 81(1): 1–15.

Engstrom, James D. 2001. "Industry and Immigration in Dalton, Georgia." in *Latino Workers in the Contemporary South*, edited by Arthur D. Murphy, Colleen Blanchard and Jennifer A. Hill. Athens, Ga.: University of Georgia Press.

Fix, Michael E., Phillip L. Martin, and J. Edward Taylor. 1997. *Poverty Amid Prosperity: Immigration and the Changing Face of Rural California.* Washington: The Urban Institute Press.

Galston, William A., and Karen J. Baehler. 1995. *Rural Development in the United States.* Washington: Island Press.

Grey, Mark A. 1999. "Immigrants, Migration, and Worker Turnover at the Hog Pride Pork Packing Plant." *Human Organization* 58(1): 16–27.

Gordon, Peter, J. W. Richardson, and Gang Yu. 1998. "Metropolitan and Nonmetropolitan Employment Trends in the U.S.: Recent Evidence and Implications." *Urban Studies* 35(7): 1037–57.

Griffith, David. 1995. "Hay Trabajo: Poultry Processing, Rural Industrialization, and the Latinization of Low-Wage Labor." In *Any Way You Cut It: Meat Processing and Small-Town America*, edited by Donald D. Stull, Michael J. Broadway, and David Griffith. Lawrence, Kan.: University Press of Kansas.

Guthey, Greig. 2001. "Mexican Places in Southern Spaces: Globalization, Work and Daily Life in and around the North Georgia Poultry Industry." In *Latino Workers in the Contemporary South*, edited by Arthur D. Murphy, Colleen Blanchard and Jennifer A. Hill. Athens, Ga.: University of Georgia Press.

Hernández-León, Rubén, and Víctor Zúñiga. 2000. " 'Making Carpet by the Mile': The Emergence of a Mexican Immigrant Community in an Industrial Region of the U.S. Historic South." *Social Science Quarterly* 81(1): 49–66.

———. 2003. "Mexican Immigrant Communities in the South and Social Capital: The Case of Dalton, Georgia." *Southern Rural Sociology* 19(1): 20–45.

Johnson, Kenneth M. 1998. "Renewed Population Growth in Rural America." *Research in Rural Sociology and Development* 7: 23–45.

———. 1999. "The Rural Rebound." *PRB Reports to America* 1(3): 1–20.

Johnson, Kenneth M., and Calvin L. Beale. 1998. "The Rural Rebound." *Wilson Quarterly* 12(Spring): 16–27.

———. 1999. "The Continuing Population Rebound in Nonmetro America." *Rural Development Perspectives* 13(3): 2–10.

Kandel, William, and John Cromartie. 2003. "Hispanics Find a Home in Rural America." *Amber Waves* 11(1):11.

———. 2004. *New Patterns of Hispanic Settlement in Rural America.* Rural Development Research Report 99. Washington: U.S. Department of Agriculture.

Kandel, William, and Emilio A. Parrado. 2003. "Industrial Transformation and Hispanic Migration to the American South: The Case of the Poultry Industry." In *Hispanic Spaces, Latino Places: A Geography of Regional and Cultural Diversity*, edited by Daniel D. Arreola. Austin, Tex.: University of Texas Press.

———. 2005. "Restructuring of the U.S. Meat Processing Industry and New Hispanic Migrant Destinations." *Population and Development Review* 31(3): 447–72.

Liang, Zai. 1994. "On the Measurement of Naturalization." *Demography* 31(3): 525–48.

Singer, Audrey. 2004. "The Rise of New Gateways." Report for the Center on Urban and Metropolitan Policy. Washington: Brookings Institution.

Stull, Donald D., Michael J. Broadway, and K. C. Erickson. 1992. "The Price of a Good Steak: Beef Packing and Its Consequences for Garden City, Kansas." In *Structuring Diversity: Ethnographic Perspectives on the New Immigration,* edited by L. Lamphere. Chicago, Ill.: University of Chicago Press.

Stull, Donald D., Michael J. Broadway, and David Griffith. 1995. *Any Way You Cut It: Meat Processing and Small-Town America.* Lawrence, Kan.: University Press of Kansas.

Suro, Roberto, and Audrey Singer. 2002. "Latino Growth in Metropolitan America: Changing Patterns, New Locations." Report for the Pew Hispanic Center. Washington: Pew Hispanic Center and Brookings Institution.

Woodrow-Lafield, Karen A., Xiaohe Xu, Thomas Kersen, and Bunak Poch. 2004. "Naturalization for U.S. Immigrants: Highlights from 10 Countries." *Population Research and Policy Review* 23(3): 187–218.

Zúñiga, Víctor, and Rubén Hernández-León. 2005. *New Destinations: Mexican Immigration in the United States.* New York: Russell Sage Foundation.

CHAPTER 5

﹀

NEW HISPANIC MIGRANT DESTINATIONS:
A TALE OF TWO INDUSTRIES

EMILIO A. PARRADO AND WILLIAM KANDEL

In the past decade, scholarly attention has focused on Hispanic population growth and immigration to small towns, cities, and regions that traditionally never experienced post–World War II immigration (Gozdziak and Martin 2005; Millard, Chapa, and Burillo 2005; Zúñiga and Hernández-León 2005). Three outcomes are associated with this trend. First, the high volume of immigration has catapulted Hispanics into the largest minority group in the United States, surpassing African Americans. Second, new metropolitan areas of destination, particularly in the American Southeast, emerged as immigrant magnets, competing with traditional destinations in California and Texas. Third, Hispanic population growth is no longer confined to urban areas; rural areas in nontraditional immigrant-receiving states have also experienced dramatic increases. As a result, for the very first time in American history, roughly half of all nonmetropolitan Hispanics now live outside the traditional five southwestern states of Arizona, California, Colorado, New Mexico, and Texas (Kandel and Cromartie 2004).

Despite the growing literature on immigrant adaptation in new destinations, the socioeconomic forces that foster the rapid growth of Hispanic populations in new receiving areas remain ambiguous. The relative newness of the trends has limited the number of quantitative analyses relating demographic and economic changes, and researchers have yet to compare rural and urban destinations systematically, thereby limiting our understanding of how labor-market processes affect the geographic diversification of Hispanics. Accordingly, our chapter has three objectives. The first is to relate Hispanic population growth to changing labor demand created by industry transformations in new destination areas. The second is to contrast these forces across rural and metropolitan areas. The third is to assess the changing socioeconomic profile of the labor force in new destination areas to distill labor-market implications.

NEW URBAN AND RURAL MIGRANT DESTINATIONS

Recent changes in the geographic distribution of Hispanics are now fairly well documented (Singer 2004; Suro and Singer 2002). Since 1990, Hispanics have grown dramatically in nontraditional receiving areas, both rural and urban, especially in the southeastern United States.[1] Between 1990 and 2000 the Hispanic proportion of metropolitan areas in the Southeast grew from 11 percent to 14 percent while declining from 61 percent to 58 percent in the Southwest (Kandel and Parrado 2004). In cities such as Atlanta and Raleigh-Durham, for instance, the Hispanic population grew by an extraordinary 362 percent and 569 percent, respectively, between 1990 and 2000, compared to 27 percent and 30 percent in Los Angeles and San Antonio. Although these figures are partly a function of the small size of the initial Hispanic population, rapid in-migration to new metropolitan destinations such as Atlanta and Oklahoma City did increase their representation of Hispanics to close to 10 percent of the total population.

The trend in rural areas is even more pronounced. Between 1990 and 2000 Hispanic growth in rural areas (67 percent) was significantly higher than in metropolitan areas (57 percent), and again, the change was particularly acute in the Southeast. Census 2000 data indicate that during the 1990s the percentage of Hispanic population in the nonmetropolitan Southeast increased from 11 percent to 19 percent while decreasing from 66 percent to 53 percent in the Southwest. To cite three not atypical examples, the total populations of Franklin County, Alabama, Gordon County, Georgia, and Le Sueur County, Minnesota, increased by 12.3 percent, 25.8 percent, and 9.4 percent, respectively, between 1990 and 2000; but for Hispanics, the corresponding figures were 2,193 percent, 1,534 percent, and 711 percent!

Several explanations have been proposed to account for the diversification of Hispanic migrant destinations. They are not mutually exclusive, but they highlight different dimensions of the migration process in rural and urban areas. A policy-oriented explanation emphasizes outcomes of United States immigration laws and policies. Douglas S. Massey and colleagues (Durand, Massey, and Charvet 2000; Massey, Durand, and Malone 2002) argue that an unintended consequence of the 1986 Immigration Reform and Control Act (IRCA), which legalized the status of close to 3 million previously undocumented persons, was to facilitate geographic mobility to new regions of the country. This change coincided with increased border-crossing enforcement in the 1990s, which caused Mexico-United States flows to fan out from well-traversed crossing points near San Diego and El Paso to numerous long-neglected portions of the border.

At the same time, the crackdown on border crossings during this period dramatically increased the cost of migrating in the form of higher smuggling fees and significantly raised the likelihood of death and injury during crossing (Massey, Durand, and Malone 2002; Cornelius 2001). Greater migration expenses and risks caused migrants to extend their stays, which increased opportunities for establishing social and economic ties, legal status, and ultimately new lives in the United States. Hence, a combination of policy outcomes that prompted Hispanics to migrate internally and others that increased the costs of migration and border crossing increased the number of people who settled permanently at new American destinations.

A second explanation for the new settlement patterns, particularly in rural areas, centers on quality-of-life factors. Evidence from several ethnographic studies suggests that the movement of Hispanics to small cities and towns outside the Southwest reflects their desire for better schools, lower crime rates, fewer street gangs, more affordable housing, and greater tranquillity in general (Fennelly and Leitner 2002; Fennelly 2005; Suro and Singer 2002; Hernández-León and Zúñiga 2000). In addition to these "pull" factors, depressed labor markets in Southern California and Texas beginning in the late 1980s also served as "push" factors, particularly for the millions of former undocumented migrants whose legal status was regularized under IRCA, making them more mobile.

A third explanation for Hispanic settlement in new destinations stresses corporate labor recruitment. Empirical evidence supporting this argument focuses on rural-based agricultural and manufacturing industries, where exceptionally high turnover rates and limitations on using the H-visa programs required companies continually to hire new workers. Firms accomplished this through active recruitment campaigns in traditional urban immigrant destinations such as Miami, Houston, and Los Angeles, as well as in migrant source countries (Johnson-Webb 2002; Jesse Katz, "Poultry Industry Imports Labor to Do Its Dirty Work," *Los Angeles Times*, December 8, 1996; Katz, "The Chicken Trail," three-part series, *Los Angeles Times*, November 10 to 12, 1996; Krissman 2000; Marisa Taylor and Steve Stein, "Network Helps Recruit Immigrants for U.S. Job Market," *Fort Worth Star-Telegram*, July 4, 1999). Other industries with active recruitment programs include carpet manufacturing (Hernández-León and Zúñiga

2000), forestry (McDaniel and Casanova 2003), and petroleum refining (Donato, Stainback, and Bankston 2005).

INDUSTRIAL CHANGE, LABOR DEMAND, AND DUAL LABOR MARKETS

Lacking in these explanations is any explicit assessment of labor demand as a factor fueling Hispanic migration. According to dual-labor-market theory (see Piore 1979), international migration to specific destinations is best understood in terms of industry-specific changes in labor demand at particular locations. Within developed societies, labor markets typically bifurcate into a capital-intensive primary sector that offers long-term, secure jobs with high wages and economic mobility, and a labor-intensive secondary sector that contains jobs offering little long-term opportunity, employment security, or mobility.

The instability of employment, seasonality of labor demand, limited occupational mobility, and poor job quality in the secondary sector implies that firms needing to expand their workforces face considerable obstacles to satisfying labor demand from domestic sources. Given the social context of employment, native workers shun low-status jobs and are unwilling to work without monetary compensation that far exceeds feasible levels given the limited skill requirements of the jobs and intensive international competition faced by companies. Jobs are also embedded within occupational hierarchies that require earnings differentials across occupational grades. Firms that raise wages for lower-skilled employees are pressured to do the same for other employees to maintain an established hierarchy, a practice most firms find too expensive and therefore resist.

Immigrants solve businesses' quandary of recruiting workers to flexible low-wage jobs because their transnational status permits them to profit economically through the arbitrage of using destination-country wages to support home-country standards of living, and their social frame of reference in their home countries ameliorates their unstable condition and low social status in destination countries. They are willing to take what natives see as "dead-end" jobs because they view their stay as temporary. A feature common to immigrant workers is a "target earner" mentality that yields a willingness to accept low wages for almost any available vacancy in the labor market.

In order to understand the diversification of Hispanic migration to new urban and rural destinations, therefore, closer attention must be directed to processes of employment growth, relocation, and structural transformation within industries of the secondary sector, as it is the generation of jobs especially tailored to migrant populations that drives migration flows. The construction and meat-processing industries have been particularly instrumental in attracting Hispanic migrants and creating new areas of settlement. Although they are not the only industries that employ Hispanics in new destination areas, they have been a primary source of immigrant jobs and their differential development has contributed to the emergence of new rural and urban destinations. Documenting the expansion and relocation of the construction and meat industries away from traditional immigrant receiving areas is thus essential for understanding the market processes fueling the diversification of destinations.

METROPOLITAN MAGNETS AND CONSTRUCTION INDUSTRY EXPANSION

In addition to trends in Hispanic population growth, the 2000 Census revealed that natives have consistently been migrating away from prior concentrations in the Northeast in favor of southeastern and southwestern destinations. William H. Frey (2002) describes this process as the emergence of the "New Sunbelt." Georgia, North Carolina, and Arizona have seen significant gains in native-born population, while New York and Illinois have experienced native-born population declines. The native-born population has not dispersed, however, but concentrated in a small number of rapidly growing metropolitan areas. As a result, urban destinations such as Raleigh-Durham, Atlanta, and Charlotte, which Frey labels "metropolitan magnets," have experienced large gains in population through in-migration of the native-born.

These states are attractive because of their growing economies and relatively low costs of living (especially housing), as well as climatic and environmental amenities. Consequently, they have received a highly select labor force. According to data from the 2003 Current Population Survey, over 65 percent of in-migrants to the South over the age of twenty-five had at least some college education, and 56 percent were employed in management, professional, or service occupations. The combination of a rapidly growing and highly skilled population in new metropolitan magnets throughout the South has triggered a significant increase in the demand for housing, which has had clear implications for growth in the construction industry.

During the last thirty years, the construction industry—which includes infrastructure construction, home building, home remodeling, and manufactured housing—has experienced substantial employment growth. In 2000 it employed 6.7 million people and generated output valued at about $800 billion, or 7.6 percent of the nation's gross domestic product (Conway, Dunn, and Khalil 2004), making it one of the largest and most dynamic industries in the country. The greatest share of this output is for private residential construction (55 percent) followed by public (25.6 percent) and private nonresidential construction (19.4 percent). The construction industry is also characterized by a relatively low level of concentration, with 80 percent of workers employed in firms with fewer than ten employees, a size that corresponds to most of the roughly 800,000 construction companies in the United States.

The industry's geographic dispersion is directly connected to population growth and concentration. As a result, the shift in American migration patterns has directly influenced the evolution of the industry and brought changes to its labor force. Between 1990 and 2004 the industry sold approximately 12 million new residential units, 5.5 million in the South (45 percent) and 3.3 million in the West (28 percent). In almost all regions, new residential development occurs at the metropolitan fringe. These trends, coupled with broader processes of economic development and historically low interest rates, have increased labor demand within the construction industry, especially in new metropolitan magnets. This increased labor demand has not been easy to satisfy, however, and industry-oriented reports contend that the industry suffers a consistent labor shortage (Goodrum 2004).

At the same time, employment opportunities in the industry have become less attractive to an increasingly well-educated domestic labor force. To counter reduced profitability during the economic downturn of the late 1980s, construction companies have relied increasingly on nonunion labor (Stepick et al. 1994); and because construction workers frequently work outdoors and use potentially dangerous tools and materials, on temporary scaffolding, and at dangerous heights, they face greater occupational safety risks than most other workers. According to Bureau of Labor Statistics data from 2002, the rate of work-related injuries for construction workers was one third higher than the mean rate for all private industries.

Together, these trends fueled a rapidly increasing demand for low-skilled workers that led to the increased incorporation of Hispanics into the industry in nontraditional receiving areas. It is no surprise, therefore, that the Associated General Contractors of America (2005) included "responding to the workforce needs of the industry with effective immigration reform" as a legislative priority for the 109th Congress.

THE RESTRUCTURING OF MEAT PROCESSING IN RURAL AREAS

In contrast to the diversification of metropolitan destination areas, the diversification of rural destination areas for Hispanics has been affected mainly, although not exclusively, by changes in labor demand within the meat-processing industry (Kandel and Parrado 2004, 2005). This growing and diverse industry, which includes the processing of beef, pork, and poultry products, has experienced important transformations that have altered its labor demands and geographic location. Although the timing and specific attributes of this process vary among producers, the restructuring follows a fairly consistent sequence: changed consumption patterns; increased demand for value-added production; industry consolidation and vertical integration that result in larger companies; the relocation of production facilities to rural areas, mainly in the Midwest and Southeast; and the declining relative attractiveness of meat-processing jobs (MacDonald et al. 2000; Ollinger, MacDonald, and Madison 2000). Together these transformations lie at the root of Hispanic migration to new rural areas of migrant destination (Kandel and Parrado 2005).

Through the 1950s, American per capita consumption of beef and pork was several times that of poultry. Beginning in the late 1950s, however, poultry producers began adopting new technologies that allowed them to process more birds at faster line speeds, precipitating a steady decline in poultry prices relative to beef that helped permanently alter Americans' eating habits over the course of two decades. Red meat and pork consumption remained stable, while poultry consumption has increased consistently over the past four decades. The meat-processing industry responded to these changes in consumption by adding "further processing" operations to their increasingly larger plants and vertically integrating their production processes. This, in tandem with changing consumer tastes toward more pre-cut and pre-processed meat products, greatly increased the demand for meat-processing labor.

These changes occurred over different time periods and at different rates for the poultry-, hog-, and cattle-processing industries, but the effect was similar: a growing control of production, from start to finish and a growing demand for large quantities of uniformly sized animals that could be processed quickly in increasingly mechanized plants. Such transformations produced an industry dominated by a few large firms that could afford the capital costs of large plants, and these firms now account for most of the meat produced in the United States. They also employ a growing number of low-skilled workers.

Geographic relocation played a key role in the process of industrial transformation (Broadway 1995). To reduce transportation costs, ensure constant supplies of animals, and maintain high year-round plant utilization, beef and hog processing plants relocated to nontraditional rural regions outside the Midwest, taking advantage of lower land and labor costs in the West, Southwest, and Southeast. Relocation to rural areas also weakened the bargaining power of many urban-based unions, resulting in a decline in wages and working conditions that decreased the attractiveness of meat-processing jobs to native-born workers. Whether this occurred as part of an active and purposeful effort to replace domestic workers with more pliant foreign-born workers remains unclear.

Together these processes contributed to a consistent pattern of low-skilled job growth in rural areas. Not surprisingly, growing consumer demand combined with plant relocation produced labor shortages in rural areas for the meat-processing industry similar to those faced by the construction industry in metropolitan magnets. Rural-based meat-processing firms found themselves short-handed in the face of an increasingly educated domestic workforce that had better employment alternatives elsewhere, resulting from the extended macroeconomic boom of the 1990s.

Although wages in the meat-processing industry remained high compared with those of low-skilled employment in other industrial sectors, they entailed relatively difficult working conditions, and consequently, many processing plants display employee turnover rates of 60 percent to 140 percent per year, or even higher (Grey 1999; Macguire 1993). Given increasing demand for value-added food products from an ever-growing population, larger plants located increasingly in sparsely populated nonmetropolitan counties, competitive wages elsewhere, and unattractive working conditions, meat-processing plants had difficulty filling the growing labor demand through the use of local workers. As a result, the industry began to recruit Hispanic migrants to new rural destinations.

CHANGING COMPOSITION OF THE LABOR FORCE

In order to document more directly the connection between changes in the construction and meat-processing industries and the diversification of Hispanic immigrant destinations, we turn to an analysis of the labor-force composition of the two industries and how it varies across metropolitan and rural areas of the United States. We start by illustrating these trends for the construction industry, using data from the 5 percent Public Use Micro Sample (PUMS) for the census of 1980, 1990, and 2000. Table 5.1 presents changes in the racial and ethnic composition of the labor force for all

TABLE 5.1   Racial and Ethnic Composition of the Construction
Industry Work Force in Metropolitan Areas,
1980 to 2000 (Percentages, Except as Noted)

	All Industries			Construction Industry		
	1980	1990	2000	1980	1990	2000
All metropolitan areas						
Non-Hispanic white	78.9	75.1	67.8	83.3	79.4	72.3
Non-Hispanic black	11.6	10.6	11.6	7.7	6.2	6.0
Other	2.6	4.3	7.0	1.7	2.5	3.7
Hispanic	6.9	10.1	13.6	7.3	11.9	18.0
Growth of workforce		8.9	21.2		23.9	33.9
Growth of Hispanic workforce		46.2	49.0		70.4	70.3
N	4,133,648	4,500,820	5,454,570	184,301	228,405	305,738
Metropolitan areas with greatest domestic migration losses						
Non-Hispanic white	67.4	62.9	54.1	74.9	63.6	56.7
Non-Hispanic black	13.2	14.1	15.0	7.7	5.9	6.2
Other	5.9	7.3	11.0	4.8	6.3	7.7
Hispanic	13.5	15.7	19.9	12.6	24.2	29.5
Growth of workforce		36.7	12.9		21.5	11.6
Growth of Hispanic workforce		46.1	36.1		84.5	30.7
N	945,217	1,291,720	1,458,363	34,015	41,314	46,094
Metropolitan magnets for domestic migrants						
Non-Hispanic white	80.7	77.0	66.8	83.0	81.6	65.6
Non-Hispanic black	11.7	12.0	13.2	8.4	7.1	6.6
Other	1.7	2.5	5.2	1.0	1.6	2.6
Hispanic	6.0	8.4	14.8	7.6	9.7	25.2
Growth of workforce		−11.9	40.1		18.1	65.8
Growth of Hispanic workforce		21.7	89.9		40.9	145.6
N	466,127	410,859	575,669	27,280	32,210	53,409

Source: Authors' compilation from IPUMS data, 1980–2000.

metropolitan areas, as well as for those experiencing the greatest domestic migration losses and those that have been magnets for domestic migrants.[2] The top panel of the table reports estimates for all industries, as well as for the construction industry in all metropolitan areas.

Results show the increasing representation of Hispanics in the American labor force over time. Between 1980 and 1990 the percentage of Hispanics in all industries increased from 7 percent to 14 percent while the percentage of whites declined from 79 percent to 68 percent and the percentage of non-Hispanic blacks stayed essentially the same. Table 5.1 also shows the growing employment capacity of the construction industry. Between 1980 and 1990 and 1990 and 2000, the American labor force expanded by 9 percent and 21 percent, respectively, but employment in the construction industry grew by 24 percent and 34 percent. When combined with the growing presence of Hispanics in the industry, this change resulted in a 70 percent increase in the number of Hispanic construction workers from 1990 to 2000, compared with a 49 percent increase across all industries.

These trends, however, vary considerably between metropolitan statistical areas (MSAs) that have experienced domestic population losses and those that have become magnets for domestic migrants. The bottom two panels of table 5.1 show these results. Especially during the period 1990 to 2000, MSAs experiencing a loss of native migrants experienced relatively stagnant labor-force growth (just 13 percent), well below the average for all metropolitan areas (21 percent). The same pattern characterizes the labor force in the construction industry, which in these places grew only 12 percent compared to 34 percent across all MSAs. These trends directly affected the ethnic composition of the construction labor force. The percentage of Hispanics in the industry grew consistently after 1980 and reached 30 percent in 1990. In absolute terms, however, this represents a 31 percent increase in the number of Hispanic construction workers, well below the average absolute growth rate of 70 percent for all MSAs.

A very different picture highlights the attractiveness of metropolitan magnets for domestic migrants, where labor-force growth averaged 40 percent between 1990 and 2000. This growth was particularly pronounced for the construction industry, which experienced an average 66 percent growth in its labor force over the same period. Moreover, the Hispanic representation increased considerably, going from 8 percent to 15 percent across all industries, and from 10 percent to 25 percent in the construction industry. In these metropolitan magnets, employment growth and increased Hispanic representation combined to yield a 146 percent increase in the total number of Hispanic construction workers between 1990 and 2000, illustrating the importance of the structural transformation of the construction industry in altering destinations for Hispanic migrants to the United States.

A similar story emerges for the meat-processing industry, though in this case the geographic distinction is between metropolitan and non-metropolitan areas. Table 5.2 shows changes in the racial and ethnic composition for the entire American labor force and separately for metro and nonmetro areas. The top panel shows that between 1980 and 2000, the Hispanic proportion of the total labor force almost doubled, from 5.7 percent to 11.1 percent, but more than tripled in the meat-processing industry, from 8.6 percent to 28.6 percent. Corresponding Hispanic workforce growth outpaced that of all workers during the 1980s and 1990s for all industries and especially for the meat-processing industry.

Similar trends appear in both metropolitan and nonmetropolitan areas, as shown in the middle and bottom portions of the table. The transformation of the meat-processing industry's labor force, characterized by the growth in the immigrant labor force and the movement of plant operations from urban to rural locations, began in the late 1970s and early 1980s (Griffith 1995). Table 5.2 indicates that during the 1980s, the meat-processing workforce shrank by 31.3 percent in metropolitan areas but grew by 41.3 percent in nonmetropolitan areas. During this same period, the absolute number of Hispanic workers increased by 19.3 percent and 98.2 percent in metropolitan and nonmetropolitan areas, respectively.

HISPANIC POPULATION GROWTH IN MULTIVARIATE PERSPECTIVE

We now compare the relative weight of employment growth in construction and meat processing with that of other industries and broader socio-economic processes. Using data from the decennial census and County Business Patterns, we model Hispanic population change for metro and nonmetro counties from 1980 to 1990 and from 1990 to 2000. Specifically, we express the dependent variable, change in the proportion of the total population that is Hispanic, as a function of labor-force distribution, macroeconomic indicators, population indicators, and geographic region. We analyze metropolitan and nonmetropolitan counties separately to differentiate the forces attracting Hispanics to metropolitan and rural areas.[3]

The critical predictor in our analysis is change in the industrial composition of the labor force. Using industrial sector categories from the census long form data, we measured the employment share in ten sectors, including construction. We divided manufacturing employment into durable and nondurable goods, and further divided nondurable goods by separating out

TABLE 5.2   Racial and Ethnic Composition of the Meat-Processing-Industry Workforce, 1980 to 2000 (Percentage, Except as Noted)

	All Industries			Meat-Processing Industry		
	1980	1990	2000	1980	1990	2000
All areas						
Non-Hispanic white	81.8	79.6	72.8	73.4	66.2	48.4
Non-Hispanic black	10.2	9.2	10.1	16.4	17.1	18.5
Other	2.3	3.5	6.0	1.6	3.3	4.5
Hispanic	5.7	7.7	11.1	8.6	13.5	28.6
Growth of workforce		15.7	12.4		7.4	31.1
Growth of Hispanic workforce		44.8	47.6		52.4	102.1
N	5,879,356	6,799,819	7,645,970	15,705	16,863	22,099
All metropolitan areas						
Non-Hispanic white	78.9	75.1	67.8	70.0	59.9	42.0
Non-Hispanic black	11.6	10.5	11.6	15.5	13.5	17.1
Other	2.6	4.3	7.1	2.2	4.7	6.9
Hispanic	6.9	10.1	13.6	12.4	21.9	34.1
Growth of workforce		8.9	21.2		−31.3	53.1
Growth Hispanic workforce		46.4	49.2		19.3	86.9
N	4,133,648	4,500,820	5,454,570	7,338	5,038	7,712
All nonmetropolitan areas						
Non-Hispanic white	88.9	88.2	85.0	76.4	68.8	51.9
Non-Hispanic black	6.7	6.6	6.6	17.2	18.6	19.2
Other	1.5	2.0	3.5	1.2	2.7	3.3
Hispanic	2.9	3.2	4.9	5.3	9.9	25.7
Growth of workforce		31.7	−4.7		41.3	21.7
Growth Hispanic workforce		35.7	37.9		98.2	114.6
N	1,745,708	2,298,999	2,191,400	8,367	11,825	14,387

Source: Authors' compilation from IPUMS data, 1980–2000.

our second subsector of interest, meat processing. We did so by computing the ratio of employment in meat processing to that in nondurable goods manufacturing, using data from the Current Population Survey for 1981 (a proxy for 1980), 1990, and 2000, and applied this ratio to decennial census data for those years. These industrial sectors resemble the dependent variable and measure change over each decade in the proportion of total employment accounted for by each sector. Sectoral employment shares in any given year and changes over the decade necessarily sum to 1.0 and 0.0, respectively.

We control for county-level economic conditions at the beginning of each decade by including the mean household wage income, the proportion of the county population earning a poverty-level income, and the male unemployment rate. Although these factors change over the decades, we feel they adequately capture variation in employment and economic conditions related to population change. To control for non-employment-related factors attracting in-migrants to rural areas, such as climate, topography, and scenic beauty, we include in each model an Amenity Scale value to capture physiographic variation associated with retirement, second home, telecommuting, and tourist destinations that have spurred economic development in many nonmetropolitan counties (McGranahan 1999).[4]

Covariates related to county population conditions include measures of total population, growth rate, and the percentage of Hispanics at the beginning of the decade, which we expect captures population momentum arising from social networks in new-destination settlements. For the analysis of nonmetropolitan counties we control for proximity to urban employment with an indicator of whether the county is adjacent to a metropolitan county. Finally, we include region to control for the overall geographic distribution of Hispanics.

Results from the models for metropolitan and nonmetropolitan counties are reported in table 5.3. Coefficients in boldface indicate significant differences in parameter estimates across the two decades. Among industrial sectors, we use services as the reference category, hence positive coefficients for a given sector indicate a greater association with Hispanic population growth relative to the services sector. Concentrating on the role of industrial characteristics, five industries are central to understanding Hispanic population growth: agriculture, construction, durable goods manufacturing, nondurable goods manufacturing, and meat processing. However, their effects vary across metropolitan and nonmetropolitan counties and across the time periods considered.

Results for metropolitan counties clearly show that even after controlling for other economic and population characteristics, Hispanic population

TABLE 5.3 OLS Regression Estimates on Percentage Change in Composition of Hispanic Population

	Metropolitan Counties		Nonmetropolitan Counties	
	1980 to 1990	1990 to 2000	1980 to 1990	1990 to 2000
Change over decade in proportion employed in:				
Agriculture	0.081** (0.035)	0.006 (0.093)	0.035** (0.010)	0.123** (0.020)
Construction	0.066* (0.036)	0.188*** (0.076)	0.035** (0.015)	0.020 (0.031)
Durable-goods manufacturing	0.064** (0.020)	0.111** (0.045)	0.032*** (0.011)	0.114** (0.019)
Nondurable-goods manufacturing	0.070** (0.024)	0.128** (0.048)	0.032*** (0.013)	0.170** (0.019)
Meat processing	0.121** (0.045)	-0.171* (0.094)	0.059** (0.015)	0.261** (0.025)
Transportation	0.052 (0.051)	0.035 (0.112)	-0.032 (0.022)	0.077 (0.043)
Communication, utilities	0.037 (0.072)	0.008 (0.088)	-0.010 (0.027)	-0.117** (0.049)
Wholesale and retail trade	0.032 (0.027)	0.088 (0.057)	-0.027** (0.013)	0.037 (0.022)
Public administration	-0.076 (0.059)	-0.098 (0.093)	-0.066** (0.030)	-0.141** (0.050)
County-level economic indicators at start of decade				
Poverty rate (percentage below)	-0.019 (0.019)	-0.036 (0.028)	-0.015** (0.007)	-0.005 (0.012)
Male unemployment rate	-0.054** (0.025)	-0.114** (0.060)	-0.048*** (0.008)	-0.145** (0.018)
Mean household wage income ($10,000)	0.002 (0.003)	0.001 (0.002)	0.001 (0.002)	-0.001 (0.002)
Amenity Scale Value	0.002** (0.001)	0.003** (0.001)	-0.001** (0.000)	-0.002** (0.001)

	(1)		(2)		(3)		(4)	
County population status								
Total population (thousands), at start of decade	0.000**	(0.000)	0.000**	(0.000)	0.000	(0.000)	0.000**	(0.000)
Population growth rate	0.003	(0.003)	0.010*	(0.005)	0.004	(0.003)	0.030**	(0.004)
Percentage Hispanic at start of decade	0.069**	(0.008)	0.088**	(0.012)	0.026**	(0.004)	0.028**	(0.006)
Adjacent to metro county					0.001	(0.001)	−0.001	(0.001)
National region variables								
Northeast	**−0.005***	(0.003)	**−0.014***	(0.004)	**−0.017***	(0.002)	**−0.026***	(0.003)
Midwest	−0.012**	(0.003)	−0.017**	(0.004)	−0.020**	(0.002)	−0.019**	(0.002)
South	−0.014**	(0.002)	**−0.014***	(0.004)	**−0.021***	(0.001)	**−0.012***	(0.002)
West	−0.006**	(0.003)	−0.002	(0.005)	−0.011**	(0.002)	−0.006**	(0.002)
Intercept	0.015*	(0.009)	0.024*	(0.013)	0.027**	(0.005)	0.023**	(0.007)
Adjusted r-squared	0.463		0.393		0.280		0.204	
N (cases)	731		731		2391		2391	

Source: U.S. decennial censuses, SF3 Files, 1970–2000: U.S. Census Bureau's annual County Business Patterns data, 1981, 1990, 2000: Economic Research Service, U.S. Department of Agriculture Natural Amenities Scale, 1999.

*p<.05; **p<.01; bolded coefficients indicate statistically significant differences across time periods (p>0.1 one-sided test).

growth is directly affected by growth in the construction industry. Moreover the effect becomes significantly stronger across time periods. Results thus confirm that rapid growth in the southern construction industry relative to other regions undergirds the expansion of Hispanic populations in new metropolitan destinations. At the same time, the role of construction diminished and became insignificant in rural areas over this same period.

Another striking result for metropolitan counties is the reversal of the effect of meat-processing employment on Hispanic population growth across periods. This reversal contradicts the pattern evident for rural counties, where meat-processing employment is associated with a significant contribution to Hispanic population growth. This change is consistent with the description presented earlier regarding the industrial and geographic transformation of the industry. As the meat-processing industry relocated out of cities to southeastern and midwestern rural areas it attracted Hispanic in-migrants and contributed to the growing diversification of destination areas.

Other industry effects are also worth noting. In general, coefficients appear to be more stable over time periods in metropolitan than in nonmetropolitan counties. There is a statistically significant increase in the size over time of the coefficients for agriculture and durable and nondurable goods manufacturing in rural counties over time, a pattern suggesting that as rural counties become more involved in these activities, they can expect growing Hispanic populations. In other words, economic processes fueling the growth of manufacturing employment in rural areas are likely to change their ethnic composition.

Estimates of the effect of control variables confirm the validity of the model's specification. Immigrants and migrant workers are relatively mobile populations that are attracted to places with employment opportunities, and our results show a consistent negative relationship between Hispanic population growth and unemployment rates and poverty. The influence of the presence of natural amenities has only a slight influence, positive for metropolitan counties that need service workers, and negative for nonmetropolitan counties where Hispanics are more likely to work in agriculture, manufacturing, and similar industries situated in midwestern and southern areas that rank low on natural amenities.

At the same time, larger initial Hispanic population sizes facilitate growth in metropolitan and nonmetropolitan Hispanic representation over time, a reminder of the importance of social networks in facilitating new Hispanic settlements. Total population growth also appears to drive

Hispanic population growth, and may be capturing total employment growth independent of changes in industry sector share. Finally, while negative coefficients associated with the four regional indicators demonstrate the relative dominance of the Southwest, where roughly half of all nonmetropolitan Hispanics reside, those for the Northeast and Southeast changed over time. Between the 1980s and 1990s metropolitan and nonmetropolitan northeastern counties grew less likely to increase their representation of Hispanics; in contrast to this, the nonmetropolitan Southeast experienced elevated Hispanic population growth during the 1990s.

CHARACTERISTICS OF HISPANICS AT NEW DESTINATIONS

The foregoing analyses illustrate the importance of labor demand in the construction and meat-processing industries for Hispanic population diversification. Yet a core tenet of dual-labor-market theory is that the socioeconomic characteristics of the Hispanic population should reflect their position in the secondary sector of the United States' economy. Specifically, we expect an increasing representation of foreign-born and low-skilled Hispanic workers in the construction and meat-processing industries, especially at new destinations (tables 5.4 and 5.5). Table 5.4 shows trends in national origin and educational characteristics for construction workers by race and ethnicity. For the urban-based construction industry we again separate metropolitan areas that have experienced domestic migration losses from those that have functioned as magnets for domestic in-migrants. For the rural meat-processing industry, we distinguish between metro and nonmetro areas.

The data in table 5.4 demonstrate an unmistakable pattern. Between 1980 and 2000 both industries experienced increased proportions of foreign-born workers, from roughly 8 percent to over 20 percent. During the same period these industries did not show a substantial decline in the least-educated proportions of their workforces, which one would expect, given the continued rise in educational attainment in the United States. In 2000 well over 20 percent of both industries' labor forces had less than a high school education. These trends highlight the relative unattractiveness of jobs in industrial sectors that are increasingly being taken by nonnative and relatively poorly educated individuals.

The change is particularly pronounced for Hispanics. While results hold for both traditional and new areas of destination, the proportion of Hispanics who were foreign-born in the construction industry in areas that have been magnets for domestic migrants more than doubled from 31 per-

TABLE 5.4   Socioeconomic Characteristics of the Construction Industry Labor Force, 1980 to 2000

	Percentage of Foreign-Born			Percentage with Less Than High School			Average Annual Wage Income[a]		
	1980	1990	2000	1980	1990	2000	1980	1990	2000
All metropolitan areas									
Non-Hispanic white	4.6	5.1	4.8	19.5	10.3	8.1	33,304	35,942	37,277
Non-Hispanic black	4.8	9.1	10.8	41.0	20.4	12.7	24,259	27,299	28,260
Other	34.5	51.7	45.4	18.7	11.9	12.9	34,894	37,602	33,763
Hispanic	44.9	64.4	72.9	50.7	44.4	46.8	26,635	26,286	24,869
Total	8.1	13.6	19.0	23.4	15.0	15.5	32,279	34,513	34,653
Greatest domestic migration losses									
Non-Hispanic white	10.3	11.6	12.2	16.6	8.3	5.7	36,734	40,655	42,954
Non-Hispanic black	11.0	20.7	24.7	34.0	14.0	10.7	27,847	32,551	32,131
Other	35.6	55.9	59.6	17.5	10.9	14.4	36,387	39,365	35,279
Hispanic	52.0	70.6	72.8	46.4	44.7	41.8	28,347	27,546	26,647
Total	16.8	29.3	34.5	21.8	17.7	17.3	35,160	37,360	37,408
Magnets for domestic migrants									
Non-Hispanic white	2.4	2.8	3.6	21.6	12.6	9.9	30,063	31,972	36,831
Non-Hispanic black	2.0	5.8	7.6	43.5	25.6	14.0	21,186	23,602	26,513
Other	21.3	32.5	33.4	25.8	17.2	13.4	27,853	30,419	31,491
Hispanic	31.3	55.8	78.5	52.7	46.8	55.0	26,181	24,185	23,195
Total	4.7	8.6	23.5	25.8	16.9	21.7	29,101	30,756	32,980

Source: Authors' compilation from IPUMS data, 1980–2000.
[a] In 2000 dollars.

cent to 78 percent between 1980 and 2000. In these areas, moreover, the percentage of Hispanics with less than a high school education remained virtually unchanged, increasing slightly from 53 to 55 percent. These findings bolster additional intra-industry occupation tabulations (not shown), which show that where 28 percent of non-Hispanic whites were employed in professional or managerial occupations in the construction industry, only 10 percent of Hispanics held similar positions. Likewise, only 9 percent of whites were employed as laborers, but the figure was 28 percent among Hispanics.

TABLE 5.5 Socioeconomic Characteristics of the Meat-Processing Industry Labor Force, 1980 to 2000

	Percentage of Foreign-Born			Percentage with Less Than High School			Average Annual Wage Income[a]		
	1980	1990	2000	1980	1990	2000	1980	1990	2000
All areas									
Non-Hispanic white	3.9	2.5	3.1	28.5	16.4	11.8	30,949	27,439	30,519
Non-Hispanic black	1.4	0.9	1.8	41.9	21.4	14.3	21,195	18,591	20,561
Other	46.9	60.2	62.0	39.5	35.3	31.6	24,707	21,996	24,103
Hispanic	49.6	70.5	81.9	65.0	60.7	62.5	26,092	21,049	20,825
Total	8.2	13.3	28.1	34.0	23.8	27.6	29,001	25,087	25,972
Metropolitan areas									
Non-Hispanic white	7.1	6.8	6.9	26.8	15.0	9.9	34,631	34,589	36,891
Non-Hispanic black	1.9	2.1	3.2	38.9	15.0	13.7	26,367	21,557	22,286
Other	54.7	80.5	79.5	32.1	38.1	34.5	26,844	24,702	26,103
Hispanic	55.8	71.8	81.1	64.7	56.3	58.9	27,291	22,952	21,912
Total	13.4	23.8	36.5	33.5	25.1	28.9	32,474	30,089	29,105
Nonmetropolitan areas									
Non-Hispanic white	1.4	0.9	1.4	29.9	16.9	12.6	27,914	24,787	27,708
Non-Hispanic black	0.9	0.5	1.1	44.2	23.4	14.5	17,082	17,700	19,747
Other	34.3	44.9	42.5	51.5	33.1	28.4	20,940	19,879	21,674
Hispanic	36.9	69.2	82.5	65.4	64.9	65.1	23,640	19,180	20,036
Total	3.6	8.8	23.5	34.5	23.2	27.0	25,916	22,931	24,293

Source: Authors' compilation from IPUMS data, 1980–2000.
[a] In 2000 dollars.

Similar results hold for the Hispanic labor force in the meat-processing industry (table 5.5). In rural areas the foreign-born proportion of Hispanics in the industry increased from 37 to 83 percent between 1980 and 2000. As a result, the percentage of Hispanics with less than a high school education remained unchanged, at 65 percent, throughout the period. As with the construction industry, this trend is further reflected in the occupational composition of the labor force by race and ethnicity. According to census 2000 data (not shown), 12 percent of whites work in professional and managerial positions in the meat-processing industry, compared with just 2 percent of Hispanics, and 44 percent of Hispanics are employed as meat cutters or other operatives, whereas only 15 percent of whites hold the same occupation.

One correlate of this shift in labor-force composition is a substantial decline in relative real wages for Hispanics in both industries. Hispanic construction workers in metropolitan areas characterized by either population losses or in-migration saw their wage incomes fall consistently across the two decades examined, in sharp contrast with those of all other racial and ethnic groups, whose incomes increased. In the meat-processing industry, Hispanic workers saw their wage incomes decline more severely during the 1980s and rebound less forcefully during the 1990s than those of workers of other ethnic or racial backgrounds.

When combined with the growth of Hispanics in both industries and the growing representation in new areas of destination previously discussed, these results highlight how, consistent with dual-labor-market theories, the foreign birth and low skill of Hispanic workers increased with their representation. As predicted, the relatively undesirable new jobs created in the construction and meat-processing industries were filled with low-skilled immigrant workers who did not compete directly with the slower-growing population of skilled natives, especially non-Hispanic whites, the only group to experience a sharp decline in representation in both industries.

CONCLUSIONS

Over the past two decades, Hispanic population growth in nontraditional metropolitan and nonmetropolitan destinations has been encouraged by several factors. These include changes in border enforcement and immigration policy, the search by migrants for more favorable employment and living conditions, and by formal and informal recruitment by firms seeking to replenish a continuously depleted supply of low-skilled workers. The dispersion of the Hispanic population to new towns, cities, and regions throughout the nation has profound implications for political outcomes, social service delivery, economic development, and social, cultural, and public policy response.

In this analysis we developed a labor-demand explanation for the increasing representation of Hispanics in new-destination areas, linking metropolitan growth to a rising demand for construction workers and rural growth to industrial restructuring in the meat-processing industry. In each case, the growth of the Hispanic populations in new destinations stemmed from a demand for labor in a major industry that hired large numbers of low-skilled workers for physically demanding and relatively hazardous work to produce two fundamental necessities, food and shelter. In the construction industry, a number of factors—a growing population, historically low interest rates, and economic growth in the Southeast and Southwest—converged to boost the demand for new housing and home renovations, especially in urban areas and their outlying regions. During the same period, the meat-processing industry experienced growing demand for its products as a result of changing consumer tastes for meat products and prepared products, population growth, and skyrocketing exports.

The construction and meat-processing industries witnessed a substantial decline in the proportion of their workers represented by labor unions, and, not coincidentally, annual wage incomes for Hispanic workers in both industries declined in real terms between 1980 and 2000. Hispanic workers in the meat-processing industry suffered income declines considerably more precipitous than those of average workers in that industry. Hispanic construction workers did even worse, experiencing income declines while the average construction worker enjoyed an increase in real income during this period.

Our results do not point to racial or ethnic discrimination as the culprit for this unusual outcome, because non-Hispanic blacks and individuals in the "other" category experienced gains during the same period. Rather, it appears that significant income declines for Hispanic workers in both the meat-processing and construction industries stem from their lower human capital endowments and, more important, from the structural conditions in both industries that create the demand for such workers. If there is one central point to our analysis, it is that Hispanic population growth in new and traditional destinations originates from the growing demand and changing preferences of American consumers for fundamental goods and services, such as food and housing.

Immigrant labor in construction and food processing follows a pattern found in crop agriculture and both nondurable and durable goods manufacturing. As education levels in the general population rise and other employment options reduce the attractiveness of employment in these industries, American firms that do not or cannot locate production overseas seek cost-cutting measures at home. A central strategy in doing so has been the shift to low-cost, low-skilled labor (David Barboza, "Meatpackers' Profits Hinge on Pool of Immigrant Labor," *New York Times*, December 21, 2001). The construction and meat-processing industries experienced substantial increases in the proportion of foreign-born workers for each racial and ethnic group we examined, non-Hispanic whites excepted. Yet education levels for Hispanic workers in both industries remained stagnant over the period, a striking contrast to the considerable improvement experienced by other racial and ethnic groups. Such outcomes are consistent with a dual-labor-market interpretation of Hispanic employment occurring in industries and occupations that native residents increasingly shun.

Opinions expressed herein do not reflect those of the Economic Research Service or the U.S. Department of Agriculture.

NOTES

1. The Southeast comprises Delaware, Maryland, the District of Columbia, Virginia, West Virginia, North Carolina, South Carolina, Georgia, Florida, Kentucky, Tennessee, Alabama, Mississippi, Arkansas, Louisiana, and Oklahoma; the Southwest comprises Arizona, California, Colorado, New Mexico, and Texas.

2. Metropolitan areas with greatest domestic migration losses are defined as those with more than a negative 3 percent net migration rate between 1995 and 2000. Magnets for domestic migrants include those metropolitan areas with more than 3 percent net migration rate during the same period. Estimates for net migration rates were obtained from William Frey (2003).

3. "Nonmetropolitan" areas follow the Office of Management and Budget definition, which is based on population and commuting patterns. A metropolitan area consists of one or more core counties with an urbanized area of 50,000 or more inhabitants, together with surrounding counties with metropolitan characteristics such as commuting patterns and population density and growth. Nonmetropolitan areas consist of all other counties and contain only open country, small towns, or small cities. Hence, counties can be grouped according to whether they are metropolitan or nonmetropolitan. The term "nonmetropolitan" is distinct from "rural," which despite its frequent general usage also refers to a Census Bureau definition for places with fewer than 2,500 inhabitants. In this paper, however, we use the term "rural" in its general context. Because population change over a decade may prompt counties to be reclassified from nonmetropolitan to metropolitan, or vice versa, we use the initial 1980 classification throughout the analysis.

4. The Amenity Scale Value is a composite measure of six indicators of climate, typography, and water body characteristics reflecting environmental qualities most people prefer. These characteristics (and their measures in parentheses) include warm winters (average January temperature), winter sun (average January days of sun), temperate summers (winter-summer temperature gap), summer humidity (average July humidity), topographic variation (topography scale), and water area (water area as proportion of total county area). Because the six characteristics are measured differently, they are normalized through

the computation of Z-scores, which are then summed and recoded to yield values ranging from 1 to 7. The ASV has not been recalibrated for periods earlier than 1999, but the environmental features it measures are unlikely to change significantly over the two-decade span of our analysis. For more information on this scale, see David A. McGranahan (1999, 2–6).

REFERENCES

Associated General Contractors of America. 2005. *Construction News.* January 11. Alexandria, Va.: Associated General Contractors of America.

Broadway, Michael J. 1995. "From City to Countryside: Recent Changes in the Structure and Location of the Meat- and Fish-Processing Industries." In *Any Way You Cut It: Meat Processing and Small Town America*, edited by Donald D. Stull, Michael J. Broadway, and David Griffith. Lawrence, Kan.: University Press of Kansas.

Conway, Hugh, Collin Dunn, and Gary Khalil. 2004. *Construction: A Report on the Industry.* Washington: Industrial College of the Armed Forces.

Cornelius, Wayne A. 2001. "Death at the Border: Efficacy and Unintended Consequences of U.S. Immigration Control Policy." *Population and Development Review* 27(4): 661–85.

Donato, Katharine M., Melissa Stainback, and Carl L. Bankston, III. 2005. "The Economic Incorporation of Mexican Immigrants in Southern Louisiana: A Tale of Two Cities." In *New Destinations: Mexican Immigration in the United States*, edited by Víctor Zúñiga and Rubén Hernández-León. New York: Russell Sage Foundation.

Durand, Jorge, Douglas S. Massey, and Fernando Charvet. 2000. "The Changing Geography of Mexican Immigration to the United States: 1910–1996." *Social Science Quarterly* 81(1): 1–16.

Fennelly, Katherine. 2005. "Latinos, Asians, Africans in the Northstar State: New Immigrant Communities in Minnesota." In *Beyond the Gateway: Immigrants in a Changing America*, edited by Elzbieta M. Gozdziak and Susan F. Martin. Lanham, Md.: Lexington Books.

Fennelly, Katherine, and Helga Leitner. 2002. "How the Food Processing Industry Is Diversifying Rural Minnesota." Working Paper 59. East Lansing, Mich.: Michigan State University, Julian Samora Research Institute.

Frey, William H. 2002. "Metropolitan Magnets for International and Domestic Migrants." Washington: Brookings Institution.

———. 2003. "Metropolitan Magnets for International and Domestic Migrants." Washington: Brookings Institution.

Goodrum, Paul M. 2004. "Hispanic and Non-Hispanic Wage Differentials: Implications for the United States Construction Industry." *Journal of Construction Engineering and Management* 130(4): 552–9.

Gozdziak, Elzbieta M., and Susan F. Martin. 2005. *Beyond the Gateway: Immigrants in a Changing America.* Lanham, Md.: Lexington Books.

Grey, Mark A. 1999. "Immigrants, Migration, and Worker Turnover at the Hog Pride Pork Packing Plant." *Human Organization* 58(1): 16–27.

Griffith, David. 1995. "Hay Trabajo: Poultry Processing, Rural Industrialization, and the Latinization of Low-Wage Labor." In *Any Way You Cut It: Meat Processing and Small Town America*, edited by Donald D. Stull, Michael J. Broadway, and David Griffith. Lawrence, Kan.: University Press of Kansas.

Hernández-León, Rubén, and Víctor Zúñiga. 2000. " 'Making Carpet by the Mile': The Emergence of a Mexican Immigrant Community in an Industrial Region of the U.S. Historic South." *Social Science Quarterly* 81(1): 49–66.

Johnson-Webb, Karen D. 2002. "Employer Recruitment and Hispanic Labor Migration: North Carolina Urban Areas at the End of the Millennium." *Professional Geographer* 54(3): 406–21.

Kandel, William, and John Cromartie. 2004. "New Patterns of Hispanic Settlement in Rural America." Rural Development and Research Report 99. Washington: U.S. Department of Agriculture, Economic Research Service.

Kandel, William, and Emilio A. Parrado. 2004. "Industrial Transformation and Hispanic Migration to the American South: The case of the Poultry Industry." In *Hispanic Spaces, Latino Places: A Geography of Regional and Cultural Diversity*, edited by Daniel D. Arreola. Austin, Tx.: University of Texas Press.

———. 2005. "Restructuring of the U.S. Meat Processing Industry and New Hispanic Migrant Destinations." *Population and Development Review* 31(3): 447–71.

Krissman, Fred. 2000. "Immigrant Labor Recruitment: U.S. Agribusiness and Undocumented Migration from Mexico." In *Immigration Research for a New Century*, edited by Nancy Foner, Rubén G. Rumbaut, and Steven J. Gold. New York: Russell Sage.

MacDonald, James M., Michael E. Ollinger, Kenneth E. Nelson, and Charles E. Handy. 2000. "Consolidation in U.S. Meatpacking." Agricultural Economic Report 785. Washington: Economic Research Service, U.S. Department of Agriculture.

Macguire, Steven R. 1993. "Worker Tenure in 1991." *Occupational Outlook Quarterly* 47(1): 25–37.

Massey, Douglas S., Jorge Durand, and Nolan J. Malone. 2002. *Beyond Smoke and Mirrors: Mexican Immigration in an Era of Economic Integration*. New York: Russell Sage Foundation.

McDaniel, Joshua M., and Vanessa Casanova. 2003. "Pines in Lines: Tree Planting, H2B Guest Workers, and Rural Poverty in Alabama." *Southern Rural Sociology* 19(1): 73–96.

McGranahan, David A. 1999. "Natural Amenities Drive Rural Population Change." Agricultural Economic Report 781. Washington: U.S. Department of Agriculture, Economic Research Service.

Millard, Ann V., Jorge Chapa, and Catalina Burillo. 2005. *Apple Pie and Enchiladas: Latino Newcomers in the Rural Midwest*. Austin, Tx.: University of Texas Press.

Ollinger, Michael E., James M. MacDonald, and Milt Madison. 2000. "Structural Change in U.S. Chicken and Turkey Slaughter." Agricultural Economic

Report 787. Washington: U.S. Department of Agriculture, Economic Research Service.

Piore, Michael J. 1979. *Birds of Passage: Migrant Labor and Industrial Societies.* Cambridge: Cambridge University Press.

Singer, Audrey. 2004. "The Rise of New Immigrant Gateways." Report for the Center on Urban and Metropolitan Policy. Washington: Brookings Institution.

Stepick, Alex, Guillermo Grenier, Steve Morris, and Debbie Draznin. 1994. "Brothers in Wood." In *Newcomers in the Workplace: Immigrants and the Restructuring of the U.S. Economy,* edited by Louise Lamphere, Alex Stepick, and Guillermo Grenier. Philadelphia, Penn.: Temple University Press.

Suro, Roberto, and Audrey Singer. 2002. "Latino Growth in Metropolitan America: Changing Patterns, New Locations." Washington: Brookings Institution and Pew Hispanic Center, Center on Urban and Metropolitan Policy.

Zúñiga, Víctor, and Rubén Hernández-León. 2005. *New Destinations: Mexican Immigration in the United States.* New York: Russell Sage Foundation.

CHAPTER 6

⋎

THE ORIGINS OF EMPLOYER DEMAND FOR IMMIGRANTS IN A NEW DESTINATION: THE SALIENCE OF SOFT SKILLS IN A VOLATILE ECONOMY

KATHARINE M. DONATO AND CARL L. BANKSTON, III

> Well, it's attitudes and skills; it's a combination of both . . . but probably definitely attitude. They come out here and it's wide open from when they start till the time they stop.
> —Louisiana oil industry employer

Recent studies indicate a new geographic dispersion of immigrants to states such as Georgia, Minnesota, and North Carolina; to cities that include Phoenix, Las Vegas, Denver, and Nashville; and to smaller towns and villages throughout the southern and western regions of the United States (Kandel and Parrado 2005; Zúñiga and Hernández-León 2005; Saenz et al. 2004; Singer 2004; Bankston 2003; Durand, Massey, and Charvet 2000; Engstrom 2001; Hernández-León and Zúñiga 2000; Grey 1999; Stull, Broadway, and Erickson 1992). What accounts for the initiation of immigration to these new destination areas? This is a key research question.

Studies suggest that the emergence of immigration to new areas of destination is related to at least three factors: labor-market opportunities, particularly in food processing and other industries generating unskilled and semiskilled employment; higher wages than in origin communities or in large urban centers where migrants may have settled in the past; and market failures in sending nations that push persons to migrate as part of a strategy to avert risk. Although these characteristics reflect the major theoretical paradigms advanced to explain international migration (Massey et al.

1994), together they fail to deal with an important dimension: the perceptions and actions of employers. Because these models view migratory decisions as rational and linked to labor demand, wages, and risk, they do not recognize the extent to which employers seek out and hire workers on the basis of perceptions of quality.

The objective of this paper is to understand why, how, and when American employers in one new destination area turned to immigrants rather than natives to satisfy their labor needs. We draw on a rich set of data that includes interviews with approximately 140 employers, labor leaders, and immigrants as well as public opinion surveys in the surrounding communities. We interviewed employers in four new destination communities in southern Louisiana, an area where deep-sea offshore drilling has rapidly increased labor demand since the late 1980s. Louisiana had not been a common destination area for immigrants in the past, but many Spanish-speaking migrants began working in ship and fabrication yards in port cities during the mid-1990s (Donato, Bankston, and Robinson 2001; Donato, Stainback, and Bankston 2005).

Our findings suggest that the volatility in labor markets during the 1980s created a new demand for immigrant labor in southern Louisiana. By the late 1990s, employers sought immigrants—especially those from Mexico. They believed immigrants were "willing subordinates" because they evaluated their treatment by American employers relative to how they would be treated in Mexican-origin communities (Waldinger and Lichter 2003, 40). Immigrants' dual frame of reference made them an attractive labor supply for onshore manufacturing employers in the oil industry, where they preferred the "soft skills" of immigrants, such as motivation to work and positive interaction with others (Kirschenman and Neckerman 1991). "Soft" skills have been defined as "abilities and traits that pertain to personality, attitude, and behavior" (Moss and Tilly 2001, 44). Consistent with prior studies documenting how employer preferences are associated with race and ethnicity, this study illustrates how the salience of subjective opinions about immigrants in the highly volatile oil industry generated a demand for immigrant labor in southern Louisiana.

EMPLOYERS AND THE INDUSTRIAL SECTOR

We begin by describing employers and the industrial sector they represent, focusing on issues related to labor supply and demand at the time of our interviews. To place their reports in a larger context, we also present data from the U.S. Bureau of Labor Statistics on changes in the rate of unemployment and the size of the local labor force. Wherever possible,

FIGURE 6.1   Map of Louisiana

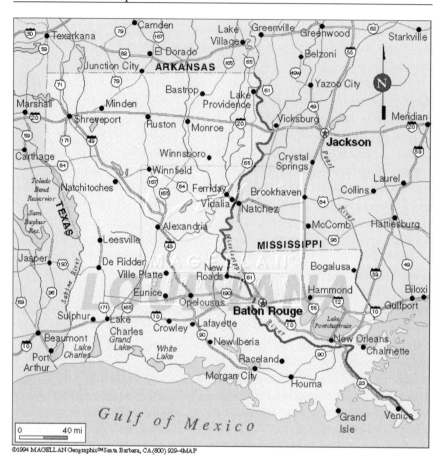

Source: Used with permission of Magellan Geographer. Created by Carl Bankston and George Woodell using Corel software.

we highlight regional differences and compare trends and patterns in our four study areas to the state of Louisiana and the nation as a whole. In addition, we augment the interpretation of these data with the employers' own words.

All the workplaces we visited—Houma, Morgan City, New Iberia, and Port Fourchon—were located in industrial areas that are part of the flat geography of southern Louisiana, near the Gulf of Mexico and interlaced with bayous and rivers (see figure 6.1). Employers in the community of New Iberia are mainly located at the Port of Iberia, a large industrial and manufacturing park just outside the city limits. Although New Iberia itself is a charming old Louisiana town, the port is a two-thousand-acre industrial complex that exports a wide variety of products to the oil industry and employs more than five thousand workers, of whom many are welders and pipe fitters. The port is situated at slightly more than five feet above sea level and contains docks that run along a channel going through the port. The channel extends eight miles, via the Gulf Intercoastal Waterway, to the Gulf of Mexico. Most respondents to our questionnaires were supervisory managers in companies at the Port of Iberia or suppliers of contract labor. Their workers made offshore platform structures, oil and gas pipes, and vessels and barges to service oil platforms.

In Morgan City, Louisiana, we visited workplaces at three locations. Several large shipbuilding companies were located at one edge of the city, alongside the Atchafalaya River and Flat Lake. Here we conducted interviews with personnel or human resource directors in administrative offices surrounded by busy shipyards filled with workers in hard hats. To the south of the city, we interviewed employers at another set of businesses that occupied a strip of land beside the Gulf Intercoastal Waterway, which intersects with the Atchafalaya. These include shipbuilding and ship and barge repair companies as well as a wide variety of other employers, including fabricators of platforms and pipes, supply companies for offshore structures, renters of equipment to shipbuilders, and suppliers of contract labor. Farther southeast of the city, located among southern Louisiana's bayous, were several large oil companies. At these locations, most jobs involved the construction of offshore oil rigs, and here managers were usually least involved with workers.

Work sites in and near Houma were even more spread out than those in Morgan City. With more waterways, the producers of offshore materials and services were scattered across locations in the city of Houma and throughout the parish. Finally, we interviewed employers in Port Fourchon, Louisiana's southernmost port. Since the 1980s it has grown to become a center of offshore oil and gas support activities. It houses the nation's only multi-use superport, the Louisiana Offshore Oil Port (LOOP), a technologically sophisticated port that serves as the central unloading and distribution point for all incoming supertankers to the region. It contains a hundred-foot-deep pipeline into which large supertankers empty millions of barrels of crude oil every day. Eventually oil is piped north to the salt dome storage areas near Galliano, in Lafourche Parish; this oil represents more than 30 percent of the oil refined in the United States.

Table 6.1 presents the characteristics of the sixty-eight companies whose employees we interviewed. The clear majority of our companies were in the oil and gas sector of the economy (78 percent). Another 12 percent were

TABLE 6.1   Attributes of Employers in Four Southern
Louisiana Communities

Characteristic	Distribution
Percentage of companies in each area	
Morgan City	25.0%
New Iberia	13.2
Houma	36.8
Port Fourchon	25.0
N	68
Primary industry	
Oil and gas	78.5%
Shipbuilding	12.3
Other	9.2
N	65
Year of business creation	
1940 to 1950s	16.7%
1960s	11.1
1970s	18.5
1980s	38.9
1990s	14.8
N	54
Company type	
Local	42.4%
Regional	15.3
National	18.6
Multinational	23.7
N	59
Company size	
Fewer than 100 workers	54.4%
100 to 499 workers	26.5
500 to 999 workers	13.2
More than 1,000 workers	5.9
Average number of workers	268.3
N	68

Source: Louisiana Immigrant Project (1999).

shipbuilding companies holding contracts from oil and gas companies to construct off-shore platforms, their parts, and the ships that service them. These corporations represent both established companies and newcomers founded after 1980 (approximately half were founded before the 1980s and the other half were founded in the 1980s or 1990s, reflecting corporate restructuring through mergers and acquisitions that began as a result of the oil bust in the early 1980s).

Interestingly, many companies (42 percent) were locally owned and another 15 percent were regional establishments. Approximately 19 percent of the businesses were national and 24 percent were multinational. In addition to being largely locally owned, half of our sample employed fewer than one hundred workers. Larger employers (with between one hundred to five hundred workers) made up another 26 percent of our sample; 24 percent reported five hundred to one thousand workers; just 6 percent had more than 1,000. The preponderance of smaller, local companies means that many employers operate in fairly informal settings, often administrative offices located on work sites.

The managers and supervisors who spoke with us often had working class backgrounds and maintained close contacts with their workers because many had prior experience in the skilled work done by their employees. Despite their shared sector location, there was considerable diversity in the primary activities of employers in our sample, as documented in table 6.2. Approximately 30 percent sold, rented, or serviced equipment to the oil and gas industry, 26 percent fabricated offshore pipes and platforms, and 11 percent reported shipbuilding as their primary activity. In addition, another 8 percent provided contract labor services, 6 percent cleaned and repaired ships, another 6 percent cleaned and repaired platforms, and a final 6 percent were engaged in offshore drilling.

Heterogeneity among employers is a consequence of the patchwork nature of the Gulf Coast oil industry. Making equipment, erecting an offshore oil structure, and building or repairing ships that serve the industry involve many tasks and create opportunities for different kinds of workers. At the same time, the various tasks draw on a similar set of skills. Carpentry, welding, and mechanics figure heavily in all of the primary activities reported by these companies, and firms providing contract laborers concentrate on supplying workers who have these skills. Even if there is job diversity, then, there is also a broad similarity in the skills workers need to perform these jobs.

During the 1990s, many companies in the industry relied on the use of contract labor—workers recruited by labor subcontractors. This practice permits employers to hire workers on an as-needed basis that corresponds

TABLE 6.2   Primary Activity and Contract-Labor Use of Employers in Four Southern Louisiana Communities

Characteristic	Distribution
Primary activity	
Oil field supply, rental, service	30.3%
Fabrication, offshore pipes and platforms	25.8
Shipbuilding	10.6
Contract labor	7.6
Ship repair and cleaning	6.1
Offshore pipes repair and cleaning	6.1
Offshore drilling	6.1
Disposal of oil field waste	3.0
Other	4.5
N	66
Use of contract labor	
Never	37.5%
Rarely	12.5
Sometimes	23.2
Often	0.7
Always	16.1
N	56
Average number of current contract workers of employers using contract labor	61.0
Level of company turnover	
Low	54.9%
High	45.1
N	51

Source: Louisiana Immigrant Project (1999).

with the ebbs and flows of the industry's business cycle. It also permits them to do so without incurring liabilities, such as the financial burdens that result from offering job benefits, and the risks and fines that may occur if unauthorized immigrant workers are found on work sites. These advantages explain why many employers now rely on contract labor. Indeed, two thirds of the employers we interviewed (see table 6.2) reported some use of contract workers, and 27 percent always or often used contract workers. These companies employed an average of sixty-one contract laborers at the time of the interviews.

TABLE 6.3   Primary Activity and Contract-Labor Use of Employers in Four Southern Louisiana Communities

Characteristic	Distribution
Racial composition of workforce	
Less than 50 percent white	15.2%
50 to 74 percent white	30.4
More than 75 percent white	54.3
N	46
Presence of Hispanic workers	
No Hispanics	50.9
One to twenty-five Hispanics	19.3
Twenty-six to 100 Hispanics	12.3
"Some" Hispanics—number unspecified	14.0
"Many" Hispanics—number unspecified	5.0
N	57
Workers with GED or high school degree	
0 to 50 percent	19.4
Greater than 50 percent	80.6
N	36

Source: Louisiana Immigrant Project (1999).

Therefore, despite certain differences, employers reported many striking similarities. All were found in central locations to service the offshore oil industry, a major industry in the United States. All were in rural or small-town settings that historically had seen relatively few international migrant workers. Approximately half were relatively small, locally or regionally owned companies that serviced the oil and gas industry in a variety of ways, from making platforms and parts to shipbuilding to cleaning and servicing vessels. Moreover, the majority of employers relied on at least some contract laborers.

Table 6.3 presents employers' descriptions of their current labor force. Most reported majority-white workforces, with approximately half reporting a workforce that was at least 75 percent white. This is surprising because, unlike many other areas of the United States, African Americans made up between 25 to 35 percent of the residents in these Louisiana Gulf Coast areas in 2000.[1] In addition, half the employers reported hiring at least some Hispanic-origin workers, a pattern consistent with other studies suggesting that since 1990, foreign-born workers have settled in nonmetropolitan areas that offer semiskilled jobs (Donato, Bankston, and Robinson 2001; Donato, Stainback, and Bankston 2005). As a consequence, approximately one fifth of the companies reported employing at least 25 Latino origin workers and 12 percent employed between 25 and 100. Other employers were vague when questioned about their Latino workforce: 14 percent said they employed "some" Latino workers and 4 percent stated that they hired "many" of them. Furthermore, although most employers reported that the majority of their employees had completed high school or the equivalent, almost 20 percent reported that half of their workforce had less than a high school education.

Table 6.4 summarizes the job characteristics described by employers. Although employers reported hiring mostly full-time workers, not one employer reported hiring unionized workers. One supervisor with a Port Fourchon company that serviced offshore structures summed up the industry's position this way: "There are very few unions in the oil field. Now in your refineries you have them. As for as the drilling aspect, production aspect, you have got a couple of helicopter companies . . . like company 10 has a union, but oil companies don't like to deal with unions so . . . they tend to shy away from people who have unions. Right now . . . you have got truckers and boats where people are trying to organize unions for the oil field . . . [but] they have been doing it for about ten years. I don't think it is going to go over. It is just like I said . . . if you become unionized, well they won't use you."[2]

Likewise, an executive with an oil field service company at the Port of Iberia emphatically stated, "Oh, God no, [not unions. . . . The company president] would have a heart attack! There have been a couple of attempts to bring in a union over the past few years, but [the company president] fought it. Don't misunderstand me. Me, I'm not anti-union at all. Sometimes they're needed. But our guys are making more than any union. There's no need for it here."

Table 6.4 also shows that three quarters of the employers in our sample reported a workforce where the majority of workers were either skilled or semiskilled. Approximately 27 percent of employers reported welding as their most common occupation. Employers also employed a relatively large number of unskilled helpers (21 percent) and roustabouts (14 percent). The demand for welders and other skilled workers was clear in our conversations with employers. One manager of a ship repair company reported that approximately 65 to 75 percent of his company's labor force consisted of craft workers and skilled workers, with the remainder being split among managerial, clerical, and unskilled workers. He told us that he always has "a lot of demand . . . for welders and fitters."

TABLE 6.4   Attributes of Jobs Reported by Employers in Four Southern Louisiana Communities

Characteristic	Distribution
Job attributes	
At least 95 percent of workers are full-time	83.0%
Unionized	0.0
At least half of workers unskilled	9.1
At least half of workers skilled or semiskilled	75.6
N	59
Most common occupation	
Other	32.3
Helper or apprentice	21.0
Tacker (welder's helper)	12.9
Welder	14.5
Roustabout	14.5
Rigger	4.8
N	62
Starting wage	
Less than $6 per hour	5.8
$6 to $9 per hour	88.5
$9 to $12 per hour	3.8
Over $12 per hour	1.9
N	52
Highest wage	
$6 to $9 per hour	44.9
$10 to $14 per hour	30.6
Over $15 per hour	24.5
N	49
Minimum wage	
All workers paid minimum wage or above	94.4
Some workers paid below minimum	5.6
N	56

Source: Louisiana Immigrant Project (1999).

Another company official estimated that three quarters of his workers were skilled or semiskilled, with most being "skilled. . . . The majority of what we do here is cut steel [and] put steel back together. . . . Doing boats like we do, all this [must] be certified . . . and all of our people are . . . certified to do the work." Moreover, the less-skilled were generally at least "semiskilled riggers . . . because we do so much construction. . . . Now [we are] building these 220-foot hopper barges, we produce three of them a week . . . for that we are constantly moving steel . . . from one area to another, and we have a very large rigging staff."

Although they held semiskilled and skilled jobs, workers preferred some work over others. Ship repair was a particularly undesirable form of work, and the least attractive to American-born workers. One employer in a ship repair company told us the work is "real dirty. You . . . go in dirty tanks, [it is] not safe to breathe all that stuff that's in there, you know. You go in there, you cut out metal without ventilation. . . . Shipyard jobs are the worst for a welder." The story was similar for the vessel repair business. Comparing his work to that found in a shipbuilding company, a manager told us, "This type of work you get into tanks. . . . you get into engine rooms and sometimes you come out looking pretty raunchy."

Although starting wages for the occupations varied, most companies reported paying well over the minimum wage for entry-level work. In fact, 89 percent of companies paid six to nine dollars as the starting wage. More variability appeared in employer reports of the highest hourly wage paid. Almost 45 percent reported that the highest hourly wage falls between six and nine dollars; an additional 31 percent reported ten to fourteen dollars; and another 24 percent reported paying fifteen dollars or more.

Table 6.5 documents that most companies (59 percent) experienced an increase in the demand for labor over the last five years and that it had become more difficult to find qualified workers than in the past. The president of a mechanical contracting company told us, "As far as the quality of help when we have to go looking for help . . . it is difficult to find good people." A recruiting manager for an oil-related heavy construction company voiced a similar concern: "There's a labor problem, definitely. There's a labor problem as for as quality people. There's your bottom line. . . . You can get anybody, you get a body, if that's all you want, but for them to be a craftsman or to be concerned about doing a good job . . . the work ethic. . . . [Well] there's the problem. I don't know if that can be solved." Finally, an executive with an oil field construction company commented on finding skilled workers: "There have been so many people that have left the industry because of the ups and downs that a lot of the quote-unquote skilled craftsmen are not in the business anymore. Probably overall, the [workforce] is down."

In sum, the prevalence of full-time employment, high wages and semi-skilled to skilled labor suggest competitive employment opportunities for workers in onshore southern Louisiana companies that supported the offshore oil industry in the late 1990s. Many of our employers were local

TABLE 6.5   Employer Opinions About Shifts in Workforce in Four
            Southern Louisiana Communities

Characteristic	Distribution
Size of workforce has increased over time	
No	32.2%
Yes	59.3
Unsure	8.5
N	59
Time frame of perceived change	
Less than five years	56.2%
Six to nine years	0.0
More than ten years	1.7
No perceived change	42.1
N	57
Now it's more difficult to find qualified workers	
Yes	59.0%
No	41.0
N	53

Source: Louisiana Immigrant Project (1999).

or regional companies, with approximately half employing less than one
hundred workers. Although most were part of the oil industry, employers' primary activities included fabricating pipes and platforms, the repair
and service of these platforms and ships, shipbuilding and repair, and offshore drilling. Moreover, partly as a consequence of stronger demand for
these workers in the last five years compared to earlier periods, employers reported more difficulty in securing a qualified workforce. Therefore,
the picture that emerges is one of a region closely linked to a single industry that had, by the 1990s, a strong demand for fairly specific, heavily
industrial, semiskilled and skilled workers.

VOLATILITY AND INSTABILITY: "TOO MANY UPS AND DOWNS"

Despite employer similarity and the strong demand for labor in the
region, trends in unemployment in these areas demonstrate that regional
rates were consistently higher and much more volatile than national
rates. Figure 6.2 presents annual unemployment rates for the nation, for

FIGURE 6.2   Unemployment Rates in the United States, Louisiana, and Selected Communities

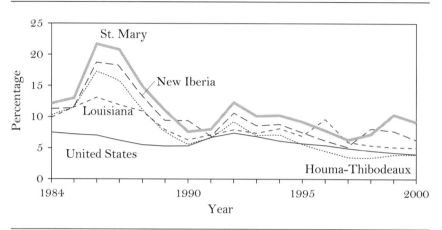

Source: Authors' compilation from Louisiana Department of Labor, Labor Market Information, and U. S. Department of Labor.

Louisiana, and for the Houma-Thibodeaux metropolitan statistical area (MSA) in Terrebonne, and for St. Mary Parish and Iberia Parish from 1984 to 2000.[3] Regional and local trends reveal a period of rapidly rising unemployment in the late 1980s, immediately after the domestic oil market crisis erupted. This was especially true in St. Mary Parish, where at least 20 percent of the local labor force was unemployed.

Unemployment in all areas began to fall by the late 1980s, and the decline continued until the early 1990s, when rates rose slightly. Since then, unemployment rates have ebbed and flowed in St. Mary and Iberia parishes, but on the whole, they modestly declined until about 1998, when we began our interviews, at a time when employers were once again complaining about labor shortages. Thereafter, unemployment began to rise, but only in St. Mary and Iberia parishes. Regional differences were also evident in the magnitude and variance of these rates.

The data in figure 6.2 suggest that labor demand has been highly volatile in southern Louisiana since the mid-1980s. This volatility has had many consequences for employers, compromising their ability to develop stable, long-term projections of labor demand and supply. Reflecting on the volatility, one president of a company that manufactures equipment for offshore pipelines lamented, "This industry is so unstable that how do you go about making projections out? Everybody was harping on how good the oil field is going to do. . . . In five or ten years it is going to be terrific. Well, I said b.s., that doesn't happen in the oil business.

When they sneeze overseas, you don't know what's going to happen to the price of oil."

In recent years, economic shifts in the region have occurred rapidly, and these became part of the immediate setting of our own study. We noticed that during the three years we were in the field (1998 through 2000), business people and community leaders changed their assessments of the economic climate. When we started, almost all were reporting that labor demand was high and that workers were scarce. For example, in July of 1998, when unemployment was still fairly low by the standards of recent history, the vice president of an oil field service company told us, "Since the fourth quarter of last year we've been to the point where we've turned work down because we don't have the people to perform the work. And so have our competitors. We're all looking for the same skilled workers to enhance the staff because there's more work than we can do."

At the same time, given their recent experiences with the local economy, employers wondered how long the strong demand for labor would last. A human resources director of an oil field equipment fabrication company, interviewed in July 1998, exclaimed, "Oh, yeah, [the company's workforce] really has been shooting up." Then he expressed reservations about the future, saying, "I don't know if it's going to go on, though, with the oil prices starting to sag."

Later on, many interviewees did report slumps in business and a number of employers said that they were laying workers off. "In the last three years when I came on board we had about 295 to 300 people," the chief operating officer of a marine construction and repair company reported at the end of 1999. "[Last year] we peaked out at about 405 but we are currently back down to 295. . . . It was strictly oil field related because [work] in the oil field has dropped off."

One employer, an executive vice president of an oil field service company, summarized the volatility this way: "The job market is a little scarce [today] but . . . if we go back to about a year and a half ago . . . well during all of 1998 everybody was prospering. . . . The shipyards were busy, the fab [fabrication] yards . . . and the machine shops were busy. Everything was busy. During that time it was difficult to find a good employee. This started to get bad for us. . . . The worst it got was around February or March of 1999. It started to get a little better after that and now it is not where it should be but it is a little better than it was."

These cycles were noted by almost all of the employers with whom we spoke. The general manager of a Port Fourchon company that leased trucks explained, "If the oil industry is busy they need more trucks. If the oil industry is not busy they don't need too many trucks. It is the oil industry that regulates how much business you are going to have and what is going on." In a similar vein, a manager of an oil field repair service specializing in repairing drilling tools reported that "when there are fewer rigs working, there is more competition for the rental companies to rent their stuff. They don't have the budgets to repair things so they tend . . . to try to get more life out of a rental item. . . . When things start picking up again, all of sudden everybody is going to want to, you know, start. . . . They are not going to walk, they are going to start running again . . . which means they [will] want it all right now."

Ultimately, the sheer unpredictability of the Gulf Coast economy has led some employers to throw up their hands in despair. In exasperation, a manager at a casing and tubing company exclaimed, "I think about a year and a half ago, there was a big demand for rigs. Rig people went up on their prices, there was a demand for boats. Well when there is a demand for rigs there will be a demand for boats. . . . Everything just balloons . . . and keeps going up and I think the oil companies just said well . . . we are going to shut this down. Now, that is what I was told and that is what I heard. I don't know. Trying to figure this oil field out? . . . I am tired of trying to figure this oil field out. There are too many ups and downs in this thing."

CONSEQUENCES OF INDUSTRY INSTABILITY

Embedded in the structure of the Louisiana Gulf Coast economy, the industry's instability has had many consequences. Three effects are especially noteworthy for understanding the labor supply and demand conditions that occurred in the late 1990s. First, industry volatility encouraged many local laborers to seek jobs in more stable fields whenever possible. Second, it led many employers to seek flexible sources of labor, such as contract workers who had needed skills but who could also be hired and fired with relative ease. Third, after many skilled workers left the area in search of employment and then, in the 1990s, labor demand began to exceed supply, some employers hired anyone they could to fill open positions, resulting in a low-quality labor supply described by many as problematic. This volatility then explains why so many employers emphasized "soft" skills, such as motivation to work and positive interaction with others, as necessary requirements for the skilled and semiskilled jobs they sought to fill.

"People Who Have Been In and Got Out Don't Want to Come Back"

Workers' own experiences in the oil industry's rapidly turning wheel of fortune encouraged them to seek jobs in more stable fields whenever possible, exacerbating the labor shortage for semiskilled and skilled jobs in the industry. This was a theme that our employers repeatedly emphasized. After the domestic oil crisis in the 1980s, many locals did not want to work in oil-related companies because the future was so unreliable and some left the region altogether. The size of the total labor force may have decreased, as in the case of St. Mary Parish, or it may have rebounded after a decrease, as in the Houma-Thibodeaux MSA (see figure 6.2). But employers reported that increasingly, fewer local workers saw value in preparing themselves for an uncertain job market or developing skills that might not pay off in a consistent manner.

Although the entire economy of the region is linked to the oil industry, some jobs were more closely linked to it than others and therefore more sensitive to short-term variations in the oil business. Because of their large size, shipbuilders in our study sites were especially vulnerable. One general manager of a multinational shipbuilding company described the reasons for the unavailability of local native-born laborers in this way: "Some of them don't want to work, and some have been in the oil industry and [left because] the oil industry is a roller-coaster ride."

Another personnel and safety manager at a company loading vessels and trucks agreed, observing that "some of the guys have gotten out of the oil field because of it going up and down and up and down. . . . One year is a great year and then next year it is rock bottom. . . . They don't want to come back because . . . there is no security. A lot of them are working. . . . They are carpenters now, they are working [and] . . . don't want to move back because it is so insecure. The money is good but it is not for long term. . . . On a lot of these projects that you get on with different oil companies, they will hire a few hundred people one year and next year they are laying off and there are a lot of companies consolidating. . . . I found [that] a lot of people . . . don't want to come back because . . . it is so unstable."

Given the repeated economic jolts as described, the pool of workers willing and qualified to work in unstable jobs steadily declined during the last two decades of the twentieth century. Sometimes this appeared as a decline in total numbers of workers. At other times, though, when the improving oil economy generated economic opportunities throughout the job market, workers would try to find jobs that would not disappear as soon as the next downturn began. Moreover, the consequences for the supply of available workers cumulated over time, as the manager of a company servicing offshore rigs and boats recognized: "Every time [the oil economy] slows down and picks up, we have a decrease in those coming back. . . . I would probably be one of them, too. If they cut me loose right now, I would get out and not come back, probably."

When workers returned to the region after leaving in search of employment, those with the most experience tended not be among them. "When the crunch went down, everybody left from the area. Now the crunch is not here. . . . The jobs are here but there is nobody qualified to do the jobs," said an official with a company that supplies drilling fluids. Other employers also reported that the volatility of the oil industry had caused the best workers to get out. In New Iberia, the vice president of operations for a oil field construction company explained, "There have been so many people that have left the industry because of the ups and downs that a lot of the quote-unquote skilled craftsmen are not in the business anymore."

A safety director of a shipbuilding company made the same point: "When the oil industry went down in the early 1980s, a lot of people that were in the industry got out of it, and found new crafts, new jobs, and in the past four years while things were picking up, you don't have that level of qualified people [due to] lack of experience." The loss of skilled labor was observed by almost all of our informants, community leaders as well as employers. We spoke with a state political representative who summarized what had happened in his region: "My understanding of . . . the employment situation in the shipyards . . . is that because of the downturn . . . in the 1980s, we lost a lot of skilled workers. When I say skilled workers, I am talking about the fitters, welders, all these people that build these gigantic oil field platforms . . . boats and barges. We lost them permanently in most cases because they were forced to relocate to Atlanta, Florida, and wherever to find suitable employment . . . that was commensurate with their work experience, skills, and what they were used to getting paid. So when business got brisk in the 1990s, those skilled workers just weren't around."

"Need a Lot of People for a Certain Period of Time"

The roller-coaster nature of the oil economy encouraged employers to turn to workers who could be quickly hired and released. Large shipyards were especially affected by the rapid growth of the 1990s. When orders for ships arrived, these companies needed sizable crews of skilled blue collar workers, including many welders, who were willing to do hard, dirty work. Once a downturn hit, fewer goods were shipped and the need for both new construction and repairs substantially slowed. Therefore, it was in the interest of shipyards to be able to locate and employ small armies of workers to whom they made little commitment.

A small shipbuilder explained that "the larger shipyards I have worked in before . . . need a lot of people for a certain period of time and then they don't need that many. It is hard to keep a stable workforce when you keep doing that." The reality of layoffs seemed almost a certainty. One shop foreman told us, "Of course when these shipyards and oil fields slack off, we definitely have to cut our force." The coordinator of a contract labor company made a similar observation about his company's rapid hiring and firing cycles: "The oil field has made its ups and downs. . . . In the last five years, I would say that right now we are at our peak, we have been over two hundred employees for about the last seven or eight months. Before that had dropped, I would say in the last five years the lowest our field employees have gone is probably about one hundred twenty-five to one hundred thirty."

One employer noted how reliance on contract labor is relatively new in the industry. "The industry has gone to contracting mainly because fluctuation in the oil field allows them to change their workforce as it fluctuates. By having contract [workers], you don't have the liability, and fifteen years ago, that was not in the oil field. Mostly all oil companies had their own employees, but as years have gone by, [employers] have gone more and more to contract employees because it gets rid of liability and . . . the [avoidance of] layoff problems . . . because every time the oil field goes in a down slump, they lay people off and you lose a lot of people that don't come back to the oil field."

As a result, employers hiring workers on a short-term basis to meet large and small contract demands was a fairly common practice. Approximately 25 percent of workers in one large employer were contractors who performed all types of skilled blue collar work, from welding to electrical. This employer summed up his reason for doing so: "It's just cheaper." Reliance on contract labor depended on the type of work some companies had. For example, one employer never used contract labor for new ship construction because "you have less control over the people you hire . . . and you are always working on a fixed-price contract." But for repair operations, he used "a lot of contractors . . . because in the repair business, the activity levels are very cyclical. . . . In the short term . . . your facility may be full today and empty tomorrow."

Another employer contracted laborers for "those who clean boat tanks and that kind of work." This type of work was nonexistent ten years ago, but as environmental concerns grew so too did a new sector of cleaning crews, who are largely contract laborers. Although boat crews used to do this work themselves, cleaning crews now apply a variety of different chemicals while boats are in close proximity in their ports. Finally, even employers who did not use contract labor recognized they would do so in the future. "It just depends on our needs. We have . . . a couple of bids right now . . . If we should get both of those bids . . . say by the end of the week . . . I will have to hire [contract] people right on the spot."

"As Long as They Behave Themselves While They're Here and They Do Their Jobs Right"

One consequence of not having enough labor to meet demand is that employers have hired workers whom they have barely screened. To our surprise many employers described a hiring process that was incomplete and subjective. For example, one employer told us that most important are the "recommendations from fellow employees rather than prior job history or references from past employers" and that "probably seventy to eighty percent of our new hires in skilled labor are referrals from employees."

Another employer who performed no type of background check on potential employees said, "We don't care what they've done, as long as they behave themselves while they're here and they do their jobs right." Yet another employer told us that an employee's skills and whether he will be hired "is proved by whether he can pass a test. If he can pass ours in-house for welding or fitting, then that's fine with us." He also said he would consider hiring potential workers if his current employees vouched for them, but that he was not able to do background checks on potential hires or check whether they have a criminal record.

Employers linked the subjectivity in their hiring process to the strength of labor demand. One employer said, "When we have demand we really can't be that picky." Our interviewer then asked, "So how picky you are depends on how badly you need them?" The employer answered, "Yeah." Another responded to our question by saying, "You have to understand that normally [past job turnover, recommendations from previous employers, and so forth] are things that you look at, has he stayed anywhere, are you able to call employers. But right now, none of that really matters. . . . If they come in and want to work and agree with what we have to offer and they want to take the physical, pass it, and come back here and want to work, they can go to work. All that past stuff really doesn't matter." Later he added, "We used to look at criminal records" but for the past year and a half, anybody who walked in and could pass the test and physical had the job.

Another manager of a vessel repair business described how he hired new workers: "I don't do much advertising . . . We make phone calls and look at applications and . . . we have . . . I think the average is something like six or eight [walk-in] applications a week that we get over here. We look for more experience than education. In this line of work . . . if I see a young person who may not have five years' experience but I know that where he worked previously, he might have been an excellent worker and he has left there because of lack of work. A lot of times that young person can really produce for you. . . . He is more energetic and he wants to make this his trade and . . . things like that. He is a good investment in this type of work."

In the face of the strong demand for labor, subjectivity in the hiring process has had implications for employers. To begin with, many hired employees who had completed fewer years of formal education than the national or state average. One employer representing a barge service company told us that of his hundred employers, none were high school graduates, including himself. Another large employer with more than six hundred workers told us, "We try to get as much education as we possible can," adding that it would be "very tough down here" to require a particular educational level for his employees. Another employer with an oil field supply company told us that there were "no educational requirements. Common sense is the only requirement."

Employers often had to hire young workers. Employers felt quite strongly that these workers did not care about their work. They were too independent, had high rates of absenteeism, showed little loyalty, and had more drug problems than older workers. As a result, many employers complained that the quality of the workforce was on the decline. The biggest problem they identified was absenteeism, and among all the employers in our sample, it was the most common reason for dismissal. "It's the number one problem. Workers just walk off . . . for more money elsewhere, but they don't even bother to let us know. They go elsewhere [or] are thrown into jail. . . . They just abandon work."

Another employer lamented, similarly, that "so many of them miss so much work. It is hard to find dedicated people. They want a paycheck and that is it. You know . . . it is like nobody cares about [loyalty]. . . . We always have these two or three that are always missing Monday, or when they get their check, then the next day they don't show up. In talking to other people it is like that all over." Asked what would be the qualities he would look for if he could choose his workers, one owner of a small company who had been in the business for forty years replied, "Right now, I would love to have someone . . . around twenty-one or twenty-two years old with a fairly decent head on their shoulders, who knows how to work. Basically someone who would come to work every day and after they get their first check, they wouldn't take two days off and expect to come in on the third day without a problem." One employer summed up the situation this way: "There are plenty of people. . . . They just don't want to work. America is lazy."

SALIENCE OF "SOFT" SKILLS IN A VOLATILE ECONOMY

Thus, volatility in the oil-based economy pushed qualified workers to search for employment elsewhere. As labor demand strengthened in the 1990s, employers hired anyone they could find, often using subjective and incomplete hiring practices. Not surprisingly, employers complained about the declining quality of their workforces, especially the difficulties they faced with young workers. Many also turned to contract labor. In the face of these shifts, what have employers told us about their requirements for filling semiskilled and skilled jobs? Do they make skill distinctions, and if so, along what lines? Below we look at the skills employers seek and rely on Phillip Moss and Chris Tilly's (2001) examination of hiring practices, using employers' reports to understand the differences between "hard" and "soft" skills. Our work overlaps with theirs in its approach and substantive focus.

In all our interviews, we asked employers about the most important qualities and skills they looked for in someone seeking a semiskilled or skilled job. Some employers pointed to "hard" skills, defined as "worker's cognitive and technical abilities" that "include basic skills such as reading, writing, arithmetic, and grammar"; more abstract abilities such as "problem solving or ability to learn; and technical abilities" such as computer or construction skills (Moss and Tilly 2001, 44). As we expected, some employers required applicants to be literate and have a high school education or GED. Other employers wanted their new hires to have "hard" skills that reflected experience with skilled blue collar work in the past. Some wanted potential employees to have skill certification papers, and for some jobs, such as machinists, employers wanted math skills and persons who were mechanically inclined.

Nonetheless, most employers recognized that few applicants for the semiskilled and skilled jobs they sought to fill would have such "hard" skills. The majority emphasized behavioral and "soft" skills, such as motivation and the ability to interact well with others. "Soft" skills are "abilities and traits that pertain to personality, attitude, and behavior" (Moss and Tilly 2001, 44). Their salience in these new immigrant destinations, we argue, derives from the unique set of circumstances that employers in southern Louisiana faced at the end of the twentieth century, and from employers' beliefs that associated immigrants with subordinate labor because they evaluate their work in the United States and compare it to employment in their communities of origin (Waldinger and Lichter 2003).

In almost all interviews, employers described how they value social skills, especially the capacity to be motivated by their work and interact well with others. The first and second most important attributes were "getting along with the rest of the workforce and loyalty. We don't want somebody that is going to be detrimental to the company." Technical skills ranked in third place. Another employer reported that the two qualities he would look for most in new employees were skill levels and work ethic. "You are looking for somebody that really wants to work. That is very important to us. . . . You would look at absenteeism . . . how often they change jobs . . . those type of things."

One employer epitomized the opinion of many when he said, "The biggest thing is the attitude of the individual. We look at that real hard, because even if an individual is not at the skill level and doesn't have the skill, if he's got that good positive attitude, the willingness to learn, you can see it in an individual, we would definitely take a strong look at that person." Another employer, describing why he ranked technical skills third, said: "It is hard to evaluate that because we couldn't use him if he didn't have any type of skills. But . . . on an equal basis . . . given two guys with the same technical skills . . . we would take the guy who . . . got along with everybody and . . . he would probably make a loyal employee. I don't know if they call that discriminating or not."

Thus, consistent with the employers interviewed by Moss and Tilly (2001), our employers strongly emphasized worker's soft skills as a key desirable attribute. Together with other challenges that employers faced in the oil industry in the 1990s, the door to hiring foreign-born workers opened. In fact, despite the fact that few immigrants other than Southeast Asian refugees had settled in the four study sites during the last fifty years, employers viewed migrant workers and their skills as the answer to existing labor problems. Consider the comments by one employer: "We found that [immigrants] had . . . pretty much the skills we wanted. The only problem that we had was a language barrier which we worked out pretty well . . . and we spent twenty-seven months trying to see how we could get them into the country to help us because we lost probably about twenty million dollars' worth of revenue by not having them."

Generally speaking, Mexican workers met employers' demands because their soft skills were especially appealing. One company president expanded the percentage of Mexican-born workers to 40 percent of his employees after struggling to make a profit with American-born workers in the past. "I went ahead and brought in seventy Hispanics. . . . Boy, I tell you, it change like night and day. It was more competitive for jobs. . . . These guys have a little work ethic, they are hard workers. . . . It really helped the local labor force out because . . . it just illustrated what other people could do. We saw reduced turnover . . . fewer worker compensation claims . . . we saw a much quicker return to work and less lost time." Another employer, a personnel manager of a company with 180 employees, of whom 50 were Mexican migrants, told us, "They have a better work ethic . . . and I guess they come from disadvantaged places and they just like to do more . . . for a lesser wage." A high-ranking official overseeing activities in one port in our study commented, "We find that Mexicans hold up real good under these (hot) conditions. It is amazing. I don't know if they have a high toler-ance for pain or what."

For many employers, positive sentiments toward Mexican migrants were also directly tied to the immigrants' dual frame of reference, which permit-ted them to be hired at low cost. "We have strictly labor from Mexico [and,] yes, it is cheaper. You know it is kind of a shame and I am going to go by . . . what was said to me from supervisors. We found [that] the majority of the time, a worker from Mexico . . . worked harder and [was] more apprecia-tive. Because of the cost of living down there and the money that could be made up here, they enjoyed it. . . . They loved it." One owner said admiringly, "The Mexicans [we] brought over . . . they don't take morning breaks or afternoon breaks. . . . They just eat a little for lunch and they work almost all day long. They work circles around the people here. They were happy to get a job and they weren't going to get run off. These jobs . . . they say we are taking them out of people's hands here . . . but American labor, whether union or otherwise, it was not there. . . . I saw it with my own eyes." Another manager had lavish praise for Mexican laborers, telling us how his company "has a lot of industry in south Texas across the border. . . . Those people [Mexicans] have very little, so they come over here and they'll give you twelve hours in an eight-hour day. They are more efficient. . . . We get more production, better service, the quality is there and all the way around it's just excellence of work when you do it that way."

CONCLUSION

The objective of this paper was to understand why, how, and when American employers in one new destination area turned to immigrants rather than natives to satisfy their labor needs. Drawing on a rich data set that includes interviews with approximately 140 employers, leaders, and immigrants as well as public opinion survey data that represent their larger communities, we examined employers' views of immigrant labor in four new destination communities in southern Louisiana, an area where deep-sea offshore drilling has rapidly increased manufacturing labor demand since the early 1990s. Although Louisiana has not been a common destination area for immigrants in the past, many Spanish-speaking migrants began working in ship and fab-rication yards in port cities in the 1990s.

Our findings suggest that immigrant settlement in this new destination exists because employers in this area have come to perceive that immigrants, especially those born in Mexico, have desired cultural traits and employ-ment habits. Consistent with prior studies that document how employer preferences are associated with race and ethnicity (see Kirschenman and

Neckerman 1991; Waldinger and Lichter 2003), this case study illustrates that employer preferences about nativity also matter. Although demand and supply are indeed relevant attributes, especially for employers that rely on workers for unskilled and semiskilled onshore jobs, such as welding, pipe fitting, and carpentry, subjective employer views about the quality of immigrant labor developed and grew from the instability and volatility experienced by this industrial sector in the 1980s. By late in that decade, many American-born workers left and sought employment elsewhere. Employers, to meet their subsequent demand for labor, then used subjective hiring practices and sought flexible and lower-quality labor. One consequence was an emphasis on soft skills and a strong demand for Mexican workers because employers recognized that immigrants evaluated their employment experience in the United States in terms of their experience in the labor market in Mexico.

We are grateful for the generous support of this project provided by the Minerals Management Service, U.S. Department of the Interior.

NOTES

1. Data on the racial composition of populations in our study areas is available from the U.S. Bureau of the Census. For example, to find the data for New Iberia, Louisiana, go to http://newiberiala.usl.myareaguide.com/census.html.
2. At the end of each quotation, we list interview number and date in parentheses.
3. Unfortunately, unemployment statistics for LaFourche Parish that include Port Fourchon are not available. However, even if they were, they would be less relevant because Port Fourchon is, to a large extent, a place where people go specifically to work.

REFERENCES

Bankston, III, Carl L. 2003. "Immigrants in the New South: An Introduction." *Sociological Spectrum* 23(2): 123–28.

Donato, Katharine M., Carl L. Bankston III, and Dawn T. Robinson. 2001. "Immigration and the Organization of the Onshore Oil Industry: Southern Louisiana in the Late 1990s." In *Latino Workers in the Contemporary South*, edited by Arthur D. Murphy, Colleen Blanchard, and Jennifer A. Hill. Athens, Ga.: University of Georgia Press.

Donato, Katharine M., Melissa Stainback, and Carl L. Bankston, III. 2005. "The Economic Incorporation of Mexican Immigrants in Southern Louisiana: A Tale of Two Cities." In *New Destinations of Mexican Immigration in the United States: Community Formation, Local Responses and Inter-Group Relations*, edited by Víctor Zúñiga and Rubén Hernández-León. New York: Russell Sage Foundation.

Durand, Jorge, Douglas S. Massey, and Fernando Charvet. 2000. "The Changing Geography of Mexican Immigration to the United States: 1910–1996." *Social Science Quarterly* 81(1): 1–15.

Engstrom, James D. 2001. "Industry and Immigration in Dalton, Georgia." In *Latino Workers in the Contemporary South*, edited by Arthur D. Murphy, Colleen Blanchard, and Jennifer A. Hill. Athens, Ga.: University of Georgia Press.

Grey, Mark A. 1999. "Immigrants, Migration, and Worker Turnover at the Hog Pride Pork Packing Plant." *Human Organization* 58(1): 16–27.

Hernández-Léon, Rubén, and Víctor Zúñiga. 2000. " 'Making Carpet by the Mile': The Emergence of a Mexican Immigrant Community in an Industrial Region of the U.S. Historic South." *Social Science Quarterly* 81(1): 49–66.

Kandel, William, and Emilio A. Parrado. 2005. "Restructuring of the U.S. Meat Processing Industry and New Hispanic Migrant Destinations." *Population and Development Review* 31(3): 447–72.

Kirschenman, Joleen, and Kathryn M. Neckerman. 1991. " 'We'd Love to Hire Them, but . . .': The Meaning of Race for Employers." In *The Urban Underclass*, edited by Christopher Jencks and Paul E. Peterson. Washington: Brookings Institution.

Louisiana Immigrant Project. 1999. Research project, Louisiana State University, Department of Sociology (PI: Katharine M. Donato).

Massey, Douglas S., Joaquin Arango, Graeme Hugo, Ali Kouaouci, Adela Pellegrino, and J. Edward Taylor. 1994. "An Evaluation of International Migration Theory: The North American Case." *Population and Development Review* 20(4): 699–751.

Moss, Phillip, and Chris Tilly. 2001. *Stories Employers Tell: Race, Skill, and Hiring in America*. New York: Russell Sage Foundation.

Saenz, Rogelio, Katharine M. Donato, Lourdes Gouveia, and Cruz C. Torres. 2004. "Latinos in the South: A Glimpse of Ongoing Trends and Research." *Southern Rural Sociology* 19(1): 1–19.

Singer, Audrey. 2004. "The Rise of New Gateways." Report for the Center on Urban and Metropolitan Policy. Washington: Brookings Institution.

Stull, Donald D., Michael J. Broadway, and K. C. Erickson. 1992. "The Price of a Good Steak: Beef Packing and Its Consequences for Garden City, Kansas." In *Structuring Diversity: Ethnographic Perspectives on the New Immigration*, edited by Louise Lamphere. Chicago, Ill.: University of Chicago Press.

Waldinger, Roger, and Michael I. Lichter. 2003. *How the Other Half Works: Immigration and the Social Organization of Labor*. Berkeley, Calif.: University of California Press.

Zúñiga, Víctor, and Rubén Hernández-León. 2005. *New Destinations: Mexican Immigration in the United States*. New York: Russell Sage Foundation.

PART II

⋎

COMMUNITY REACTION TO NEW IMMIGRANT GROUPS

CHAPTER 7

PREJUDICE TOWARD IMMIGRANTS IN THE MIDWEST

KATHERINE FENNELLY

The literature on contemporary immigrant-host relations in the United States has generally focused on large urban areas, yet during the past ten to fifteen years rural communities in many states experienced a large influx of immigrants attracted by job prospects in the food-processing industry (Fennelly and Leitner 2002; Stull 1998; Griffith 1999; Fennelly 2005). Especially in the midwestern United States, the relocation of meat and poultry processing plants out of urban centers into rural towns spurred the diversification of formerly white, Anglo-Saxon, and Scandinavian-origin communities. This movement was accelerated by business tax incentives, the proximity of water and grain supplies, and the opportunity to recruit non-union, low-wage workers (Benson 1999; Cantu 1995; Fennelly and Leitner 2002; Griffith 1999; Yeoman 2000).[1]

In the Midwest, most of those working on meat and poultry industry "disassembly lines" are documented and undocumented immigrants from Mexico and Central America, though some towns also contain refugees from Africa and Asia. During the 1990s, foreigners moved to rural communities in such numbers that they helped reverse population losses of the previous decades (Minnesota Planning 1997). In some cases the arrival of large numbers of culturally different residents revitalized rural communities and led to the formation of pro-immigrant coalitions of local citizens and nonprofit agencies, but in other cases immigration led to xenophobia and prejudice among natives, who perceived them as threatening competitors for resources, group identity, and power.

The relatively rapid change from predominantly white, European-origin populations to diverse communities with sizable percentages of immigrants

151

offers a natural laboratory for analyzing the perceived threats. In this chapter I present qualitative data gathered in the summer of 2001 for a close-up view of the attitudes of American-born residents toward immigrants in a rural town with a large meat-processing plant. In doing so I compare perceived symbolic and economic threats across three groups of Euro-Americans: community leaders (CL), middle class citizens (MC), and working class residents (WC). Participants' own explanations of their attitudes are used to describe native sentiments within a context of rapid demographic change. The analysis sheds light on the nature of anti-immigrant prejudice and the kinds of public policies that might foster greater empathy.

BACKGROUND

Prejudice, broadly defined, is the acceptance of negative stereotypes that relegate groups of people to the category of "other" (Sniderman, Tetlock, and Carmines 1993). Racism is the extension of prejudice to an ideology or belief system that ascribes unalterable characteristics to the "othered" groups. Such belief systems are used to justify negative attitudes and social avoidance of out-groups (See and Wilson 1988). Prejudicial beliefs can also enhance a sense of positive group distinctiveness (Sniderman, Hagendoorn, and Prior 2004). Conversely, perceived threats to cultural unity are both a product of prejudice, and a source of reinforcement for prejudicial beliefs.

Such "symbolic threats" to national identity have a long history in the United States. In the late nineteenth and early twentieth centuries, they were kindled over concerns related to the integration of European immigrants (Castles and Miller 2003; Conzen et al. 1992; Nevins 2003). John Higham (1955) describes how notions of racial superiority and exclusiveness that characterize racism were developed in the nineteenth century and emerged in the early twentieth century as fully formed nativist ideology (131). Contemporary nativists compare the difficulties experienced by recent waves of immigrants—particularly Latinos—with the mythical success of previous generations of Euro-Americans (see, for example, Huntington 2004). These contrasts feed stereotypes that attribute a lack of initiative and talent to contemporary immigrants. Both historically and currently, immigrants' perceived linguistic challenges to English as the national language constitute an important component of their symbolic threat, both as a determinant of prejudice and as a justification for preexisting xenophobic attitudes.

A related symbolic threat in the Midwest is what might be termed "rural nostalgia": the belief that demographic changes are a primary cause of the demise of pristine rural areas. Part of this nostalgia has to do with notions of ethnic solidarity, or what Caroline Tauxe (1998) describes as a "normative, self-reliant European-American community." The sentiment is notably prevalent in rural areas where increases in immigrants coincide with other dramatic economic and social changes, such as losses of population, school closings, and the displacement of small and mid-sized farms by large agribusinesses (Fennelly and Leitner 2002; Amato and Amato 2000). Rural nostalgia and xenophobia are fomented by anti-immigrant groups, who couch their opposition to immigration in the cloak of social and environmental protection.

In addition to symbolic and linguistic threats and rural nostalgia, economic threats growing out of a perceived competition for scarce resources represent an important source of negative attitudes toward out-group members (Esses et al. 2001; Stephan and Finlay 1999; Fennelly and Federico forthcoming). People viewing immigrants as a threat commonly view society as a "zero-sum" competition in which resources are finite, so that gains by immigrants necessarily imply equivalent losses by natives. People of low socioeconomic status are most susceptible to the perception of immigrants as a competitive threat (Oliver and Mendelberg 2000). For example, national surveys show that lower-income, less-educated adults in the United States are especially likely to believe that immigrants are a burden to the country and that they take away jobs from native-born Americans (Public Agenda 2000). Perceptions of economic threat are also particularly strong among those who adhere to an interpretation of the "Protestant work ethic" that attributes low status to a lack of self-reliance and hard work (Levy 1999; Reyna 2000; Esses et al. 2001; Oyamot, Borgida, and Fischer 2006). In contrast, persons of higher socioeconomic status feel less threatened by economic competition from immigrants and other minority-group members (Burns and Gimpel 2000).

STUDY SITE AND METHODS

By the year 2000, more immigrants in metropolitan areas lived in suburbs than in cities (Singer 2004) and large numbers had moved into nontraditional gateway states, including Minnesota. Overall, the foreign-born population of Minnesota rose by 50 percent during the 1990s. Over the same period, the Latino-origin population increased by 166 percent—more than in any other state in the Midwest, and almost three times the rate for the nation as a whole (McConnell 2001). Latinos include both native- and foreign-born individuals, although the distinction may not be apparent to many white European Americans. Mexicans have long come to the region as seasonal agricultural workers, but in the 1990s a strong economy and the availability of jobs in food processing and manufacturing led to a surge in their numbers (Fennelly and Leitner 2002). By 2000, the state contained some 42,000 Mexicans and over 137,000 Spanish speakers (U.S. Census Bureau 2000). Mexicans constitute the largest share of foreign-born residents in both the nation (27.6 percent) and Minnesota (16 percent).

"Euro" Focus Groups

In order to obtain a deeper understanding of the causes of prejudice against Latinos and other immigrants in a rural community, we empaneled a series of focus groups in a town selected to meet the following three criteria: the presence of immigrants of diverse origins; major ethnic-racial diversification within the past ten years; and the existence of a large meat-processing plant. The community that we call Devereux fulfilled these requirements. It is a midwestern community of 20,000, mostly white residents of European ancestry with a large meatpacking plant that has expanded over the past decade, attracting hundreds of Latino, Asian, and African workers. The meat plant is one of the major employers in Devereux, but in the mid-1990s most of the European-origin blue collar workers (henceforth called "Euros") left the plant after it was shut down and reopened as a non-union shop.[2] At the time of our interviews 96 percent of the employees on the plant disassembly line were immigrants (the disassembly or evisceration line is where the animal is cut up for packaging). The foreign-born population of the town included over three thousand Latinos—predominantly from Mexico—about two hundred fifty Somalis, a similar number of Nuer people from southern Sudan, and over four hundred Asians, principally Cambodians and Vietnamese.[3]

The data on Devereux's Euros come from conversations with three focus groups of older, white, American-born residents who had lived in the community for at least ten years—long enough to have observed the demographic changes that are the subject of the study.[4] Older residents were selected for the Euro groups because they have come to represent an increasingly large fraction of rural communities as Minnesotans age, and as younger white adults leave rural areas to seek employment in the cities.

Participants were assigned to the three groups—community leaders (CL), middle class residents (MC), and working class residents (WC)—on the basis of their employment and status in the community. Table 7.1 briefly profiles participants in these three groups, with each person assigned a pseudonym. Members of the CL group were recruited through a list of town leaders provided by the head of the local Chamber of Commerce; MC group members were recruited through community organizations, such as the Chamber of Commerce, the PTA, and the Rotary Club; WC participants

TABLE 7.1   Descriptions of European Americans Interviewed
in Devereux Focus Groups

Group and Respondent	Description
Community leader group (CL)	
Joe:	White male in early seventies; some college; retired from business management job. Born and raised in Devereux. Married to Elizabeth. Has an adopted daughter born outside of the United States.
Elizabeth:	White female in early sixties, retired from white collar job; some college; lived in Devereux for most of her life; has an adopted daughter born outside of the United States.
Gary:	White male in his early fifties; small business owner; married to an immigrant.
Cheryl:	White female in her early fifties; small-business owner; has lived in Devereux for over thirty years.
Phyllis:	White female in her early sixties; college graduate; small-business owner; lived in Devereux for most of her life; married to a European immigrant.
Ron:	White male in his mid-sixties; some college; business manager; born elsewhere in the Midwest, but grew up in Devereux
Matthew:	White male in his mid fifties; white collar service job; some college; born elsewhere in Midwest; long-term resident of Devereux; worked in meat-processing plant while in high school.
Middle Class group (MC)	
Sue:	White female in mid forties; college graduate; office worker; born elsewhere in Midwest; long-term resident of Devereux; has taught English to immigrants.
Dale:	White male in late sixties; some college; born and raised in Devereux; currently works part-time in retail.
Herb:	White male in mid sixties; small-business manager; high school graduate; born and raised in Devereux; parents were immigrants from Western Europe.
Jeff:	White male in mid-seventies; some college; born and raised in Devereux; retired from a white collar job; mother was an immigrant from Western Europe.
Sally:	White female in mid-sixties; no high school diploma; worked in meat plant for fifteen years and in childcare; currently retired; born and raised in Devereux.
Vicky:	White female in mid-seventies; high school graduate; currently retired from work as secretary; born and raised in nearby town.

(Continued)

TABLE 7.1   Descriptions of European Americans Interviewed
in Devereux Focus Groups (*Continued*)

Group and Respondent	Description
Ed:	White male in early fifties; college graduate; owner of retail business; born elsewhere in Midwest; long-term resident of Devereux; married to Heidi.
Heidi:	White female in late forties; college graduate; school teacher; born elsewhere in Midwest; long-term resident of Devereux; married to Ed.
Sharon:	White female in early fifties; college graduate with some graduate school; part-time store clerk; lived in Devereux most of her life.
Working Class group (WC)	
Lilly:	White female in early sixties; did not graduate from high school; has worked various low-wage, part-time jobs; born and raised in nearby town; long-term resident of Devereux; worked at meat plant for twenty years; currently retired.
Leanne:	White female in late thirties; has an associate degree; blue collar worker; born and raised in Devereux; worked for many years at meat plant; lives in trailer court; has relative married to a Mexican; sister of Andrea.
Andrea:	White female in early forties; college graduate; commutes to small town outside of Devereux for blue collar work; born and raised in Devereux; lives in trailer court; sister of Leanne.
Deborah:	White female in mid fifties; some college; commutes to another town for blue collar work; born elsewhere in Midwest; long-term resident of Devereux.
Daniel:	White male in early sixties; did not finish high school; born and raised in nearby town; moved to Devereux six years ago; currently unemployed; previous work in food-processing plant supervising Mexican and Asian workers.

Source: Author's compilation.

were referred by a local resident who had run job retraining programs for former meat plant employees and by former employees themselves.

Each focus group was assigned two trained moderators, one to serve as the facilitator and the other, as the note taker. The moderators prepared verbatim transcriptions from tape recordings of the sessions. The transcripts, intake questionnaires, debriefing notes, and observations were entered into the NUDIST text analysis program, which was used to complement repeated close readings of the transcripts. Statements about immigrants and diversity were analyzed several ways. In the initial coding we evaluated each statement made about an immigrant or groups of immigrants, categorized the nature of the comment (language, values, physical characteristics, and so forth) and coded statements as "positive," "negative" or "neutral or mixed." Two co-investigators and a graduate student did this coding independently, and later discussed and reconciled their discrepancies. We also kept coded information on each participant's background characteristics.

After the initial coding, one of the investigators went back over the transcripts to make more refined distinctions among the various statements. This included coding "interjections"—instances in which participants voiced the first positive or negative comment about immigrants in response to a neutral question, or which presented a view that differed from the previous speakers' comments about immigrants. We did this because one of the risks of focus-group discussions is the likelihood that individuals will be influenced by preceding positive or negative comments. We surmised that participants who volunteered the first positive or negative statement about immigrants in response to a neutral question were most likely to be voicing their own attitudes, rather than merely assenting to those of previous speakers.

The same might be said of participants who interjected opposing views to those of the previous speaker. For example, early in the MC focus-group session, several individuals described their fears of going downtown because of the presence of immigrants. After several comments, one member disagreed, said, "I think it's your perception," and went on to argue that immigrants congregated on the sidewalks downtown because they didn't have suburban yards, adding, "That's where they live. They're, you know, either that, or your choice is inside." In the middle of this comment, a woman interrupted and said, "I live down at the north end of town and it's scary down there. . . . Sometimes . . . groups of maybe ten go by my house and scream and yell and it's very scary." We coded the first person's statements in the preceding dialogue as the interjection of a positive comment about immigrants, and second person's as the interjection of a negative comment.

FINDINGS

Although members of the CL, MC, and WC focus groups were differentially recruited on the basis of position and reputation, the groups actually differed little in terms of background variables (see table 7.2). The CL group had a larger proportion of individuals with some college education

TABLE 7.2   Characteristics of Members of the Three European-Origin Focus Groups (Percentage)

Variables	Community Leaders	Middle Class	Working Class
Education			
High school or less	14.3%	44.4%	40.0%
Postsecondary	85.7	55.6	60.0
Annual income			
Less than $50,000	40.0	55.6	80.0
More than $50,000	60.0	44.4	20.0
Marital status			
Married	77.8	100.0	80.0
Divorced or Single	22.2	0.0	20.0
Gender			
Male	57.1	44.4	20.0
Female	42.9	55.6	80.0
Age			
Mean age	59.7	60.0	51.6

Source: Author's compilation.

and with incomes over $50,000, but these differences were not statistically significant. The mean age of participants in each group was over fifty. This preponderance of older adults is characteristic of many rural communities where the lack of employment opportunities has led to an exodus of younger Euro-American residents to urban areas.

Before presenting qualitative data from each of the three focus groups, we summarize the number of positive and negative statements made by group members about immigrants, and the number of positive and negative "interjections." As can be seen in table 7.3, the three focus groups varied greatly in the relative number of positive and negative statements members made about immigrants, ranging from a ratio of 22:19 positive-to-negative among the CL group to 58:70 in the MC group to 75:113 in the WC group. Thus, only Community Leaders made more positive than negative statements about immigrants, although they also made the fewest statements of either kind.

Conversations about changes in Devereux provoked a lengthy conversation about economic development on the part of the CL group, in contrast to the other two groups, in which the question immediately elicited comments about immigrants. The WC group clearly voiced the most negative

TABLE 7.3   Number of Positive, Negative, and Empathic Evaluative Comments Made About Immigrants in European-American Focus Groups

Groups and Respondents	Positive Statements[a]	Positive Interjections	Empathetic Statements	Negative Statements[a]	Negative Interjections
Community leaders					
Joe	5	1	3	2	1
Elizabeth	6	0	0	3	0
Gary	1	0	0	3	0
Cheryl	1	1	3	3	0
Phyllis	3	1	2	1	0
Ron	0	0	0	1	0
Matthew	6	1	10	6	1
Total	22	4	18	19	2
Middle class					
Ed	9	5	16	6	0
Heidi	5	0	3	4	1
Sue	4	1	4	10	3
Dale	6	1	5	28	6
Herb	9	2	3	7	4
Jeff	6	2	3	4	1
Sally	3	0	0	8	4
Vicky	9	3	1	3	0
Sharon	7	2	4	0	0
Total	58	16	39	70	19
Working class					
Lilly	17	0	3	26	4
Andrea	10	3	3	35	6
Deborah	10	1	0	27	0
Leanne	19	0	3	25	3
Daniel	19	1	3	39	2
Total	75	5	12	113	15
Grand total	155	25	69	101	36

Source: Author's compilation.

[a] Positive and negative interjections are instances in which participants offered the first positive or negative comment about immigrants in response to a neutral position, or presented a view that contradicted the previous speaker's comment.

opinions about immigrants, but they also made the largest absolute number of positive statements. It may be that their greater proximity to immigrants in the workplace and low-income neighborhoods resulted in a greater variety and intensity of opinions. The three focus groups also varied in the numbers of positive and negative interjections. The rank order of the ratio of positive to negative interjections for the three groups was the same as for the general comments described earlier: Community Leaders had fewer interjections but voiced more positive than negative opinions than other groups, 4:2, compared with 16:19 for the MC group and 5:15 for the WC group.

Community Leaders

Conversations in each focus group were initiated with a question about how long each member had lived in Devereux, followed by a general question: "What are some of the changes that you all have observed in life and in work in Devereux over the past five to ten years?" Members of the CL group were older, longer-term residents of the town and included a former mayor, a bank president, and a number of small-business owners. Not surprisingly, their perspectives on immigration reflected their roles as entrepreneurs concerned with the economic vitality of the community. Their group discussion began with comments about the growth of the community, expansion of the interstate highway, competition for small-business owners from Wal-Mart and other corporate chains, and the importance of business diversification in the town.

Members of the CL group were most likely to view ethnic and racial diversity as a generally positive "side product" of economic growth. The first mentions of the topic came in the form of comments about the segmented labor market in which immigrants take jobs that American-born residents eschew:

> Phyllis: They fill a definite niche. There are some industries that Caucasians and young preppy college students aren't going to work in, and we need the economic base to be diversified.

> Joe: I don't know how else to put this, but this white face is probably not going to work at the meat plant, and we have people willing to come to Devereux and to do the work; I'm willing to buy the meat and eat it but I have a lot of feeling for the people willing to take these jobs.

Immigrants were not perceived to pose direct economic threats to most CL group members, but a few expressed concerns about the effect of immigration on retail businesses. Gary, for example, worried that the presence of Mexicans and Somali immigrants downtown was scaring older Euro-American customers away from his store, and Phyllis added that concentrations of immigrants were ghettoizing sections of the commercial area:

> Phyllis: There is a housing problem because they don't have money to move to residential neighborhoods. . . . The retail neighborhoods and trailer courts are becoming ghettos, and this is not good.

Another participant expressed concern over more indirect economic threats in the form of negative influences on school budgets, property values, and business in general:

> Matthew: I worry about the impact on school system. The state has a formula per student; the impact of providing ESL is huge on our community.

Overall, members of the CL group made few statements that revealed that they perceived symbolic threats from the immigrants, but close inter-actions between immigrants and members of the CL group were infre-quent. Cheryl observed that although she rented apartments to Sudanese and Somali residents, she has had little contact with them, and Matthew commented on the superficiality of the relationships between the American- and foreign-born:

> Matthew: I'm going to use a difficult word; you just get along. I think the community gets along, but I don't think the community under-stands the various backgrounds. We've started a diversity center but the communication is painfully slow.

Middle Class Focus Group

Participants in the MC focus group were all long-term residents of Devereux. The group included several older white collar workers and retirees who did not have college diplomas, as well as four members between the ages of forty-four and fifty-one who were college graduates. In the MC group the introductory question on changes that participants had observed over the last five to ten years immediately elicited examples of symbolic threats. Fear of the unknown and nostalgia for a more homogeneous town population combined to foster negative attitudes toward immigrants among these MC residents:

> Sharon: We used to feel like we knew everybody. I mean, you used to walk around town and you could walk down [Main Street], and you knew everybody, you knew all of the faces. And now, you don't know all the faces and so, I think sometimes you feel a little isolated, or maybe vulnerable, just because you're not familiar with that person's background.

Some of the MC group alternated positive statements about the changes in town with an acknowledgment of fear. Sue had taught English to immigrants in Devereux, and though she initially commented that the town had become "more exciting" now that there were new Latino and African businesses, she also admitted feeling afraid:

> Sue: One time we did walk up this way. . . . We walked really fast down [Main Street] just simply because of the different nationalities, the Hispanics. . . . We just didn't feel safe.

Another participant interjected that there were no yards by the downtown apartments, and that this led many Latinos and Africans to congregate in the street in the summer. Others continued to dwell on perceived physical threats, sometimes drawing upon hearsay. Herb mentioned the high crime rate in a Texas town where his sister had lived as a reason for his concerns about Latinos in general. His description of "what look like very moral" Texas Latinos hiding weapons reveals a deep distrust that he transfers to Latinos in Devereux:

> Herb: And so you see this, what look like very moral people, just like I see 'em here in town, and yet everybody's carrying a knife? Or something like that . . . well in the last five–ten years, it's very common that somebody gets stabbed or maybe two or three of 'em in one fight. So these are some of the things that are changing in that regard.

Rates of serious crimes in Devereux actually decreased over the five years prior to the focus-group study, but innuendo and selective recall of crime and traffic accident reports mentioning immigrants contribute to the perception of increased crime:

Dale: There's more trouble in town too. . . . Well, you look in the paper, you can see it in the paper. A lot of driving violations. A lot of fights and stuff like that. In other words, you kind of wonder about walking downtown Devereux at night.

One of the most prominent themes from the MC focus group was the symbolic importance of language as a means of defining membership in the community. English-language proficiency was perceived not as a skill but as the reflection of core American values by the MC Euro-Americans. The implication is that immigrants voluntarily chose whether or not to speak English, and that this choice indicated acceptance of American mores and the desire to be integrated into American society. Immigrants who did not master English were portrayed as unwilling to be "assimilated," as in this comment:

Jeff: The Mexicans—because there's quite a few of 'em—it's too easy for them to speak their own language. They are not gonna make the attempt. I think there's gotta be more pressure, from somewhere, to, uh, learn.

Negative comments about immigrants who do not speak good English were most often directed toward Spanish speakers. This may be because they represent the largest group of immigrants in Devereux. The use of Spanish was cited more than once as an example of deviousness—that Latinos who knew how to speak English were intentionally pretending not to understand or to be able to communicate in that language:

Herb: I think they've gotta put the right foot forward more than they do. . . . A lot of 'em talk just as good a English as good as the rest of us. But you'd never know it. . . . So, hey, come clean. If you talk English, talk English to me. If you don't, then learn.

These quotes are clear examples of internal attribution of responsibility for disadvantaged status. As Sue and Ed described it, immigrants who speak in their native languages are "creating their own isolation":

Sue: If somebody's speaking Spanish or Somalian or whatever, and we don't know it, we can't, you know, if they're sitting down to coffee and conversing in Spanish—

Ed: —and you're bein' mutually excluded, yup—

Sue: —you're not gonna join in. So they're kind of creating their own isolation once again there.

After the last comment, the moderator asked, "So is it all about just learning English? What else, besides?" to which Dale and Jeff replied:

Dale: Culture, our culture. Blending with us, I think. You know, getting away from their culture more or less, what they've had.

Jeff: I still think the quicker assimilation of these people is, the sooner, the quicker, the better. They'll get along much better. They'll feel more comfortable.

Some speakers implied that immigrants were being given unfair preferential treatment that would not be accorded to the white Euros if their situations were reversed:

Vicky: Well I think they should learn English as fast as possible. If we went to Mexico or someplace we'd have to learn Spanish right away or we wouldn't get very far.

MC group members also made an implicit connection between communication skills and American values. In a fascinating response to the moderator's question, "What does it mean to be American?" Dale responded, "Don't be clique-ish," and went on to elaborate:

Dale: You talk to people. Say hello. I notice it, I'm up in the morning early and they're walking down to the meat plant. I say good morning to 'em, some of 'em say hi and nod. The rest just keep on walkin'.

There seemed to be no awareness of the significant time and effort that many of the immigrants were investing in learning the English language. Furthermore, English proficiency was viewed as the sole desired goal, with little support for bilingualism or retention of one's native language. To the Euro-Americans in this group, English-language acquisition is seen as an essential step toward the "assimilation" of immigrants. In the words of one respondent, "Instead of English as a second language it should be English as the first language."

Like the CL group, members of the MC group described a pervasive segregation of immigrants into enclaves with little interaction with Euro-Americans:

> Sharon: I feel like we have maybe three communities existing right here, and you know, we overlap at the grocery store or the gas station or whatever, but basically they kind of go to their little areas, and we kinda go to our little areas, and . . .
>
> Moderator: What are the three communities?
>
> Sharon: Well, actually there are probably more, but I mean you know, the European—the white Europeans—the Hispanic, and I would say the African. Because, like I said, I think that the Asians have really become almost part of the European.

Gary, who is married to a Latina, was one of the only members of the group who mentioned close friendships and interactions with immigrants—in this case, Latinos. Other examples cited as friendships were generally neighborhood acquaintances or casual working relationships.

Unlike the CL group, where only a few members mentioned economic threats or concern over immigrant use of public resources, several MC residents attributed lower school achievement and declining property values to immigrants. Jeff and Dale's comments were typical:

> Jeff: I was curious, back on some of the, um, immigrants that we have if they, the parents, support the kids in school. That's gotta be a problem, cuz you know schools get criticized because, well, their SAT scores and everything's down. . . . Uh we get criticized by the governor and whatever, how the schools are not doing as well, and I think the immigration is bringing that down.
>
> Dale: My opinion is the rentals, the houses, the real estate will go down. Cuz they have cars all over, and junk; they don't take care of the yards and stuff.
>
> Jeff: A friend in town had a house for sale for I think over three hundred thousand. And unfortunately next door was a rental property with a, uh, Spanish-Mexican family, and they had about three cars in the yard. . . . It just looks bad. Three, two, cars with all covered in junk.
>
> Dale: I hear a lot of people talk about the tax dollars, too. They don't wanna see the tax dollars spent teaching people how to read. . . . I think that's definitely wrong, you know, but I do hear it. And I hear it downtown.

Assessments of immigrant initiative varied among MC group members. In these conversations Latinos or Mexicans were often singled out, and there were fewer references to Cambodian, Vietnamese, Somali, or Sudanese immigrants. In the views of some participants, Latinos were hard workers, but with limited expectations and drive compared to Euro-Americans or Asians, as noted by Herb:

> Herb: The good part of the Spanish working for the minimum wage area is they can live on it. They have less wants and so on, and so they're probably happier as workers than the locals.
>
> Heidi: They [Hispanics] have a very different attitude towards education too. . . . I think it has a lot to do with their economic status. I mean, to them, education is not as important as earning a living.

But Latinos are not always described as conforming to the American worth ethic. Jeff, for example, broadly characterized Mexicans as less reliable than Somalis.

> Jeff: Some of 'em [Mexicans] don't even realize that, hey, you have to be on work on time and this kind of thing. You can come to work any time you want. . . . Other, uh, other of the nationalities like the Somalians, I hear they're good workers.

Of all the Euros in the MC group, only Ed appeared to recognize the diversity that exists within the various immigrant groups, as well as selection process that attracts low-income Mexicans to the United States. In the following statement he described the role of poverty driving many low-income Mexicans to emigrate to the United States:

> Ed: You obviously are not getting the elite of Mexico up here, from a standpoint particularly from finances—and education. So uh . . . you're getting a community here either that is very, very hard-working or sees an opportunity to work—or maybe not to work. Maybe they come up here and take advantage of another situation. And, uh, I've found both, ya know. I've had experience with people that I'd just soon not associate with, and people that I wouldn't mind livin' next door to.

Other examples of empathetic statements came from Euros with family members who were born in Europe. Although Herb was quoted earlier, demanding that immigrants speak English, he later recalled his own parents' struggles learning the new language:

> Herb: I think it's important to remember, uh, we're in a big hurry here I think to integrate them into our society. My folks both came from Holland years ago, and they came through the same thing we're talking about here. When my older brothers and sisters started getting close to going to school, they were still talking Dutch at home.

At another point Jeff made a similar admission:

> Jeff: I can compare . . . like, even my mother came over from Denmark. Couldn't speak a word of English when she came over, but she'd do housework and so forth. And uh, it was a struggle.

In addition to these empathetic expressions, there was open acknowledgment of Euro-American prejudice at several points in the conversation. At one point Dale directly acknowledged the existence of racism. After Sue's story of the isolation of her daughter's Somali classmate he stated:

> Dale: I think it's us. . . . If you're white, you're prejudiced against the colored automatically, cuz you're born and raised [muffled], you can deny it. . . . Now there's two Irish people in town, immigrants that I got to know pretty well. No problem at all. They're white. But now, if they were black, or yellow or something else . . . I think there'd be a reservation there.

Working Class Focus Group

The WC focus group participants in our study had the closest contact with immigrants because they had worked in the meat-processing plant with Mexican, Vietnamese, and Cambodian employees, and some lived in a trailer court with many immigrant neighbors. In spite of this high level of exposure to immigrants, their reactions convey deep prejudice and stereotyped attitudes. WC participants and many of their family members had worked at the Devereux plant in the early 1990s, when workers were represented by the United Food and Commercial Workers Union, before the closing and deunionization of the plant and its subsequent shift to a predominantly immigrant workforce.

The subject of the plant closure naturally came up in the WC focus group. Somali immigrants were mentioned in this conversation, even though they were only recently arrived in Devereux and represented a small share of immigrants:

> Andrea: [The company] is not there to support the town; they're there to support their own pockets.
>
> Daniel: Right.
>
> Leanne: And the town let 'em do it. I think that hurt a lot of people.
>
> Daniel: They gave 'em a bond to build a bigger [plant]. Well then they went downhill real quick. They busted the—they laid everybody off to bust the union. Now they gotta . . . they're the ones that brought the Somalians in. . . . Not a lot of people wanted to go back to work there after that.

What is particularly interesting about Daniel's comment is that, in his mind, the influx of Somalis and the plant closure are conflated, and both contribute to the former workers' lack of interest in returning to the plant.

A question about how Devereux had changed over the years immediately elicited nostalgic comments from the WC group members who described an idealized past and the ways that demographic change had altered it:

> Andrea: You don't know your neighbors anymore.
>
> Leanne: We had softball.
>
> Daniel: Oh, you went outside? You played softball there in the summer?
>
> Leanne: We played till dark. And you knew who lived in what house and when they were home . . . and you'd go and walk in and talk to them.
>
> Daniel: Oh, God, now you wouldn't wanna do it. You know.
>
> Leanne: Even when [my son] wants to go play with a friend up at what we call the trailer court up there, I don't want him there, and the friend's white, I just don't trust him going up there. Again, it's a trailer court. . . .
>
> Andrea: When we were growing up, everybody was the same. This is something different coming in, so we don't know how to talk to 'em.

The line between the image of a pristine countryside and its symbolic "pollution" by an influx of non-European immigrants becomes blurred in the focus-group discussions:

> Andrea: I don't mind the minority, just so, we're getting so over-populated. There's nowhere to drive and see trees and stuff. . . .

Lilly: You used to drive around the countryside . . .

Andrea: Yeah.

Lilly: . . . and look at nice beautiful . . .

Andrea: . . . leaves.

Lilly: Now there isn't.

Daniel: I mean, yeah, you'd go a mile and you'd see a farmhouse. Now you can go ten miles without seeing a farmhouse.

Andrea: Without seeing the trees too. [*Chuckles.*]

Daniel: Really changing.

Loss of jobs, overpopulation, and the demise of a rural agricultural economy are thus fused with descriptions of immigrants. As Andrea stated clearly, "This is something different coming in."

Among members of the WC group, immigrants were generally described in stereotypic terms as an undifferentiated "other," receiving what were perceived as unwarranted advantages. Several of the members of the group had direct experience with welfare cuts themselves, but they had exaggerated notions of the benefits for which immigrants are eligible. In their minds all immigrants get long-term government help:

Andrea: They do get a tax break.

Daniel: That's another thing. They don't pay taxes for, what? Five to seven years?

Leanne: I think they changed it now. Three to five.

Daniel: Well, I think the government's going overboard with 'em. I mean, they should treat 'em all the same, whether they're Mexican or whatever, wherever they come from. They should all be treated the same. You know, whether they get kicked out of their own country, whether they wanna come over here. You know, but they shouldn't be treated better than we are. We're the ones that are payin' for what they're gittin'. If they're gonna run around act like they're better than we are, we ain't gonna, we ain't gonna appreciate that at all.

Daniel's comments are a clear statement of what some researchers have called the "modern prejudice belief system"(Levy 1999). As overt statements about the lesser abilities or characteristics of minorities are increasingly viewed as politically incorrect in the United States, such views have been replaced by assertions that discrimination no longer exists, and that minority-group demands for economic and political power are unwarranted. In studies of white attitudes toward blacks, this prejudice is reflected in high levels of agreement with statements such as "Over the past few years, the government and news media have shown more respect for blacks than they deserve" and "Blacks are getting too demanding in their push for equal rights" (Eberhardt and Fiske 1996, 375).

On the one hand, immigrants are stereotyped as a "burden" on society—individuals who do not subscribe to a work ethic and who receive welfare and other "undeserved" state benefits. On the other hand, their potential economic and political success is simultaneously seen as threatening. This twin attribution is made explicit in the following conversation, where economic and political power are both clearly viewed as zero-sum games in which gains by immigrants threaten the majority status of white Americans.

> Moderator: Can you imagine the different groups we're talking about becoming full-fledged members of the community?
>
> Deborah: But I mean, like, as far as, like, I don't know if that's what you meant, like, becoming more in our community, but you think of school board, and you think of city council and you think of Chamber, and—
>
> Deborah: Well, yeah, it would be kind of scary, but I mean I just can't imagine it would even happen, like, in the next ten or fifteen years. I would hope.
>
> Leanne: It would be almost scary, yeah, I guess, that scary feeling they may change it . . .
>
> Deborah: Well, I mean, maybe if enough of 'em all get here they could all vote them in . . .
>
> Leanne: I still think we'd be kind of afraid that they wouldn't have our best interests at heart. That they'd have their group.

A concern over the potential loss of majority power is also implicit in this fragment of the discussion; the fear becomes explicit in the next statements:

> Lilly: Yeah, but if they keep on bringing, bringin' 'em over here, as many as they are for the last five years, man where is everybody else gonna be? There's no homes for 'em now.

Deborah: I think that is, was one of the concerns that was brought up about how many more people are gonna be here before we . . .

Andrea: . . . get overpopulated . . .

Deborah: . . . like I said, yeah, feel like the minority.

What is particularly revealing about several of the WC group participants is that they not only express fears and stereotypes of immigrants, but also recognize their prejudices. In the following conversation, Andrea, Leanne, and Daniel compare contemporary stereotypes of immigrants with the racism directed toward African Americans that they learned while growing up. They openly acknowledge that immigrants are the "new blacks."

Andrea: But you always heard growing up—blacks are bad, they don't work, they work but they, you know, steal from ya, they steal ya blind.

Leanne: And you gotta be afraid of 'em cuz they will hurt ya.

Andrea: And now you're more afraid of the immigrants that are coming in instead of the blacks that we've had here. I don't know, it just seems like no one talks about black people anymore. They must be okay and accepted now because there's somebody else not to like.

Daniel: [*Laughs.*] That's about it.

Andrea: You know? I s'pose it was the Indians before the blacks, I don't know.

Remarkably, these same individuals who openly articulate nativist attitudes and admit to racism also express the hope that their children will grow up without prejudice:

Daniel: Yeah, it is. Really. [Diversity] is good for the kids.

Leanne: You know, they're growing up not prejudiced.

Daniel: Well, it's gonna hurt and help both. I don't think they're gonna love 'em all. I mean they're gonna find out they're just like the white people, there's good, there's bad, ugly, there's cute.

This admission is one of several contradictions demonstrated by different Euro-Americans in our study, and even within the same individual.

On the one hand, Daniel expresses anger and resentment toward immigrants who "shouldn't be treated better than we are." On the other hand, he mentions going out for drinks with Vietnamese and Mexican coworkers and acknowledges that not all immigrants are the same, and that "just like white people, there's good, there's bad, ugly, there's cute." These sentiments were echoed by other WC group members when at the end of their conversation the moderator asked, "What do you think is the most important thing that we've talked about today?"

> Daniel: It takes all kinds to make a state, or a city.
>
> Andrea: Yeah, we believe there's good and bad . . . different nationalities within themselves.
>
> Leanne: I think it's important too that, we, you know there's changes and our kids are accepting the changes.
>
> Daniel: Gotta give 'em a chance.

Although tolerance and the importance of cross-cultural understanding were clearly not themes of the WC conversation, this is the summary statement that Daniel, Andrea, and Leanne wish to make. It is unclear why positive statements about diversity are proffered in a group that has had no compunctions about revealing deep-seated stereotypes and negative attitudes toward immigrants.

CONCLUSIONS AND DISCUSSION

As rural midwestern communities lose population, they offer incentives to meatpacking companies to relocate and expand their meat-processing and manufacturing plants. The nature of the work and the demise of labor unions make the work unattractive for native-born residents, but the opportunities for steady, full-time work at wages well above the federal minimum wage are a lure for documented and undocumented immigrants from Mexico and Central America, and for refugees from Africa and Asia. As Joseph Amato and Anthony Amato (2000) have noted, these newcomers arrive as strangers, and their primary motivation is to work. This all-consuming focus and their low levels of English-language ability and education pose formidable challenges to community integration. Together, language barriers and socioeconomic class differences relegate many immigrants to a permanent category of outsiders. In Devereux, some of the so-called "newcomers" have lived in the community for over a quarter of a century.

Socioeconomic and language barriers reinforce existing status differences between American- and foreign-born residents. In the words of Louise Lamphere (1994), integration and change occur in the context of specific institutions where newcomers and established residents interact and have differential access to power. Interactions between Euro-Americans and immigrants usually occur in formal settings where relationships are defined and circumscribed by role relations, such as manager-worker, owner-tenant, or teacher-student. These scripted roles establish individuals of European origin as the ones who hold the power and immigrants as those at the bottom of the social hierarchy. Indeed, in the year of our focus-group study, 96 percent of the jobs on the disassembly line in the Devereux meat plant were held by immigrants, and only 4 percent by Euro-Americans. In contrast, the Euros held jobs in management and administration, as supervisors, mechanics, or human resource specialists. These power differentials are of course exacerbated by the undocumented status of many Latino workers, and by fear and uncertainty regarding rights and expectations experienced by all immigrants, regardless of legal status.

The extent of native interaction with immigrants varied greatly across the three focus groups and permitted us to reflect on the theoretical model first put forth by Gordon Allport (1954) over half a century ago. He hypothesized that proximity to out-groups would diminish perceived differences linked to prejudice. However, the combined implications of contact research and studies of the association between social class and prejudice are ambiguous regarding expected relations between working class native-born and foreign-born residents. It is working class whites who live and work in closest proximity to immigrants in rural communities, but whites of low socioeconomic status also perceive the greatest threats from immigrant workers. Several working class focus-group members had worked side by side with immigrants in the meat-processing plant before being laid off, and they lived together with them in local trailer courts. Because they were closest to immigrants in economic and social status they felt most threatened by their presence. This finding underscores the complex effects of "contact" on race relations.

In towns with large meat-processing plants the role of contact in promoting empathy may be reduced if white workers feel that they have been displaced by immigrants. Although a number of studies have shown that immigrants generally do not take jobs away from native-born American workers (Leitner 2000), meat-processing firms have implemented a strategy that entails relocating to rural areas, closing unionized plants, reopening non-union plants, and lowering wages to a level that attracts only immigrant workers. Competition is particularly evident when American-born unionized workers are discouraged or prevented from reapplying for jobs in the newly reopened facility. In these settings, contact and proximity to immigrants are likely to produce conflicting attitudes among low-income white residents because they make the economic threat of foreign-born workers appear more immediate and more serious.

The end result is that many Euro-Americans may have friendly relations with some individual immigrants, while simultaneously harboring resentment and supporting broad negative stereotypes of groups. Such attitudes appear to be a manifestation of what a number of social scientists have described as "ambivalence," or internalized conflict over racial policies. R. Michael Alvarez and John Brehm (1997) attribute such ambivalence in native-born Americans' attitudes toward African Americans to competing interpretations of the Protestant work ethic and humanitarian-egalitarian orientations. In the case of the working class group in Devereux, ambivalence is exhibited by the juxtaposition of statements about the value of diversity with expressions of fear over undeserved benefits accorded to immigrants, and indignation (as articulated by Daniel) that "they shouldn't be treated better than we are."

As Jennifer L. Hochschild (2006, 44) has succinctly stated:

> Americans find it very difficult to sustain their dedication to equality when it is defined as anything more robust than a thin equality of opportunity synonymous with liberty. . . . People define their group as people like them in some crucial way, and they seek justice, here defined mainly as greater equality, for that group. They perceive those outside the group more dimly and care less about whether justice is done to them, or they sometimes perceive outsiders as threats or even enemies, who must be stalled or defeated in order for justice to be done.

Although Daniel espouses the virtues of teaching his children to be more tolerant than he is, these statements are less convincing than his outrage over the perceived marginalization of his social group, and the perception that immigrants are "being treated better than we are." This conclusion corroborates the findings of other studies—that it is members of the lowest socioeconomic groups who feel most threatened by economic competition from immigrants or other minority groups (Burns and Gimpel 2000).

Alvarez and Brehm (1997) distinguish between ambivalence, which cannot be resolved with additional information, and uncertainty. One senses that the working class group's objections to immigrants stem less from concern that they violate the Protestant work ethic (as described by the middle class group), than from WC anger over their own marginalization. In contrast, the community leaders are elites whose principal concerns were economic development and diversification. They generally perceived immigrants as economic assets, by virtue of their role as laborers in expanding industries. From their isolated and privileged vantage points, few CL focus-group members viewed immigrants as economic or symbolic threats. The middle class group, in contrast, included a majority of white collar workers who openly expressed fears toward immigrants, whom they perceived as both a physical menace and as a threat to the cultural and linguistic cohesion of the white majority. As blue collar workers and former employees of the town's meat-processing plant, WC group members did not express the same fear of immigrants as the MC group, but they were vehement in their perceptions of the foreign-born as a threat to white-majority power and in their conviction that immigrants were receiving unwarranted advantages. These dual sentiments, first described by Gunnar Myrdal (1944) almost half a century ago, are the result of an internal struggle between racism and internalized notions of socially desirable behavior. They are also the logical result of socialization in a society that sanctions and promotes negative stereotypes of immigrants, while simultaneously lauding equal opportunity and the "American Dream."

NOTES

1. Fieldwork for this study was conducted in collaboration with Professor Helga Leitner of the Department of Geography, University of Minnesota.
2. In the early 1990s the plant employees belonged to the United Food and Commercial Workers Union (UFCW). In 1992 management asked the union to make wage concessions, but the UFCW refused. In December of 1993 the company closed the Devereux plant and many employees left to find other jobs. The plant was re-opened the following month, but when the union contract expired at the end of that year, neither party opened negotiations. Large numbers of immigrant employees were hired to work on the disassembly line. In January 1995, existing employees voted to decertify the union. Production expanded in the following years, and by 2001 (the year of our study), the plant had added a second shift and employed about 600 workers. In that year 96 percent of the disassembly line workers were immigrants.
3. These estimates are based on a combination of census data and reports from agencies and churches serving immigrant groups.
4. The exception was one resident who had lived in Devereux for six years.

REFERENCES

Allport, Gordon W. 1954. *The Nature of Prejudice.* Reading, Mass.: Addison-Wesley.

Alvarez, R. Michael, and John Brehm. 1997. "Are Americans Ambivalent Towards Racial Policies?" *American Journal of Political Science* 41(2): 345–74.

Amato, Anthony J., and Joseph Amato. 2000. "Minnesota, Real and Imagined." *Daedalus* 129(3): 55–80.

Benson, Janet E. 1999. "Undocumented Immigrants and the Meatpacking Industry in the Midwest." In *Illegal Immigration in America: A Reference Handbook*, edited by David W. Haines and Karen E. Rosenblum. Westport, Conn.: Greenwood Press.

Burns, Peter, and James G. Gimpel. 2000. "Economic Insecurity, Prejudicial Stereotypes and Public *Opinion on Immigration Policy.*" *Political Science Quarterly* 115(2): 201–25.

Cantu, Lionel 1995. "The Peripheralization of Rural America: A Case Study of Latino Migrants in America's Heartland." *Sociological Perspectives* 38(3): 399–414.

Castles, Stephen, and Mark J. Miller. 2003. *The Age of Migration.* Basingstoke, U.K.: Palgrave Macmillan.

Conzen, Kathleen N., David A. Gerber, Ewa Morawska, George E. Pozzetta, and Rudolph J. Vecoli. 1992. "The Invention of Ethnicity: A Perspective from the U.S.A." *Journal of American Ethnic History* 12: 4–51.

Eberhardt, Jennifer, and Susan T. Fiske. 1996. "Motivating Individuals to Change: What Is a Target to Do?" In *Stereotypes and Stereotyping*, edited by Miles Hewstone. New York: Guilford Press.

Esses, Victoria M., John F. Dovidio, Lynne M. Jackson, and Tamara L. Armstrong. 2001. "The Immigration Dilemma: The Role of Perceived Group Competition, Ethnic Prejudice, and National Identity." *Journal of Social Issues* 57(3): 389–412.

Fennelly, Katherine. 2005. "Latinos, Asians, Africans in the Northstar State: New Immigrant Communities in Minnesota." In *Beyond the Gateway: Immigrants in a Changing America*, edited by Elzbieta M. Gozdziak and Susan F. Martin. Lanham, Md.: Lexington Books.

Fennelly, Katherine, and Christopher Federico. Forthcoming. "Rural Residence as a Determinant of Attitudes Toward US Immigration Policy." *International Migration.*

Fennelly, Katherine, and Helga Leitner. 2002. "How the Food Processing Industry Is Diversifying Rural Minnesota." JSRI Working Paper WP-59. East Lansing, Mich.: Michigan State University, Julian Samora Research Institute.

Griffith, David. 1999. "Social and Cultural Bases for Undocumented Immigration into the U.S. Poultry Industry." In *Illegal Immigration in America: A Reference Handbook*, edited by David W. Haines and Karen E. Rosenblum. Westport, Conn.: Greenwood Press.

Higham, John. 1955. *Strangers in the Land: Patterns of American Nativism, 1860–1925*. New Brunswick, N.J.: Rutgers University Press.

Hochschild, Jennifer L. 2006. "Ambivalence About Equality in the United States, or, Did Tocqueville Get It Wrong and Why Does That Matter?" *Social Justice Research* 19(1): 43–62.

Huntington, Samuel P. 2004. *Who Are We: The Challenges to America's National Identity*. New York: Simon & Schuster.

Lamphere, Louise, Alex Stepick, and Guillermo Grenier. 1994. *Newcomers in the Workplace*. Philadelphia, Penn.: Temple University Press.

Leitner, Helga. 2000. "The Political Economy of International Labor Migration." In *A Companion to Economic Geography*, edited by Eric Sheppard and Trevor J. Barnes. Oxford: Blackwell.

Levy, Sheri R. 1999. "Reducing Prejudice: Lessons from Social-Cognitive Factors Underlying Perceiver Differences in Prejudice." *Journal of Social Issues* 55(4): 745–54.

McConnell, Eileen. 2001. "The Midwest in Transition: An Examination of the Unprecedented Growth in the Hispanic Population." Paper presented to Third Upper Midwest Conference of Demographics for Policy Analysts. November 2001, Minneapolis, Minn.

Minnesota Planning. 1997. "Reasons for 'Rural Rebound' Are Diverse." *PopBites* 97(July): 12.

Myrdal, Gunnar. 1944. *An American Dilemma: The Negro Problem and Modern Democracy*. New York: Harper.

Nevins, Joseph 2003. *Operation Gatekeeper: The Rise of the "Illegal Alien" and the Making of the U.S.-Mexico Boundary*. New York: Routledge.

Oliver, J. Eric, and Tali Mendelberg. 2000. "Reconsidering the Environmental Determinants of White Racial Attitudes." *American Journal of Political Science* 44(3): 574–89.

Oyamot, Clifton M., Eugene Borgida, and Eric L. Fischer. 2006. "Can Values Moderate the Attitudes of Right-Wing Authoritarians?" *Personality and Social Psychology Bulletin* 32(4): 486–500.

Public Agenda. 2000. "Distinct Views on the Proverbial Melting Pot." *American Demographics* 22(12): 24.

Reyna, Valerie F. 2000. "Lazy, Dumb or Industrious: When Stereotypes Convey Attribution Information in the Classroom." *Educational Psychology Review* 12(1): 85–110.

See, Katherine O., and Wilson, William J. 1988. "Race and Ethnicity." In *Handbook of Sociology*, edited by Neil J. Smelser. Newbury Park, Calif.: Sage.

Singer, Audrey. 2004. *The Rise of New Immigrant Gateways*. Washington: Brookings Institution.

Sniderman, Paul M., Louk Hagendoorn, and Markus Prior. 2004. "Predisposing Factors and Situational Triggers." *American Political Science Review* 98(1): 35–50.

Sniderman, Paul M., Philip E. Tetlock, and Edward G. Carmines. 1993. *Prejudice, Politics, and the American Dilemma*. Palo Alto, Calif.: Stanford University Press.

Stephan, Walter G., and Kristyna Finlay. 1999. "The Role of Empathy in Improving Intergroup Relations." *Journal of Social Issues* 55(4): 729–43.

Stull, Donald D. 1998. "On the Cutting Edge: Changes in Midwestern Meatpacking Communities." The Rural and Regional Essay Series. Marshall, Minn.: Society for the Study of Local and Regional History.

Tauxe, Caroline. 1998. "Heartland Community: Economic Restructuring and the Management of Small Town Identity in the Central U.S." *Identities* 5(3): 335–77.

Yeoman, Barry. 2000. "Hispanic Diaspora." *Mother Jones* July–August: 36–77.

CHAPTER 8

⌄∕

NEW MIDWESTERNERS, NEW SOUTHERNERS: IMMIGRATION EXPERIENCES IN FOUR RURAL AMERICAN SETTINGS

DAVID GRIFFITH

Since the late 1980s, the midwestern and southern United States have witnessed high levels of immigration from Mexico, Central America, Asia, and Africa; census figures on immigration in some regions display increases of several hundred percent from 1990 to 2000. During the 1990s, research generally focused on changes taking place in new receiving communities as a result of concerted efforts by employers to recruit immigrants into rural industries such as meatpacking, seafood processing, and poultry processing (Stull, Broadway, and Griffith 1995; Grey 1999; Griffith 1993; Fink 2003). These recruitment efforts built on and at times mirrored techniques common in agriculture (Commission on Agricultural Workers 1993; Hahamovich 1997; Griffith et al. 1995). Subsequent studies have considered the network basis of labor recruitment, relations between labor supplies and housing stock, the growth and human consequences of labor subcontracting, occupational injury and the problem of high labor turnover, and other dimensions of rural labor markets experiencing high levels of immigration. With few exceptions (for example, Benson 1990), researchers paid less attention to the processes by which immigrants elaborated their residence within communities: enrolling children in school, attending church, accessing health care, and generally settling in.

Coincidental with settlement, new immigrants have been moving out of traditional occupations such as agriculture and food processing and into construction, tourism, fast-food services, and manufacturing, and have also been engaging in entrepreneurial activities oriented toward other immigrants. Social dispersion into schools, churches, adult education programs, human rights organizations, ethnic organizations, and other settings has accompanied the geographical and economic dispersion, and related to these processes has been a fundamental change in immigrant groups, from primarily young, single males to families, including women, children, and elderly. At the same time, new sending areas have developed in Latin America, Asia, and Africa, introducing more indigenous language speakers and more ethnic diversity into migrant streams. Finally, in both new and old receiving areas, more complex class and ethnic relations among immigrants and between immigrants and natives have developed in response to pressing problems such as housing, health care, translation services, and immigrant consumption patterns.

This chapter draws on two and a half years of research on new immigrants in four new American destination areas: southwestern Minnesota, focusing primarily on the town of Marshall and other nearby communities; Marshalltown, in central Iowa; southeastern North Carolina; and the town of Adel and surrounding areas of Cook County, Georgia. This research, funded by the U.S. Department of Agriculture's Fund for Rural America Program, consisted of initial site visits to ten American communities and subsequent ethnographic and survey research in six: two in the South, two in the Midwest, and two on the West Coast. In addition to conducting research in the four communities listed, I also conducted site visits in Wachula, Florida, and Beaufort County, North Carolina, and my colleague, Ed Kissam, conducted research in Arvin, California, and Woodburn, Oregon.[1]

I was thus responsible for five of the ten initial site visits and four of the six subsequent case studies. Following a brief overview of the four communities under consideration here, I discuss several dimensions of new immigration in these areas, including the role of historical reporting, the importance of the food industry, the key integrating practices of churches, work places, schools, and health systems, and processes of differentiation occurring within immigrant groups.

OVERVIEW OF STUDY COMMUNITIES

The comparisons between the four communities shown in table 8.1 illustrate differences among the regions that have direct consequences for immigrant and native groups. Immigrant families in the two southern regions, for example, maintain strong ties to agricultural labor, with some household members continuing to take work in local harvests during the summer months. They also maintain ties to other regions they pass through to work during other parts of the year, including Florida, Kentucky,

TABLE 8.1   Comparisons of the Four Study Communities' Histories with Immigrants

Area and Length of Experience	Groups Present	Approximate Number	Share of Population	Primary Occupations	Legal Statuses
Southwest Minnesota Since early 1990s	Somalis, Hmong, Latinos	1,000 to 1,200	6 to 10%	Food processing, electronics, gardening, retail trade, services	Refugees, documented and undocumented; U.S.-born citizen children[a]
Marshalltown, Iowa Since late 1980s	Michoacános, other Mexicans	8,000 to 9,000	24 to 39%	Meatpacking, fast food, casino work	Documented and undocumented refugees; U.S.-born citizen children[a]
Southeastern North Carolina Since early 1990s	Mexicans, Salvadorans, Guatemalans	15,000 to 16,000	9 to 16%	Poultry processing, hog processing, construction, light manufacturing, agriculture	Documented, undocumented, U.S.-born citizen children[a]
Adel and Cook Counties, Georgia Since late 1990s	Mexicans	100 to 200	1 to 2%	Welding, steel fabricating, boat building, box and lumber manufacturing, agriculture	Documented H2 workers, undocumented, U.S.-born citizen children[a]

Source: Author's compilation.
[a] Although U.S.-born children are not immigrants, I include them here because they live in immigrant households and play important roles in the settlement process.

Tennessee, eastern Virginia and Maryland, upstate New York, and southwest Michigan. Southeastern North Carolina, however, is distinct from south-central Georgia in that many of its agricultural laborers are legal temporary foreign workers from Mexico who hold H-2A visas, which are allocated to workers in industries such as agriculture (Griffith 2006). Although workers holding H-2A visas do work in Georgia (in forestry), we encountered none in Cook County.

In the two midwestern communities, in contrast, nonrefugee immigrants arrived directly from Mexico, from other meatpacking areas of the Midwest, or by somewhat more circuitous routes (usually by way of southwestern states, including California). Most coming to the Midwest are specifically seeking work in meatpacking or are family members of meatpacking workers. Marshalltown, Iowa, draws somewhere between 60 and 80 percent of its new immigrant Mexicans from one village, Villachuato, in the state of Michoacán (Grey and Woodrick 2002). Over the past decade, immigrants in Marshalltown have changed from primarily single males to families with young children, and have moved into fast food, roofing, casino work, dairies, and other economic sectors. Many families have some members who are American-born and thus American citizens, whereas others are undocumented. Such mixed status allows families partial access to educational resources, employment opportunities, and social services while still inhibiting full participation in civil society. Southwestern Minnesota is further distinguished from the other communities in its ethnic diversity, receiving significant numbers of Somali and Hmong refugees as well as Latino immigrants.

Paralleling these migrations, all regions have experienced secondary migrations of immigrants with prior experience in the United States, stable legal statuses, English-language ability, and often more education and business acumen. These families have established businesses that cater primarily to immigrants but in many cases also to natives. Most common among these have been ethnic stores, restaurants, and bars, but others provide legal and translation services, labor contracting and employment services, real estate services, and auto repair. Many individuals from these families also have emerged as informal leaders in these communities, acting as liaisons between native and immigrant groups, though formal community leaders, such as mayors, often fail to recognize or acknowledge their importance. Others who occupy such leadership positions, however, use them to take advantage of new immigrants by functioning as labor contractors, landlords, employers, service providers, and business partners.

Adel, Georgia

Located on Interstate 75 in southern Georgia, twenty miles north of Valdosta, Adel (pronounced AY-del), in Cook County, is a community of five thousand to six thousand. It has a long history of seasonal populations of migrant Latino farmworkers, and more recently around one hundred Latino families from the farm-labor stream have settled permanently. The population of Cook County is three times that of Adel and its settled Latino population is about twice Adel's. Most settled Latino families reside in the neighboring towns of Sparks, which adjoins Adel to the north, Cecil, five miles to the south, and Lennox, eight miles north. A handful of families also live in trailers and houses in the countryside.

The region, along the northern edge of a swampy swath that stretches across southern Georgia, enjoys a long growing season with mild winters and easy access to urban markets to the north (Macon and Atlanta) and the south (Tallahassee and Tampa–St. Petersburg) along I-75. Although Adel is home to the largest steel fabrication center east of the Mississippi, much of its economy remains closely tied to agriculture and forestry, principally the production of fruits, nuts, vegetables, and lumber products. Growers around Adel produce pecans, strawberries, peaches, and other agricultural products, and agricultural services in Adel include box and pallet companies that employ varying numbers of people throughout the year. All of these sectors depend to some degree on Latino, usually Mexican, labor. Several large lumber yards round out Adel's economy. Many of these hire immigrants, and a pleasure-boat-building plant in a nearby community has increased its hiring of Mexican immigrants over the past five years. Other Adel businesses include several retail shops in a struggling outlet mall along the interstate highway, a handful of motels, downtown banks, restaurants, and retail stores (including one Latino shop), as well as government services.

Adel's settled immigrant population is quite recent, having been there for less than six years, and dates to a split between a farm-labor contractor and some members of his crew. According to one of the early immigrant settlers, the split occurred when the labor contractor attempted to find work for his crew members outside of agriculture during a dead time between harvests. The farm-labor contractor owned a Latino store in downtown Adel, which provided contacts for finding employment. This off-season employment enabled some members of his crew to become familiar with work at a local nursery, where they were able to secure better-paid, year-round employment. When the harvests began again, these crew members refused to return to farm work. Other members of the crew, their families, their siblings' families, and other relatives and friends, followed suit.

Since then, one hundred to two hundred families have settled in and around Adel. Nevertheless, most of the native community members we interviewed continue to view the Latino population in Cook County as a temporary "migrant" population. This perception is related to the continuing seasonal migration into the area for agricultural work, combined with the tendency of some Latinos to take on seasonal work even after they have settled, notably in local box and pallet companies. Others work in steel fabrication plants, pleasure-boat-building factories, and lumber companies.

A few businesses and services in Adel have attempted to upgrade their services to meet the needs of Latino residents—for example, by hiring translators at the local hospital—but generally the community seems to have adopted a neutral stance toward Latinos. On the one hand, local leaders, police, realtors, and service providers haven't made any special effort to make the Latinos feel welcome, assist them in buying houses, or extend banking or licensing services to them. On the other hand, neither have there been overt demonstrations of racism or excessive police surveillance of the Latino population. Most of the Latinos we interviewed view the community as quiet and peaceful ("muy tranquilo" is a phrase they use) and seem pleased with the work they have found. There are indications, however, that resentments between the farm-labor contractor and his former crew members linger.

Southwestern Minnesota

The study area in southwestern Minnesota consists of eighteen counties that stretch into the state 70 to 100 miles east of the South Dakota border and around 125 miles north of the Iowa border. They are primarily rural counties dotted with regional marketing centers such as Marshall (located at the center of the region), Montevideo, Willmar, Hutchinson, Glencoe, Granite Falls, Redwood Falls, and Worthington. The largest of the counties, Kandiyohi, has slightly more than 40,000 residents, although most communities have fewer than 15,000 inhabitants. The region's total population, based on the Census Bureau's estimate for 2001, was 285,871. Comparing this figure to previous census years points to one of the region's principal problems: population loss. The 2001 figure is lower than the 2000 figure of 287,627 and only slightly higher than the 1990 figure of 283,514, and it is far below the 1980 figure of 304,276 (Roy and Owen 2001, 12).

Like Adel, southwest Minnesota is a wet environment, with a complex network of irrigation canals and river systems that local historians have termed "the great oasis" (Amato, Timmerman, and Amato 1999). It is heavily agricultural, although its wetlands, rich in waterfowl and wildlife, annually attract large numbers of hunters of deer, duck, geese, and other fauna. Most of our work took place in and around the town of Marshall, where a turkey-processing plant began hiring Latino immigrants in the late 1980s. Marshall is best known in the region (and perhaps the nation) as the home of Schwan's Foods, a national food company with beverage and food plants here and in other parts of the country. Its founder, Marvin Schwan, was for many years one of the town's most influential citizens, and the company continues to wield power in the community, donating to various causes and hiring immigrants.

In addition to Latinos, Marshall also received Hmong immigrants during the 1980s and 1990s; most of these were secondary migrants from the Twin Cities who found work in a local electronics manufacturing plant. By around the turn of the twenty-first century, many had returned to the Twin Cities just as there was another migration of Hmong from St. Paul to Walnut Grove, thirty minutes southeast of Marshall. Finally, in the early 1990s, Somali refugees began arriving in the area and found work in local electronics and poultry plants; after the factories employing them closed, however, many of these families left for other parts of the state.

Community leaders throughout southwestern Minnesota have adopted a proactive stance toward immigrants. City and county officials, including school system personnel, have worked hard to make them feel a part of the community and to assure that their children remain. Some immigrant leadership has emerged to join public employees in these efforts. Many community leaders and members view the immigrants as a source of future vitality, although this sentiment is not shared universally throughout the native population. Community leaders in Walnut Grove, in particular, report that the Hmong have revitalized the local housing market, prevented a school closure, established a cultural center, and have begun establishing new businesses. As in Adel, most immigrants find rural Minnesota a tranquil environment, yet most also report that they will remain only as long as their economic prospects are sound. In early 2004, one of the principal employers of Latinos and Somalis, the turkey processor Heartland Foods, stimulated some emigration of these new immigrant families when it closed its plant. A new turkey company, Turkey Valley Farms, has since reopened the plant, and once again immigrants are being hired.

Southeastern North Carolina

Duplin, Sampson, and Pender counties, in southeastern North Carolina, constitute a region known for its poultry, pork, and pickle industries, all of which have integrated immigrant labor into their operations. All three industries are vertically integrated, with interlinked sectors for growing, servicing, feeding, and processing their primary products (turkeys, chickens, hogs, or cucumbers). Thus, the new immigrants, nearly all Latino, have found work in the cucumber fields, on hog and poultry farms, and, most important, in the various food-processing plants. Although most of the Latinos are from Mexico, notably Mixtecs from Oaxaca, the region has attracted a growing number of Honduran refugees and immigrants since the devastation of Hurricane Mitch, along with Salvadorans and Guatemalans.

As in southern Georgia, immigrants have long been present seasonally as migrant farmworkers, gradually replacing African Americans beginning in the early to mid-1980s. Besides working in the cultivation of pickle cucumbers, migrants are employed in the production of tobacco, blueberries and strawberries, ornamental plants, sweet potatoes, and assorted other vegetables. Many of the agricultural workers are legal immigrants from Mexico, with temporary H-2A visas, who are imported by a large labor-contracting firm that calls itself the North Carolina Growers Association (NCGA). In August 2004, the association signed a union contract with the Farm Labor Organizing Committee, a new labor union based in Ohio that organizes cucumber workers in the United States and Mexico.

In part to serve the migrant population, a regional health network currently hires many people with the language and cultural skills necessary to deal with the Spanish speakers. There are no large cities and only a few small towns in the region, all with populations under ten thousand, although the nearby city of Wilmington and nearby New Hanover County, on the Lower Cape Fear River, together constitute one of the fastest-growing regions of the United States. The booming construction industry draws many immigrants out of meatpacking and farmwork, and is home to a handful of agencies and organizations that serve the Latino population in some capacity. The large Catholic church in Newton Grove, Our Lady of Guadalupe, has attracted large numbers of Latinos, in part owing to its name (the church antedated Latino immigration by nearly twenty years), but it does not engage in social justice issues, leaving that to an Episcopal ministry in the region that is part of a statewide network of activist Episcopal clergy.

Marshalltown, Iowa

Central Iowa's Marshalltown, an easy drive from the capital city of Des Moines and two other major urban areas, Cedar Rapids and Waterloo-Cedar Falls, is a community of 28,000 to 30,000 with a Latino immigrant population of some 8,000 to 9,000, or about a third of the total population. Its immigrant population is unique among all those discussed here in that the majority come from one village in Mexico: Villachuato, Michoacán. Links between the American and the Mexican cities have been fostered with the encouragement of the New Iowans Center, an active group of anthropologists and other academics located nearby at the University of Northern Iowa, and there have been several cultural and material exchanges. Marshalltown leaders and agency personnel have visited the Michoacán community to improve their appreciation of the immigrant population in Iowa.

Latinos were originally recruited in the late 1980s to work a large pork-packing plant in Marshalltown. Over the past fifteen years, the immigrant population has changed from primarily young, single males to immigrant families. Although still concentrated in meatpacking work, Latinos in Marshalltown have networked into a variety of other sectors in the economy, finding jobs in a nearby Mesquakie Casino, in fast-food restaurants, in manufacturing, and in other sectors. Two major national companies, Fisher Controls and Lennox Heating and Air Conditioning, are based in Marshalltown, and recently staff from their personnel office have been speaking with the local job service about training and hiring Latinos. As with Schwan's in Marshall Minnesota, the heads of these two companies have been influential in Marshalltown in the past and the companies continue to wield power today. One of the heirs of the Fisher family, Mary Ellen Tye, established a foundation dedicated to local cultural matters, and recently it has been funding activities related to immigrants, including underwriting the cost of local leaders' travel to Mexico.

As in Minnesota, many of Marshalltown's leaders view new immigrants as a source of vitality, in stark contrast to the aging native population. This is in line with Iowa state policy: the governor and several agencies and organizations have actively promoted a pro-immigration position, establishing task forces to examine workforce, housing, health, and other state needs that could be taken care of in part by increased immigration (see, for example, Grey et al. 2001). Such policy positions are consistent with past state initiatives, such as the Iowa governor's enthusiastic response to President Carter's plea for states to absorb Vietnamese and other Southeast Asian refugee populations in the late 1970s.

These state positions have met with uneven popular support. Some in the state have backed English-only initiatives and other anti-immigration policies, and newspapers around the state continue to run editorials portraying Iowa's immigrants in negative terms. In Marshalltown, however, the voices against immigration seem to have been drowned out by the voices supporting them.

SHARED AND DIVERGENT EXPERIENCES

New immigrant destinations typically experience several common developments. In these four communities, we found that immigrant incorporation was facilitated by invoking history, the role of the food industry, churches, schools, and the health care system.

Remembering

Immigration into each of these communities, while recent, is neither wholly new nor entirely unique. The United States is a nation of immigrants, and in each of these regions, those who support immigration and immigrants routinely invoke the historical record to justify their stance. Thus, the local historian Joseph A. Amato (1996, 3), who has written several short histories of Marshall and the region, states:

> The Minnesota state constitution was originally printed in English and several other languages, including Welsh. By 1896, official election instructions were being issued in nine languages: English, German, Norwegian, Swedish, Finnish, French, Czech, Italian, and Polish. In 1910 over half the people living in most counties of southwestern Minnesota had been born outside the United States.

Similarly, in each of the guides produced for their "Welcoming New Iowans" series, the anthropologists Anne Woodrick and Mark Grey (2002, 1) open with brief histories of immigration into the region: "Indeed, with the exception of small groups of Native Americans, without immigrants there would be no Iowans. The thousands of European immigrants who arrived in the 1800s and early part of the 1900s settled this state and established many towns and cities."

Similarly, in North Carolina, when Congresswoman Eva Clayton addressed a gathering interested in immigration in Rocky Mount, she spoke of earlier migrations into the state, and employers hiring new immigrant laborers in southern Georgia were quick to point out that migrant farmworkers had been passing through the region since Emancipation.

Highlighting continuity to a shared past and established tradition is clearly intended to make immigration palatable to those who are uneasy about the influx of foreigners; invoking history in communities and regions experiencing new waves of immigration also implies that recent immigrants, like those before them, will eventually assimilate into the dominant culture, shedding all but quaint residues of their language, dress, religion, and indeed every other cultural element—except, of course, their food. In some cases, assimilation is imagined to come at the cost of values that had characterized earlier waves of immigrants, particularly their work ethic but also such characteristics as dedication to family, religious conviction, and cooperative spirit. Thus, local employers of Latinos routinely praise their work ethic and characterize them as "churchgoing, family-oriented people." In Walnut Grove, Minnesota, one leader in the public school system went so far as to say: "We used to build houses and barns together. We used to take care of our elderly instead of send them to old folks homes. We used to bring the whole family together for meals. We don't do any of those things anymore; but the Hmong do."

Such comments invoke powerful images. They resonate with many local residents who might otherwise view immigration as a threat to nationalism, the English language, security, Christianity, and central cultural values. Although they have not been sufficient to quell anti-immigration sentiments in the regions, they have been able to moderate those sentiments enough to open the door to arguments for immigration based on materialist considerations.

The Food Industry and the New Immigrants

In all four regions, economic well-being is directly tied to the food industry. The heavy dependence of so many food-processing industries on immigrant labor is significant because of these firms' notorious power, huge workforces, high capital concentration, and the evolving relationship between foods and drugs in the field of genetically modified organisms (see Nestle 2002; Pringle 2003; Schlosser 2001). Echoing Daniel Rothenberg's central metaphor of immigrants' and shoppers' hands touching indirectly (1998), a tobacco grower in rural North Carolina once said to me, "One day Mexicans are going to wake up and realize their power. They're going to realize that everything we buy in a grocery store has been touched by a Mexican."

This statement may have been somewhat of an exaggeration, but in our few case studies we have repeatedly encountered Latinos "touching" a wide range of food products, some of which are produced by independent

companies but most of which are produced by giant food industry corporations that make up the food oligopoly: ConAgra, RJR-Nabisco, Altrea
(formerly Philip Morris), Nestlé, Pepsico, Unilever-Bestfoods. These and
a handful of other companies account for the bulk of foods produced and
distributed in the United States and much of the world (Nestle 2002,
11–14). Many of their products—Healthy Choice, Hunt's Tomato Sauce,
Hebrew National hot dogs, Butterball Turkeys, Chef Boyardee, and Slim
Jims, to name just a few of ConAgra's products—depend on brand recognition and high-quality production regimes (ConAgra Foods 2004). Their
ability to maintain quality in turn depends on a combination of consistent
production processes and labor that performs fast, repetitive work with a
minimum of complaint.

The food industry's heavy dependence on immigrant labor is not something that federal, state, or local policymakers can take lightly. Federal
immigration policies and border enforcement practices have always been
cognizant of food industry needs (Calavita 1992; Hahamovich 1997;
Griffith et al. 1995). At local levels, families such as the Schwans and companies such as Swift or Carolina Turkey wield considerable power as large
employers, taxpayers, and consumers of public and private services.
Initiatives targeted at immigrants' problems must involve these companies in some capacity, whether the initiatives are as benign as providing
English-language classes or as threatening as raising community awareness about the underreporting of occupational illness (Stull, Broadway,
and Griffith 1995; Stull and Broadway 2004).

Within food industry workplaces, integration is taking place even if
in a segmented fashion, forcing employers to accommodate the new
immigrants by learning some of their language, encouraging immigrants to learn English, or, more commonly, hiring or promoting a
bilingual staff to work in personnel offices, on factory floors, and in
other settings. In most studies of immigrants, the search for work is
seen as the principal driving force behind migration (Bump 2005;
Gozdziak and Martin 2005; Massey et al. 1993; Portes and Bach 1985;
Portes 1994). In rural areas, the food industry is the driver of work-
related migration, even among refugees. Hmong and Somali refugees in
southwest Minnesota are largely secondary migrants, recruited out of
the Twin Cities and attached to places only as long as opportunities for
work remain.

The links among immigration, food production, and food policy are,
however, more complex than the food industry's importance as the principal employer of rural immigrant labor. The food industry's interests
shape research agendas at land grant colleges, thereby influencing county

extension agents, who are strategically located to address immigration issues. Thus, Iowa State University's extension services have attempted to reach out to immigrants in rural areas by developing an "Iowa Community Voices Program for Spanish-Speakers." The specific purposes of the program (Quinn, n.d.) are:

> (1) To give new Spanish-speaking residents the knowledge and confidence to actively participate in community, school and government activities; (2) to help Spanish-speaking residents make their voices heard in the community, school and local government; (3) to introduce the leadership of the community (established English-speaking residents) to the new Spanish-speaking residents and open a dialogue; and (4) to identify issues impacting the Spanish-speaking residents and develop a plan to address these issues.

Sponsoring meetings conducted in Spanish for twenty to twenty-five adults over six consecutive Saturdays in different locations around rural Iowa (mostly in meatpacking towns), the initiative has met with uneven success.[1] Some extension service agents view their primary loyalty as being to food producers, and such efforts strike them as too activist or, more simply, not part of their basic mission. In southwest Minnesota, for example, a woman who had lived for several months in Mexico and was fluent in Spanish was hired by the Worthington area's agricultural extension service as a diversity specialist, a job that involved attempting to incorporate new immigrants into the various activities, such as 4-H (the youth agriculture program), that could enhance youths' lives. Unfortunately, she lasted only a year at the job, for reasons that become clear in notes from an interview with her.

> Patricia, a diversity specialist, quit because she said she has had practically no support from the local staff and in some cases her work was even sabotaged.[2] Her tale offers a classic story of field office personnel butting heads with the central administration. Her position was mandated by the state, but stuffed down the throat of the local office of the extension service. Many of the locals have been working for the extension service since they graduated from high school—women with home economics backgrounds and men with limited technical training—and they have used youth agricultural programs such as 4-H as local power bases to husband resources feeling threatened by minority initiatives. She said that it was ironic that, even though 4-H was originally developed to empower marginalized rural populations, the locals turn a deaf ear asked to reach out to people of color.[3]

At Cornell University, recently, the Migrant Program—founded in 1981 as an advocacy and rural services organization that assisted migrant farm-workers with problems ranging from accessing banking services to protesting living conditions in labor camps—was dismantled after regional food industry representatives claimed that it was encouraging "labor activism" and brought pressure to end the program. This closure is being contested by labor advocates, and meanwhile state officials have proposed transferring the program from the Department of Rural Sociology to the School of Agriculture (Gray 2005). Once there, the program is more likely to become more of a farm labor contracting organization than an advocacy program.

Churches

At the Hispanic Ministry at St. Mary's Catholic Church, in Marshalltown, one of the stories people tell is of the 1992 procession of the statue of the Virgin of Guadalupe. This march occurred after the Lutheran minister in Marshalltown began holding services in Spanish in his church and allowed immigrant Latinos to keep a statue of the Virgin of Guadalupe in the church, despite its obvious symbolic importance as a Roman Catholic icon in Mexico. St. Mary's, the Catholic church, had refused to reach out to Latinos in any significant way, in part because of resistance from the native congregation, but when the Lutheran minister began preaching in Spanish, the diocese realized that St. Mary's had made a mistake and in 1992 the parish brought in a Spanish-speaking priest to begin holding Mass in Spanish.

Following the priest's arrival, in high ceremony, the Latino Catholics of Marshalltown carried the Virgin from the Lutheran church to St. Mary's, placing the statue in a prominent position in the rear of the church. It was a moment that local Catholics describe as "rife with ecumenical implications."[4] The Virgin's procession from one church to another was a particularly dramatic event, yet it underscores the important role that churches play in welcoming new immigrants. In Marshall, the Catholic church even reached out to Muslims and Hmong, and in all of the regions under study churches have been among the first to see that the basic needs of immigrants are met.

Churches usually provide much more than spiritual fulfillment, including one or more of a range of services that immigrants generally want or need, such as English-language classes, translation assistance, orientation to the community, education about immigrants' rights, and transportation. As Kerry Preibisch (2003) noted in her work on Mexican and Caribbean guest workers in Canada, churches also provide alternatives to workplaces and neighborhoods where immigrants can gather and socialize. In our survey work, slightly more than one third of those interviewed reported significant interactions with churches during their first weeks in the community, and 94 percent of those who reported such interactions characterized them as positive.[5]

Among the kinds of help reported were language training, food provision, assistance finding work, help with legal documents, and encouraging native-born community members to learn Spanish so everyone could communicate better. The latter effort was particularly important to many of the clergy we interviewed. They appeared to be almost as interested in teaching native community members about immigrants as they were in orienting new immigrants to the community. This attitude in part reflects the perception that new immigrants are particularly devout, as one Catholic nun suggested:

> On the Sunday nearest to December 12 (the day of the Virgin of Guadalupe), their church managed to collect $1,604 in donations from Latino families, specifically for the purchase of roses. They made a deal with a large local grocery with a floral service to make wreaths that the families then used to build a mountain of roses around the Virgin in the front of the church. When one of the Anglo parishioners saw this, she said, "What a waste of money." But Sister Mona said that this was actually a revelatory experience for her, showing her, as a daughter of God, how important the Virgin was to Catholicism. She said that the Latinos should be credited for their willingness to come up with so much money for ritual.

Sister Mona believes that—just as some Latinos have taught her, a woman of the church, a new perspective on the Virgin Mary—other residents of Marshalltown and Iowans generally could benefit from better communication with members of the Latino community. Part of her job has been to speak to several community organizations and groups, including the other Catholic church across town (an Anglo church), to educate them about the Latino community. Among the important pieces of information she seeks to pass along is the idea that many of the Latino families, particularly those with children, are here to stay.[6]

Like the efforts of agricultural extension services, the church's embrace of the immigrant community has met with a mixed response from long-time congregation members. In Sister Mona's church, attendance at the Spanish-language Mass began surpassing Anglo attendance as Anglo parishioners moved from her church, which was near the struggling downtown, to a church in a more affluent part of town. She viewed this as

directly related not only to the church's expanding its Latino congregation but also to the provision of services to immigrants, which included
assisting the undocumented, responding to complaints about landlords,
and advocating for improved working and housing conditions.

Given the tendency of churches to welcome new immigrants, some
have become more involved in immigrant problems than others. I noted
earlier that the priest at the Catholic church in Newton Grove, North
Carolina, had stayed away from involvement in workers' rights and other
social justice issues, confining himself to more strictly religious rituals
and practices, such as holding Mass in Spanish, baptisms, blessing immigrants' pickup trucks, hearing confessions, and so forth. Instead, a local
Episcopal ministry network advocated for improved conditions for immigrants, distributing free food after Sunday services, and referred immigrants to health, legal, and other services. The Episcopal church is located
less than a mile from the Tri-County Health Center, which is part of a
health network built in part on attention to migrant workers' health, and
its clergy and their helpers have vans to shuttle migrant farmworkers as
well as settled immigrants between the church and their homes.

Schools

Like workplaces, schools have been at the forefront of immigrant integration; some are clearly more devoted to training in English as a second language (ESL) than others. School leaders in the northern communities, in
particular, view new immigrant youths as a potential source of vitality,
culture, education, and revenues. Southern school systems, while clearly
less sanguine in their reception of new immigrants, are nevertheless making efforts to accommodate the new students. Whereas principals and
other school officials in North Carolina and Georgia, when interviewed,
merely listed the kinds of ESL training they offered, school officials at
both midwestern sites were far more enthusiastic about the ways in which
they had embraced new immigrant schoolchildren.

These differences are reflected in the top panel of table 8.2, which shows
the percentage of immigrants who believe that elementary schools are
doing a good job. All of the midwestern respondents agreed that elementary schools were doing a good job, but the figure was only 83 percent
among those in the South, a statistically significant difference. Positive
evaluations of schools appear to have influenced overall evaluations of the
community. As the bottom panel of the table shows, midwestern locations
fared better than southern locations when immigrants were asked to state
their degree of liking for the community. Whereas 44 percent of midwest-

TABLE 8.2   Perceptions Among Immigrants of Community
in Which They Live (percentage)

Perceived Condition	Midwest	South
Elementary schools doing a good job		
Yes	100.0	82.8
No	0.0	17.2
Degree of liking for community		
Like it a lot	43.5	29.0
Like it quite well	50.7	51.6
Don't like very much	5.8	19.4

Source: Author's compilation.

ern immigrants said they liked their community a lot, only 29 percent of southern respondents did so. Likewise, only 6 percent of those in the Midwest said they didn't like their community very much, whereas 19 percent of those in the South did so.

Schools in the two northern sites have gone well beyond merely teaching English to new immigrants. In Marshall, the director of instruction for the public school system has taken a number of steps, in addition to offering ESL classes, to teach and retain new immigrant students. First, he took the time to learn about the cultural backgrounds of immigrant children in order to understand how such backgrounds might clash with school policies or organizational structures. He learned that Somalis come from extremely hierarchical and patriarchal tribal groups that do not conform well to the democratic organization of the public schools and that at times make it difficult for female teachers to direct male Somali students.

Second, he brought in a victim of Somali torture to speak to the staff about surviving state brutality so that teachers had a better understanding of what some Somali families may have gone through. Third, to deal with ethnic tensions among Anglo, Somali, Latino, and Asian youth, he held focus groups with members of the student body and brought in volunteer bilingual adult members of each of the immigrant groups to facilitate communication among the students and to develop "funds of cultural knowledge" among families. This was part of his continuing attempt to involve parents in their children's education. Finally, he has hired immigrants onto the staff as teachers' aides.

Each of these initiatives fed into a general strategy common throughout the region: training new immigrant youths in ways that make these youths feel welcome enough to make southwest Minnesota their home while fostering increased understanding of new immigrant cultures among native Minnesotans. Community service leaders and the public school officials, using the catchy phrase "growing our own," speak of how they hope to help their communities grow and respond to labor and business needs by providing skills to young immigrants that are relevant to the local economy.

This strategy is not confined to youth. In a meeting organized to present the benefits of adult education and ESL training to local businessmen, officials, and state political representatives, emphasis was placed on the ways in which people trained through adult education and ESL programs used their skills in the local economy. One Somali man testified that he landed his job as a clerk at K-mart only after attending ESL classes, and his manager from the store was on hand to add that without the program he wouldn't have begun hiring Somalis; now he hires them directly out of the high school and finds them to be superior employees.

As positive as Marshall's public schools and adult education programs have been, perhaps the most positive experience in the region has been that of Walnut Grove, where an influx of new Hmong students between 2000 and 2003 revitalized the local elementary school, saving it from closing. The school superintendent was grateful for the Hmong immigration:

> W. is obviously pleased with the presence of the Hmong, reporting that his own fate is tied to theirs. He purchased a farm near town and has five children. He said that having the Hmong in town is "wonderful for a parent," especially one with five children because it shows them that his size of family isn't so strange as it might be elsewhere. He said that his children don't have to go elsewhere to experience another culture, that school enrollments are up, and that because the classes are small it's impossible to not have Hmong friends. Out of nineteen new enrollments in their Kindergarten class this year, eleven are Hmong. He said that in his former position, another rural community in Minnesota, he kept seeing enrollments drop, along with state funds of $5,000 per child. They had to cut back on teachers and programs year after year. The Hmong have kept this from happening in Walnut Grove.

Like the Minnesota educators, Marshalltown school officials have expressed their enthusiasm for new immigrants by developing an innovative center of instruction based in its Woodbury Elementary School. The center is a bilingual educational program with 50 percent Latino youths and 50 percent English-speaking youths who together receive instruction in both Spanish and English with the goal of making both groups fluent in both languages. They have a waiting list and have children registered up until 2005, as well as having some English-speaking parents seeking instruction in Spanish to help their children. Parents have to agree to a five-year commitment to the program and the center has facilitated increased communication among American-born and immigrant families.

Much of the program's success is due to the background and tireless efforts of the center's director, Shelly Sosa, along with the support of the school principal, who was among one of the early local officials to visit Villachuato. Sosa's sensitivity to Latino issues and problems derives from working at the local meatpacking plant for several years, in the human resources department, where she experienced first-hand the difficulty that many Latinos in Marshalltown faced. In addition to teaching and developing curriculum for the center, she does many of the same things here for parents and children of immigrants that she did at the plant: taking a busload of people to Iowa City once a month for dental checkups, handling translations and interpreting, developing awareness of attention deficit disorder among Latinos, helping with job training, getting eyeglasses for students and mothers who don't have insurance, and so forth. She also assists school nurses with students who speak little English.

Through her position at Woodbury School, Sosa has been able to facilitate other efforts aimed at improving relations between immigrants and Marshall's native citizens. She has worked closely with the University of Iowa's New Iowans Program on the visits to Villachuato, assembling educational materials for the school there. Her husband is from Villachuato and she is assisting with the production of a video that the police are developing for new immigrants. As director of the Center for Bilingual Education, Shelly stays in touch with developments in the community that may be beneficial to her students and their families. For example, she informed the community that the police had hired a bilingual police officer and was trying to hire another, and, significantly, that it had hired a number of Hispanic jailers. "That might not sound like much," she said, "but in Marshalltown it is."

The use of the school as a platform for more successful integration was emphasized during a focus group held to assess opportunities to support Latino art and culture in Marshalltown, as well as in an exhibit at a local gallery of students' artwork. In the focus group, one participant spoke of a celebration of the Virgin of Guadalupe as follows:

> December 12th, the celebration of the Virgin of Guadalupe, [was]
> held at Woodbury School. The program lasted 2.5 hours and more

than 250 people attended. We identified with that kind of program because it was adapted to our culture. In the school, now my kids have a concert and they sing pieces in Spanish—American kids together with our kids, singing in Spanish!

Health Systems

One of the changes that our study sites have all experienced, noted in the introductory paragraphs, has been the far-reaching demographic shift from young, primarily single male migrants to somewhat older (though still young) families of immigrants. The settlement of families implies more women and children, who are more likely to access local health care systems. Rural health providers in each of the regions concur that mothers and women of childbearing age are the people most likely to access local health care systems. From interviews with rural health providers in each community, I gleaned the following list of concerns:

1. Reproductive and child health issues, including pre- and postnatal care, pregnancy and childbirth services and reproductive technologies, inoculations, and child dental care. Nearly all health providers interviewed listed these as the top health priorities among immigrants. Some added that the first thing immigrant women want to do in the United States is have children. Rural health providers were particularly concerned that many regions are isolated, with poor or nonexistent public transportation systems, and that immigrant women either do not seek adequate prenatal care or cannot access such care. Thus, major concerns among these professionals are health education and outreach.

2. Sexually transmitted diseases (STDs), particularly herpes and AIDS. The concern over STDs was highest among rural health providers in regions, notably North Carolina and Georgia, where substantial numbers of migrant farmworkers live for extended periods in the area. Nevertheless, rural health providers in the two midwestern sites listed STDs among health problems facing immigrants. This may be related to skewed sex ratios, with males still outnumbering females, the use of prostitutes, and the large numbers of young people in immigrant populations (see Kandel 2004 for data on age and sex ratios in Latino as compared to native populations). It is not uncommon in these communities to hear stories of native Anglo women who visit the houses of young male workers for serial sexual acts and have multiple partners over short time periods, with or without the expectation of being paid.

3. Alcoholism and substance abuse. Again, this seems to be more common in areas migrants continue to pass through. Studies of the farm labor force has found that substance abuse is often a part of labor-camp life, at times encouraged by labor contractors as part of schemes to keep workers in debt (Griffith et al. 1995). Substance abuse is not confined to farmworkers, however. In the mid-1990s, *U.S. News and World Report* portrayed Marshalltown as a major distribution point for methamphetamines and linked the problem to the presence of new immigrant workers.

4. Health risks associated with driving, including drunken driving and driving cars that are old and poorly maintained, thus creating hazards for drivers and for others on the road. Driving drunk may derive from home-country driving conditions, where there may be fewer cars on more isolated roads and driving drunk is considered less objectionable than in the United States. In the case of driving old and poorly maintained cars, this is related to licensing and auto insurance problems. Difficulties obtaining licenses in some areas increase the probability that, if apprehended by police, immigrants' automobiles will be impounded. Fines and impoundment fees may make it economically more feasible to abandon a car than negotiate for its return, in which case buying cheaper, older cars is more rational than buying newer and presumably safer models.

5. Domestic violence. Health providers who listed domestic violence among the problems facing immigrants usually understood that different standards of gender and age relations applied to new immigrant populations than applied to American-born citizens. While they were no more likely to forgive domestic violence because of this, they were able to place it in a context in which there were unanticipated consequences. In Minnesota, for example, one community leader mentioned that Somali women loved to dial 911, but that they were often surprised by the police response. They wanted their husbands restrained but not arrested or jailed, yet the police often had no choice but to incarcerate them. Health providers in Georgia and Iowa made similar comments in connection with Latinos.

6. Poor nutrition. When health providers cite problems associated with poor nutrition, they are usually referring to obesity, high rates of diabetes and hypertension among adults, and youth obesity from eating at fast-food restaurants. In eastern North Carolina, educating families about the health risks of obesity has become a priority

FIGURE 8.1   Hmong Healing Ritual Performed in Walnut Grove, Minnesota

Source: Photo by Harry Yang.

area in research and outreach efforts, particularly because large numbers of African Americans suffer from diabetes. This has burdened the region's principal medical center at East Carolina University so much that one physician recently commented that all the medical centers in this part of the state "dump their worst cases on us."[7] The university's AgroMedicine Center, a center dedicated to health issues in rural areas, has been conducting a research and educational effort entitled "Growing Up Fit" to deal with youth obesity in the region.

7.   Noncompliance with drug regimens and drug interactions with alternative therapies. Our information about native "curanderas," midwives, and others who provide alternative therapies is limited and anecdotal, but field workers did encounter stories of native healers. The photographs (figures 8.1 and 8.2) are of a Hmong shaman performing a healing ritual and a soul retention ritual in Walnut Grove; Ann Fadiman's (1994) profile of a Hmong child with epilepsy in Merced County, California, offers piercing evidence of the problems that can develop when both conventional and alternative curing methods are used. In eastern North Carolina, health providers mentioned that they

FIGURE 8.2   Hmong Soul Retention Ritual Performed in
Walnut Grove, Minnesota

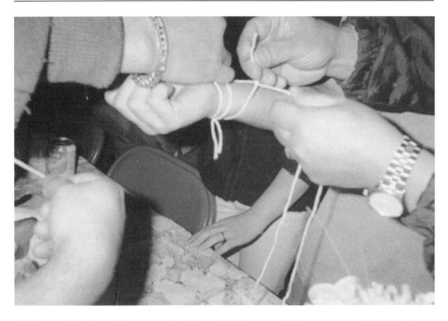

Source: Photo by Harry Yang.

believed Honduran immigrants were sponsoring the migration of
native healers. One of the principal Honduran entrepreneurs in the
state was trained as a physician in Honduras; although he cannot
practice in the United States, he consults with local physicians to
assure accurate diagnoses, reporting that a great deal of noncompliance with drug regimens derives from translation problems. Others
reported that Latin ideas about hot and cold foods influenced whether
or not immigrants followed health providers' advice.

8.   Other problems. Although not perceived as high-priority areas, individual health providers also mentioned lead poisoning from renting
old homes, tuberculosis, lack of health insurance and consequent use
of emergency rooms, and occupational injury. The failure of most
health providers to acknowledge occupational injury as a primary
health risk facing immigrants is odd, given the high rates of injury
common in many branches of the food industry (Stull, Broadway, and
Griffith 1995; Stull and Broadway 2004).

The health problems facing new immigrants in these communities
have been exacerbated by problems generally facing rural health centers.

Beyond chronic shortages of rural health providers, particularly physicians, a major challenge in dealing with immigrants is finding suitable translators. In regions that have long had a migrant farm-labor force, such as eastern North Carolina, health centers have hired several Spanish-speaking staff members over the years, yet even these individuals have difficulty translating adequately for new waves of indigenous-language speakers from Mexico (for example, who speak Mixtec), let alone translating for Somalis, Sudanese, Hmong, or other ethnic groups. Many rural health centers have relied on bilingual children in immigrant households to translate, but many have moved away from this because of the obvious problems of relying on children to translate difficult or embarrassing medical information. But hiring adults from the community is not always a feasible option: in southern Georgia, for example, one of the principal adult translators at a local health center was a Georgia woman who was married to a Latino man and spoke very rudimentary Spanish; in other cases, speakers of Tex-Mex, a mixture of Spanish and English, have been used with limited success.

Limited Spanish on the part of rural health providers, particularly physicians, has led to problems with establishing trust between patients and health providers and between health centers and immigrant communities. Several rural health providers mentioned that developing trusting relationships with new immigrants was a challenge not only because of language difficulties but also because of the amount of information health centers require, the problems with undocumented immigrants, and differences between medical practices in the home country and the receiving region. The Honduran physician mentioned above has been developing a new Spanish intake form to deal with at least some of these concerns.

Finally, two other problems noted by health providers and by our field observations were the lack of public transportation in rural areas and health centers that served one ethnic group to the exclusion of others. The solution to the first issue is fairly straightforward, but the second is more complicated, as it occurs primarily in the southern regions and derives from mistrust between African Americans and Latinos. This mistrust occurs especially in places where Latinos are seen as displacing African Americans from specific jobs, such as poultry processing (Griffith 1993). New immigrant Latinos in the South commonly report that African Americans discriminate against them more than Anglos, and it is not uncommon to hear Latinos make racist comments about African Americans.

As a result of these intergroup tensions, over time the staff and clientele of some rural health centers have become dominated by either African Americans or Latinos, and efforts to reach out to the other group have become frustrated by an indifference on the part of other staff members or discomfort on the part of patients sitting in waiting rooms among people toward whom they may feel hostility. This hostility is encouraged by access to different funding streams as well: centers whose funding comes from migrant health networks may focus on Latinos to the exclusion of African Americans.

INTERNAL DIFFERENTIATION OF IMMIGRANTS

Local observers may consider immigrant groups homogeneous, but it is clear that they are not. The ways in which new immigrant populations are becoming differentiated from one another are among the more fascinating aspects of the immigrant settlement process. Here I discuss a case from Marshalltown, Iowa, that illustrates some of the processes by which immigrant groups have become internally differentiated.

Entrepreneurs and Meatpackers

This case contrasts entrepreneurial and meatpacking immigrants in Marshalltown, where relations of trust and mutual cooperation have developed among higher-class Latino immigrants in Marshalltown. Based on ethnic background, region of origin, and level of entrepreneurship and education, a small group (<50) of Jalisco-based new Latino immigrants in Marshalltown have become differentiated from the much larger (8,000 to 9,000) group of new Latino immigrants primarily from Villachuato, Michoacán. Most of the Villachuato immigrants work at the pork-packing plant; most also come directly from Mexico, with family members who are already in Marshalltown financing their travel.

By contrast, the Jalisco group own new businesses in Marshalltown; they arrived as part of a step-migration process, settling first in California, then moving from California to Chicago, and from Chicago learning about the growing Latino population in Marshalltown. They came from backgrounds in business or working in businesses owned by family members or friends, although a few have also spent time in factories or other unskilled, low-wage work while learning English. Significantly, too, they have all worked to secure permanent resident status for themselves and their children, while many of the Michoacán immigrants remain undocumented. In Marshalltown, the Jalisco group members I discuss here include one realtor, one owner of an auto mechanic shop, one store owner, and one restaurant owner. These businesses account for over 70 percent of the Latino-owned businesses in Marshalltown, and their stability and success is in part due to the connections that exist among themselves and with

FIGURE 8.3   Relations Among Jalisco-Based Entrepreneurs in Marshalltown

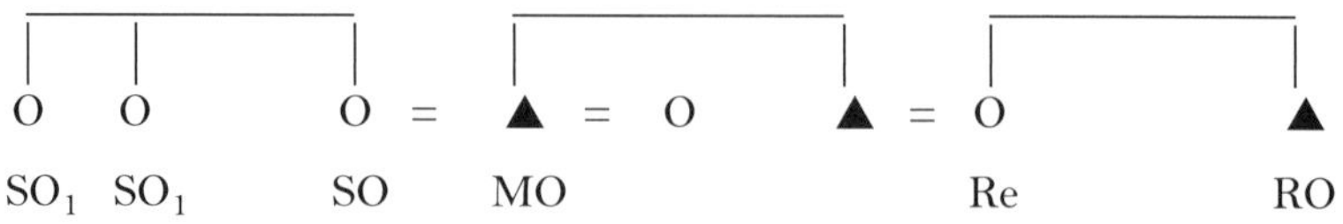

SO = Store Owner
Re = Realtor
RO = Restaurant Owner
MO = Mechanic Owner
SO$_1$ = Store Owner in another town
= friendship or business adviser tie

Source: Author's compilation.

other Latino business owners in Iowa. Figure 8.3 outlines these connections, which include family and friendship or business adviser ties. For example, although no family ties exist between the store owner (SO) and the auto mechanic shop owner (M), the store owner listed the mechanic as a key person she relies on for business advice in Marshalltown.

With the exception of the auto mechanic, who caters primarily to Anglos, the Latino entrepreneurs rely primarily on Michoacán Latinos as customers and have emerged as informal Latino leaders in the town. The store and restaurant owners also hire local Latinos to work in their businesses, as do the owners of the stores in the other towns. The restaurant is one of the oldest Latino businesses in Marshalltown and was one of the first venues for Latinos to learn about the problems facing other Latinos in town, including those from Michoacán.

Interactions between the Jalisco entrepreneurs and the Michoacán immigrants do not end at work. Formal leaders of the town, such as the police chief or the mayor, typically rely on the Jalisco entrepreneurs as informal cultural liaisons, brokers, and translators in cases where problems between new immigrants and local residents have occurred. In addition, most of the members of the Latino entrepreneurial class have at one time or another assisted a new immigrant family in some way as well as established significant fictive kinship ties or relationships approximating kin ties with one or two local Marshalltown residents. The realtor, in particular, has been active in assisting new immigrants not only with finding housing but also with accessing medical care, educational services for their children, and advising local businesspeople about how to better interact with the Latino community. She also has formed friendship and fictive kinship ties with several members of the community, including local Anglo activists for the Latino community and an elderly retired engineer who has encouraged her daughters to pursue engineering in college. The others have, at times condescendingly, performed translation and other services for newly arriving Spanish-speaking immigrants, despite the fact that a large knowledge base about adjusting to Marshalltown exists within the working class Michoacán immigrants.

Many families from Michoacán have some children who are United States citizens and others who remain undocumented. As younger Latinos enter the workforce with English-language skills, some are moving into other sectors of the economy, although still primarily as unskilled or semi-skilled laborers in jobs such as bank teller or fast-food worker, and still others are seeking educational opportunities. Persistent high Latino school dropout rates, however, indicate that many youths are moving into meat-packing and similar jobs as soon as they can, reproducing the Latino working class in Marshalltown.

Many of these Latino children have few if any ties to their parents' Mexican communities, despite the strong general tie that exists between Villachuato and Marshalltown. The Jalisco group has not participated in the exchanges with Villachuato in any significant way. Their positions in the community remain largely informal, vis-à-vis both the new immigrant Latinos and the formal leadership of Marshalltown, and are based on network ties among one another and to native residents of Marshalltown who recognize their business abilities.

CONCLUSION: CLASS, TRUST, AND STATE FRAGMENTATION

Class relations among immigrants overlie their ethnic and linguistic similarities and their shared religious, cultural, and political histories without significantly altering the material consequences that unequal class positions entail. In addition, they tend to be multifaceted rather than restricted to a single dimension, such as an employer-employee or land-lord-tenant relationship. Like class relations in general, class relations among immigrants range from highly exploitative, potentially dangerous relations, as between networks of labor smugglers or contractors and new immigrants, to the more paternal relations between Jalisco and Michoacán immigrants in Marshalltown. These different manifestations reflect the dominant class positions toward immigrants in general, which also range from highly exploitative to combinations of paternalism and exploitation,

sometimes grounded in partnerships and other mutually beneficial relations, and their variability in some cases helps disguise them. In all
cases, however, class relations depend on a combination of organized
power (specifically the state's ability to confer legal status, enforce immigration law, and so forth) and ties within and between dominating classes.
In many cases, too, shared ethnic and linguistic backgrounds inside otherwise hostile, foreign environments can reinforce class relations through
relations based largely on trust. This occurs within as well as between
classes of immigrants, where trust becomes an important component of
solidifying one's class position and of maintaining class divisions.

These observations speak directly to one of the guiding theoretical perspectives in immigration research today: considering immigrants primarily as actors in "transnational social fields" (Glick-Schiller 1999, 97; Basch,
Glick-Schiller, and Szanton Blanc 1994; Guarnizo 2001). Among the more
important elements of this perspective is its focus on the active participation of migrating families in at least two states simultaneously, and
its emphasis on political activity in sending and receiving countries.
Through transnational social fields, sending states expand the reach of
their sovereignty, encouraging their citizens living abroad to participate
in receiving-country politics and thereby to influence international relations. These activities differentiate previous generations of transnational
immigrants from their contemporary counterparts because earlier immigrants tended to leave their home countries as those states were still in
the process of nation building; they thus had little sense of national identity (Foner 1997). Others consider transnationalism today as qualitatively
and quantitatively distinct from nineteenth- and early-twentieth-century
forms because improved telecommunications have stepped up the rate and
frequency of exchange and allowed the development of qualitatively distinct communications (Portes, Guarnizo, and Landolt 1999). Proponents
of the notion of transnationalism also emphasize the construction of hybrid
identities that derive from continual and frequent exchanges of people, information, goods, money, cultural knowledge, and other contacts between
sending and receiving nations.

Our research suggests that transnational processes are occurring at the
same time that developments within these communities reduce the ability of immigrants to sustain these processes over time. The cultural
exchanges between Villachuato, Michoacán and Marshalltown, Iowa, for
example, now formalized through funded and institutionalized connections involving mayors, school principals, and other community leaders,
are evidence that the elaboration of transnational social fields can draw
upon local political and economic resources in receiving settings to widen
and deepen international communication. Yet the active attempts by local

school authorities in Marshall and Marshalltown to encourage youths to remain in Minnesota and Iowa, if sustained, are likely to undermine the attachments that immigrant youths and the American-born children of immigrant families feel toward sending countries. Some parents had phased back ties to their home countries, visiting less frequently, as their children grew more attached to receiving communities.

Our work also raises several issues to consider in formulating new research into the formation, elaboration, reproduction, and dissolution of transnational social fields. First, a disproportionate amount of attention devoted to political activity, including state communications and the rhetoric of party politics, implies that both sending and receiving states, as well as immigrants themselves, are more internally homogeneous in their interests than the above discussion suggests. In each of the communities profiled, divisions within immigrant populations derive from several sources, including class backgrounds and legal status, and different legal statuses of members of the same family can affect access to state resources, particularly education. These divisions influence the propensity for immigrants to engage in political activity, as well as the quality of such engagement. Class and ethnicity have always influenced political participation, and in this chapter I have pointed out the ways that class- and ethnic-based divisions emerge within immigrant populations from the same nation-states. Further, states are fragmented entities, and state positions, activities, and policies penetrate immigrant families' lives unevenly, influenced by such factors as class, legal status, language ability, education, occupation, the propensity of state and municipal governments to enforce federal immigration law, and immigrants' perception of being welcome or unwelcome.

More generally, the information presented above suggests that research on transnational social fields needs to consider the influence of local settings on the propensity for new immigrant families to form attachments to adopted, receiving communities, to embrace transnational social fields, or to develop hybrid identities and allegiances that allow meaningful participation in sending and receiving communities. The comparisons between southern and midwestern locations suggest that local communities can influence immigrants' attitudes toward schools and other community institutions, which in turn affect the propensities of immigrant families to remain in communities indefinitely, return to natal communities, or move elsewhere. Settlement is occurring unevenly in all the communities we studied. Our focus on the process of settlement inevitably drew our attention to the ways that immigrant families are elaborating their ties to the local economy, churches, schools, health care systems, and other community institutions, including the participation of community natives in these processes. Local settings condition immigrants' experiences in ways that influence their social and cultural ties to regions, to communities, and to each other. Although comparisons between southern and midwestern new immigrant destinations imply regional differences in these processes, a fruitful area of future research would be to consider whether or not rural and urban locations stimulate qualitatively distinct processes of settlement.

The author would like to thank the many immigrants and natives who made this study possible, as well Ed Kissam, of Aguirre International, and the USDA's Fund For Rural America for a productive research relationship. Thanks also to my research assistants Silvia Aleman, Felixa Amato, Ana Maria Araos Chavez, Gustavo Estrada, Edith Fernández-Baca, Anna García, Isabel Gutierrez-Montes, Emily Jo Jackson, Lucy Lopez, Paul Nielson, Jose Carlos Requena, and Harris Yang. Finally, thanks to Neal and Jan Flora at Iowa State University, Mark Grey at University of Northern Iowa, and Joe Amato and Anthony Amato at Southwestern State University in Marshall, Minnesota.

NOTES

1. Personal communication from Jan Flora, sociology professor, Iowa State University.
2. With the exception of authors and other known figures, all the names used here are pseudonyms.
3. Author's field notes, May 3, 2002.
4. Author's field notes, January 2001.
5. The survey data consist of 377 structured interviews across the four regions: 271 were with immigrants and 106 with natives. Sampling was done either randomly or through a cluster sampling design. By region, we interviewed 86 immigrants in Minnesota, 71 in Iowa, 72 in North Carolina, and 52 in Georgia.
6. Author's field notes, January 2001.
7. Personal communication from Dr. Ed Janowsko, urologist.

REFERENCES

Amato, Anthony, Janet Timmerman, and Joseph Amato, editors. 1999. *Draining the Great Oasis*. Marshall, Minn.: Crossings Press.

Amato, Joseph A. 1996. *To Call It Home: The New Immigrants of Southwest Minnesota*. Marshall, Minn.: Crossings Press.

Basch, Linda, Nina Glick-Schiller, and Cristina Szanton Blanc. 1994. *Nations Unbound: Transnational Projects, Postcolonial Predicaments, and Deterritorialized Nation-States*. Langhorns, Penn.: Gordon & Breach.

Benson, Janet. 1990. "Good Neighbors: Ethnic Relations in Garden City Trailer Courts." *Urban Anthropology* 19(3): 361–86.

Bump, Micah. 2005. "From Temporary Picking to Permanent Plucking: Hispanic Newcomers, Integration, and Change in the Shenandoah Valley." In *Beyond the Gateway: Immigrants in a Changing America*, edited by Elzbieta Gozdziak and Susan Martin. Lanham, Md.: Lexington Books.

Calavita, Kitty. 1992. *Inside the State: The Bracero Program, Immigration, and the INS*. New York: Routledge & Kegan Paul.

Commission on Agricultural Workers. 1993. "Appendix I: Case Studies and Research Reports." Washington: U.S. Government Printing Office.

ConAgra Foods. 2004. *Healthy, Slim & Reddi: 2004 Annual Report*. Omaha: ConAgra Foods.

Fadiman, Ann. 1994. *The Spirit Catches You and You Fall Down*. New York: Farrar Straus & Giroux.

Fink, Leon. 2003. *The Maya of Morgantown*. Chapel Hill, N.C.: University of North Carolina Press.

Foner, Nancy. 1997. "What's New About Transnationalism? New York Immigrants Today and at the Turn of the Century." *Diaspora* 6(3): 366–75.

Glick-Schiller, Nina. 1999. "Transmigrants and Nation-States: Something Old and Something New in the U.S. Immigrant Experience." In *The Handbook of International Migration: The American Experience*, edited by Charles Hirschman, Philip Kasinitz, and Josh DeWind. New York: Russell Sage Foundation.

Gozdziak, Elzbieta, and Susan F. Martin. 2005. *Beyond the Gateway: Immigrants in a Changing America*. Lanham, Md.: Lexington Books.

Gray, Margaret. 2005. "Latino Farmworkers in New York: Power, Constraints, Advocacy, and Backlash." Paper presented at Cumbre 2005, Re-Visioning Latino America: New Perspectives on Migration, Transnationalism, and Integration. University of Nebraska, Omaha, April 22, 2005.

Grey, Mark A. 1999. "Immigrants, Migration, and Worker Turnover at the Hog Pride Pork Packing Plant." *Human Organization* 58(1): 16–27.

Grey, Mark A., and Anne Woodrick. 2002. "Unofficial Sister Cities: Meatpacking Labor Migration Between Villachuato, Mexico, and Marshalltown, Iowa." *Human Organization* 61(4): 364–76.

Grey, Mark A., Andrew Lonead, Maureen Boyd, and Ann Woodrick. 2001. *Marshalltown New Iowans Pilot Community Assessment*. Cedar Falls, Iowa: UNI New Iowans Program.

Griffith, David C. 1993. *Jones's Minimal: Low-wage Labor in the United States*. Albany, N.Y.: State University of New York Press.

———. 2006. *American Guestworkers: Jamaicans and Mexicans in the U.S. Labor Market*. University Park, Penn.: Penn State University Press.

Griffith, David C., Ed Kissam, Jeronimo Camposeco, Anna Garcia, Max Pfeffer, David Runsten, and Manuel Valdés Pizzini. 1995. *Working Poor: Farmworkers in the United States*. Philadelphia, Penn.: Temple University Press.

Guarnizo, Luis Eduardo. 2001. "On the Political Participation of Transnational Migrants: Old Practices and New Trends." In *E Pluribus Unum? Contemporary and Historical Perspectives on Immigrant Political Incorporation*, edited by Gary Gerstle and John Mollenkopf. New York: Russell Sage Foundation.

Hahamovich, Cynthia. 1997. *The Fruits of their Labor*. Chapel Hill, N.C.: University of North Carolina Press.

Kandel, William. 2004. "Hispanics in the United States." Keynote address to the first annual conference on Working with Latinos and Hispanics in the United States. October 27, 2004, San Juan, Puerto Rico.

Massey, Douglas, Joaquin Arango, Graeme Hugo, Ali Kouaouci, Adela Pellegrino, and J. Edward Taylor. 1993. "Theories of International Migration: A Review and Appraisal." *Population and Development Review* 19(3): 939–99.

Nestle, Marion. 2002. *Food Politics: How the Food Industry Influences Nutrition and Health*. Berkeley, Calif.: University of California Press.

Portes, Alejandro. 1994. "Introduction: Immigration and Its Aftermath." *International Migration Review* 28(4): 632–9.

Portes, Alejandro, and Robert Bach. 1985. *Latin Journey: Cuban and Mexican Immigrants in the United States*. Berkeley, Calif.: University of California Press.

Portes, Alejandro, Luis Eduardo Guarnizo, and Patricia Landolt. 1999. "Introduction: Pitfalls and Promise of an Emergent Research Field." *Ethnic and Racial Studies* 22(2): 217–37.

Preibisch, Kerry. 2003. "Social Relations Practices Between Seasonal Agricultural Workers, Their Employers, and the Residents of Rural Ontario." Report to the North-South Institute, Ottawa, Canada. Guelph, Ont.: University of Guelph.

Pringle, Peter. 2003. *Food, Inc.: Mendel to Monsanto—The Promises and Perils of the Biotech Harvest*. New York: Simon & Schuster.

Quinn, Tom. N.d. "Iowa Community Voices Program for Spanish-speakers." Fact sheet. Ames, Iowa: Iowa State University, Extension Service.

Rothenberg, Daniel. 1998. *With These Hands: The Hidden World of Migrant Farmworkers Today*. New York: Harcourt Brace.

Roy, Corinna, and Greg Owen. 2001. *Southwest Minnesota: A Needs Assessment*. Report prepared for the Community Action Agencies of Southwest Minnesota. St. Paul, Minn.: Wilder Research Center.

Schlosser, Eric. 2001. *Fast Food Nation: The Dark Side of the All-American Meal*. New York: Farrar, Straus & Giroux.

Stull, Donald, and Michael Broadway. 2004. *Slaughterhouse Blues: The Meat and Poultry Industry in North America*. Belmont, Calif.: Wadsworth/Thomson.

Stull, Donald, Michael Broadway, and David Griffith, editors. 1995. *Any Way You Cut It: Meat Processing and Small Town America*. Lawrence, Kan.: University of Kansas Press.

Woodrick, Anne, and Mark A. Grey. 2002. *Welcoming New Iowans: A Guide for Christians and Churches*. Cedar Falls, Iowa: University of Northern Iowa, Welcoming New Iowans Program, and Ecumenical Ministries of Iowa.

CHAPTER 9

HISPANIC IMMIGRATION, BLACK POPULATION SIZE, AND INTERGROUP RELATIONS IN THE RURAL AND SMALL-TOWN SOUTH

HELEN B. MARROW

American immigration scholars are rapidly gaining interest in "new immigrant destinations"—locales that have little historical experience of post-1965 immigration but which are now receiving immigrants (Durand, Massey, and Charvet 2000; Massey, Durand, and Parrado 1999; Zúñiga and Hernández-León 2005). Implicit in this new interest is the assumption that "context matters." New immigrant destinations raise eyebrows because of the various ways, both objective and subjective, that geographic place and demographic context affect lives. The size and characteristics of cities, towns, and rural areas can be expected to influence how immigrants experience the United States and interact with local Americans; how local Americans react to new immigrants and receive them; and how existing institutional structures, cultures, and historical memories factor into the long-term incorporation of immigrants at the "new" destinations, versus "old" historical destinations in major cities.

The sheer range of new immigrant destinations sets the stage for comparative research on how new destination contexts matter to immigrant incorporation processes at various levels of analysis (Jones-Correa 2005, 88; Marrow 2005). Here, I use results from participant observation and in-depth interviews in a new destination area to examine how the size and relative status of the local African American population affects Hispanic newcomers' experiences of incorporation in the rural and small-town South.[1] What stands out most about the majority (but not all) of new immigrant destinations across the American South are their larger proportions of African Americans and their stronger "binary" conception of

211

race and racial hierarchy, compared to other places in the United States (see McClain et al. 2006). That is, the American South continues to be the home of a majority of the nation's African Americans, the urban South continues to be disproportionately black and white, and southern blacks still identify more cohesively as a racial group in census data (that is, identifying themselves as "blacks" alone) than do non-southern blacks. Moreover, recent demographic trends have reinforced the region's unique racial profile. The region witnessed greater in-migration of native whites and blacks than of nonwhites and nonblacks in the 1990s (Frey 2001, 2002; Greenbaum 1998; Kochhar, Suro, and Tafoya 2005; McClain et al. 2003; Stack 1996). In this way, the pattern noted by some, whereby "recent immigrants have tended to concentrate in cities in the Southwest and in coastal cities that contain relatively smaller numbers of African Americans but relatively larger numbers of Hispanics" (Bean, Van Hook, and Fossett 1999, 34) is reversed: for now, native African American populations in many southern locales outnumber new immigrant populations (Schmidley 2003).

The American South thus provides a unique opportunity to examine the effects of Hispanic newcomers and African Americans on each other in places where the African American community is proportionately large and cohesively identified, and where Hispanic populations are newer, less established, and not as large as they are in traditional immigrant-receiving states and cities. In fact, when we hear that immigrants are now settling in the South, it is precisely the region's higher proportions of African Americans and historical memory and current lived reality of black-white tension that piques our concern about how newcomers will fare, get along with local residents, and affect local residents' relative standings in the social hierarchy.

BLACK-HISPANIC RELATIONS IN THE SOUTH

Generally speaking, the existing literature on immigrant incorporation and intergroup relations in the United States documents serious black-Hispanic tensions. Even in national-level public opinion data, black-Hispanic relations are viewed as more negative than others, including white-Hispanic ones. For example, "In another Gallup poll in 2004, almost three quarters of Americans agreed that relations between whites and blacks, and between whites and Hispanics, are 'very' or 'somewhat' good. They judged white-Asian relations to be a little better and black-Hispanic relations to be a little worse" (Hochschild 2007, 165).

Three basic theoretical models attempt to account for more negative black-Hispanic compared to white-Hispanic relations by focusing on black-

Hispanic competition for economic and political local resources: two economic interest models (personal and group) and the sociological group position model.[2] Keeping these three models in mind, how might the higher proportions of African Americans in the South affect black-Hispanic relations as compared to the situation in other regions and major immigrant-receiving cities? Here, I review two contrasting hypotheses, which I then utilize to guide my analysis of how and why black-Hispanic relations vary across two rural southern counties with different proportions of African Americans.

The first hypothesis is that higher proportions of African Americans in the South will smooth black-Hispanic tensions compared to what often occurs elsewhere. The argument here is that the higher proportions of African Americans in the South may reduce African Americans' feelings of being threatened because of the effect of their own "strength in numbers." That is, higher proportions of African Americans may serve as a shield to feelings of individual-level or group-level socioeconomic or political threat from Hispanic newcomers, potentially smoothing black-Hispanic relations.

More generally, according to this "strength-in-numbers" line of reasoning, higher proportions of African Americans in the South may translate into more opportunities for black-Hispanic contact and, consequently, cooperation and coalition building than would be the case in places with smaller African American populations. In particular, the large number of progressive organizations in the region, which have grown out of the civil rights movement, may help smooth black-Hispanic relations by engaging in proactive coalition building strategies (Smith 2003, 30). Perhaps the more numerous these organizations and the larger the populations of African American constituents they reach, the more progress toward smoothing black-Hispanic relations in the South we will see.

A contrasting hypothesis is that higher proportions of African Americans in the South will exacerbate black-Hispanic tensions. Although it is the case that higher proportions of African Americans in the South may produce more opportunities for black-Hispanic contact and, consequently, cooperation and coalition-building than they would in places with smaller African American populations, it is also the case that they may produce more opportunities for black-Hispanic competition and conflict, as greater numbers of African Americans begin to see themselves in either individual or group-level competition with Hispanic newcomers. Together, these hypotheses represent two directions black-Hispanic relations might go in a heavily African American region of the country, as would be loosely predicted by contact theory.

One ongoing research project, directed by Paula McClain in Durham, North Carolina, offers some preliminary evidence in favor of the second hypothesis—that higher proportions of African Americans in the South are likely to exacerbate rather than smooth negative black-Hispanic relations in comparison to other places. In the year 2000, African Americans constituted almost half of Durham's population: 46 percent of Durham's population identified as white, 44 percent as black, 0.3 percent as Native American, 4 percent as Asian, 5 percent as "other race," and 9 percent as Hispanic or Latino of any race. Durham also has a long-established history of biracial politics and has historically had a very prosperous upper and upper middle class black community (McClain et al. 2003, 19).

Using survey data of 500 residents and twenty-two interviews with elite leaders in Durham, McClain and colleagues found that "relations between the older established black community and the new Latino immigrants are strained and stem from a dislike of each other," and that "the fact that these strains exist at this early stage does not bode well for future social and political relations in Durham" (McClain et al. 2003, 42–43). McClain and colleagues uncovered several disturbing findings: that "Latino immigrants do indeed feel that they have more in common with whites than with blacks," that "contact between blacks and Latinos seems to increase the probabilities that Latino immigrants will see a difference between themselves and blacks," that while "blacks are divided on whether Latinos are taking jobs from blacks, close to two-thirds feel that if Latino immigration continues at its present rate, black economic opportunity will be threatened," that "while an overwhelming majority of Durham blacks believe that Latinos have too little political influence in life and politics, almost half believe that if Latino immigration continues at the present rate blacks will lose political power and influence," and finally, that "blacks are more likely [than whites] to see their political power threatened" (41–42). In a later publication, McClain and colleagues (2006) reconfirm that Latino immigrants hold very stereotypical views of blacks (even more so than whites do), and that contact specifically in neighborhood settings intensifies blacks' and Latinos' stereotypes of each other as well as Latinos' likelihood of feeling they have more in common with whites than with blacks.

OVERVIEW OF FINDINGS

My research findings show that the proportion of African Americans at the local county level does indeed affect Hispanics' incorporation experiences in the rural and small-town American South, but that it does not affect them uniformly. Rather, it affects incorporation differently in the socioeconomic and political arenas. In the socioeconomic arena, I will show that the higher proportion of African Americans in majority-black Bedford County compared to majority-white Wilcox County (both pseudonyms for the two counties in North Carolina where I conducted my research) exacerbates black-Hispanic tensions by elevating African Americans' sense of individual- and group-level threat. In contrast, in the local political arena, I will show that the higher proportion of African Americans in majority-black Bedford County compared to majority-white Wilcox County smoothes black-Hispanic tensions by protecting African Americans from feelings of threat, at least initially.

On the one hand this reflects the fact that Hispanic newcomers in both counties currently wield more economic than political power. Although most work, many are undocumented labor migrants and thus are automatically excluded from participating in electoral politics, and others are recent immigrants still learning the ropes of the American political system. In fact, Hispanic respondents, such as Lidia, an immigrant from Oaxaca, Mexico, living in Wilcox County, readily acknowledge their lack of political power in the area, frequently contrasting it with their ability to "work hard" (economic power):

> Lidia: I think the needs of blacks compared with the needs of Latinos are very different. In first place, blacks are [American] citizens. They can express all their rights. And in contrast, Latinos aren't citizens. And they can't ask politicians for special attention. All they can do is . . . their economic impact, that is the only source of strength that Latin Americans have in this country. Latinos are not public charges. They are hardworking people who come here to fight for a better well-being for their families. And I think that for that aspect, the politicians should pay them a little more attention.

In both counties, then, Hispanic newcomers' presence is not as immediately threatening to blacks' political positions as it is to blacks' socioeconomic positions.

On the other hand, I argue that this also reflects how African Americans' "strength in numbers" and progress have been accrued primarily in the political, not the economic, arena since the civil rights movement, especially in the rural South, where the black middle class is weak. African Americans in both counties thus enjoy a significant "competitive edge in the public and political arena" (Morawska 2001, 61) that they do not necessarily enjoy in the low-wage private sector, where Hispanic newcomers pose a greater threat to their socioeconomic positions. I will show that this is especially the case in majority-black Bedford County, where the high proportion of African Americans creates a greater degree of political security than exists in Wilcox County; this protects them from an immediate sense of political threat in a way that it does not do in the socioeconomic arena.

In other words, I show that black-Hispanic tensions in the rural and small-town South are indeed structured by demographic context (the size of the local African American community) but also by institutional arena of incorporation (where African Americans and Hispanic newcomers hold and exert most of their power). Together, these findings strengthen the call to pay more attention to both demographic context and institutional arena of incorporation in research on immigrant incorporation and intergroup relations (Jones-Correa 2005, 88), including in new immigrant destinations.

SITE SELECTION

I selected two "new" rural southern immigrant destination counties in the state of North Carolina (called here Bedford and Wilcox Counties) for three reasons. First, according to the designations used in the 2000 United States Census, North Carolina experienced the highest rates of growth in its "Hispanic/Latino" (394 percent) and "immigrant" (274 percent) populations out of all states during the 1990s (McClain et al. 2006, 576; Mohl 2003, 38; Suro and Singer 2002). Second, the national economic downturn of the early 2000s was manifested as significant downsizing and restructuring in four major areas that, when viewed together, negatively affected North Carolinians as much as residents of any other state, owing to North Carolina's particular industrial mix: tobacco (agricultural restructuring), textiles (blue collar restructuring), telecommunications (white collar restructuring), and antiterrorism companies (general restructuring).[3] Finally, to compare two counties at the local level we need to hold some higher-level factors constant; here, state-level economic conditions and opportunities and state-level attitudes toward immigration are held constant.

These two counties are similar in other regards. Both counties are non-metropolitan as well as southern, and both are located in the same generally impoverished rural eastern region of North Carolina.[4] United States census data for 2000 show that both counties' populations are more heavily engaged in agriculture and transformative industries such as construction and manufacturing, and less engaged in professional, financial, and arts services and activities than either the total national or total North Carolina state populations. Moreover, both counties' populations are less well educated, earn less income, post higher unemployment rates, and are more heavily represented below the poverty line than either the national or state averages for these indicators. In fact, their unemployment rates were at least twice that of the national rate before the onset of the recession of the early 2000s, their individual poverty rates are just under 20 percent each, and Bedford County only left its "persistent poverty status" in the 1990s (Miller and Weber 2004).

Together, these characteristics mean that even though North Carolina has historically been considered more progressive than other southern states (Key, Jr. 1949/1984, 205), its rural eastern region resembles the rest of the Deep South more than do its central Piedmont or western mountain regions (215). And within North Carolina, the greatest growth in the Hispanic population has occurred along the I-85 corridor in the central Piedmont region (near the major metropolitan areas experiencing rapid population and economic growth) and near major military bases (Kochhar, Suro, and Tafoya 2005, 20; Johnson, Jr., Johnson-Webb, and Farrell 1999). Hispanics and immigrants have settled in small towns and rural areas throughout the state, but they are fewer in number and have received much less academic or policy attention to date for that reason, as well as for the relative lack of resources in small towns and rural areas compared to their metropolitan counterparts. Thus, the choice of these two counties reflects my interest in the increasing geographic dispersion of immigration outside of metropolitan areas as well as outside of traditional immigrant-receiving regions and states (see also Kandel and Parrado 2004; Saenz and Torres 2003).

Despite their overall similarities, there are important differences in the local economic and social receiving contexts of these two counties that fall along four general dimensions:

- The nature and operation of their primary immigrant-receiving economies

- Their rates of population growth over the 1990s

- The absolute and relative proportions of their "Hispanic/Latino" and "immigrant" populations

- The demographic relationship of their "Hispanic/Latino" populations to their African American populations

On the one hand, Wilcox County posted a 23 percent increase in its population over the 1990s, which is slightly higher than the population increase for all of North Carolina and well above the 13 percent national increase. Much of the population increase here is tied to immigration, especially in the county's large agricultural sector and booming poultry- and hog-processing sectors, which withstood the recession of the early

2000s relatively well. Consequently, in Wilcox County the proportion of "Hispanics/Latinos" and "other race" persons identified in the 2000 United States census is very high—15 percent and 11 percent, respectively—at least compared to the North Carolina state averages of 5 percent and 2 percent. Finally, in Wilcox County, the proportion of Hispanics (15 percent) is approximately half of the African American population (29 percent).

On the other hand, Bedford County was one of only three counties in North Carolina to lose population over the 1990s—and according to one local county commissioner, the only county in the state to lose population over both the 1980s and 1990s. This loss was partly due to a devastating flood in the fall of 1999, but even more so to the cumulative negative impact of job losses and industry relocations in both its white collar telecommunications and blue collar textile and manufacturing industries over the 1980s and 1990s. Consequently, while immigration has been occurring in Bedford County, primarily in the agricultural and "transformative" (manufacturing and construction) sectors, the proportions of Bedford County's "Hispanic/Latino" and "other race" populations in 2000 are low—3 percent and 2 percent, respectively—even by North Carolina state standards and certainly by national standards. Furthermore, these proportions remain far lower than the very high proportion of African Americans in this majority-black county (58 percent). In fact, today Bedford County ranks fourth in the state of North Carolina in the proportionate size of its African American population, and it is a historical center of North Carolina's section of the southern "black belt" (Key, Jr. 1949/1984).

Overall, these county-level demographic differences between Bedford and Wilcox Counties serve as a proxy for two distinct local social, racial, and economic contexts in the rural South that new immigrants are entering today, even though the two counties lie in the same generally impoverished eastern region of North Carolina and have African American population proportions high enough to be characteristic of the racially divided rural American South (Reed 1993, 7–8):

> [In 1920] a band of rural counties with substantial black populations . . . traced the area of cotton cultivation and plantation agriculture, in a long arc from southeastern Virginia down and across to eastern Texas, with arms north and south along the Mississippi River. This is the Deep South—what a geographer would call the "core area" of the region defined by its staple-crop economy. . . . Two out of three Southerners are now urban folk, and most rural Southerners work in industry anyway, but the fossil remains of this old South can still be found as concentrations of poor, rural black Southerners.

Most specifically, these county-level differences provide a valuable opportunity to analyze and compare Hispanics' experiences and intergroup relations in the context of stagnating or declining low-wage industries, such as tobacco agriculture and routine manufacturing and textiles, with their experiences in the context of expanding low-wage industries, such as food processing, and in a majority-black county versus a majority-white county. In this chapter, I focus on the latter.

For ease and consistency, all pseudonyms for geographic places in majority-black Bedford County will begin with the letter *B*, and all pseudonyms for geographic places near majority-black Bedford County will begin with letters close to *B* (roughly, *A* through *E*). Likewise, all pseudonyms for geographic places in majority-white Wilcox County will begin with the letter *W*, and all pseudonyms for geographic places near majority-white Wilcox County will begin with letters close to *W* (roughly, *U* through *Z*).

METHODS

Data and results come from ethnographic research and 129 individual semi-structured interviews conducted by the author from June 2003 to June 2004 in Bedford and Wilcox Counties, North Carolina. Slightly over half of the 129 interviews (70, or 54 percent) were conducted with Latin American immigrants of varying nationalities, in either Spanish or English. These foreign-born respondents hail primarily from Mexico (39), but also from South America (16), Central America (14), and Cuba (1). Approximately one seventh of the interviews (18, or 14 percent) were conducted with American-born Hispanics, in either Spanish or English.[5] These native-born Hispanic respondents are from New York (6), Puerto Rico (6), Texas (3), Florida (2), and "other states" (3); none were from California.[6] And approximately one third of the interviews (41, or 32 percent) were conducted with "key native-born informants," in English. These native-born respondents are both white (27) and black (14).

Interview respondents were located by combining theoretical sampling and snowball sampling designs. In the broader project, individual interviews were spread across four arenas:

1. Local workplaces (economic arena)

2. Local elementary school systems (sociocultural arena)

3. Local courts and law enforcement systems (sociocultural arena)

4. Local politics (political arena)

In order to analyze differences in incorporation processes across institutional boundaries, I first employed a theoretical sampling design to generate categories of interview respondents in each of these arenas based on the probability that these types of individuals might have unique and theoretically informative experiences regarding important issues I wanted to examine. My methodology was similar in each of the arenas, such that interview respondents in the project would ultimately include lower-status Hispanic workers as well as some native- and foreign-born line managers and supervisors and salaried employees in workplaces; Hispanic school officials, former students, or parents of Hispanic children in school as well as some native-born school officials familiar with educational issues affecting the local Hispanic population; Hispanic personnel in local courts or law enforcement agencies as well as some native-born legal personnel familiar with legal issues affecting the local Hispanic community; and established or emerging Hispanic political leaders and some native-born political leaders in local and state politics.

To locate these interview subjects, I drew on existing social networks to contact the employers of the three workplace settings that I wanted to study—a tobacco farm and a textile mill in Bedford County and a large poultry processing plant in Wilcox County[7]—as well as several local politicians and service providers who I thought or had heard would be familiar with each county's Hispanic populations. Through these initial contacts, I met various Hispanic "key informants" who in turn helped me locate other Hispanic interview respondents through an informal snowball sampling design over the course of the year.

Interviews lasted from thirty minutes to three hours (most lasted for one and a half to two hours), and respondents were asked a battery of questions regarding their migration history, family background, racial and ethnic-group identification, employment history, opinions and views about race and immigration, opinions and views about other racial and ethnic groups, opinions and views about southern history and culture, and electoral or nonelectoral political participation. Employers, school personnel, legal personnel, and political leaders were asked additional questions about their experiences with Hispanics and their views on the local Hispanic community. All interview subjects were offered ten dollars in cash in return for an individual interview; I donated all inducements turned down by interview subjects to an organization or charity of their choice or to the two emergent Hispanic associations that allowed me to attend and observe their meetings and other activities.

Finally, I supplemented all of these interviews with additional activities:

- Making observations in the three workplace settings.

- Attending some local school board meetings, PTA meetings at elementary schools, and traffic courts (as well as monitoring published county commissioner meeting agendas) in each county.

- Reviewing local newspaper archives for reference to Hispanics or immigration in each county.

- Attending emergent Hispanic association meetings as well as groups formed by local American politicians and service providers to assess Hispanics' needs in each county; in a few circumstances, I also examined these local leaders' connections to Hispanic political groups and initiatives at the state level.

After my field work was completed, I coded all interview material using Atlas.ti, a software program that allows for the qualitative analysis of large bodies of textual, graphical, audio, and video data. To ensure the anonymity of my interview subjects, all names were changed, and I have also altered identifying information (such as interview subjects' sex, states and countries of birth, years of arrival in the United States, migration trajectories, occupations and departments of work, and so forth), so that any resemblance to actual persons is coincidental.

NEGATIVE BLACK-HISPANIC SOCIOECONOMIC RELATIONS

Most broadly, my research findings confirm that in the socioeconomic arena, Hispanics' characterizations of African Americans and the dynamics of black-Hispanic conflict in these two counties closely resemble those already found in the immigrant incorporation and intergroup relations literatures elsewhere in the United States. Despite reflecting the complex and often contradictory array of patterns of intergroup relations that have been located and discussed in the literature (Bobo and Johnson 2000, 81; Hochschild 2007)—including internal ambivalence on the part of many interview respondents (Hochschild 1981, chapter 8)[8]—the predominant patterns that emerge from my research in both of these counties are as follows:

- Hispanics view whites as being of "higher status" than African Americans, on the basis of whites' higher levels of education, and cultural factors in general.

- Hispanics note better white-Hispanic than black-Hispanic relations.

- But most Hispanics are careful to point out that there are often positive and negative relations with both whites and blacks, usually conditioned by class status (see also Hernández-León and Zúñiga 2005; Leitner 2003; Rich and Miranda 2005, 201–6).

Thus, the intersection of race and class helps explain Hispanics' perceptions of better white-Hispanic than black-Hispanic relations in eastern North Carolina. In both counties, blacks are socioeconomically disadvantaged relative to whites at both the individual and group levels, and consequently, blacks are perceived as being more likely than whites to feel as though they are being (or will be) displaced or "leapfrogged" by Hispanic newcomers, and reacting more negatively to newcomers in return.[9]

I will illustrate a brief example of each pattern. First, Pilar, an immigrant from Lima, Peru, living in Bedford County, draws on her personal postmigration experiences to make the observation that blacks are less educated and motivated (in other words, "lower status") than whites in rural eastern North Carolina today:

> Pilar: At my job, you see? I've seen that. There aren't any blacks in the offices. They are all whites. All of them. There is not even one black in the offices. And obviously it's because of their education. The majority of whites in the offices are engineers or they are people who—in contrast, on the other side of the plant, they are all blacks. There are almost no whites. I mean, I've never counted but the majority of them are blacks. And so, whites are people who want to move forward, out of the place where they're from—that's the idea I get, right? Because, just by looking. Not because I've talked with them, but by looking. The whites always want to move forward and make something of themselves. Blacks, getting a job and earning enough, that's sufficient and they stay there. That's the idea that I get. Well, because I don't see anyone in an office who's black, that's probably why. Because they haven't studied, so they stay where they are. They are operators, they implement— they are manual laborers, right?

Second, Álvaro, an immigrant from Coahuila, Mexico, living in Bedford County, describes local white-Hispanic relations as better than black-Hispanic ones:

> Interviewer: In general, how would you characterize the interactions and the relationships here between Hispanics or immigrants and American whites?

Álvaro: I would say that fifty percent of whites, they have a good attitude to the Hispanics. But the other fifty percent, that's where I would say that it's a bad attitude to the Hispanics. It's like everybody says, there are bad apples and good apples. But at least to me, it's a kind of half and half. I see more white people, Caucasians, doing or trying to do, positive things to the Hispanic community versus the African American people. With a better attitude, with a better approach. They are being more kind. But on the other hand, you know, the bad fifty percent—they really don't care. They're always trying to avoid you, do not talk with you, don't help. . . . Thinking that we are stealing jobs, that we are the kind of people just for cleaning or the workforce. That we don't deserve to be a part of the community. That's the other fifty percent, that's my conception.

Interviewer: How would you describe the relationship between Hispanics or immigrants and American blacks here?

Álvaro: I can't say good. Because my opinion is that a big part of the African American population, they really don't accept the Hispanic community. We are intruders. Just a small part, one probably quarter of the population—they are the ones who realize or can see us as allies.

Interviewer: But you say only about twenty-five percent?

Álvaro: Right.

Third, Alicia, an immigrant from Santiago, Chile, living in Bedford County, shows how class can mediate both white-Hispanic and black-Hispanic relations in rural eastern North Carolina, such that a less favorable class distribution among local blacks (as compared to local whites) contributes to more negative black-Hispanic than white-Hispanic relations overall:

Interviewer: Have you ever been discriminated against for being Hispanic or being an immigrant in this country?

Alicia: Yes, I think everyone feels it.

Interviewer: Can you give me an example of this?

Alicia: At the post office. I go to the post office every day. I get the mail every day. And there are a lot of African Americans. [*Whispers quietly.*] And they are, well, fairly aggressive, vulgar. I mean, it's very difficult to say if it's because I'm Hispanic or just because they don't like me. It's very difficult. But because I'm Hispanic, I see it from that point of view. Do you understand? And sometimes here in the office, there are people I know who don't like Hispanics. And I get a feeling from them . . . how would I explain it you? Very cold. And so they think that I am a person who, that Hispanics are people who are worth less. But I also have a conception of them . . . how would I explain it to you? The fact that someone can't treat me or anyone else well, or is vulgar. I think we have to make those people understand that we are not strangers to them. We have to give them the possibility of some time to get to know us.

Interviewer: Does this happen more with white Americans or black Americans?

Alicia: More with black Americans.

Interviewer: How come?

Alicia: Well, and like, with the white people that here you call "rednecks." It's social class that accounts for it.[10]

These more positive depictions of white-Hispanic than black-Hispanic socioeconomic relations, frequently mediated by class status, do not only hold in Wilcox County. They also mirror those found at the aggregate national level and in major immigrant-receiving cities, and they have even been noted in other studies of immigration in both the rural (Griffith 2005, 66; Studstill and Neito-Studstill 2001, 75–81) and urban South (McClain et al. 2003; Rich and Miranda 2005, 201–6). They demonstrate how Hispanic respondents in eastern North Carolina tend to locate the source of black-Hispanic tensions in elements of both individual- and group-level socioeconomic competition. On an individual level, the broad socioeconomic differences between whites and blacks in these two counties (regardless of their causes) mean that blacks are disproportionately underrepresented as both employers and skilled workers. Consequently, many whites and Hispanics have incentives to relate to one another in a complementary rather than competitive way (for example, when a white employer wants to hire more workers), while many blacks and Hispanics have incentives to relate in a competitive rather than complementary way (for example, when they vie to obtain jobs in a region where employers are predominantly white).

A Mexican immigrant expresses this in less technical terms when he reports that he "has not yet met a single Latin who works for a black man" (Studstill and Neito-Studstill 2001, 78). Eduardo, an immigrant from Quetzaltenango, Guatemala, living in Wilcox Country, describes poor relations between black and Hispanic line workers in Poultry Processing Plant, Inc., which he ascribes to blacks' perceptions of direct and indirect economic competition, compared to better (but still self-interested) reactions by higher-status white employers and managers to Hispanic line workers:

Eduardo: The white American race likes Hispanics a lot. And the black race does not like Hispanics very much.

Interviewer: Why not?

Eduardo: Because they think that we are taking away their jobs.

Interviewer: And how come?

Eduardo: Because they say that because of us, they earn less. And the white American race likes us because we do the work like they want.

Interviewer: So white Americans like Hispanics to do those jobs? And the African Americans are scared that Hispanics are going to do their jobs, or are going to take away their jobs?

Eduardo: Or like, well, they don't like that because of us, [whites] don't raise their wages.

Interviewer: So you think that the majority of Hispanics have better relations with American whites than with American blacks?

Eduardo: Yes, because they have more communication because whites say, "Do you think that you can do this job?" And so we tell them, "Yes." And blacks say, "No, it's very hard." So because of that, at work white Americans always talk with Hispanics, if it is possible for them to do the work. And Hispanics will, because we like to work. They give us things, and Hispanics are going to do that work. And I think that white Americans always talk to Hispanics.

Furthermore, even when not singling out specific instances of individual-level socioeconomic competition, Hispanic respondents in these two counties already perceive that blacks are more likely than whites to perceive them as a socioeconomic threat to their group as a whole. Significantly, their perceptions are shared by many key native respondents, including both blacks and whites. For example, Don, a white Bedford County commissioner, muses:

Don: Oddly, I think there would probably be more tension between blacks and Spanish immigrants than white and Spanish immigrants. And it's just a perception. I tend to feel like many blacks feel like that the immigrants are taking their jobs.

Tyrone and Quincy, two African American truck-tractor drivers at Tobacco Farm, Inc., in Bedford County, go further to illustrate an acute group-level sense of African Americans' declining socioeconomic worth and power relative to Hispanic newcomers, even though they themselves have not been displaced from their jobs. (Notice how they respond to questions about African Americans and Hispanics' local political power with descriptions of socioeconomic power instead):

> Interviewer: Do you feel that African Americans have sufficient political power in your area?
>
> Tyrone: Ah, we ain't got no power left! [*Both men laugh.*] Blacks ain't got no power left. We just make it by. Especially on this farm anyhow, we just make it. Like I said, like I said you know, it's all about the white person here. Whites going to take over this farm here. The black ain't gonna have no chance over here. The white and the Mexican. They going to take over, 'cause it's hard on the black on the farm, like I said.
>
> Interviewer: And what about Hispanics? Do you feel that Hispanics or immigrants have sufficient political power?
>
> Quincy: They doin' all right [economically]. From what I seen, doin' all right.
>
> Tyrone: After a while we get enough Spanish down here, they gonna run the white out! [*Laughs.*] I really believe that. They gonna run the white out. They get enough of 'em over here, they gonna try to run 'em out. After a while this place might end up turnin' to Mexico. Gonna have 'em all down, family and all of 'em. But they good people, but they come down every year, you know, come down every year and work and get dream cars and stuff.

Such interpretations are compounded by Hispanic respondents' attempts to explain their better relations with (and reactions from) whites than African Americans by focusing not only on perceived job competition between Hispanics and African Americans at the lower end of the class spectrum but also on the social tensions spurred by demographic change in neighborhoods and schools and the feeling that blacks are being displaced by new Hispanics in a larger social as well as economic sense (see also Dunn, Aragonés, and Shivers 2005, 176; Rich and Miranda 2005, 205). That is, one significant finding from my research is that black-Hispanic tensions are most tense outside the workplace, specifically in several neighborhoods and trailer parks, where Hispanics now reside in locales previously occupied by African Americans, and in local public schools, especially middle schools. Even in several elementary schools, some Hispanic students are making such rapid academic progress that local teachers and administrators are beginning to wonder why African American students—their historical minority group—are not keeping pace. Bedford Elementary School Vice Principal Randy White describes a strong degree of resentment among African American teachers and administrators in response to feelings that African Americans students are being displaced or "leapfrogged" in terms of educational progress:

> Randy White: We are aware that a number of our Hispanic children do well on their course work, as well as their end-of-grade tests. Only in conversations with black colleagues and community members, they're feeling . . . I'm not sure what the feeling is. They're feeling threatened. They're feeling some anger. Resentment. But I don't know that they themselves can put their finger on why. I don't know that they have really thought through and analyzed. But they do know these people who they consider as foreigners have come in, and are now being successful in their school system, where a lot of their people are not being as successful. So there is a resentment there. I mean, you know, you can look at our test scores, and we can point out where some of our Hispanic children have been and where they are now, and how they are becoming more and more successful.

In sum, black–Hispanic socioeconomic tensions are already a serious concern in eastern North Carolina today. At a local milling company where I almost conducted some of my workplace interviews, several employers and employees laughed at me when I told them I was interested in investigating relations between African Americans and Hispanics there to see what kinds of tensions or forms of cooperation existed between the two groups. They reported that there was "nothing but bad blood" between the two groups and suggested that "investigating part of the issue of Hispanics becoming the more prominent minority group [over blacks] might be interesting for me to do" instead.[11] This illustrates how, in both Bedford and Wilcox Counties, respondents explain black–Hispanic tensions by pointing not only to African Americans' objective conditions of economic deprivation or disempowerment but also to African Americans' "low or diminishing socioeconomic status" vis-à-vis Hispanic newcomers and to their "historically and collectively developed judgments about the positions in the social order" that African Americans should rightfully occupy above Hispanic newcomers. This lends greatest support to the group position model's explanation of black–Hispanic tensions (Bobo and Hutchings 1996, 955; Morawska 2001, 49).

Perhaps the clearest example of this threat to African Americans' current socioeconomic standing can been seen in a question posed by an African American businesswoman to Alexandria County Democratic congressional candidates in Archer Bluff: "she asked directly—even bluntly—what black constituents could expect for their votes from the candidates as a quid pro quo, in terms of economic development, reparations for slavery, and the effect of Latino immigration on the standard of living for blacks in the district" (*Archer Bluff Times* [a pseudonym], June 13, 2004). As she makes clear, many African American residents of Bedford and Alexandria Counties are concerned about their "declining standard of living," and some even draw a connection between new Hispanic immigration and stagnation in African Americans' larger struggle for socioeconomic justice.

BLACK POPULATION SIZE AND SOCIOECONOMIC THREAT

I found that black-Hispanic socioeconomic relations were more negative in Bedford County, which is majority black, than in Wilcox County, which is majority white. Not only were reports of black-Hispanic tensions stronger and more prevalent in Bedford County than in Wilcox County, but also, as mentioned earlier, they are disconcerting in the arenas where they are cited most frequently—lower-class neighborhoods (mostly local trailer parks) and public elementary schools (mostly middle schools). For example, although several white and Hispanic respondents in both counties expressed common negative stereotypes of African Americans as lazy, violent, nonworking, or welfare recipients, I was able to locate few descriptions of black-Hispanic tensions in Wilcox County that could mirror those that I heard in Bedford County. Most reports in Wilcox County were more neutral than in Bedford County, such as in the following response by Josefa, an immigrant from San Salvador, El Salvador:

> Interviewer: In general, how would you describe the relations between Hispanics and American whites?
>
> Josefa: Well, at work we have a daily relationship. When we're not at work, we go to the stores, or we meet someone and we say hello.
>
> Interviewer: In general, how would you describe the relations between Hispanics and American blacks?
>
> Josefa: There isn't any problem between the two races.
>
> Interviewer: Do you think that having more Hispanics or immigrants here affects the way blacks think about their race—about what it means to be black here?

Josefa: I think right now it doesn't have anything to do with that. Probably maybe a long time ago, in the time of slavery. But right now, I don't think there is any problem.

Even though some teachers and administrators in Wilcox County share concerns about the balance between Hispanic and black students' educational progress at the elementary school level, those concerns were less heated than those in Bedford County during the time of my research.

To probe this difference further, I began asking Wilcox County respondents who did not note much black-Hispanic conflict in the heavily white and Mexican eastern part of the county or in Weakley Elementary School, which is predominantly white and Hispanic, whether they knew or had heard of any such conflict either in the heavily African American and Honduran western part of the county or in schools other than Weakley Elementary, where more African American students are enrolled. But still, nothing came close to the negative reports voiced in Bedford County. For example, even Jaime Wilson, a North Carolina–born Hispanic who identifies himself as "American of Spanish origin, Hispanic Caucasian," told me that his eldest daughter had not experienced any conflict with African American students at her predominantly black local high school, even though he had been prepared to confront that when she first enrolled there:

Jaime Wilson: My oldest [daughter] is seventeen. She'll be going to Governor's School this year. She turned down the N.C. School of Math and Science because she did not want to leave her high school. She enjoyed it so much there.

Interviewer: Which school is that?

Jaime Wilson: Wilcox High School. She loves it there. It's supposed to be one of the worst high schools in the county as far as blacks and racism and gangs, but she's the drum major. She's on soccer, she's on volleyball, she's on every committee that comes through there. She loves it. And her lowest grade that she's ever brought home was a 94.

Similarly, Eva, an immigrant from Buenos Aires, Argentina, who taught at Wright Elementary School and Wilcox High School before coming to Weakley Elementary, agreed that "it is very different on the other side of Wilcox County," where there are many more African Americans and the towns are generally a lot poorer than they are near Weakley Elementary on the northern side of the county. But even at those two schools, which have more African American students than Weakley Elementary, she reports that most conflict "was more between the immigrants, even there," not between African Americans and Hispanics.

These more neutral depictions of black-Hispanic relations in Wilcox County contrast starkly with decidedly negative reports in Bedford County, including African American students harassing and picking on Hispanic students in local middle and high schools and on school buses, "diversity" problems concerning African American schoolteachers not treating their Hispanic students or coworkers well, serious problems concerning robberies committed against Hispanics by African Americans in local trailer parks—to the point where one Hispanic interview respondent told me he had contacted a local Bedford police officer and the Bedford County sheriff about starting a community watch program for Hispanic residents of one local trailer park[12]—and accusations that local African American community groups are not being 100 percent forthright in their efforts to reach out to Hispanics when and where such efforts are made. There are too many of these negative reports to present here; two will illustrate the seriousness of black-Hispanic tensions in majority-black Bedford County today.

Anita, an immigrant from Michoacán, Mexico, is characteristic of Hispanic respondents who perceive that they or their children are more discriminated against by blacks than by whites:[13]

> Anita: Right, because there's another case, too, with my oldest daughter. When she goes to Bedford Middle School, she wears her gold necklace there. She said that some of the black students pick on her a lot, and they even tried to grab her necklace to try and take it off her. And she spent a couple of days scared. And her father told her, "Just ignore them, because if they go to school and don't show respect for other people, well, you can't do anything about it. And sometimes it's not worth worrying about it, if they can't hold themselves back. But if they demand it from you, then there will be problems." And honestly that's what you have to do.

> Interviewer: And how do we find a solution for this conflict between blacks and Hispanics?

> Anita: Well, it's difficult because you're always thinking about them. Whenever the children go to school—well, in my cases it's daughters because they're all girls—but I'm always hoping that they leave and come home okay. Because with those [black] boys you never know what can happen. That's how you try to protect them like that. When it's time for my daughter to come home and she isn't home,

and it's almost time for her to come home and she hasn't come home, you worry. It's not because you want something to happen, but it's because you are conscious that the blacks are people who sometimes even among themselves, they don't hold themselves back or don't think about what they are going to do.

Elisa is an immigrant from Tamaulipas, Mexico, who works as a migrant education program recruiter and parent facilitator in the Bedford County public school system. In her interview, Elisa expressed frustrations with several African American coworkers, who she feels have not adequately supported her either on an individual level, in her occupational missions to provide support to Hispanic students who are experiencing problems in school or to collect donations to give to needy Hispanic migrant workers in the area, or on a group level, in terms of including Hispanics as equal partners in planned community events:

Elisa: Well, I kind of feel that the black people don't want Hispanics here. I don't mean that bad, but I don't think that they really care for them to be around. And you know, sometimes I got that feeling of, like, "Why are you here?" And also, once I was invited to come speak at a gathering that they were holding. They wanted the black and the Hispanic communities to be there. But I don't know, I guess they had canceled the gathering at the last minute. But they didn't tell me! So I showed up and nobody was there. And then I guess they also rescheduled the gathering for the next week. But they didn't tell me about that either! They went out of their way not to tell they had canceled one meeting and rescheduled another. So I felt like they didn't really want us there. I had wanted to bring some of the Hispanic community, to get them to show up. I even took pictures. I always have my camera on me, you know to take my pictures everywhere, and I took some pictures of everything here and there. Just to show, you know, that I didn't forget about it and that I really did show up. I don't know how the gathering went the next week, because I didn't know about it, but there were no Hispanics there.

These more negative depictions of black-Hispanic relations in Bedford County than those in Wilcox County lend support to hypothesis 2—that higher proportions of African Americans in many locales across the South exacerbate black-Hispanic socioeconomic conflict at the local level. In fact, Davíd, an immigrant from Medellín, Colombia, living in Bedford

County, speculates that this will also be the case at the regional level in the South:

> Interviewer: There are more African Americans in the South than there are in other regions of the country. Do you think this is affecting the experiences of Hispanics or immigrants here in any way?
>
> Davíd: Yes.
>
> Interviewer: How so?
>
> Davíd: Like I said before, I feel the blacks don't like us. And that it is worse than with the whites.

Here it is very important to stress that demographic and structural factors, such as the size of the Hispanic and immigrant population or the local political structure at the county level, cannot account for the more prevalent black-Hispanic tensions I find in Bedford County versus Wilcox County. African Americans constitute 58 percent of Bedford County's local population in 2000 while Hispanics only constitute 3 percent, a gap that suggests full socioeconomic displacement is still a long way off for blacks in Bedford County. Moreover, sheer demographics would have led us to expect to find more evidence of perceived socioeconomic threat in Wilcox County, where blacks constitute 29 percent of the local population and Hispanics constitute 15 percent, yet the reverse is the case. The two counties' local political structures are similar; both currently operate on a "county manager" form of government and have a group of six to seven elected county commissioners, each of whom represents one of the county's electoral districts.[14]

Of course, these findings do not mean that there are no efforts to build coalitions between blacks and Hispanics in Bedford County, or that there are no individual-level examples of cooperation between blacks and Hispanics in workplaces, schools, or neighborhoods there. On the contrary, such efforts are indeed present, but black-Hispanic conflict simply seems to outweigh black-Hispanic cooperation there, at least for now.

BLACK POPULATION SIZE AND POLITICAL THREAT

Yet what happens in the political arena differs from what happens in the socioeconomic arena. My research shows that the greater proportion of African Americans at the local level in Bedford County affords them some protection from feelings of political threat as Hispanic newcomers enter their midst, rather than elevating a sense of black-Hispanic political competition. During my field research in 2003 and 2004, I either came into contact with or observed more instances of formal political black-Hispanic coalition-building efforts at the North Carolina state level, where African Americans constituted 22 percent of the state population in 2000, and in Wilcox County, where African Americans constituted 29 percent of the county population in 2000, than I did in Bedford County, where African Americans constituted 58 percent of the county population in 2000.[15]

At the state level, black-Hispanic coalition building is one of the principal goals of the North Carolina Coalition on Black and Brown Civic Participation, a state-level subsidiary of the National Coalition on Black Civic Participation formed in 2003 to foster black-brown coalition building and promote long-term voter registration and education projects at the state level, with the goal of networking down to the local level. In Wilcox County, the most visible example of formal, local-level, black-Hispanic coalition building is the Wilcox County Center for Leadership Development's use of external grant money to expand an eight-week leadership training course (originally designed to promote underrepresented African American leadership in the county) to the newer Hispanic community in Spanish, beginning in 2002 and repeated through 2005. No formal efforts of this sort were located in Bedford County,[16] although black-Hispanic coalition building was reported to be "on the agenda" in the Bedford County chapter of the NAACP (I was unsuccessful at contacting local-level NAACP leaders in Wilcox County).[17]

What could account for these differences? In particular, African Americans in Bedford County are reported by whites, blacks, and Hispanics alike to wield substantial political power at the local level, and as Clarence Brown, Bedford County's African American county manager, points out, this power rests largely on their large population size at the county level:

> Interviewer: Do you feel that African Americans have sufficient political power in this area?
>
> Clarence Brown: Sufficient political power? I would have to say yes.
>
> Interviewer: How come?
>
> Clarence Brown: How come? Well, in quite a few leadership roles, you have African Americans in those positions. One of the things that I've said more than once is that African Americans have not participated in the political process long enough to "know how to play the game." But I think that in this area, with the population of the county being 55 percent African American,[18] that there is a good representation of African Americans. There are some wards and districts that

have been great for African Americans' participation in the political process. Before that time, you could look at boards and commissions, and all of their representatives were basically living in one neighborhood or one geographic area. And by splitting everything up into wards and districts, you almost assure yourself of having a diverse group of people being political leaders.

Interviewer: You mentioned that the African American population here is 55 percent, which is much higher than the national average. How do you think this compares to their political representation at the national level? Do you think they have sufficient political power at the national level?

Clarence Brown: Blacks? No.

Interviewer: So you think it's better for them here?

Clarence Brown: Oh yeah. Yeah.

Interviewer: Do you think that having more Hispanics or immigrants here affects the way that blacks think about their race?

Clarence Brown: No.

Interviewer: Why not?

Clarence Brown: Why not? Because we have not been significantly impacted by Hispanics being here in this county. I mean, the groups of black people I've been around in general don't sit around and talk about or perceive the Hispanic population as being threatening.

The feeling that Hispanics are not yet challenging African Americans' formal political power yet because so far they lack the similar organization or "numbers" at the local county level (even while Hispanics may be making great political strides at the national level) is also expressed by some whites in Bedford County, as Don, the county commissioner quoted earlier, explains:

Don: My understanding is that the Spanish community is already the largest minority group in the country. And as I hear political debate and strategies, I hear 'em going after the Latino vote and so forth. So I think certainly on a national level it's a recognized stronghold of potential votes, much more so than, than, as I say, here on a local level. And I think when you think of it nationally, they are probably a lot more organized than they are on a local level.

Interviewer: Do you think that African Americans have sufficient political power in this county?

Don: Definitely.

Interviewer: How come?

Don: Well, they have fought for it and they've been successful. In Bedford County, they are a majority in reality. The majority voters in Bedford County are black. They have control of the city council in Archer Bluff, majority control. They have had majority control of the Bedford County commissioners, so they have shown that when they get united behind an issue that they can carry, they will. And they are well represented, I think, although that I am sure some black communities would disagree. They're well represented on all of our elected boards and appointed boards. I think the two communities [white and black] are trying to work together, and certainly their voice is heard strong on every issue. That certainly is not true in the Spanish community.

As these two responses show, African Americans' formal political power in Bedford County is considered relatively secure and so there have been few organized efforts to promote black-Hispanic cooperation to date, despite more black-Hispanic tensions there than in Wilcox County, because such efforts are not considered necessary in terms of numbers yet.

More generally, my research findings diverge between the local socioeconomic and political arenas. They lend support to hypothesis 2 in the local socioeconomic realm—that higher proportions of African Americans in the South will exacerbate black-Hispanic tensions by elevating African Americans' sense of socioeconomic threat, as is evidenced in majority-black Bedford County as compared to majority-white Wilcox County. But they also lend support to hypothesis 1 in the local political realm—that higher proportions of African Americans in the South will smooth black-Hispanic tensions by protecting African Americans from an elevated sense of political threat, as is also evidenced in majority-black Bedford County as compared to majority-white Wilcox County.

In contrast to the "strength-in-numbers" line of reasoning in hypothesis 1, however, my research findings suggest that higher proportions of African Americans in the South may translate into fewer rather than more opportunities for black-Hispanic contact and coalition building than they would in other places with smaller African American populations if African American political leaders and civil rights organizations feel secure due to those numbers and do not sense the strategic need to develop positive black-Hispanic relations by engaging in proactive coalition-building strategies with Hispanics. Although African Americans are certainly considered to be socioeconomic and racial minorities in both Bedford and Wilcox Counties, the fact that their population size has translated into more formal political power (and therefore less of a political minority status) in Bedford County seems to have depressed blacks' efforts to reach out to new Hispanics at the local political level there. In contrast, at least some leaders in Wilcox County (particularly at the Wilcox County Center for Leadership Development) have already begun to envision local Hispanics as a "political minority group" in a similar position to African Americans at the local county level—in need of political support.

The latter case resonates with at least one other study of immigration in the South. In Dalton, Georgia, a small city of about 28,000 residents in 2000, even though African American responses to new Latinos are varied and have not always been smooth, "Black leaders have organized meetings with their Latino counterparts to find a common political agenda," including beginning a drive to register new Latinos within the local chapter of the NAACP (Hernández-León and Zúñiga 2005, 267). Interestingly, these coalition-building efforts are being pursued by the leadership of a small African American population—in 2000, Dalton's population was identified as 66 percent white, 8 percent black, 2 percent Asian, 21 percent "other race," and (according to a separate question on Hispanic origin ethnicity) 40 percent Hispanic or Latino of any race, and blacks constituted just 4 percent of Dalton's surrounding Whitfield County (248).

In fact, Rubén Hernández-León and Víctor Zúñiga (2005) show that African American leaders' efforts to find a common political agenda with Latino newcomers there partially reflect their feeling that "in the wake of a massive inflow of Latino immigrants" they were at risk of becoming "irrelevant" (267). This suggests that in contrast to what I find in majority-black Bedford County, the presence of smaller African American populations may encourage greater black-Hispanic coalition building for strategic demographic reasons, instead of or in combination with visions of shared structural status or what Michael C. Dawson (1994) calls "linked fate":

> [A]lthough in the words of their leadership, black Daltonians have no power, politically active African Americans have seen Latino immigration as a way to overcome their marginal status (Hernández-León and Zúñiga 2005, 267).

At the same time, it is worth noting that several Hispanic political and community leaders in Bedford County were starting to show frustration over inattention from black political leaders during the time of my research, even though they were not actively voicing it yet.[19] This suggests that black-Hispanic political competition in Bedford County could emerge in the future as Hispanics become more politically organized and begin to vie for formal political power with the local African American as well as white political leadership. In this case, my research findings in the political arena, which currently lend support to hypothesis 1, could begin to lend more support to hypothesis 2—that higher proportions of African Americans in the South will exacerbate black-Hispanic tensions by elevating African Americans' sense of political threat *after* an initial period of security due to their strength in numbers. This would lend qualitative support to the idea that competition arises among various groups "when the size of one group obviates the need to form coalitions with other minority groups" (McClain and Tauber 2001, 115).

In fact, if this occurs, it could be that the initial period of protection from political threat that the higher proportion of African Americans affords blacks in Bedford County compared to Wilcox County could exacerbate black-Hispanic political competition in Bedford County once it arises, owing to Hispanics' perceptions of inattention now. Such a possibility does not seem far-fetched, given what has happened in other majority-black locales where new immigrants have settled, such as Compton, California, where it has taken heated black-Latino conflict to bring to light Latinos' concerns over "absence of Latino representation" in local politics and limited access to institutional resources (Camarillo 2004). And it underscores the need for proactive black-Hispanic coalition-building efforts even in rural new immigrant destinations with large, politically secure African American populations.

SUMMARY

In this chapter, I have discussed one reason why Hispanic newcomers in eastern North Carolina feel that, on the whole, they are treated better by whites than African Americans: how race interacts with the local class structure in the rural American South. In both Bedford and Wilcox Counties, blacks are socioeconomically disadvantaged relative to whites at both the individual and groups levels. Consequently, they are perceived as being more likely than whites to feel as though they are being (or will be) displaced or "leapfrogged" by Hispanic newcomers, both inside and outside the workplace. In academic parlance, respondents note that blacks perceive a greater degree of socioeconomic and symbolic "threat" from Hispanic newcomers than do whites, and that in response to this threat, their reactions to Hispanic newcomers are more negative than are those of whites, contributing to more tense black-Hispanic relations overall.

Within this picture of class-based racial group threat, furthermore, I have shown how local-level differences in black population size interact with institutional arena of incorporation to structure intergroup relations in the rural South. In the local socioeconomic arena, the higher proportion of African Americans in majority-black Bedford County compared to majority-white Wilcox County exacerbates black-Hispanic tensions by elevating African Americans' sense of individual and group-level threat. In the local political realm, by contrast, the higher proportion of African Americans in majority-black Bedford County compared to majority-white Wilcox County smoothes black-Hispanic tensions by protecting African Americans from similar feelings of threat, at least initially. Interestingly, this initial political security seems to reduce the strategic demographic incentives that blacks in Bedford County have to reach out to Hispanic newcomers to engage in coalition-building strategies there.

These findings demonstrate how intergroup relations in new immigrant destinations are indeed nuanced by demographic context. The larger size of the local African American population in Bedford County compared to Wilcox County does impact Hispanic newcomers' incorporation experiences in various arenas, including in workplaces, schools, neighborhoods, and local political systems. Viewed alternately, however, these findings demonstrate how the specific demographic contexts that new immigrants are entering are influenced by the institutional arena of incorporation. That is, black-Hispanic tensions in Bedford and Wilcox Counties are structured not only by the size of the African Americans population at the local level but also by the arenas where African Americans and Hispanics hold and exert most of their power—primarily in the local political arena in the case of rural southern African Americans and primarily in the local economic arena in the case of rural southern Hispanics.

Together, these findings strengthen the call to pay more attention to both demographic context and institutional arena of incorporation in research on immigrant incorporation and intergroup relations (Jones-Correa 2005, 88), including in new immigrant destinations. That Hispanic and other newcomers are now entering a variety of locales across the country raises important questions about how majority-minority and interminority relations will play out in various arenas outside major immigrant-receiving states and cities. My research findings foresee a fairly bleak scenario for black-Hispanic socioeconomic conflict in rural locales with large populations of relatively disenfranchised African Americans who are beginning to feel their standing threatened by the entry of Hispanic newcomers. In contrast, my research findings foresee greater initial political tension, but perhaps also earlier efforts to promote black-Hispanic coalition building, in rural locales with smaller populations of African Americans who are beginning to feel threatened with political irrelevance.

Preparation of this article was supported by a National Science Foundation Graduate Research Fellowship, a National Science Foundation Integrative Graduate Education Research Traineeship, a David Rockefeller Center for Latin American Studies Summer Research Grant, a Center for American Political Studies Dissertation Fellowship in American Politics, and a partial Rural Poverty Research Institute Rural Poverty Dissertation Fellowship. Any opinions, findings, conclusions or recommendations expressed in this publication are those of the author and do not necessarily reflect the views of supporting sources. Special thanks to Susan Brown, Rafaela Dancygier, Jennifer Hochschild, Hiroshi Motomura, Mary C. Waters, William J. Wilson, and members of the 2004 to 2005 Migration and Immigrant Integration Research Workshop at Harvard University for feedback on earlier drafts.

NOTES

1. I focus on Hispanic rather than all immigrant newcomers, since the overwhelming majority of immigrants who arrived in the South during the 1990s are (using the Census Bureau categories) "Hispanics/Latinos," the great preponderance of them foreign-born, primarily in Mexico (Smith 2003, 3). The United States Census Bureau currently defines the terms "Hispanic" and "Latino" interchangeably to refer to all "persons of Mexican, Puerto Rican, Cuban, Central or South American, or other Spanish culture or origin, regardless of race" and regardless of whether they are born in the United States or abroad (U.S. Office of Management and Budget 1995, 1997). I am aware of the many debates concerning the appropriateness of, as well as the differences between, the terms "Hispanic" and "Latino" as they relate to different subpopulations of people with ties to Latin America. Elsewhere in my research I pay close attention to how "Hispanic/Latino" respondents understand, define, accept, or resist these terms as racial and ethnic self-identifications. However, for two reasons I employ the term "Hispanic" loosely throughout this chapter. First, it is a convenient way to refer to all individuals in eastern North Carolina who fit the United States Census Bureau's official definition of "Hispanics/Latinos." Second, and more important, it reflects how both of the terms "Hispanic" and "Latino" are used in eastern North Carolina today—largely interchangeably and referring to both foreign- and American-born individuals of Latin American heritage—while maintaining consistency by using only one term as much as possible.

2. For an introduction to the personal economic interest model, which emphasizes individual-level economic competition between immigrants and American-born natives, especially low-skilled Hispanics and African Americans, see George J. Borjas (1998); Kristin F. Butcher (1998); and Daniel

S. Hamermesh and Frank D. Bean (1998). For an introduction to the group economic interest model, which emphasizes group-level competition between immigrants and American-born natives, see Peter Burns and James Gimpel (2000) and Jack Citrin et al. (1997). For a review of the group position model, which emphasizes both "objective conditions" of economic and political deprivation or disempowerment and "subjective" beliefs and representations toward one's own and other groups, see Lawrence D. Bobo and Vincent L. Hutchings (1996); Bobo and Devon Johnson (2000); and Ewa Morawska (2001). For other research on various aspects of competition between African Americans and Latinos and other immigrants, see Frank D. Bean and Gillian Stevens (2003, chapter 9); Albert M. Camarillo (2004); Jeff Diamond (1998); James H. Johnson, Jr., Walter C. Farrell, and Chandra Guinn (1999); Nestor Rodríguez (1999); Michael J. Rosenfeld and Marta Tienda (1999); Roger Waldinger (1996); Waldinger and Michael I. Lichter (2003).

3. Personal communication from James H. Johnson, Jr., July 17, 2003.

4. Divisions between the rural east and the central Piedmont are strong in North Carolina: "North Carolina has more-tender sectional sensibilities than any other state in the South, including even tripartite Tennessee.... The bulk of population, money, and productive activity now rests west of the fall line and gives that [central Piedmont] section the pre-eminence long ago held by the agricultural counties of the [eastern] coastal plan and tidewater" (Key, Jr. 1949/1984, 218–20). For a more detailed description of eastern North Carolina, see also David Griffith (1995a, 1995b, 2005) and Rebecca M. Torres, E. Jeffrey Popke, and Holly M. Hapke (2006).

5. These proportions capture the dominance of Mexicans among North Carolina's Hispanic and Latino population, which was 65.1 percent Mexican, 8.2 percent Puerto Rican, 1.9 percent Cuban, and 24.8 percent "other" Hispanic or Latino (generally meaning from other Spanish-speaking Central and South American countries) in 2000 (Mohl 2003, 40).

6. Several of the foreign-born respondents migrated indirectly to North Carolina through California, but none of the American-born Hispanics was born there. Torres, Popke, and Hapke (2006) also find that migrants in Greene County, eastern North Carolina, are now arriving primarily from abroad, not in response to post-IRCA "push" factors in traditional receiving states, especially California.

7. All three are "traditional, low-wage southern industries" that immigrants in the South have entered disproportionately (Kochhar, Suro, and Tafoya 2005; Smith 2003). For research on immigration and manufacturing/textiles in the region, see James Engstrom (2001); Rubén Hernández-León and Víctor Zúñiga (2000, 2005); and Rachel Willis (2005). For research on immigration and poultry processing in the region, see Altha J. Cravey (1997); Leon Fink (2003); Elzbieta Gozdziak and Micah Bump (2004); David Griffith (1995a, 1995b, 2005); Greig Guthey (2001); William Kandel and Emilio A. Parrado (2004); and Steve Striffler (2005).

8. Other studies have also identified mixed reactions to immigrants in receiving communities, including internal ambivalence among individuals. Mark A. Grey and Anne C. Woodrick (2005, 140–41) uncover mixed reactions to immigrants in Iowa communities, grouping them together in what they term the "twenty-sixty-twenty rule": "In any rural Iowa community, about 20 percent of the people actively welcome immigrant newcomers or they are at least open to making it work. At the other end of that spectrum, we usually run into about 20 percent of the population that is dead set against immigrant influxes. Motivated by any number of concerns or biases, they have made up their minds that newcomers are bad for their community and nothing will change their perspective. The large 60 percent of the population is not sure about newcomers. They are not actively welcoming immigrants, but they are also not actively working against their arrival either. This portion of the population is ambivalent and often fearful of change. Most take a wait-and-see attitude. Many are open to learning more" (141). Brian L. Rich and Marta Miranda (2005) also "identify an ambivalent mixture of community responses toward immigrants, which include paternalistic, benign, and cooperative assistance, as well as negative racialized attitudes" (Zúñiga and Hernández-León 2005, xxii). Finally, Barbara Ellen Smith (2003) also uncovers internal ambivalence among African American respondents in the form of "contradictory and varied responses" to immigration (24).

9. In North Carolina, United States census data for 2000 show that the economic profile of African Americans living in nonmetropolitan areas is considerably weaker than that of their counterparts living in metropolitan areas. In terms of education, 29.3 percent of nonmetropolitan African Americans age twenty-five to sixty-four had not completed high school in 2000, compared to 17.8 percent of their metropolitan counterparts. In terms of labor force participation, 5.5 percent of nonmetropolitan African Americans age twenty-five to sixty-four were unemployed in 2000, compared to 4.4 percent among their metropolitan counterparts. In terms of occupational distribution, 20.2 percent of nonmetropolitan African Americans age twenty-five to sixty-four and in the labor force were employed in managerial or professional occupations in 2000, compared to 25.8 percent of their metropolitan counterparts, while 46.4 percent of nonmetropolitan African Americans age twenty-five to sixty-four and in the labor force were employed in production, craft, or repair occupations in 2000, compared to 28.8 percent of their metropolitan counterparts. Finally, in terms of income, the median wage or salary income for nonmetropolitan African Americans age twenty-five to sixty-four and in the labor force was $18,500 in 2000, compared to $23,000 for their metropolitan counterparts (Ruggles et al. 2004, weighted data, author's calculations). These figures reflect the rural South's lack of an established black middle class. Indeed, generally speaking, whites in Bedford and Wilcox Counties belong either to the middle class or to the poor and working classes (for a discussion of this class division among whites in the "highland" southern city of

Dalton, Georgia, see Hernández-León and Zúñiga 2005). Blacks' socioeconomic position is much weaker than whites'; most African Americans in both
counties belong to the poor and working classes, and only some belong to the
middle class. In Bedford County, one white resident notes, "It is sad, but you
know, really, I could count them [local middle class blacks] on my hands.
And I know who all of them are" (post-fieldwork notes, November 26, 2004).

10.   The term "redneck" denotes elements of cultural orientation as well as
social class. Nonetheless, it is significant that Pilar associates many white
"rednecks" with lower class status.

11.   Field notes, Victoria Milling Company (a pseudonym), June 23, 2003.

12.   Field notes, Marco Ramírez, March 3, 2004.

13.   Griffith (2005, 66) and Rich and Miranda (2005, 204) also document Hispanics'
perception that they are more discriminated against by blacks than whites.

14.   In both counties, the county manager serves as the spokesperson for the
County Board of Commissioners, whose main responsibilities include
adopting a budget, establishing the property tax rate, enacting ordinances,
establishing policies and procedures for the operation of county programs,
and hiring and overseeing county staff.

15.   I did not attempt a comprehensive review of all local- or state-level coalition-
building efforts or African American responses to Hispanics in this project.
Rather, I attempted to gauge the incidence or visibility of such efforts
through individual interviews with Hispanics and some African American
respondents as I conducted my research, and to take note of any efforts
that came to the attention of the emerging Hispanic associations or local-
level service-provider meetings that I attended and observed during my
research. While this may not constitute a comprehensive review of existing
coalition-building efforts, it does document which efforts were currently
salient or important to Hispanics in these two counties at that time, primarily from their point of view.

16.   In both counties, there are more examples of black-Hispanic cooperation in
service and nonprofit agencies than in the electoral political arena. For example, Hispanics are increasingly employed (and also most visible in their positions) as interpreters in county and municipal service agencies, such as county
health departments, community colleges, town clinics, and even nonprofit
agencies such as local Partnerships for Children, where they come into contact with African American coworkers and often become good acquaintances.
But as of 2003 to 2004 no Hispanic occupied any formal political leadership
position in either county, such as a local school board member, town council
member, or county commissioner. Regina, an African American Bedford
County commissioner, illustrates this when she says, "I've worked with several people in nonprofit organizations who are working with the Spanish-
speaking population and that kind of thing. But none who are actually in the
political arena." In Archer Bluff, Hispanic political leader respondents speak
positively of an African American mayoral candidate who has expressed interest in the local Hispanic community, and Kendra, an African American human

relations representative for the Archer Bluff city government, is an active member of Latinos Unidos and has provided this emerging Hispanic association with much-needed institutional as well as personal support. However, as of 2004 there was nothing in Bedford or Alexandria Counties that could rival the Hispanic Leadership Course developed by the Wilcox County Center for Leadership Development in an explicit attempt to build a black-Hispanic coalition in the realm of political and civic leadership development.

17. Interestingly, after my field research was completed, I learned that Bedford County Manager Clarence Brown had invited an emerging local Hispanic school and political leader to head up planning for the county's 2005 Martin Luther King, Jr. Day festivities (*Bedford Newspaper* [a pseudonym], December 22, 2004).

18. In the 2000 United States census, African Americans constitute 58 percent of Bedford County's population.

19. Field notes of an informal conversation after a Hispanic Assistance Council meeting, March 3, 2004.

REFERENCES

Bean, Frank D., and Gillian Stevens. 2003. *America's Newcomers and the Dynamics of Diversity*. New York: Russell Sage Foundation.

Bean, Frank D., Jennifer Van Hook, and Mark A. Fossett. 1999. "Immigration, Spatial and Economic Change, and African American Employment." In *Immigration and Opportunity: Race, Ethnicity, and Employment in the United States*, edited by Frank D. Bean and Stephanie Bell-Rose. New York: Russell Sage Foundation.

Bobo, Lawrence D., and Vincent L. Hutchings. 1996. "Perceptions of Racial Group Competition: Extending Blumer's Theory of Group Position to the Multi-Racial Social Context." *American Sociological Review* 61(6): 951–72.

Bobo, Lawrence D., and Devon Johnson. 2000. "Racial Attitudes in a Prismatic Metropolis: Mapping Identity, Stereotypes, Competition, and Views on Affirmative Action." In *Prismatic Metropolis: Inequality in Los Angeles*, edited by Lawrence D. Bobo, Melvin L. Oliver, Jr., James H. Johnson, Jr., and Abel Valenzuela. New York: Russell Sage Foundation.

Borjas, George J. 1998. "Do Blacks Gain or Lose from Immigration." In *Help or Hindrance? The Economic Implications of Immigration for African Americans*, edited by Daniel S. Hamermesh and Frank D. Bean. New York: Russell Sage Foundation.

Burns, Peter, and James Gimpel. 2000. "Economic Insecurity, Prejudicial Stereotypes, and Public Opinion on Immigration Policy." *Political Science Quarterly* 115(2): 201–25.

Butcher, Kristin F. 1998. "An Investigation of the Effect of Immigration on the Labor-Market Outcomes of African Americans." In *Help or Hindrance? The Economic Implications of Immigration for African Americans*, edited by Daniel S. Hamermesh and Frank D. Bean. New York: Russell Sage Foundation.

Camarillo, Albert M. 2004. "Black and Brown in Compton: Demographic Change, Suburban Decline, and Intergroup Relations in a South Central Los Angeles Community, 1950 to 2000." In *Not Just Black and White: Historical and Contemporary Perspectives on Immigration, Race, and Ethnicity in the United States*, edited by Nancy Foner and George M. Frederickson. New York: Russell Sage Foundation.

Citrin, Jack, Donald P. Green, Christopher Muste, and Cara Wong. 1997. "Public Opinion Toward Immigration Reform: The Role of Economic Motivations." *Journal of Politics* 59(3): 858–82.

Cravey, Altha J. 1997. "The Changing South: Latino Labor and Poultry Production in Rural North Carolina." *Southeastern Geographer* 37(2): 295–300.

Dawson, Michael C. 1994. *Behind the Mule: Race and Class in African-American Politics*. Princeton, N.J.: Princeton University Press.

Diamond, Jeff. 1998. "African-American Attitudes Towards United States Immigration Policy." *International Migration Review* 32(2): 451–70.

Dunn, Timothy J., Ana María Aragonés, and George Shivers. 2005. "Recent Mexican Immigration in the Rural Delmarva Peninsula: Human Rights Versus Citizenship Rights in a Local Context." In *New Destinations: Mexican Immigration to the United States*, edited by Víctor Zúñiga and Rubén Hernández-León. New York: Russell Sage Foundation.

Durand, Jorge, Douglas Massey, and Fernando Charvet. 2000. "The Changing Geography of Mexican Immigration to the United States: 1910–1996." *Social Science Quarterly* 81(1): 1–15.

Engstrom, James. 2001. "Industry and Immigration in Dalton, Georgia." In *Latino Workers in the Contemporary South*, edited by Arthur D. Murphy, Colleen Blanchard, and Jennifer A. Hill. Athens, Ga.: University of Georgia Press.

Fink, Leon. 2003. *The Maya of Morgantown: Work and Community in the Nuevo New South*. Chapel Hill, N.C.: University of North Carolina Press.

Frey, William H. 2001. "Census 2000 Shows Large Black Return to the South, Reinforcing the Region's 'White-Black' Demographic Profile." Population Studies Center Research Report No. 01-473. Ann Arbor, Mich.: University of Michigan, Institute for Social Research.

———. 2002. "Three Americas: The Rising Significance of Regions." *APA Journal* 68(4): 349–55.

Gozdziak, Elzbieta, and Micah Bump. 2004. "Poultry, Apples, and New Immigrants in the Rural Communities of the Shenandoah Valley: An Ethnographic Case Study." *International Migration* 42(1): 149–64.

Greenbaum, Susan. 1998. "Urban Immigrants in the South: Recent Data and a Historical Case Study." In *Cultural Diversity in the U.S. South: Anthropological Contributions to a Region in Transition*, edited by Carole E. Hill and Patricia D. Beaver. Athens, Ga.: University of Georgia Press.

Grey, Mark A., and Anne C. Woodrick. 2005. " 'Latinos Have Revitalized Our Community': Mexican Migration and Anglo Responses in Marshalltown, Iowa."

In *New Destinations: Mexican Immigration to the United States*, edited by Víctor Zúñiga and Rubén Hernández-León. New York: Russell Sage Foundation.

Griffith, David. 1995a. "*Hay Trabajo:* Poultry Processing, Rural Industrialization, and the Latinization of Low-Wage Labor." In *Any Way You Cut It: Meat Processing and Small Town America*, edited by Donald D. Stull, Michael J. Broadway, and David Griffith. Lawrence, Kan.: University of Kansas Press.

———. 1995b. "New Immigrants in an Old Industry: Blue Crab Processing in Pamlico County, North Carolina." In *Any Way You Cut It: Meat Processing and Small Town America*, edited by Donald D. Stull, Michael J. Broadway, and David Griffith, eds. Lawrence, Kan.: University of Kansas Press.

———. 2005. "Rural Industry and Mexican Immigration and Settlement in North Carolina." in *New Destinations: Mexican Immigration to the United States*, edited by Víctor Zúñiga and Rubén Hernández-León. New York: Russell Sage Foundation.

Guthey, Greig. 2001. "Mexican Places in Southern Spaces: Globalization, Work, and Daily Life in and Around the North Georgia Poultry Industry." In *Latino Workers in the Contemporary South*, edited by Arthur D. Murphy, Colleen Blanchard, and Jennifer A. Hill. Athens, Ga.: University of Georgia Press.

Hamermesh, Daniel S., and Frank D. Bean, editors. 1998. *Help or Hindrance? The Economic Implications of Immigration for African Americans*. New York: Russell Sage Foundation.

Hernández-León, Rubén, and Víctor Zúñiga. 2000. " 'Making Carpet by the Mile': The Emergence of a Mexican Immigrant Community in an Industrial Region of the U.S. Historic South." *Social Science Quarterly* 81(1): 49–65.

———. 2005. "Appalachia Meets Aztlán: Mexican Immigration and Inter-Group Relations in Dalton, Georgia." In *New Destinations: Mexican Immigration in the United States*, edited by Víctor Zúñiga and Rubén Hernández-León. New York: Russell Sage Foundation.

Hochschild, Jennifer. 1981. *What's Fair? American Beliefs About Distributive Justice*. Cambridge, Mass.: Harvard University Press.

———. 2007. "Intergroup Relations." In *The New Americans: A Guide to Immigration Since 1965*, edited by Mary C. Waters and Reed Ueda. Cambridge, Mass.: Harvard University Press.

Johnson, Jr., James H., Walter C. Farrell Jr., and Chandra Guinn. 1999. "Immigration Reform and the Browning of America: Tensions, Conflicts, and Community Instability in Metropolitan Los Angeles." In *The Handbook of International Migration: The American Experience*, edited by Charles Hirschman, Philip Kasinitz, and Josh DeWind. New York: Russell Sage Foundation.

Johnson, Jr., James H., Karen D. Johnson-Webb, and Walter C. Farrell Jr. 1999. "A Profile of Hispanic Newcomers to North Carolina." *Popular Government* 69(1): 2–13.

Jones-Correa, Michael. 2005. "Bringing Outsiders In: Questions of Immigrant Incorporation." In *The Politics of Democratic Inclusion*, edited by Rodney E. Hero and Christina Wolbrecht. Philadelphia, Penn.: Temple University Press.

Kandel, William, and Emilio A. Parrado. 2004. "Hispanics in the American South and the Transformation of the Poultry Industry." In *Hispanic Spaces, Latino Places: Community and Cultural Diversity in Contemporary America*, edited by Daniel D. Arreola. Austin, Tex.: University of Texas Press.

Key, Jr., V. O. 1949/1984. *Southern Politics in State and Nation*. Knoxville, Tenn.: University of Tennessee Press.

Kochhar, Rakesh, Roberto Suro, and Sonya Tafoya. 2005. "The New Latino South: The Context and Consequences of Rapid Population Growth." Report. Washington: Pew Hispanic Center, July 26, 2005.

Leitner, Helga. 2003. "Inscriptions and Contestations of the Color Line in Small Town America." Paper presented at the Color Lines Conference. Harvard Law School, Cambridge, Mass., August 29 to September 1, 2003.

Marrow, Helen B. 2005. "New Destinations and Immigrant Incorporation." *Perspectives on Politics* 3(4): 781–99.

Massey, Douglas S., Jorge Durand, and Emilio A. Parrado. 1999. "The New Era of Mexican Migration to the United States." *Journal of American History* 86(2): 518–36.

McClain, Paula D., and Steven C. Tauber. 2001. "Racial Minority Group Relations in a Multiracial Society." In *Governing American Cities: Inter-Ethnic Coalitions, Competition, and Conflict*, edited by Michael Jones-Correa. New York: Russell Sage Foundation.

McClain, Paula D., Niambi M. Carter, Victoria M. De Francesco, J. Alan Kendrick, Monique L. Lyle, Shayla C. Nunnally, Thomas C. Scotto, Jeffrey D. Grynasviski, and Jason A. Johnson. 2003. "St. Benedict the Black Meets the Virgin of Guadalupe: Intergroup Relations in a Southern City." Paper presented at the Color Lines Conference. Harvard Law School, Cambridge, Mass., August 29 to September 1, 2003.

McClain, Paula D., Niambi M. Carter, Victoria M. DeFrancesco Soto, Monique L. Lyle, Jeffrey D. Grynasviski, Shayla C. Nunnally, Thomas C. Scotto, J. Alan Kendrick, Gerald F. Lackey, and Kendra Davenport Cotton. 2006. "Racial Distancing in a Southern City: Latino Immigrants' Views of Black Americans." *Journal of Politics* 68(3): 571–84.

Miller, Kathleen K., and Bruce A. Weber. 2004. "How Do Persistent Poverty Dynamics and Demographics Vary across the Rural-Urban Continuum?" *Measuring Rural Diversity* 1(1): 1–7.

Mohl, Raymond A. 2003. "Globalization, Latinization, and the Nuevo New South." *Journal of American Ethnic History* 22(4): 31–66.

Morawska, Ewa. 2001. "Immigrant-Black Dissensions in American Cities: An Argument for Multiple Explanations." In *Problem of the Century: Racial Stratification in the United States*, edited by Elijah Anderson and Douglas S. Massey. New York: Russell Sage Foundation.

Reed, John Shelton. 1993. *My Tears Spoiled My Aim and Other Reflections on Southern Culture*. San Diego: Harcourt Brace.

Rich, Brian L., and Marta Miranda. 2005. "The Sociopolitical Dynamics of Mexican Immigration in Lexington, Kentucky, 1977 to 2002: An Ambivalent

Community Responds." In *New Destinations: Mexican Immigration to the United States*, edited by Víctor Zúñiga and Rubén Hernández-León. New York: Russell Sage Foundation.

Rodríguez, Nestor. 1999. "U.S. Immigration and Changing Relations Between African Americans and Latinos." In *The Handbook of International Migration: The American Experience*, edited by Charles Hirschman, Philip Kasinitz, and Josh DeWind. New York: Russell Sage Foundation.

Rosenfeld, Michael J., and Marta Tienda. 1999. "Mexican Immigration, Occupational Niches, and Labor Market Competition: Evidence from Los Angeles, Chicago, and Atlanta, 1970–1990." In *Immigration and Opportunity: Race, Ethnicity, and Employment in the United States*, edited by Frank D. Bean and Stephanie Bell-Rose. New York: Russell Sage Foundation.

Ruggles, Steven, Matthew Sobek, Trent Alexander, Catherine A. Fitch, Ronald Goeken, Patricia Kelly Hall, Miriam King, and Chad Ronnander. 2004. Integrated Public Use Microdata Series, version 3.0, machine-readable database. Minneapolis, Minn.: Minnesota Population Center. Accessed at http://www.ipums.org.

Saenz, Rogelio, and Cruz C. Torres. 2003. "Latinos in Rural America." In *Challenges for Rural America in the Twenty-First Century*, edited by David L. Brown and Louis E. Swanson. University Park, Penn.: Pennsylvania State University Press.

Schmidley, Diane. 2003. "The Foreign Born Population in the United States: March 2002." In *Current Population Reports*. Washington: U.S. Government Printing Office.

Smith, Barbara Ellen. 2003. "Across Races and Nations: Toward Worker Justice in the U.S. South." Paper presented at the Color Lines Conference. Harvard Law School, Cambridge, Mass., August 29 to September 1, 2003.

Stack, Carol. 1996. *Call to Home: African Americans Reclaim the Rural South*. New York: Basic Books.

Striffler, Steve. 2005. "We're All Mexicans Here: Poultry Processing, Latino Migration, and the Transformation of Class in the South." In *The American South in a Global World*, edited by James L. Peacock, Harry L. Watson, and Carrie R. Matthews. Chapel Hill, N.C.: University of North Carolina Press.

Studstill, John D., and Laura Neito-Studstill. 2001. "Hospitality and Hostility: Latin Immigrants in Southern Georgia." In *Latino Workers in the Contemporary South*, edited by Arthur D. Murphy, Colleen Blanchard, and Jennifer A. Hill. Athens, Ga.: University of Georgia Press.

Suro, Roberto, and Audrey Singer. 2002. "Latino Growth in Metropolitan America: Changing Patterns, New Locations." In *Survey Series, Census 2000*. Washington: Brookings Institution.

Torres, Rebecca M., E. Jeffrey Popke, and Holly M. Hapke. 2006. "The South's Silent Bargain: Rural Restructuring, Latino Labor and the Ambiguities of Migrant Experience." In *The New South: Latinos and the Transformation of Place*, edited by Heather A. Smith and Owen J. Furuseth. Aldershot, England: Ashgate Press.

U.S. Office of Management and Budget. 1995. "Standards for the Classification of Federal Data on Race and Ethnicity; Notice." *Federal Register* 60(166).

————. 1997. "Revisions to the Standards for the Classification of Federal Data on Race and Ethnicity; Notice." *Federal Register* 62(210).

Waldinger, Roger. 1996. *Still the Promised City? African Americans and New Immigrants in Post-Industrial New York.* Cambridge, Mass.: Harvard University Press.

Waldinger, Roger, and Michael I. Lichter. 2003. *How the Other Half Works: Immigration and the Social Organization of Labor.* Berkeley, Calif.: University of California Press.

Willis, Rachel A. 2005. "Voices of Southern Mill Workers: Responses to Border Crossers in American Factories and Jobs Crossing Borders." In *The American South in a Global World*, edited by James L. Peacock, Harry L. Watson, and Carrie R. Matthews. Chapel Hill, N.C.: University of North Carolina Press.

Zúñiga, Víctor, and Rubén Hernández-León, editors. 2005. *New Destinations: Mexican Immigration to the United States.* New York: Russell Sage Foundation.

CHAPTER 10

✕

NASHVILLE'S NEW "SONIDO": LATINO MIGRATION AND THE CHANGING POLITICS OF RACE

JAMIE WINDERS

> Even Nashville . . . has a new sonido: the norteño music booming from its three Spanish-language radio stations. Los Tigres del Norte compete with Garth Brooks and chipotle complements chitterlings across a vast stretch of the South, in urban "Little Mexicos" . . . like Nashville's Nolensville Road district.
>
> Mike Davis (2000, 4)

In 2000, the urban and labor scholar Mike Davis wrote that "even Nashville ha[d] a new sonido"(sound) and was feeling the effects of Latino migration. In a clever rhetorical maneuver, Davis highlighted the ubiquity of Latinos across the United States by calling attention to their presence in the most unlikely of places, Nashville, Tennessee, the country music capital of the world and a city virtually absent from the map of urban and immigration studies. Davis mentions Nashville to signal the reach of Latino influence to the very edges of urban America and, in so doing, alludes to a historically powerful trope of southern distinctiveness and exceptionalism (Woodward 1960/1968, 1971; Greeson 1999; Winders 2005b). His allusion to this discourse of southern exceptionalism is, however, meant to be ironic and to mark its contemporary failure. Southern cities, long positioned outside the influences of transnational migration, are increasingly central to Latino movements to and within the United States, a fact which, for Davis, offers irrefutable evidence that Latino migration is a powerful force across the country. If "even Nashville" is swinging to the rhythms of a norteño beat (a style of music popular in northern Mexico), Latinos clearly deserve a central place in urban studies.

Even as Davis quipped about how Latino culture had penetrated the bastion of the urban South, Nashville's rapidly growing Hispanic population was challenging the image of southern cities as exceptional. By 2000, "even Nashville" had a Latino community that numbered somewhere between the official metropolitan census count of just over 40,000 and local estimates of 110,000. In response to this growing Latino population, Nashville was grappling with a new regime of social services and urban politics and was witnessing the expansion of a Latino business district across southern parts of the city. By the beginning of the twenty-first century, "even Nashville" was retuning the "old-fashioned black-and-white screen" upon which its social relations and urban politics had historically been calibrated to accommodate what Davis (1999, 7) describes elsewhere as "the living color of the contemporary big city."

This chapter examines the retuning of Nashville's black-and-white screen and the city's reaction to the "living color" of Latino migration. Focusing on how Latino migration has influenced both understandings of race and belonging and social interactions between racialized communities in Nashville (Straughan and Hondagneu-Sotelo 2002), it analyzes how the arrival of Latino men and women has been framed within two key social spaces: Nashville's public sphere, especially public discourse around the city's changing racial politics and composition; and its local labor market, especially its low-wage work sites and their transition toward an increasing dependence on Latino workers. In considering these two contexts, the chapter examines changing racial formations and ethnic relations (Omi and Winant 1986; Peake and Kobayashi 2002) and investigates how understandings of race are redefined through daily practice by immigrants and non-immigrants alike in the Music City (Goode and Schneider 1994; Pulido 2004). In cities like Nashville, with almost no previous experience with voluntary international migration, critical attention to the ways that long-term residents adjust to new arrivals—and that new arrivals adjust to their new home—can shed light on the reworking of community boundaries of race, ethnicity, and belonging more broadly (Zúñiga et al. 2001).

To develop this argument, the chapter proceeds in two parts. The first reviews existing research on the emergence of southern American towns and cities as popular destinations for domestic and international Latino migrants and points to some of the differences between Nashville's experiences and those documented in other, particularly rural, southern locales. This background information lays the groundwork for the chapter's second part, which examines Latino migration's effects on understandings of race and belonging in Nashville's public discourse and low-wage work-places. By comparing how Latino migration is framed in these two social spaces, the analysis highlights this migration's uneven effects across Nashville's social institutions and underscores the need for both multi-sited ethnographic research on Latino migration to southern cities and more attention to the social spaces and contexts within which understand-ings of this migration are constructed.

LATINO MIGRATION'S NEW GEOGRAPHY

As has been well documented by newspapers, think tanks, academic sym-posia, activist conferences, and other sources, the South's racial and ethnic composition has changed dramatically since the early 1990s through the arrival of Latino men and women. Perhaps the most dramatic sign of this trend has been the increase in the Mexican-born population, the largest immigrant group in the United States. According to Elizabeth Grieco (2003), eight of the ten states with the greatest percentage change in the foreign-born Mexican population between 1990 and 2000 were southern states, led by Tennessee's 2,166 percent shift. In 2001, the Center for Immigration Studies announced that 59 percent of the immigrant gate-ways that they called "New Ellis Islands" were in the South, where numer-ous states were the location of more than ten such gateways (Camarota and Keeley 2001). These dramatic demographic shifts are changing the public image of southern cities in ways not imagined ten years ago and are rais-ing new issues for immigrant-receiving areas in the region.

Much of the growth of Latino migration to southern communities is attributable to the region's strong rural and urban economies, low liv-ing costs, and, until recently, relatively weak anti-immigrant sentiment (Cravey 1997, 2003; Smith 1998; Hernández-León and Zúñiga 2000, 2003; Mendoza, Ciscel, and Smith 2000; Murphy, Blanchard, and Hill 2001; Fink 2003; Johnson-Webb 2003). In addition, however, this migration has been influenced nationally by American economic restructuring in the 1990s and a large-scale amnesty offered to undocumented migrants during the late 1980s. Internationally, it has been affected by political and economic difficulties in Central America and Mexico. As stories of new opportuni-ties in the American South spread south of the Mexico-United States bor-der itself, transnational flows of people, capital, and culture began to form between and among communities of the American South and sending regions throughout Latin America, transforming cities such as Nashville in a matter of years.

Just as Latino migration has grown dramatically in the South over the last ten years, research on the topic has also expanded exponentially.

Scholars across the social sciences have examined this migration's economic effects and demographic characteristics and are making important contributions to understanding the new geography of Latino migration (Durand, Massey, and Charvet 2000; Hernàndez-Leòn and Zúñiga 2000; Murphy, Blanchard, and Hill 2001; Johnson-Webb 2003). To date, however, most studies of Latino migration to the American South have offered descriptive analyses that do not engage the region's historical and contemporary geographies of race and racism or address its shifting racial politics in any detail (for a fuller version of this argument, see Winders 2005a). In this way, studies of immigration to southern communities, with the exception of those by Emily Selby, Deborah Dixon, and Holly Hapke (2001) and Rubén Hernández-León and Víctor Zúñiga (2005), have yet to analyze how Latino migration is affecting broader understandings and practices of race within the region, despite frequent calls to do so (Smith 1998).

This relative silence on questions of Latino migration and race in the South reflects more than a gap in the secondary literature. It also signals, I argue here, a general haziness about Latino migration's effects on racial formations, categories, and intergroup relations within affected communities. Latino migration's cultural, political, and economic consequences in southern communities are often fairly evident, but other effects of this migration, particularly with respect to racial formations, are not so readily apparent (Velázquez 1999). Indeed, the arrival of Latin Americans, a population that fits uneasily within a black-white racial taxonomy, raises new questions about southern race relations and racial categories more broadly (Hill 1998). How, for example, will the South's racial framework adjust to a group whose "difference," both from long-standing communities and within the category "Latino" itself, is simultaneously racial, linguistic, ethnic, national, and cultural (Oboler 2002)? Where will Latinos get placed in the region's changing racial grammar?

These questions linger for a variety of reasons, including the newness of Latino migration to the South, the rapid rate of population growth, and the variety of local responses to it. Complicating this situation is a secondary literature focused on small communities in rural Georgia and North Carolina. Studies suggest that in these states, Latin American population growth began in the mid- to late 1980s and has been predominantly Mexican in origin (Cravey 1997, 2003; Murphy, Blanchard, and Hill 2001; Selby, Dixon, and Hapke 2001; Zúñiga et al. 2001). Latino workers in these areas have reportedly congregated in particular industries, such as poultry processing and light manufacturing, which dominate not only local economies but also, in some cases, political systems (Hernández-León and Zúñiga 2005). The connections between Latino migration to these smaller southern locales and movements to larger urban centers, such as Nashville and Atlanta, however, have yet to be explored (Odem 2004; Winders 2005a). As the remainder of this chapter shows, Latin American immigrants in Nashville display a wider range of national origins and are employed in a wider range of jobs than those in smaller southern communities. These differences, which may reflect intraregional distinctions between interior and coastal destinations or between rural and urban locales, merit further attention as the literature on this topic grows.[1]

Nashville's New "Sonido"

Although Latin Americans have been a minor presence in rural Tennessee as migrant workers since the 1930s (Cantu 1999), Nashville did not come to have significant Latino communities until the mid-1990s, almost a decade after Hispanic communities in Georgia and North Carolina hit their growth spurt. Despite this late start, by 1995 Nashville's Latino population was experiencing what one local advocate described as an "in-your-face type of explosion."[2] Within a few years, Latino communities in the Music City had become "more organized" and more visible; and the city's new sonido had grown louder.

As has been documented in other studies (Fink 2003; Hernández-León and Zúñiga 2003), Latino migration to Nashville began as a movement of young *mexicanos* away from Texas and California, as cooling economies and growing anti-immigrant sentiment in those states made Nashville more appealing. This secondary migration, however, rapidly became transnational and extended to other regions of Latin America. It also became more complex, as growing numbers of Latina women, young children, and older migrants came to the city through formal and informal family reunification.

Latino migration to Nashville, in contrast to patterns described in smaller southern communities (see Cravey 1997, 2003; Murphy, Blanchard, and Hill 2001; Selby, Dixon, and Hapke 2001), has been predominantly, but not exclusively, Mexican. According to the 2000 census, 62.4 percent of the 25,774 Hispanics in Davidson County, Tennessee, were of Mexican origin. From 1990 to 2000, the county's Central-American population increased by a factor of 88, from 154 to 13,540 persons (Cornfield et al. 2003, 9); and in the last five years, a smaller number of South Americans have also come to Nashville, a trend noted in Atlanta as well (Odem 2004). Well-educated, and often well-heeled, these immigrants from Colombia, Venezuela, and other parts of South America typically bring higher levels of social capital and a different understanding of the permanence of their presence in Nashville than do their Mexican counterparts.

Although South and Central Americans are outnumbered by Nashville's Mexican population, many non-Mexican Latinos hold leadership positions in community and business organizations. This situation highlights, and sometimes sharpens, tensions around class and nationality among the city's Hispanic population. In the words of a state director of minority-health initiatives, "You can see class divisions and strata" between "South American professionals" and "subliterate Californian and Mexican workers and transients," as members of the first group develop social services for the latter. These distinctions influence who speaks with authority for and about Nashville's "Hispanic community" and who remains seen but not heard in the Music City (Velázquez 1999).

Much of the increase in Nashville's Latino population is attributable to the city's recent economic and population growth (Winders 2006b). Between 1980 and 2000, Nashville's metropolitan population increased by nearly 45 percent, to just over 1.2 million residents (MDC 2002). During the same period, the number of jobs increased by over 90 percent, to nearly 900,000 (MDC 2002). This expansion created a tight labor market, particularly in construction, services, and the hospitality industry. With unemployment rates hovering around 3 percent to 4 percent, this tight labor market quickly became a staple aspect of discussions of immigration, making the words "Latino" and "labor" all but inseparable. Davidson County's construction workforce grew by 50 percent from 1993 to 2001, and as many as half of those workers were Hispanic by 1998 (Drew Sullivan, "Jobs Draw Hispanics to State," *The Tennessean*, September 5, 1998, 1A).

Latino migration to Nashville has also been influenced by broader economic transitions in Middle Tennessee, of which the construction boom has been a key part. During the mid-1990s, Middle Tennessee's economic geography shifted from light manufacturing around Nashville to the provision of services within Nashville (Winders 2006b). Simultaneously, Nashville was ranked as a very "livable" city and attracted a growing number of young professionals (Wall 1999), resulting in a 9.1 percent net internal migration rate from 1990 to 1997. As Nashville's population expanded into adjacent counties, construction and services boomed, creating low-wage, seasonal jobs that were increasingly filled by Latino workers.

Through these and other factors, the number of Latin Americans coming to Nashville grew dramatically in the late 1990s. By 2003, the Census Bureau estimated that Nashville's metropolitan area was home to more than 50,000 Hispanics, which is likely a conservative figure, given previous census figures. In 2000, the Nashville Catholic Diocese surveyed 4,824 Latinos at Spanish-language masses across Middle Tennessee to determine how many participated in the census. Of the almost 5,000 respondents, 40.5 percent said they had not participated in the census, so the diocese calculated a 2000 population estimate of 110,000 Latinos and Latinas in its geographical area.[3]

Although the exact number of Latinos in Nashville remains unclear, their influence in the city is easier to detect. The language of low-wage laborers is changing at many Nashville work sites, as is the language of play at area schoolyards and playgrounds. Social-service providers, as well as local businesses, are learning to speak Spanish, and local banks and lending agencies are finding creative ways to finance loans for a population whose ambiguous legal status is trumped by its unambiguous buying power (Mendoza, Ciscel, and Smith 2000). From the series of mystery novels set in Nashville's Hispanic neighborhoods (Villatoro 2001, 2003) to the strips of Mexican "tiendas" (shops) lining south Nashville's major roads, Nashville, as Davis aptly noted, has brought a new sonido and a new beat to the Music City.

My examination of this new *sonido* is based on ten months of fieldwork in Nashville during 2002 and 2003. My research centered on two primary questions: How did Nashville become a popular destination site for Latino migrants in the middle to late 1990s? And what effects has Latino migration had on Nashville's racial formations and intergroup relations (Omi and Winant 1986)? To answer the first question, a variety of data sources were used, including quarterly regional economic reports published from 1996 to 2003 by Middle Tennessee State University's Business and Economic Research Center; 2000 census data, along with local population estimates and immigrant community assessments; and articles published in Nashville's major newspaper, *The Tennessean*, from 1995 to 2003. An analysis of these sources revealed the broad contours of Latino migration to Nashville and constructed a narrative about the development of Latino communities within the city. From this general narrative, key issues concerning Latino communities were highlighted for further examination in the study's second part, which centered on Latino migration's influence on racial formations and intergroup relations in Nashville.

This second phase of my research drew on semistructured interviews and participant observation conducted with two groups in Nashville. The first included approximately fifty key actors involved in the city's racial and immigrant politics, a group comprising Latino, white, and black business and community leaders, activists, advocates, service providers, and social workers. The second group was approximately sixty workers and supervisors from six low-wage work sites where managers had recently begun to hire Latino workers to work alongside white, black, refugee, and other foreign-born workers already there. These two sources of data were analyzed, first, to discern Latino migration's effects on public discourse about the nature of the "Hispanic community" and changing intergroup relations and, second, to characterize interpersonal interactions between and among Latino and non-Latino workers and supervisors at specific work sites.

Part of the story these interviews tell is familiar and aligns with other studies of Latino migration to the South to document rapid Latino community growth, overwhelmed social service agencies, and dramatic changes generated by the arrival of Latinos. Another part of this story is less familiar, particularly in relation to emerging arguments about changing work sites across southern communities (Johnson, Johnson-Webb, and Farrell, Jr. 1999; Mohl 2002; Cravey 2003; Johnson-Webb 2003). This less-familiar story highlights the effects of Latino workers on workplace social relations and practices in Nashville, by drawing on workers' perspectives regarding demographic changes in the low-wage workforce of hotels, fast-food restaurants, and small businesses. For some Nashville workers and supervisors who daily negotiate multilingual and multi-ethnic work sites, the dramatic effects of Latino migration noted in newspapers, citywide task forces, and other public venues seemed less impressive. Their framings of Latino migration, I argue, provide an important counterpoint to more familiar stories of drastic change across the region and an impetus to examine more critically how these different framings can coexist across shared urban social spaces.

LATINO MIGRATION TO NASHVILLE: AN INCOMPLETE STORY?

When Latino migration to Nashville began to accelerate in the 1990s, it constituted a rapid and unprecedented development. In 1996, Nashville's major newspaper, *The Tennessean*, announced that "Nashville's lamp [was] draw[ing] thousands" (Bonna M. de la Cruz, "Midstate Hispanics' Clout Grows," *The Tennessean*, May 2, 1996, 1B; Bonna M. de la Cruz, "Nashville's Lamp Draws Thousands." *The Tennessean*, September 16, 1996, 1A.), and articles began to chronicle the challenges faced by both immigrant newcomers and the city. By 1998, headlines revealed that Nashville's "growing Hispanic community [was] influencing local Catholicism" (Ray Waddle, "Growing Hispanic Community Influencing Local Catholicism," *The Tennessean*, September 27, 1998, 1A) and that the "immigration boom [had] hit schools" (Leon Alligood, "Immigration Boom Hits Schools," The Tennessean, November 17, 1998, 1A). Subsequent reports found churches "scrambling to fill needs of local Hispanics" (Monica Whitaker, "Church Scrambling to Fill Needs of Local Hispanics," April 21, 2000, 1A) and "bank workers learn[ing] to speak 'en español' " (Gethan Ward, "Bank Workers Learn to Speak 'en Espanol,' " *The Tennessean*, November 9, 2000). By the time the 2000 census figures were released, the "wake-up" call these numbers sounded about Nashville's expanding Hispanic population was growing in intensity.

These newspaper headlines provide some indication of the speed and scope of changes that Latino migration precipitated in Nashville and the increasing visibility that Latinos commanded in public discourse during the late 1990s. By 1996, Nashville had thirteen Spanish-language church programs, almost thirty Hispanic-owned restaurants, twenty-two Hispanic soccer teams, two Spanish-language newspapers, and two Spanish radio stations (Bonna M. de la Cruz, "Midstate Hispanics' Clout Grows," *The Tennessean*, May 2, 1996, 1B). At the same time, members of Nashville's Metropolitan Police Department were learning "survival Spanish" while seeking Spanish-speaking workers for 911 call centers (Deborah Highland, "Spanish Lessons Give Police Backup When English Fails," *The Tennessean*, December 1, 1996, 4B). By the end of the decade, Nashville's Latino population reportedly had "exploded," as "whole villages from Mexico" appeared "overnight" to work and live in the Music City.

This "explosion," by all accounts, "crept up" on Nashville's social-service and nonprofit organizations. According to one state agency director, government departments whose directors repeatedly asked in the early 1990s whether translators and bilingual material were really necessary found themselves "behind the eight ball" in the late 1990s. "Unaware of Hispanic needs" until Latinos were standing in the doorways, these agencies—with the sense of surprise reported in other new destinations throughout the South (Fink 2003)—scrambled to process, and even understand, the growing number of phone calls and requests from Spanish-speaking clients.

Partially in response to this seeming lack of preparedness for immigrant clients, Latino political and business organizations began to lobby for bilingual services and community recognition in Nashville. By 1997, Latino leaders from across Tennessee were strategizing in Nashville ("Hispanic leaders Focus 1st Meeting on Voting Impact," *The Tennessean*, April 1, 1997, 5B), and two years later, two Hispanic Chambers of Commerce were at work (and often at odds) in Nashville (Lisa Benavides, "Hispanic Voice Echoes Through New Chamber," *The Tennessean*, October 24, 1999, 1E; Monica Whitaker, "Second Hispanic Chamber Forming," *The Tennessean*, December 6, 1999, 1E). Nonetheless, compared with immigrant networks in gateway cities such as Los Angeles and New York, Nashville's formal and informal networks for new Latino arrivals were significantly smaller, and the city remained a more challenging place for Latinos to settle.

Despite Nashville's lack of preparedness for and experience with Latino migrants, its ready supply of jobs, slower pace of life, and—at least initially—relatively welcoming sentiment compensated new arrivals for the city's weaker social infrastructure. It is important to note, however, that although Nashville in the late 1990s may have lacked the baggage of cities that have long been home to Latino migrants, immigrants who came to the Music City did not walk into a blank-slate situation. Instead, they entered a setting already crosscut by racial and class divisions that they had to negotiate, understand, and potentially redefine, both as individuals and as a social group. In the process of immigrants' finding a place in this racialized and classed social landscape, differences among Latinos in Nashville were often erased, especially in the context of public discourse. For example, class and nationality distinctions for Latinos from different parts of the United States and Latin America and from different socioeconomic backgrounds all but disappeared in public discussions and debates in the Music City, as "the Hispanic community" became, in an all-too-familiar trend (Oboler 2002), a homogenous group to be located relative to a historically powerful racial dichotomy.

This act of working out where Latinos, as a racialized group, fit vis-à-vis a racial binary remains in flux in Nashville. In this study, even getting key actors in immigrant and racial politics to discuss the topic proved to be difficult. In response to questions about Latinos and race relations, one Latino business leader quipped, "It depends on whether you want to be honest or dance," and his reluctance to engage the question was not unusual. A state director involved with refugees in Nashville described Latinos and race as a "publicly avoided" topic, and it repeatedly proved to be one that made participants in this study hesitant and visibly uncomfortable. This ambiguity about where Latinos fit within a racial binary was particularly clear in an interview I undertook with a South American director of programming at a Nashville nonprofit agency. When I asked about the effect of Latino migration on local race relations, he gave this answer:

> In Nashville, there are two groups: black and white. Now, Hispanics, are they white? Are they black? What kinds are they? Sometimes they behave like African Americans; sometimes like whites. But . . . there are racial stereotypes. "Blacks don't like to work. Hispanics are taking our jobs . . ." Hispanics are the middle, like "un colchón," a mattress.

This "in between" location that Latinos are seen to occupy within Nashville's racial system—somehow similar to both groups yet distinct from them—surfaced throughout my interviews with community leaders and advocates, as participants seemed unsure about where to place Latinos within Nashville's historical understanding of race. Many discussions started with the comment "It depends on who[m] you're talking to," as people sought appropriate language for a topic perceived to be inappropriate for speculation. In part, this reluctance—or, I would suggest, inability—to find a language well suited for discussing Latino migrants and race reflects a broader issue facing Nashville: the effect of Latino migration on racial formations is still under construction. Over and over, people remarked that although "fear of the unknown" could be found, Nashville was an "open" place that was still working out the details of how and where to be a multicultural, multi-ethnic city.

Latinos' location within Nashville's racial categories may have been unclear, but their effects on the city's racial politics, particularly around issues of social justice, were quite evident. By the late 1990s, according to some immigrant advocates, Nashville's social-service agencies had discovered "a new population to serve," and one that they could serve "successfully." This characterization has important, if unspoken, racial undertones. As a new population to serve, Latinos increasingly jostle for access to scarce urban services and visibility within Nashville's political arena. In the process, Latinos, as a new "minority" community, have had a particularly strong effect on African American communities. Although Latinos may have moved African Americans "off the radar" of active discrimination and police scrutiny, as one civil rights attorney remarked, they may also have moved black communities off the radar of social service organizations and civil rights struggles themselves.

This shift in focus of social-service provision and even social justice has arguably been subtle, but it has sometimes led to tense relations between black civil rights organizations and Latino community leaders. For example, at the onset of Latino migration to Nashville, in the mid-1990s, a prominent black community leader resigned from the Metropolitan Human Relations Commission—which had been formed in response to Nashville's 1965 racial tensions—over his concern about the "diluting" of black political power through Latino migration (Bonna M. de la Cruz, "Relations Panel Deep in Turmoil," *The Tennessean,* September 15, 1996, 1B). When a Latino community leader was nominated for the open post and received support from Nashville's overall Metro Council (Mark Ippolito, "Hispanics Ask for Representation," *The Tennessean,* October 21, 1996, 5B), the politics surrounding being "the favored minority" in Nashville became clear.

A few years later, in 1999, the Nashville branch of the National Association for the Advancement of Colored People (NAACP) extended a formal membership invitation to *Unámonos,* Nashville's most prominent Latino organization at the time (Monica Whitaker, "NAACP, Hispanics Explore New Alliance," *The Tennessean,* August 16, 1999, 1A). When the leader of Unámonos questioned the different histories of discrimination faced by Latinos and African Americans and publicly doubted the possibilities of this merger, the invitation was tabled. Within a short time, even the possibility of such a partnership was shattered by a series of events that crystallized Nashville's racial and political fault lines in the late 1990s.

Rumors and complaints of police mistreatment of Latinos surfaced throughout the 1990s, but these criticisms took on a new tenor in late 1999 when a local newspaper reported accusations that white off-duty Metro Police officers employed by a private security firm had abused and harassed Latino residents at area apartment complexes (Kathy Carlson, "Metro Police Investigating Claims That Hispanics Were Abused," *The Tennessean,* October 26, 1999, 1A). A Spanish-language newspaper ran translated versions of the newspaper report, and the story quickly circulated across Nashville's increasing diverse communities. The situation of off-duty police officers harassing Hispanic residents became even more complicated as the debate increasingly focused on the Metro police chief, who was also the first African American to hold this post in Nashville. In the process, the incident spiraled into a citywide debate involving a mayor's task force on justice (Thomas Goldsmith, "Mayor Vows Action on Hispanic Concerns," *The Tennessean,* October 27, 1999, 1B) and an FBI investigation, becoming a flashpoint in Nashville's racial politics.

Although the abuse scandal at root involved white off-duty police officers accused of abusing Latino residents and conflating being Hispanic with being "illegal," it became something much more contentious because of the black leadership of the police department. When a local Latino leader called for the chief's resignation because of his alleged involvement with one of the accused officers, the NAACP publicly denounced the Latino community leader's actions (Monica Whitaker, "NAACP Backs Police Chief," *The Tennessean,* November 7, 1999, 1B). As a result of this controversy, black and Latino civil rights groups took opposite sides of a debate that increasingly focused not on the ongoing abuse investigation but on the figure of the police chief and the broader shift in black leadership he represented. With this reorienting of the debate, the abuse scandal pitted one minority group against another within different understandings of racial and social justice and different approaches to sustaining progress in race relations in the midst of Nashville's transformation from a biracial to a multicultural, multi-ethnic city.

However this story was viewed locally—as clear-cut racism and police abuse; as a well-handled, though politically charged, situation; or as gross misunderstanding of off-duty police officers "doing their job" as security guards—it was a "watershed moment" in Nashville, as one local official put it. Until public exposure of these incidents and, unfortunately, others like them, Latinos were not conceptualized as a group that could enter local debates about race relations and racial politics or that could bear significant burdens of racism and discriminatory actions. After this scandal, Latino communities earned a place within Nashville's racial politics, even if that place had yet to be clearly specified.

The ambiguous place that Latinos continue to occupy within Nashville's racial politics is sustained partly by the "exotic" position they hold in Nashville. One immigration lawyer lamented, "People here don't have a clue about diversity" in relation to Latino communities. Because of stark residential segregation (Cornfield et al. 2003) and rapid Latino population growth, Nashville, it seems, has not come to grips with "diversity." Although racial and ethnic diversity is visible within specific circuits and spaces, particularly the city's immigrant and refugee networks and community forums (Winders 2006a), the overall attitude toward Latinos remains "Hispanic communities will continue to grow, but we'll deal with it later," one advocate said. In this way, a Latino advocate said, the image of Latinos in Nashville, as well as their place in the city's racial classification system, remains "incomplete."

Some of the ambiguities with respect to this incomplete picture disappear, or at least are reconfigured, when the focus shifts from Nashville's sites of public discourse to its spaces of low-wage labor—from the perspectives of community leaders to the views of low-wage workers. One Latino business leader quipped, "Nashville isn't sure what to think [about Latinos and Latinas], . . . unless they've seen them work." Through this connection between Latinos and labor, the "incomplete" story of Hispanics in Nashville is being filled in as a story of bodies at work. In hotel housekeeping departments where older African American women supervise Mexican and refugee women, at construction sites where young *mexicanos* try to avoid Mexican foremen who are "too hard" on their *paisanos,* and at fast-food restaurants where everyone learns enough Spanish to translate the menu, the details of where Latinos fit within a racial binary are being worked out on a daily basis.

The remainder of this chapter focuses on one work site in particular, the housekeeping department of what I call Hotel Nashville, to highlight some of the ways that the details about Latinos' place within Nashville's social relations and racial formations are being negotiated through daily work activities. The arrival of Latinos in Nashville—which took state agencies, businesses, hospitals, and other institutions by surprise—seems to have attracted less attention from workers in Hotel Nashville's housekeeping department, where the entry of Hispanic workers and the changes this group has precipitated in daily workplace activities have more or less been taken in stride. Although more research on changing workplaces in southern cities is needed to be able to contextualize Hotel Nashville within regional or interurban trends, a discussion of this transitioning work site in the Music City points to the complexities and contradictions surrounding Latino migration and its uneven effects on and across southern communities.

"Everyone Starts in Housekeeping"

"Everyone starts in housekeeping," remarked Janice, an Eastern European refugee and now a housekeeping supervisor, who began her tenure at Hotel Nashville as a room attendant in the mid-1990s.[4] "Everyone," in Janice's comment, referred to a fifty-member workforce that reflects the multicultural, multilingual, and multi-ethnic realities of contemporary low-wage work sites across the United States (Waldinger and Lichter 2003). As recently as the 1980s, Hotel Nashville's workforce was composed primarily of African American women. In the late 1980s, however, the hotel, like others in the city, began to see racial and ethnic transitions in its labor force, which followed the waves of refugees coming to Nashville initially from Southeast Asia and later from a variety of global hot spots (Winders 2006a). By the late 1990s, increasing numbers of Latino workers, particularly Mexican women, were joining this stream of workers at Hotel Nashville. During this time period, when labor shortages drove some Nashville hotels to fly in room cleaners from other cities, Hotel Nashville turned to Latino labor to avoid siphoning off workers from other hotels and "outbidding" their competitors by paying higher wages.

Hotel Nashville's current workforce includes white and black workers from Nashville and other American cities, Latino workers from Mexico and elsewhere in Latin America, and political refugees from around the world. Among this collection of employees are Mexican women who bring no formal work experience to their jobs, African American women who bring almost two decades of housekeeping experience, refugees who held government office jobs in their home countries, and Mexican men who have worked at low-wage work sites in Nashville and beyond. As Janice went on to stress in her comments, in housekeeping "it doesn't matter if you're educated or not." What matters is a willingness to do physically demanding and repetitive actions in room after room, day after day, in what Roger Waldinger and Michael Lichter (2003, 61) describe as the best example of "dead-end jobs." In Hotel Nashville, "everyone" may start in housekeeping; but as this study showed, some, particularly older African American women, end up staying there.

For six weeks in the spring of 2003, I spent my afternoons in Hotel Nashville's break room, interviewing and observing workers and supervisors in groups and individually. I asked what workers and supervisors thought about their department's rapid demographic shift and the arrival of a growing Latino workforce. How did hospitality workers interpret the changes that had caught social-service agencies and government officials so off guard and had reconfigured portions of Nashville's urban fabric and politics? What did Nashville's shifting racial and ethnic composition look like to Latino and other workers laboring in the city? These questions seemed important to ask within the context of the workplace, since social interactions at the workplace, and the place of work itself in workers' lives, form key elements in processes of identity formation (Salzinger 2003; Mullings 2005). Therefore, this case study examined the details of working at Hotel Nashville, and the meanings attached to this work, through the lens of participants' work histories at the hotel and elsewhere and their comparison of work experiences across time and space in their employment trajectories.

In asking questions about work experiences in the hotel and elsewhere and in observing daily interactions at Hotel Nashville itself, I began to see a fairly consistent downplaying of the importance of demographic changes on daily workplace activities. When I asked native-born workers about the biggest changes they had seen in their tenure in housekeeping—which for some stretched back almost twenty years—they rarely mentioned their department's ethnic and racial change. When I asked Latino immigrant workers to compare their work experiences in Nashville to their work experience elsewhere, I received a variety of answers that offered glimpses into the effects of a more structured American workplace on older Mexican men or, for newly single Mexican women, the simultaneously liberating and limiting experiences of being working mothers. These responses, however, like those of native-born workers, rarely mentioned the different racial and ethnic composition in American, as compared to Mexican, work sites.

This pattern surprised me, given preliminary reports of workplace conflicts involving Latino workers in southern communities (Johnson, Johnson-Webb, and Farrell, Jr. 1999; Mohl 2002; Cravey 2003; Johnson-Webb 2003). To make sense of Hotel Nashville's seeming ill fit with these arguments, I turned to the hotel's microgeography of work. Various workplace studies (Pratt and Hanson 1994; Wright 1998; Selby, Dixon, and Hapke 2001; Salzinger 2003; Stepick et al. 2003) have shown that the geographies of the workplace itself—the ways specific tasks are structured and performed spatially and the ways that workers encounter one another in the process of completing these tasks—powerfully affect workplace social interactions.

Within Hotel Nashville, the crew of room attendants is by far the largest and most ethnically diverse segment of housekeeping, with Mexican, Bosnian, Haitian, African American, and white female (and a few male) workers. This diversity, however, does not always translate into a racially or ethnically interactive workforce. Room attendants typically work alone in the hotel, as they clean a set number of rooms each day. Despite the fact that some room attendants work together and help one another on slow days and in cases of illness, ethnicity and race often contour who helps whom and in what language workplace conversation is conducted. Thus, the multicultural mix of room attendants at Hotel Nashville does not necessarily translate into a socially integrated and cohesive workforce. Instead, the combination of a labor geography of spatially separate and discrete rooms to be cleaned and a labor structure of individual room attendants assigned to particular rooms and floors reproduces a racially and ethnically separated, if not divided, workforce in the midst of marked diversity.

Among Hotel Nashville's laundry attendants, by contrast, Colombian, Mexican, and African American workers spend almost the entire day working side by side in a tight work space. Consequently, they are more dependent on mutual understanding to complete their assigned tasks. Through the spatial and social structure of their work, laundry attendants had a different experience of workplace diversity than did room attendants, and thus developed more extensive relationships across linguistic, cultural, and ethnic boundaries. Furthermore, these relationships often continued outside both the laundry room and the workday itself, as laundry workers interacted socially more than did room attendants.

For example, Beto, a young Mexican man from Guerrero, first encountered African Americans in the hotel's laundry room. In the laundry room, language is more important for workers than it is among room attendants, because verbal communication among laundry workers affects the pace of work in a department expected to produce a constant flow of clean linen. According to one worker, the laundry room is "the most hectic [space] in housekeeping;" and constantly switching between English, Spanish, and hand gestures can slow down work. For Beto, thus, black coworkers became a primary source of job, as well as English-language, training.

In the laundry room, informal interaction and learning takes place frequently and is central to the work itself. As Spanish- and English-speaking workers find a common language to sort the laundry, they also sort out cultural differences between *los mexicanos* and *los colombianos*. Learning to navigate such cultural differences is a key aspect of learning to negotiate new social relations at the workplace. Just as supervisors have had to learn to manage an increasingly multilingual, multiethnic, and multicultural workforce, some workers have had to do the same. In the hotel laundry room, such processes facilitate the completion of work in ways not found—perhaps because not so necessary—among the more ethnically diverse but also more structurally and spatially separate room attendants.

These microgeographies of race, ethnicity, and labor at Hotel Nashville clearly influence social interactions among workers (Waldinger and Lichter 2003) and create a hypervisibility of Latino workers in areas like room cleaning and a relative invisibility elsewhere in the hotel. The spatial structure of work, however, is only part of the story. Since many employees at Hotel Nashville worked elsewhere before taking their current positions, their experiences at the hotel are always understood vis-à-vis previous work experiences. This led me to initiate conversations about how working at Hotel Nashville compared to working elsewhere, particularly in terms of the differences between current and former coworkers, to tease out how workers understood Nashville's new *sonido* in comparison to its old sound.

In these conversations, many black and white native-born workers seemed either not to notice or to give much weight to the changing faces of their coworkers. For example, Evelyn, a young African American woman who had worked at Hotel Nashville for four years, described her current coworkers and her former coworkers at a laundry-processing facility in Nashville as "about the same—black and white in both places." This comment, variations of which were offered by other workers, raises the possibility that for some African American workers, "white" has become a catch-all category for nonblack workers, Latinos included. Further research on how racial categories such as "white" are defined differently by various racial and ethnic groups is needed; but this comment points to the shifting processes through which Latino workers may be rendered invisible as "Latino" by their inclusion in the category "white" or by their wholesale removal from the workplace's racial grammar by native-born workers in new-immigrant destinations.

As I changed my questions to be more explicit about what workplace changes interested me; as I asked more questions about how participants' work experiences had changed over time; and as I sometimes pointed out changes that I thought were obvious (such as that participants' coworkers were all native-born at one hotel and now were a mixture of Mexicans, Colombians, Bosnians, and Americans), it became increasingly clear that these demographic changes may not have been so visible or so meaningful for hospitality workers as they were for city officials and community leaders. Instead of framing the entry of Latinos into the work site as a significant event, some workers used phrasing that echoed cultural-sensitivity training used in contemporary work sites. For example, Tonya, a black room attendant, remarked, "It's better to have a diverse workforce." Violet, an African-American lobby attendant, stated that at a "multicultural work site, you can learn more." Abby, a young white woman in rooms control, described her current work situation as much better than other places she had worked because "here, there is a diverse staff, which makes for a better work site." Perhaps most important, a surprising number of workers only referred to these demographic changes when I pressed the issue. When multiple workers remarked that current and former work experiences were "basically the same," I began to consider the possibility that in Hotel Nashville, Latino migration carried a different meaning and import than it did in Nashville's public sphere and that this difference was wrapped up with the difference that space and place make in understandings and practices of race and ethnicity (Peake and Schein 2000).

CONCLUSION

What can be made of Hotel Nashville, where transitions in its workforce from African American women to Southeast Asian refugees to Mexican workers in the last twenty years have proceeded with relatively little conflict or even notice (Selby, Dixon, and Hapke 2001)? Where does this story fit within studies of exclusionary practices through which particular groups gain control over hiring practices and reproduce ethnic divisions of labor (Waldinger 1997; Waldinger and Lichter 2003)? If, as has been argued for Atlanta (Wang and Pandit 2003), ethnic niching occurs very early in the formation of immigrant communities, what role do Hotel Nashville and other low-wage workplaces in Nashville play in this trend?

Although there were instances of supervisors actively working with or against Latino hiring networks at the Nashville work sites I examined, in other cases, immigrant hiring networks operated alongside employee referrals from other racial and ethnic groups, the placement of refugees at work sites by resettlement agencies, and random hiring when applicants wandered in to apply for a job. Ethnic niching is undoubtedly at work in Nashville, as Latinos are concentrated in service-sector jobs, landscaping, and other low-wage employment opportunities and service-sector jobs like hotel housekeeping continue to be both an entry and a dead end for some African American workers, particularly older women. The exclusionary closure where one ethnic group gains control over hiring practices to the detriment of other groups documented in Los Angeles (Waldinger and Lichter 2003), Miami, or New York, however, may not have fully reached the Music City. This situation in Nashville, I suggest, raises questions about what happens when there is continued ambiguity about how social interactions along and across racialized lines will settle out not only in the workplace but also in Nashville's broader urban landscape and social terrain.

Raymond Mohl (2003, 48) has argued that "blacks and Hispanics have been at odds over jobs, neighborhoods, and cultural differences for almost a decade" in the South. Citing academic and newspaper reports of a "tension-filled shop-floor situation" in North Carolina, Mohl (2003, 48) notes that "as a consequence of recent Hispanic migration, new patterns of racial and ethnic conflict linger unresolved throughout the South" (see also Johnson, Johnson-Webb, and Farrell, Jr. 1999). While not disputing these claims, I echo arguments from recent ethnographic work to suggest that representations of ethnic conflict in public discourse and the lived realities of these relations at a more intimate scale are not always congruent (Hartigan 1999; Brubaker 2002; Lee 2002). In southern cities such as Nashville, the complexities of racial and ethnic interactions sit uneasily within broad-brush claims about definite regional trends, not least because these patterns of ethnic and racial conflict and coalition are still under design and discussion.

At the work sites I examined across the city, instead of generating strong inter-ethnic conflict or even interaction, the new realities of a multicultural, multilingual, and multiethnic work site were in some cases no more trans-formative than the arrival of new equipment. Within these sites, workplace social encounters seemed to follow what Selby, Dixon, and Hapke (2001, 249) describe as a "superficial politeness" among workers spatially proximate but socially distant. This is not to minimize what has been a dramatic transition in Nashville's low-wage labor market in the last ten years. Even if Latino and non-Latino workers did not attribute a great deal of significance to the racial and ethnic shifts across these work sites, almost all agreed that these transitions have changed how work gets done at each site, and other studies of immigrant experiences in Nashville point to hostile work environments, particularly for refugees (Cornfield et al. 2003).

What did not surface in this study was the sense that a new racial and ethnic composition at work sites mattered in the same way that such changes mattered within Nashville's public sphere. What was described as an "explosion" across the city appeared more like an ongoing process of coming to grips with changing workers at the workplace, where room attendants continued to have to clean the same numbers of rooms each day, orders still had to be filled as quickly as possible, and supervisors still had to find ways to help workers do their jobs. Although it is too early in the process of incorporating Latino workers into the local labor force in new-immigrant destinations to draw firm conclusions about how this incorporation will proceed in terms of ethnic and racial relations and formations, the differences to which this chapter points raise questions about the similarities and differences between workplace relations and public discourse in new immigrant-receiving cities such as the Music City and those documented in gateway cities such as Los Angeles (Waldinger 1997).

As I suggested earlier, Latino migrants complicate Nashville's urban politics, heretofore defined in terms of a racial dichotomy, because they call into question the ways that race, ethnicity, and belonging are understood and addressed in Nashville, particularly in its public sphere. When the scale of analysis shifts from "the Hispanic community" to specific Latino workers, however, the picture changes. In Nashville's low-wage workplaces, racial and ethnic differences, though affecting how and in what language work gets done, were not interpreted in the same way as in the city's public discourse. Within Hotel Nashville, the racial and ethnic transitions that seemed to have caught the city by surprise and forced a reconsideration of what race and ethnicity mean in Nashville's urban politics were frequently seen as just another shift in a highly dynamic workplace where employees worked around new challenges brought about by a multilingual and multiethnic workforce.

The geographer Kay Anderson (2002, 25) has asked, "How might we loosen the interpretive grid of race that we impose, albeit critically, on the data of social relations without obscuring race's glaringly pernicious efficacy as a social force?" I suggest that one way to keep race from becoming a stale category of analysis is by paying attention to the ways that race and ethnicity matter in different ways at different scales and within different social spaces (Marston 2000). When Latino migration and its effects on southern cities are examined in this way, the stories told shift from "a straightforward, linear master narrative toward diverse and possibly conflicting accounts" (Nagar et al. 2002, 280). Only through careful consideration of these "conflicting" accounts of Latino migration and its influence across scales of social interaction, however, can we come to understand Latino migration as the complex process it is and begin to understand the different situations it produces in southern cities. Race relations and racial formations may still be "an uncharted area in the New South" (Schmid

2003, 152), but this "unfinished story" is better understood, I argue, when it is examined across social spaces and institutions in southern cities.

Through studies attentive to the difference that place and space make in how Latino migration is framed and acted upon in new-immigrant urban destinations such as Nashville, a richer and more complex picture of Latino migration and its effects can be achieved. Analyzing Latino migration's consequences within and across social spaces such as public schools, residential neighborhoods, and public spaces will not entirely fill in the "incomplete" picture of Latinos in new-immigrant destinations. It can, however, begin to expose, and perhaps challenge, the exclusionary practices whereby new immigrants continue to be perceived as "out of place" in southern locales and, thus, contribute to the reconceptualization of community boundaries to include Nashville's new *sonido* within the Music City's daily rhythms.

NOTES

1. The same is true for the "Deep South Triad" of Alabama, Mississippi, and Louisiana, which have also received less attention. For preliminary arguments, see Katherine Donato, Carl L. Bankston III, and Dawn T. Robinson (2001), Patricia Campion (2003), and James R. Elliott and Marcel Ionescu (2003).
2. I include both paraphrases of interview conversations and exact quotations, and identify sources of the latter. I have not identified the specific speaker if the thought was not unusual; for example, the remark that Latino migration "exploded" in the late 1990s was expressed in many interviews.
3. This survey also points to the geography of census participation. In urban Nashville parishes, 67 percent of survey participants reported census participation. In suburban parishes around Nashville, approximately 50 percent participated. In parishes at some distance from Nashville, the participation rate dropped to 33 percent.
4. All respondent names are pseudonyms.

REFERENCES

Anderson, Kay J. 2002. "The Racialization of Difference: Enlarging the Story-Field." *Professional Geographer* 54(1): 25–30.

Brubaker, Rogers. 2002. "Ethnicity Without Groups." *Archives Européennes de Sociologie* 43(2): 163–89.

Camarota, Steven A., and John Keeley. 2001. "The New Ellis Islands: Examining Non-Traditional Areas of Immigrant Settlement in the 1990s." New York: Center for Immigration Studies.

Campion, Patricia. 2003. "One Under God? Religious Entrepreneurship and Pioneer Latino Immigrants in Southern Louisiana." *Sociological Spectrum* 23(2): 279–301.

Cantu, Norma E. 1999. *Report on Latino Culture and Traditional Arts in Tennessee.* Nashville, Tenn.: Tennessee Arts Commission.

Cornfield, Daniel B., Angela Arzubiaga, Rhonda BeLue, Susan L. Brooks, Tony N. Brown, Oscar Miller, Douglas D. Perkins, Peggy A. Thoits, and Lynn S. Walker. 2003. "Final Report of the Immigrant Community Assessment." Prepared for the Metropolitan Government of Nashville and Davidson County, Tennessee.

Cravey, Altha J. 1997. "Latino Labor and Poultry Production in Rural North Carolina." *Southeastern Geographer* 37(3): 295–300.

———. 2003. "Toque una ranchera, por favor." *Antipode* 35(3): 603–21.

Davis, Mike. 1999. "Magical Urbanism: Latinos Reinvent the U.S. Big City." *New Left Review* 234: 3–43.

———. 2000. *Magical Urbanism: Latinos Reinvent the US City.* London: Verso.

Donato, Katharine M., Carl L. Bankston III, and Dawn T. Robinson. 2001. "Immigration and the Organization of the Onshore Oil Industry: Southern Louisiana in the Late 1990s." In *Latino Workers in the Contemporary South*, edited by Arthur D. Murphy, Colleen Blanchard, and Jennifer A. Hills. Athens, Ga.: University of Georgia Press.

Durand, Jorge, Douglas S. Massey, and Fernando Charvet. 2000. "The Changing Geography of Mexican Immigration to the United States: 1910–1996." *Social Science Quarterly* 81(1): 1–15.

Elliott, James R., and Marcel Ionescu. 2003. "Postwar Immigration to the Deep South Triad: What Can a Peripheral Region Tell Us About Immigrant Settlement and Employment?" *Sociological Spectrum* 23(2): 159–80.

Fink, Leon. 2003. *The Maya of Morganton: Work and Community in the Nuevo New South.* Chapel Hill, N.C.: University of North Carolina Press.

Goode, Judith, and Jo Anne Schneider. 1994. *Reshaping Ethnic and Racial Relations in Philadelphia.* Philadelphia, Penn.: Temple University Press.

Greeson, Jennifer Rae. 1999. "The Figure of the South and the Nationalizing Imperatives of Early United States Literature." *Yale Journal of Criticism* 12(2): 209–48.

Grieco, Elizabeth. 2003. "The Foreign Born from Mexico in the United States." Migration Information Source. Washington: Migration Policy Institute, October 1.

Hartigan, John, Jr. 1999. *Racial Situations: Class Predicaments of Whiteness in Detroit.* Princeton, N.J.: Princeton University Press.

Hernández-Leon, Rubén, and Víctor Zúñiga. 2000. "'Making Carpet by the Mile': The Emergence of a Mexican Immigrant Community in an Industrial Region of the U.S. Historical South." *Social Science Quarterly* 81(1): 49–66.

———. 2003. "Mexican Immigrant Communities in the South and Social Capital: The Case of Dalton, Georgia." *Southern Rural Sociology* 19(1): 20–45.

———. 2005. "Appalachia Meets Aztlán: Mexican Immigration and Inter-Group Relations in Dalton, Georgia." In *New Destinations of Mexican Immigration in the United States: Community Formation, Local Responses and Inter-Group Relations,* edited by Víctor Zúñiga and Rubén Hernández-León. New York: Russell Sage Foundation.

Hill, Carole E. 1998. "Contemporary Issues in Anthropological Studies of the American South." In *Cultural Diversity in the U.S. South: Anthropological Contributions to a Region in Transition*, edited by Carole E. Hill and Patricia D. Beaver. Athens, Ga.: University of Georgia Press.

Johnson, James H., Jr., Karen D. Johnson-Webb, and Walter C. Farrell, Jr. 1999. "Newly Emerging Hispanic Communities in the United States: A Spatial Analysis of Settlement Patterns, In-Migration Fields, and Social Receptivity." In *Immigration and Opportunity: Race, Ethnicity, and Employment in the United States*, edited by Frank D. Bean and Stephanie Bell-Rose. New York: Russell Sage Foundation.

Johnson-Webb, Karen Denise. 2003. *Recruiting Hispanic Labor: Immigrants in Non-Traditional Areas*. New York: LFB Scholarly Publishing.

Lee, Jennifer. 2002. *Civility in the City: Blacks, Jews, and Koreans in Urban America*. Cambridge, Mass.: Harvard University Press.

Marston, Sallie. 2000. "The Social Construction of Scale." *Progress in Human Geography* 24(2): 219–42.

MDC, Inc. 2002. "State of the South 2002: Shadows in the Sunbelt Revisited." Chapel Hill, N.C.: MDC, Inc. Accessed at http://www.mdcinc.org/knowledge.

Mendoza, Marcela, David H. Ciscel, and Barbara E. Smith. 2000. "El impacto de los inmigrantes Latinos en la economía de Memphis, Tennessee" ["The impact of Latino immigrants on the economy of Memphis, Tennessee"]. *Revista de Estudios Migratorios Latinoamericanos* [*Review of Studies of Latin American Immigration*] 46: 659–75.

Mohl, Raymond A. 2002. "Latinization in the Heart of Dixie: Hispanics in Late-Twentieth-Century Alabama." *Alabama Review* 55(4): 243–74.

———. 2003. "Globalization and the Nuevo New South." *Journal of American Ethnic History* 22(4): 31–66.

Mullings, Beverley A. 2005. "Women Rule? Globalization and the Feminization of Managerial and Professional Workspaces in the Caribbean." *Gender, Place and Culture* 12(1): 1–27.

Murphy, Arthur D., Colleen Blanchard, and Jennifer A. Hill, editors. 2001. *Latino Workers in the Contemporary South*. Athens, Ga.: University of Georgia Press.

Nagar, Richa, Victoria Lawson, Linda McDowell, and Susan Hanson. 2002. "Locating Globalization: Feminist (Re)reading of the Subjects and Spaces of Globalization." *Economic Geography* 78(3): 257–84.

Oboler, Suzanne. 2002. "The Politics of Labeling: Latino/a Cultural Identities of Self and Other." In *Transnational Latina/o Communities: Politics, Processes, and Cultures*, edited by Carlos G. Vélez-Ibáñez, Anna Sampaio, and Manolo González-Estay. Lanham, Md.: Rowman & Littlefield.

Odem, Mary E. 2004. "Our Lady of Guadalupe in the New South: Latino Immigrants and the Politics of Integration in the Catholic Church." *Journal of American Ethnic History* 24(1): 26–57.

Omi, Michael, and Howard Winant. 1986. *Racial Formation in the United States: From the 1960s to the 1980s.* New York: Routledge & Kegan Paul.

Peake, Linda, and Audrey Kobayashi. 2002. "Policies and Practices for an Antiracist Geography at the Millennium." *Professional Geographer* 54(1): 50–61.

Peake, Linda, and Richard H. Schein. 2000. "Racing Geography into the New Millennium: Studies of 'Race' and North American Geographies." *Social and Cultural Geography* 1(2): 133–42.

Pratt, Geraldine, and Susan Hanson. 1994. "Geography and the Construction of Difference." *Gender, Place and Culture* 1(1): 5–29.

Pulido, Laura. 2004. "Race, Immigration and the Border." *Antipode* 36(1): 154–57.

Salzinger, Leslie. 2003. "Re-forming the 'Traditional Mexican Woman': Making Subjects in a Border Factory." In *Ethnography at the Border*, edited by Pablo Vila. Minneapolis, Minn.: University of Minnesota Press.

Schmid, Carol. 2003. "Immigration and Asian and Hispanic Minorities in the New South: An Exploration of History, Attitudes, and Demographic Trends." *Sociological Spectrum* 23(2): 129–57.

Selby, Emily F., Deborah P. Dixon, and Holly M. Hapke. 2001. "A Woman's Place in the Crab Processing Industry of Eastern Carolina." *Gender, Place, and Culture* 8(3): 229–53.

Smith, Barbara Ellen. 1998. "The Postmodern South: Racial Transformations and the Global Economy." In *Cultural Diversity in the U.S. South: Anthropological Contributions to a Region in Transition*, edited by Carole E. Hill and Patricia D. Beaver. Athens, Ga.: University of Georgia Press.

Stepick, Alex, Guillermo Grenier, Max Castro, and Marvin Dunn. 2003. *This Land Is Our Land: Immigrants and Power in Miami.* Berkeley: University of California Press.

Straughan, Jerome, and Pierrette Hondagneu-Sotelo. 2002. "From Immigrants in the City, to the Immigrant City." In *From Chicago to L.A.: Making Sense of Urban Theory*, edited by Michael J. Dear. Thousand Oaks, Calif.: Sage Publications.

Velázquez, Loida C. 1999. "Finding a Voice: Latinas in the South." In *Neither Separate Nor Equal: Women, Race, and Class in the South*, edited by Barbara Ellen Smith. Philadelphia, Pa.: Temple University Press.

Villatoro, Marcos McPeek. 2001. *Home Killings: A Romilia Chacón Mystery.* Houston, Tex.: Arte Público Press.

———. 2003. *Minos.* Boston, Mass.: Kate's Mystery Books.

Waldinger, Roger. 1997. "Black/Immigrant Competition Re-Assessed: New Evidence from Los Angeles." *Sociological Perspectives* 40(3): 365–86.

Waldinger, Roger, and Michael I. Lichter. 2003. *How the Other Half Works: Immigration and the Social Organization of Labor.* Berkeley, Calif.: University of California Press.

Wall, Howard J. 1999. " 'Voting with Your Feet' and Metro-Area Livability." *Regional Economist* April 1: 10–11.

Wang, Qingfang, and Kavita Pandit. 2003. "The Emergence of Ethnic Niches in New Immigrant Destinations: An Examination of Atlanta's Labor Market, 1980–1990." *Southeastern Geographer* 43(2): 159–80.

Winders, Jamie. 2005a. "Changing Politics of Race and Region: Latino Migration to the U.S. South." *Progress in Human Geography* 29(6): 683–99.

———. 2005b. "Imperfectly Imperial: Northern Travel Writers in the Postbellum U.S. South, 1865–1880." *Annals of the Association of American Geographers* 95(2): 391–410.

———. 2006a. " 'New Americans' in a 'New South' City? Immigrant and Refugee Politics in the Music City." *Social and Cultural Geography* 7(3): 421–35.

———. 2006b. "Placing Latinos in the Music City: Latino Migration and Urban Politics in Nashville, Tennessee." In *Latinos in the New South: Transformations of Place*, edited by Heather A. Smith and Owen J. Furuseth. London: Ashgate Publishing.

Woodward, C. Vann. 1960/1968. *The Burden of Southern History*. Rev. ed. Baton Rouge, La.: Louisiana State University Press.

———. 1971. *American Counterpoint: Slavery and Racism in the North-South Dialogue*. Boston, Mass.: Little, Brown.

Wright, Melissa W. 1998. "Maquiladora Mestizas and a Feminist Border Politics: Revisiting Anzaldua." *Hypatia* 13(3): 114–31.

Zúñiga, Víctor, Rubén Hernández-León, Janna L. Shadduck-Hernández, and María Olivia Villarreal. 2001. "The New Paths of Mexican Immigrants in the United States: Challenges for Education and the Role of Mexican Universities." In *Education in the New Latino Diaspora: Policy and the Politics of Identity*, edited by Stanton Wortham, Enrique G. Murrillo Jr., and Edmund T. Hamman. Westport, Conn.: Ablex.

CHAPTER 11

⋎

THE AMBIVALENT WELCOME: CINCO DE MAYO AND THE SYMBOLIC EXPRESSION OF LOCAL IDENTITY AND ETHNIC RELATIONS

DEBRA LATTANZI SHUTIKA

On May 5, 2001, the Borough of Kennett Square, Pennsylvania, hosted its first annual Cinco de Mayo festival. Hailed as a turning point in local ethnic relations, the Cinco de Mayo was initiated as the first large-scale public event that was hosted by the town's English-speaking majority on behalf of the Mexican families who had been settling in the area since the mid-1980s. Mexican settlement had prompted mixed reactions for the English-speaking majority in this small farming village, ranging from outright hostility to reluctant acceptance. Intended as a multi-ethnic community event to celebrate local Mexican culture, the Cinco de Mayo came to symbolize acceptance and inclusion in Kennett Square and the end of a troubled era of ethnic relations in the community.

The questions that inform this chapter have developed from my exploration of festivals in Kennett Square and examines the concepts of community and belonging. How does one define "community" in places like Kennett Square, where communal membership and belonging have long been contested categories? What is the nature of the sense of place during periods of transformation and fracture, such as in an emerging multi-ethnic suburb or in a small town? The formation of new destination communities that resulted from changes in United States immigration patterns after the passage of the Immigration Reform and Control Act (IRCA) of 1986 have prompted dramatic population shifts in rural and suburban communities such as Kennett Square. These demographic changes have disrupted the long-standing homogeneity we associate with American small towns and have forced a reconsideration of local identity and sense of place for everyone who lives in these communities.

Kennett Square offers an example of one such rural community. Kennett Square is located in the heart of the Brandywine River Valley some thirty miles southwest of Philadelphia and twenty miles west of Wilmington, Delaware. Located in Chester County, one of Pennsylvania's wealthiest counties, Kennett Square has been the home of the nation's largest commercial mushroom industry for the last century. Despite its rural ambiance and history as a farming community, Kennett Square is a sophisticated town that is home to a number of upscale boutiques and restaurants, and maintains its own symphony orchestra. The village is approximately one mile square, and is home to some 5,000 residents. Politically, Kennett Square, like surrounding Chester County, is known as a politically conservative community and Republican Party stronghold. Founded as a Quaker settlement in 1855, Kennett Square has a local reputation of being a socially progressive community, a point that is frequently emphasized by local residents (Kashatus 2002; Taylor 1995/1999, 1976/1998).

Since the late 1960s, men from the Mexican state of Guanajuato have been migrating to work in the mushroom industry, then returning to Mexico to spend part of the year with their families.[1] In the years since the passage of the IRCA, which meant amnesty for previously undocumented workers, Mexican families have begun settling in increasing numbers in and around this small farming village—once a community of Quakers and others of Anglo-European descent—with the most dramatic changes taking place since 1990. Today every aspect of life in Kennett Square is touched by Mexican settlement and culture. The total population of 5,373 is now 33 percent Mexican and Latino, and increasingly, Mexican families are purchasing Kennett Square's modest single-family homes (U.S. Census Bureau 2000).

In order to examine Kennett Square's transition from a community that historically housed seasonal migrant workers to one that is now a new destination site for Mexican families, I will analyze several of Kennett Square's public display events, including the Cinco de Mayo festival. Although Kennett Square puts on up to a dozen street fairs and family events throughout the year, the Cinco de Mayo festival in 2001 was the first time the town had officially recognized its growing Mexican population through a large-scale public celebration. The festival commemorates the victory over the French of Mexican forces in the Battle of Puebla on May 5, 1862. During the early years of Mexican settlement in the late 1980s and early 1990s, the initial response by the local elected officials and the English-speaking majority was to attempt to forestall Mexican settlement and to segregate the Mexican population. The Mexicans that I interviewed in the mid 1990s shared stories about living in a community where they were not wanted, and most often, these narratives provided insight to the boundaries that had emerged between Mexicans and others in town.[2] Migrant workers and their families were considered transients and were routinely excluded from community events, such as the annual Mushroom Festival. Thus the Cinco de Mayo festival was hailed as a turning point for Kennett Square's majority English-speaking population, who for years had openly expressed ambivalence, and at times hostility, toward the Mexican families who were settling in the area.

The Cinco de Mayo festival was indeed a turning point for Kennett Square's Mexican settlers, and it was true that the Cinco de Mayo marked a change in the community was accurate—but not in the way that Kennett Square's English-speaking population intended. They wanted to demonstrate acceptance of Mexican settlers and reinforce Kennett Square's image as an inclusive community. The former goal was achieved; the latter goal probably was not achieved. In addition, however, something else occurred: by opening the community to Mexican participation, the Cinco de Mayo simultaneously opened the door to encourage Mexican emplacement, facilitating what I term locality formation.

Locality is the process of place attachment; it is constituted through interpersonal relationships that are place-specific and continue through repeated contact that ultimately produces systems of shared meanings and a sense of social alliance between those who reside in a specific locale. Locality formation is above all a process of developing meaningful interpersonal relationships beyond the bounds of biological family or fictive kin networks,[3] and characteristically it occurs in fits and starts. In many ethnographic accounts of immigrant communities in the United States, it is understood that after a period of consistent migration and settlement, former migrants living in close proximity form discernible enclaves, and the period of transition gives way to locality production.

This process is more than the straightforward development of new friendships. It also encompasses the expansion of meaningful relationships and social networks, especially between newcomers and the established community so that they are connected to each other and their new locale. Newcomers are no longer seen as transients, but "people who belong." In this sense, the boundaries between newcomers and long-term residents begin to subside. Newcomers assume ownership of the locale symbolically and materially, through communal participation or through ownership of homes or property. Through these processes, newcomers alter the social scene and re-inscribe it with distinctive cultural meanings. Their presence is acknowledged in the narrative events of community life; in essence, they become part of the story of the place. Through their participation locality is produced; they in turn become integral to the locality.

Although ethnographers often assumed locality production occurs automatically, it is in fact a process that requires persistent energy and investment on the part of all members of a given group. Shared cultural practices such as initiation rituals, rites of passage, and folklore are the processes through which locality is produced (Appadurai 1996). The importance of these cultural processes for human relations indicates that locality should not be taken for granted, as it requires a great deal of effort to maintain. Indeed, the social dynamics of Kennett Square illustrate exactly how tenuous locality production can be. During the first decade of settlement, locality formation was virtually unthinkable for Mexicans in Kennett Square, but the Cinco de Mayo marked a shift in social relations. Not only was the English-speaking population willing to openly acknowledge Mexican cultural heritage, but also the festival provided an occasion for Mexicans to begin their locality formation.

RITUAL BELONGING: THE COMMUNITY FESTIVAL

In contemporary contexts the small town festival is often seen as a dying custom.[4] Community celebrations are expensive and time-consuming, they require the coordination of the municipal and sometimes state government, citizen volunteers, local entrepreneurs (who often underwrite the event) and participation by local residents. The fact that Kennett Square continues to put on these events—its neighboring municipalities do not—is a feature that draws some middle and upper class English-speaking families to settle in the town. During a Mushroom Festival parade in 1999 an Anglo couple told me that they moved to Kennett Square because "we wanted our children to grow up in a community where there they still have parades and people know each other."

Although there are other ways that communities can display collective identity, the festival carries particular weight as a public display event. Festivals require communal participation and cannot take place in locales that lack people with a strong commitment to the event and sense of corporate identity. Festivals also hark back to notions of a past that sharply contrast with contemporary life. Such associations are suffused with romantic ideas of rural America, where face-to-face interaction was the norm and neighborly relations were believed more common. Cultural scholars often overlook American community festivals as objects of study because they so often appear apolitical and innocuous to the casual observer. Yet given the organizers' efforts to initiate and sustain a festival, these events represent more than a day of family fun and entertainment. Festivals are symbolic performances of how its organizers—be it a family, community, or social group—sees itself. These celebrations "attempt[s] to manifest, in symbolic form, what [the community] conceives to be its essential life, at once the distillation and typification of its corporate experience" (Turner 1982, 16).

Despite their folksy associations, festivals are expressions of power and resistance. In the United States, festivals are typically used as a means to represent a group's ideas of itself and the community's values—an example of such values may be the ideal of the harmonious multicultural community. Festivals are also used to demonstrate the social group's image of itself and how the members of the group would like others to see them and their community. Thus, as a cultural performance the festival provides a means to allow a group to extract select attributes of the community, such as a particular tradition or cultural practice, and display it as if it were a true representation of the entire group. Festivals showcase cultural differences while simultaneously allowing disparate groups to access one another's normally isolated worlds. Robert Cantwell (1993) argues that in a festival's most positive expression, it offers the possibility of mutual understanding, but is just as likely to sanitize and reshape the group it endeavors to represent, stripping away less desirable features such as poverty and discrimination.

At their core, festivals are multi-sense events that can express divergent, contradictory, or ambivalent meanings. Festivals such as Kennett Square's Cinco de Mayo are not merely sources of entertainment; they are also complex cultural performances that expose social and political relations in the communities where they are celebrated. They also offer an opportunity to examine local change in the making. People are attracted to festivals because of what they represent: liberation from social constraints, the ability to contest the social order, and conviviality among friends and strangers. These events break with the mundane aspects of daily life, and foster a sense of "communitas," the sense of local identity and the relationships formed through sharing a common space (Turner 1969, 96). This identity is frequently expressed in terms of power relations within the community. Festivals are spectacles replete with music, food, dance, and drama, but they do more: they also validate and contest the established social order. In short, they are occasions that are "intimately and dynamically related to the political order and to the struggle for power within it" (Cohen 1993, 4).

The Cinco de Mayo festival in Kennett Square is an opportunity to shape local ethnic relations and articulate the English-speaking community's ideas and attitudes about their Mexican neighbors and their place in the local community. The event is best understood as a cultural performance, an "occasion[s] in which as a culture . . . we reflect upon and define ourselves, dramatize our collective myths and history, present ourselves with alternatives, eventually change in some ways while remaining the same in others" (MacAloon 1984, 1). The festival as cultural performance is not only a demonstration of how a group imagines itself, but also a means to reconfigure intergroup relations and to integrate those who are outside the boundaries of the group. During the Cinco de Mayo festival, Kennett Square's State Street became a stage where local actors performed their identities in relation to their perceived place in the community, and to one another (Schechner 1985), and the festival unexpectedly became a means to reshape locality for Mexicans and their English-speaking neighbors.

The Cinco de Mayo celebration was intended to be an unequivocal welcome to Mexican families and to celebrate Mexican contributions to the local community; to work toward constructing a totality from disparate groups who need to find a way to share a social space and coexist harmoniously.[5] It was also viewed as a means to set right past transgressions against Mexican families, who had been overlooked or excluded in the planning and execution of other community events. As is the case with other large-scale public display events, the Cinco de Mayo expressed more than these positive virtues, and in fact gave voice to a deep ambivalence in community sentiment: the English-speaking population's conflicting emotions regarding Mexican settlement, particularly the changing sense of place in Kennett Square.

INTERCULTURAL AMBIVALENCE

Ambivalence is the result of conflicting emotions or the state of feeling two opposing emotions toward the same person or object. Everyone has experienced ambivalence at one time or another, whether it is felt toward a job, a family member, or neighborhood.

Emotions are often mistakenly considered to be the opposite of reason, but in fact emotions are complex bodily phenomena that result in part from judgments that are directed toward someone or something. We feel our emotions, but they are informed by mental acts of understanding or judgment. Thus an individual's reasoning is not overcome by his or her emotions; emotions are bodily perceived feelings that are informed in part by intellectual processes. For instance, the emotion of falling in love is rooted in part in judgments made on the basis of interactions with another person and an appraisal of his or her behavior (Koch 1987).

Ambivalence can arise on the communal as well as the personal level, when broader community or cultural values conflict with individual wants or desires, or when the interests of one fraction of a community or group conflict with communal principles of inclusion, justice, or equity. Suppose a political candidate supports a woman's legal access to abortion, but also maintains that her values would prohibit exercising that choice. Or a small-business owner agrees with current immigration laws that prohibit low-skilled workers from entering the United States legally, but also hires undocumented workers in order to maintain his profit margin or to keep his small business afloat. Similarly, a family may purchase a new home in a subdivision that was once a family farm, while at the same time opposing any further development of existing open land surrounding their community. In these instances, the beliefs, and the exceptions to these beliefs, are not merely instances of ethical duplicity, but a "dilemma of competing virtues or evils" (Shore 1999, 171). The ideals that are the basis on which principled choices are made often have competing standards that would, at first glance, seem to undermine them. It is possible for the broader values of a community, such as acceptance, equality, and inclusion, to run counter to the individual preferences for a community that is familiar and unified in class, language, or ethnicity. These instances of conflict between the communal value of acceptance and the desire for constancy are what I call intercultural ambivalence.

CHANGE AND THE CRAFTING OF LOCAL IDENTITY

The central conflict in Kennett Square has long been between the appropriateness of welcoming Mexican settlers as part of the community and the certainty that their permanent settlement inevitably means change. Kennett Square's communal identity is strongly associated with agriculture and the local mushroom industry; it is regionally known as the Mushroom Capital of the World. Although the industry relies on Mexican labor, the permanent settlement of Mexican families has produced a mixed reaction from the English-speaking population. A historically agricultural community, Kennett Square has also been influenced by rapid upscale suburban development in the surrounding area. Thus, this once out-of-the-way farming community has been experiencing growth and change in two directions: an influx of predominantly wealthy, highly educated Anglo-American professionals who work in Philadelphia and Wilmington and the surrounding suburbs, and an influx of a population that is predominantly Mexican and low-income and has had limited access to education.

Not surprisingly, Kennett Square's older English-speaking community has been more receptive to the growing upscale suburban population than to the Mexicans. Like many other growing municipalities, Kennett Square's elected officials are interested in attracting people to the area who provide a stable tax base and will be productive members of the community. As a means of setting the tone of the community, the official website stresses Kennett Square's Anglo-European heritage and its connections to significant historical events, such as the Battle of the Brandywine and the town's role in the Underground Railroad. In addition, the Historic Kennett Square website emphasizes that "[m]any talented individuals have been attracted to the town and found Kennett Square a good place to make their home. For a borough that has always been less than 5,000 in population, a surprising number of private educational and cultural activities have flourished." The site also provides important statistical information, including the town's average annual household income, $85,975, and compares this to the average household income for the United States for the same time period— $64,338. Similarly, it states that 9.9 percent of the population over the age of 25 has earned a graduate or professional degree and 16.8 percent had earned a bachelor's degree. For anyone researching the area as a possible future home, these statistics craft an image of Kennett Square's population as wealthy, well educated, and culturally sophisticated (see "About Kennett Square," http://www.historickennettsquare.com/about.htm).

The Kennett Square Borough website anticipates that Kennett Square will be a growing community into the next decade, and notes an expected population increase to 6,713 by 2010, but there is no mention of the fact that Mexican settlers are chiefly responsible for the past and predicted population increases. The calendar of events does list the Cinco de Mayo as a "family celebration of Mexican food and culture," but the celebration is in no way linked to the local Mexican population. In fact, there is no mention of the Mexican in-migrants or their influence on the local culture anywhere on the site.

For over a century Kennett Square has been home to a thriving agribusiness. Although the mushroom industry has always attracted newly arrived immigrants and other low-wage workers, Kennett Square has rarely become a permanent home to mushroom laborers. Mushroom pickers from a variety of ethnic and minority groups, especially Puerto Ricans, eventually moved away from picking mushrooms and also moved out of Kennett Square to find better employment. Today the sizable population of Puerto Ricans in Wilmington, Delaware, is one result of this. The historical flow of low-wage mushroom laborers out of the area has allowed Kennett to maintain its Anglo-European character. The Mexican farmworkers have been the first non-European immigrants to settle permanently in and around Kennett Square, even as many of these men move into more lucrative work, such as landscaping and construction. The fundamental reason for this shift is the availability of work. The rapid suburbanization of Kennett Square's surrounding county has produced a demand for cheap local labor to build large suburban homes and maintain the lawns of these residences, thus eliminating the need for laborers to move away to acquire better reliable employment.[6]

Why would local governing officials minimize or hide Kennett Square's growing Mexican community, particularly in light of an influential social movement dedicated to incorporating them into the community? The information provided on the official Kennett Square websites exposes an underlying class tension that has been evident since the early days of Mexican settlement, and that I also observed during my fieldwork in the community. Mexican families on the whole are low-income and the average Mexican settler has 5.4 years of education (Mexican Migration Project 2004). The class distinctions among Mexican settlers and their citizen neighbors are great and are reinforced by the fact that both populations are monolingual. These incongruities are only compounded by differences in the two groups' cultural tastes.[7] In spite of these marked differences, neither group has shown signs of wanting to leave Kennett Square to escape the other. Thus the initiation of the Cinco de Mayo festival was indeed significant in that it created an opportunity for these two groups to come together and symbolically share the community through a public festival.

CONCEPTUALIZING PUBLIC AND PRIVATE SPACE

In the early years of my fieldwork, Mexicans who spoke to me often lamented the life they had left behind. Many of these women and men, even after years of living in the United States, still reported that they had never felt "at home." Most told me they still owned homes in Mexico, and hoped one day to return. Although I understood the concept of homesickness and feeling out of place, it was not until I lived in Textitlán, a town in Guanajuato where many of Mexicans in Kennett Square are from, that I fully realized what these families had lost in their pursuit of economic opportunities north of the border.[8]

When I reflect on my own experiences in Textitlán, the images I have are of the street life at dusk. It is several hours before dinner, and the families have reconvened and are hanging out in the street in front of their homes. Neighbors stroll down the streets to visit friends. Chairs are pulled onto the sidewalks and women gather to discuss the events of the day, family life, and local gossip. Men are also on the streets, but stand together in small groups apart from the women and children. Earlier in the day, young men, "muchachos," gathered at certain street corners throughout the town's neighborhoods. I have unpoetically named these places "muchacho stands," simply because that is what the muchachos do there: stand, hang out, chat, and whistle at the young women who walk by. In these ways the street becomes an extension of the home, and because the space is used in common, the sense of individual ownership is lessened. While I was living in Textitlán it was not uncommon for my neighbors to congregate on my stoop for most of the night talking, leaving a pile of garbanzo bean hulls and beer cans on the sidewalk in front of my home. The refuse would mysteriously be swept away in the morning by one of the señoras on my street. And I as I worked late into the night on my field notes and transcriptions, I often heard the muffled whispers of my neighbor's daughter, Lia, as she and her sweetheart sat talking by my front door.

In contrast, day-to-day life in Kennett Square offered a dramatic difference, and family life is much more isolated and work-centered. After I moved to Virginia, I returned to Kennett for a field visit in 2002 as the guest of the Lopez family. I had rented their house when my family lived in Mexico, and our families had become close in the course of my fieldwork. Their oldest daughter, Marta, was getting ready to return for the spring semester at Penn State, and she kindly offered me her room, as she was departing in a few days. The Lopez house was a small, two-story single-family home with three bedrooms and one bath. The first floor consisted of two large rooms, a living room and an eat-in kitchen. Upstairs Mario and Ofelia shared the master bedroom with their youngest son, Miguel. Marta occupied the smallest bedroom alone, and her younger sisters, Rosa and Lisa, shared another room. During the summer months, Ofelia's brother rented a room in their basement. From time to time other extended-family members, primarily one of Mario's siblings and their families, would share the house as well. It was rare for so many people to be living in the house for more than a few weeks. Like many Mexican families, particularly those who were established in their own homes, the Lopez family felt obligated to help their relatives when they arrived in the United States.

During my first night with the Lopez family, I woke up unexpectedly. Although it was early January, the room I was in was so hot I could not sleep. Their house was heated by an ancient furnace, Ofelia complained to me earlier, and the rooms in the house alternated between too hot or too drafty. I looked up and saw a dim glow of stars on an unfamiliar ceiling. The stars were press on glow-in-the-dark disks that I imagined she must have put on her ceiling years ago, certainly before she went to college. Marta's room was small and full of furniture, old stuffed animals, dried flowers, and a variety of used textbooks. I sat up in bed and reached for the window, feeling guilty for opening the window in the dead of winter, but the room was insufferable. I compromised with myself and cracked the window slightly and left the bedroom door ajar, hoping to coax in enough air to make the room temperature bearable.

After a few minutes I began to doze off, but then I heard someone moving in the hallway. Checking my watch, I saw that it was 3 A.M. After a few minutes I realized that Mario had gotten up to get ready for work. He had told me that he went into his job at a restaurant early to prepare food for the day. He drives a food truck for a Mexican restaurant that vends Mexican food to several mushroom farms. A few minutes later, he left the house. I realized this early work call was why he was always so tired in the afternoons.

Ofelia was up by 7 A.M. to get the younger children fed and ready for school. After the children were off, she would spend the morning cleaning the house and cooking. Ofelia, an outstanding cook, worked at the same local Mexican restaurant as Mario, and she would sometimes bring food home with her at the end of the day. Other times, she would prepare a dish that Mario could easily heat up for dinner when he returned in the afternoon.

Mario and Ofelia made arrangements so that one of them would be home with the children after school. Mario's day ended around two o'clock in the afternoon, and he would drive back to the house and take Ofelia to work, as she had never learned to drive. He would then return to the house and wait for the children to return from school at 3:30. It was not unusual to find Mario napping on the sofa in the afternoons. Mario and Ofelia made a commitment to be the primary caregivers of their small children, but it was obvious that Mario was too exhausted after a normal workday to be actively involved in his children's lives. Most often, Miguel and Lisa would play in the house or watch television. Each evening Ofelia would return from the restaurant near eleven o'clock, usually driven by a coworker. Her children might be waiting up for her; Mario would retire to bed by eight o'clock most evenings. Because the parents worked opposite schedules, it was rare for the family to eat dinner together, except on Tuesdays, the one day of rest that Mario and Ofelia allowed themselves.

While visiting with the Lopez family, I often stayed up late chatting with Ofelia when she returned from work. Like her husband, she often complained of being exhausted, and I asked her if she ever considered working less. She explained, "We earn well, Mario and I, but we have to work so many hours. I always worry that there are so many expenses living in the United States We have to pay for our house, our car, and for Marta's college. The children need things, too, always toys, clothes, something. We have to work, because we never know if we'll need money for something."

I understood Ofelia's concern for keeping ahead: she and Mario were minimum-wage employees, and they needed the income they earned working six days a week. Like many of their peers in Kennett Square, they had to work long hours if they wanted to maintain their modest, but comfortable, lifestyle. Their work lives also essentially eliminated any possibility of a social life, however. Ofelia said that they were willing to take a day off for a special occasion, such as when Marta graduated from high school, but these occasions were not common. They rarely engaged in recreational activities simply because of their work schedules.

In Textitlán, the street life was an important part of social life, and the absence of this and other communal aspects of their lifestyle is a source of distress for the Lopez family and other Mexicans in Kennett Square. There have been complaints from the English-speaking community of Mexicans "loitering." Such gatherings are seen as threatening or undesirable. Although these families have homes and apartments, their access to common or public spaces has been limited by long work hours, zoning laws, community disapproval, and a decade of hard feelings. Opposition to Mexicans moving into what was previously an exclusively English-speaking space no doubt discourages other activity at communal events or in public places. The activities of Mexican residents who live in Kennett Square's apartments are an example of this. Although some young men congregate in the parking lots and the patchy unkempt yard in front of the apartments, families typically remain inside and avoid public interaction.

Separated from their extended families and friends, unable to recreate a semblance of the life they had in Mexico, it is understandable that Mexican families have been frustrated by the lack of community life and that they have felt out of place in Kennett Square. Thus, the initiation of the Cinco de Mayo festival was a significant event for Mexicans and the majority population, as nearly everyone in Kennett recognized the Mexican community's need for this type of social recreation.

SOJOURNERS AND NEIGHBORS

Festivals are a common occurrence in Kennett Square. This is due in part to the community's commitment to its rural heritage. Neighboring towns have similar agricultural histories, but Kennett has a particularly strong attachment to folk customs typically associated with rural America, parades and festivals being the most frequent. Thus it is not surprising that the community decided to celebrate a festival to acknowledge their Mexican neighbors. The town hosts nearly a dozen annual public events, including the Mushroom Festival, which usually draw large crowds from Kennett Square and the surrounding county.

What is surprising, however, is that English-speaking community hosted the Cinco de Mayo festival at all. Unprepared for the rapid expansion of Mexican settlement in the early 1990s, these long-term residents of Kennett Square resisted changes in their community related to Mexican settlement, including neighborhood and school integration and bilingual services. Before 1986, the majority of Mexicans were single men who had families in Mexico and worked seasonally picking mushrooms. Carefully hidden out of site on mushroom farms where they lived in barracks or trailers, these men were seen as transients and not included in local events. Although these men were vital to the mushroom industry, they were essentially invisible to the English-speaking community. Peggy Harris, a nurse practitioner who has worked at the local migrant clinic since 1976, described the situation in 1995, saying, "Well the [Mexican] community is basically a hidden community. I'm not sure how . . . what happens in the school system. The kids seem to be pretty much okay there. But I know that in all other aspects it doesn't seem . . . there's no mixing. I'm not seeing much of the Mexicans being involved in the community life overall here. They're still a hidden community" (author interview, December 1, 1995).

Although a sizable Mexican population was well established by 1995, the English-speaking majority was simply unwilling to share their neighborhoods and public spaces with Mexican families. As Mexican families moved in, long-term residents joined together in an attempt to forestall settlement. In 1995 they organized to protest the redevelopment of dilapidated properties in town that would eventually house Mexican families. A year later a local dance hall that had become a favorite gathering place for Mexican couples was closed and later torn down, and a vacant field where Mexican men gathered in the evenings after work to play soccer was plowed under. Then, in early 1997, a neighborhood association organized English-speaking residents and asked them to place yellow ribbons in front of their homes to protest Mexicans who were purchasing houses and moving into their neighborhood. Although these actions were scattered events, the effort to keep Mexicans out of Kennett did not go unnoticed by Mexicans and many in the English-speaking community.

These actions eventually brought accusations of racism from within the English-speaking community and exposed fracture within the majority population. Those who had participated in the protests bristled at the idea that their actions were racist and insisted that their actions were being misinterpreted. Although it is difficult to determine exactly how many of the English-speaking majority participated in the activities to create obstacles to Mexican settlement, these events were frequent enough to provide ample evidence of a racist sentiment on the part of those who had organized them. Nevertheless, for those who did not take part in the actions—including local advocates of the Mexican population, social-service providers, and citizens who simply refused to get involved in such activities—the notion of being labeled a racist community did not fit the image that most Kennett Square residents had of themselves or their town, and many insisted that Kennett Square was still a progressive and inclusive small town (Shutika 2005).

In 1997 a local social movement called Bridging the Community was formed to deal with community conflict. The movement was led by community activists from the English-speaking majority and successfully quieted some of the overt opposition to Mexican settlement. At the same time, Bridging the Community leaders attempted to reframe the discussions surrounding Mexican settlement, emphasizing the positive features of having a diverse, multiethnic community. Members of the movement also launched a variety of volunteer programs to help the youths of the community. Bridging the Community helped Kennett Square rehabilitate its image as a "progressive" community and encouraged a sense of openness (Shutika 2005). It was in this context that the idea for a Cinco de Mayo festival took shape.

La Fiesta Agringada: The Gringo-Style Festival in Kennett Square

Why did the predominantly English-speaking population opt to put on a festival in order to embrace and promote Mexican culture in their community? To fully appreciate the Cinco de Mayo celebration that was initiated in May 2001, we must first look back a few years to 1998, the year of the formation of the Alianza Cultural Latina, the Latino Cultural Alliance.

Alianza was formed through local efforts of primarily Mexican families and the Catholic priest serving the Mexican population, but the group expanded to include a Latino college professor, a social-services director, and two graduate students conducting research in the area, of which I was one. I joined Alianza in the summer of 1999 to assist with the second annual celebration of Mexican Independence Day celebration, the 16 de Septiembre. Much like July 4, this is a large-scale national celebration not only in Mexico but also in areas in the United States where large populations of Mexicans have settled. Although the Mexican consulate in Philadelphia hosts an impressive event on Penn's Landing every year, most Kennett Square Mexicans lacked transportation to the city and so they rarely took part. Thus the Alianza board decided to celebrate the 16 de Septiembre locally because it provided an opportunity for Mexican settlers to freely express and celebrate their identity as Mexicans in a community that seldom offered such opportunities.

The first two years of the event, 1998 and 1999, were well supported by Alianza and local Mexican families. The first year about 300 attended, and the next year, about 1,500. After the first year the event was moved to Nixon Park, which is located centrally in Kennett Square and is within walking distance of many Mexican families' homes. The Alianza board invited food vendors, organized a program of volunteer performers from the area, and paid a Mexican band to play at the event. By 2000, the successes of the previous two celebrations were well known in the community, and the number of participants increased to 4,000. The event had grown to an extent that Alianza's president decided it was time to request underwriting from the English-speaking business community, especially those that interacted the most with Mexican families, such as grocery stores, drug stores, and mushroom farms.

The board's attempts to raise money were unsuccessful. Local entrepreneurs expressed discomfort about celebrating a Mexican national holiday in the United States. One farm owner told me, "It just doesn't make sense. They're in America now," implying that celebrating the 16 de Septiembre indicated that the settler community lacked proper allegiance to the United States. Although Alianza raised enough money to pay for the event by vending sodas and selling souvenirs, the 2000 event was the last time the organization sponsored the celebration. The group folded later that year as the board members, overwhelmed by the work of staffing the event, concluded that Alianza lacked widespread community support. They also recognized that sustained financial support for the organization was unlikely.[9]

Although not willing to offer financial support, several members of the English-speaking community nevertheless considered Alianza's work to make Mexican settlers feel welcome a worthy endeavor. The English-speaking business community was hesitant to underwrite an event by the Mexican-led Alianza, but they were enthusiastic about sponsoring the Cinco de Mayo—a well-known holiday among Americans in the United States but not widely celebrated in the Mexican Republic outside of the states of Puebla and Mexico in Central Mexico. For the Mexicans living in Kennett Square, who are from western Mexico, this date had little significance before the initiation of the Kennett Square celebration.

This is not to say the holiday cannot represent Mexican identity in the United States. In fact, Mexicans and Chicanos in other parts of the U.S. often employ Cinco de Mayo for this purpose. Festival organizers frequently promote events such as Cinco de Mayo parades and other organized public display events as a means of exhibiting community identity.

Often the festivals function to expand ideas of inclusion and belonging, a fact documented in the evolution of the Cinco de Mayo festival in Corona, California (Alamillo 2003). In the early 1930s, Mexican Americans used the festival to redefine the interests of their ethnic community and to demonstrate that they had become a political force. The festival was transformed in the post–World War II era and became a bicultural event with participation by Mexicans and English-speakers to promote "good neighborly" relations (72).

A similar evolution took place in the transformation of the Cinco de Mayo celebrations in San Francisco in the 1980s. This festival was an exclusively Mexican and Chicano celebration that grew to include many Central and South American cultural forms. These changes were self-consciously initiated to express a broader Latino solidarity when the Central and South American populations in the city increased. In these cases, the Cinco de Mayo festival was initiated and directed by a core Mexican American group who self-consciously elected to transform the festival to meet political objectives and to promote pan-ethnic relations (Sommers 1991). In fact, academic studies of Cinco de Mayo festivals in the United States document this pattern: a Mexican or Chicano leadership initiating a festival and adapting its direction to fit a particular cultural or political milieu.

Although Cinco de Mayo is a Mexican holiday, it is much more widely celebrated as a popular ethnic crossover event in the United States than in most regions of Mexico. During the last two decades it has grown from an obscure regional Mexican holiday most frequently celebrated in California and the Southwest to a national event that is commemorated by Latinos, African Americans, and Anglos in a variety of contexts. Actively promoted by restaurants, bars, and beverage companies, Cinco de Mayo has become particularly popular among English-speaking Americans as a means of "understanding" or acknowledging Mexican culture (Saxton 1992; Turcsik 1996). Thus, it is not uncommon for schoolchildren throughout the United States to celebrate Cinco de Mayo as part of a multiethnic curriculum or for young adults to mark the holiday at a local bar that is hosting a Cinco de Mayo "fiesta." However, its popularity among the general population, along with the commercialization of the day, is a cause for concern for some Mexicans and Chicanos. For example, the California-based campaign Cinco de Mayo con Orgullo (Cinco de Mayo with Pride) is actively trying to reclaim the holiday as a celebration of ethnic pride and distance it from its current associations with the alcohol industry (Staples 2001).[10] Despite this and similar efforts, many Anglo Americans continue to believe mistakenly that Cinco de Mayo is Mexico's Independence Day and continue to associate the day with excessive alcohol consumption.

Thus the conceptualization of Cinco de Mayo by the population celebrating the event is the most likely factor in shaping the meaning of the event for participants. Cinco de Mayo can be used effectively to accurately represent Mexican identity, but this is most likely when the festival is initiated, or at least governed, by a Mexican leadership. Yet the meanings of Cinco de Mayo festivals are multiple, ranging from a true cultural representation to a commercial endeavor to promote the sale of Mexican-brand beers. In Kennett Square the Cinco de Mayo is associated with a particular idea of Mexican culture and identity as understood by the English-speaking majority and is not necessarily associated with other conceptions of the event in other parts of the United States. It is a cultural symbol that is easily misread as a neutral and objective representation and "celebration of Mexican culture," as Historic Kennett Square has it on their website, rather than as an interpretation of Mexican culture by English-speaking citizens.

The reasons that the English-speaking community in Kennett Square selected Cinco de Mayo as their means of celebrating Mexican settlement are multiple. The timing of the event, in spring, was convenient as there were no other festivals scheduled at that time. The community's largest festival celebrating the mushroom industry takes place during the second weekend in September, which effectively ruled out the possibility of a 16 de Septiembre celebration. Perhaps more significant, in the United States Cinco de Mayo has fewer associations with Mexican nationalism than the more popular 16 de Septiembre. Cinco de Mayo has long been a pliable symbol of Mexican identity in the American imagination. Vince Ghione, the chairman of the Kennett Square Cinco de Mayo festival, put it succinctly when he said, "Cinco de Mayo is a function of the Anglo community. . . . It's a commercial venture" (all of Ghione's comments are from my interview with him on September 6, 2004). Thus, what Americans "know" about Cinco de Mayo reflect common stereotypes about Mexican culture. But Kennett Square's Cinco de Mayo celebration did not adhere to the stereotypes of drinking and partying, the themes most commonly promoted by the alcohol industry and Mexican-themed restaurants. Instead, it was conceived as a family event with the hope of drawing members from all facets of the community.

Planning for the first Cinco de Mayo began shortly after what turned out to be the last 16 de Septiembre festival in Kennett Square, in 2000, and was sponsored by a broad community coalition, including the Kennett Square Borough Council, the mushroom industry, and local residents. The first Cinco de Mayo festival, in 2001, was well attended and so was then added to the list of annual events that would be sponsored in the community.

Although Kennett Square hosts many family-oriented fairs throughout the year, most have been poorly attended by Mexican families. In fact, the Cinco de Mayo was the first Kennett Square festival that was widely attended by Mexican families. The first Cinco de Mayo was held from one to six in the afternoon on May 5, 2001, and was located on State Street, the main thoroughfare in town. It was attended by about a thousand people. The second year the event organizers invited three Mexican-owned restaurants to sell food, and the borough also sponsored free activities for children, including pony rides and face painting. The local Giant grocery store donated two hundred ears of sweet corn, which were steamed and served on sticks covered with cheese and chili powder, Mexican style. There were also a number of invited vendors, some of whom sold Mexican-themed crafts and souvenirs, including straw sombreros and wooden maracas. Many of the vendors, however, were social-service agencies and companies who serve, or would like to serve, Kennett Square's Mexican population. For example, Project Salud and La Comunidad Hispana, the local migrant clinic and social service center, had booths promoting state-funded health insurance for children and information on the prevention of AIDS and Lyme disease. State Farm Insurance was on hand to provide information on auto and home insurance, complete with bilingual materials demonstrating that they were there to attract Mexican clientele. On the south end of State Street there was a stage for a rotation of Mexican performances by a folk-dance troupe, a mariachi band, and a Mexican deejay.

Some of the performers were from the local Mexican community. On the surface, these were standard entertainments. The folk dancers were a group of Mexican middle and high school students who wore bright indigenous costumes emblazoned with the image of the Virgin of Guadalupe across the back, signifying the combination of Mexico's Spanish and indigenous roots. The costumes, purchased in Mexico, were an apt symbol of contemporary Mexican nationalism. The Mexican deejay donned an unusually large straw sombrero with "Viva los Cabrones Mexicanos" (Long Live the Mexican Bastards) embroidered in red across the brim (see figure 11.1)—in essence, a caricature of Mexican culture. Many English-speaking festival participants also wore such sombreros, without the embroidered message. The embroidered message on the deejay's sombrero was emblematic of the type of dissent made possible by the festival. To the festival organizers and English-speaking participants, the deejay appeared to be engaging in the same kind of "fun" as many of the non-Mexican participants who wore the sombreros. But the rude message inscribed across the brim simultaneously subverted the playfulness of his action, indicating a subtle rebellion obvious only to those who read Spanish.

FIGURE 11.1   "Viva los Cabrones" Mexican DJ at the
2002 Cinco de Mayo Festival

Source: Photograph by Debra Lattanzi Shutika.

In the afternoon there was also a short parade featuring the same Mexican folk dancers, a float highlighting the dangers of Lyme disease, and a parade of flags. These were national flags representing the countries of origin of the English-speaking Kennett Square population, and included flags from countries in Europe, Asia, and Africa.[11] The event culminated with a dance at the north end of State Street with live music from a popular local Mexican band. By the end of the day, the street was packed with Mexican families and couples wearing t-shirts imprinted with the Mexican flag, the Virgin of Guadalupe, and other Mexican national symbols.

There were two other noteworthy aspects of the event. The first was the bilingual information provided by the Chester County Republican Party. Chester County is overwhelmingly Republican, and this booth provided information on the party in Spanish, and voter registration forms. Second, the ever-present bicycle police were outfitted with uniforms clearly marked "policia." The presence of the Republican recruiter indicates that, to the GOP, at least, Cinco de Mayo represents more than a friendly gesture to the Mexican community.[12] In their attempt to include Mexicans in the then majority political party, the GOP is not only acknowledging their presence in the community but also assuming that they will eventually become a political force in the county, and are working to attract them to their party. Similarly, by inscribing "policia" on the police officers' uniforms, while other official signage is not bilingual, the local government

FIGURE 11.2   Lyme Disease Awareness Float,
2002 Cinco de Mayo Festival

Source: Photograph by Debra Lattanzi Shutika.

indicated that it feels the need to make Mexicans aware of the local police and perhaps encourage them to manage their behavior carefully during the festival.

The booths dedicated to social services and the Lyme disease parade float were also telling (see figure 11.2). To festival organizers the Cinco de Mayo was an occasion to educate the Mexican population about available social services and how to avoid unsafe health behaviors, elements that were not part of the other festivals during the year. These exhibits not only demonstrate the English-speaking community's paternalistic attitude toward Mexican settlers, they presume that Mexicans are less informed about health issues than other members of the community and that the English-speaking community is responsible for protecting and educating them. Thus the festival was utilized as an opportunity to influence what festival organizers consider deficiencies in Mexican health behavior.[13]

According to the *Kennett Paper*, festival organizers and local business owners along State Street were pleased with the 2002 event. The estimated attendance was some 6,000 people, an increase from 1,000 in 2001. The majority of the participants were Mexican or Latino (Chris Barber, "Cinco de Mayo Delights Crowd," *The Kennett Paper*, May 9, 2002, 1A). The day ended with one small hitch. When Vince Ghione, the festival chairperson, at 5:55 P.M. instructed the band to play their last song so the event could end at six o'clock as scheduled, the "final" song they played went on for about twenty-five minutes, causing a slight rift between the Kennett Square chief of police and Ghione.

Participation by the English-speaking population was essential if the festival was to succeed as a demonstration of the community's acceptance of Mexicans, an image that Kennett Square is anxious to present. The festival was advertised as an "authentic" Mexican fiesta in hopes of attracting participants from all groups, but particularly the English-speaking community. Vince Ghione explained that Cinco de Mayo "is something different. We will never do anything that is artificial . . . [but will have] the authentic Mexican food . . . the folk dancers. . . . Because the people who are going to come are the Anglos. There are only so many Latinos in the area, and they're all welcome, but the people who will drive the attendance will be the Anglos."[14] Ghione went on to explain that his primary goal is to create a large festival that is also a commercial success, and strong participation is central to achieving this. His strategy for accomplishing this is to draw attention to the distinct cultural aspects of the festival such as Mexican folk dancers, food, and mariachis, and to emphasize that these entertainments are not available at other venues. The participation by the English-speaking population is particularly important in order to maintain widespread support of the event. Given Kennett Square's history with the 16 de Septiembre celebration, it seems unlikely that the community would be willing to underwrite any event that primarily serves the Mexican population.

Despite the efforts to attract a multiethnic crowd, the majority of participants at the 2002 festival were Mexican and Latino. There were a few English-speaking families present, but they were more numerous early in the day and participated in the children's activities such as face painting, pony rides, and watching the parade. As the afternoon progressed, the street was packed with Mexicans who had come to hear the band and dance. The event transformed Kennett Square's typically peaceful, quiet streets into a loud, exuberant celebration. It was remarkable in that for the first time since they began to settle in Kennett Square, Mexicans were given free rein in the streets, and they took full advantage of the opportunity to express their national heritage and pride, and simply to be comfortable being Mexican (see figure 11.3).

Although the event began and ended much earlier than a true Mexican fiesta, which would typically begin after dark and end in the early morning, even my informants who have typically been unhappy with life in Kennett Square were pleased that the event took place and that the

FIGURE 11.3   Street Crowd During the 2002 Cinco de Mayo Festival

Source: Photograph by Debra Lattanzi Shutika.

English-speaking majority made the attempt to make them feel welcome. The Cinco de Mayo provided an opportunity for Mexican settlers to lay claim to their place in the community, their numbers alone indicating that they are a force that must be recognized, and that they were ready to take part in the community.

FESTIVAL, LOCALITY, AND THE SENSE OF PLACE

The influence of a public festival extends well beyond the day of the celebration. Festivals and the memories they produce communicate the participants' ideas regarding local identity and the sense of place throughout the year, yet they rarely express a seamless local identity. In fact they often do the contrary and illuminate social distinction and discord. The Cinco de Mayo festival emerged at the start of the new millennium and was envisioned by its organizers as a means to call attention to Kennett Square's evolving community, to promote social cohesion, and to reinforce the idea that the town's majority population community values inclusion and accepts its newest neighbors. At the same time the festival brought to light several complex, and often contradictory, expressions of local identity. Most important, the Cinco de Mayo clearly articulated the English-speaking majority's ambivalence about Mexican settlement.

These contradictions were obvious in the 2002 festival, which demonstrated that the English-speaking majority's agenda for the festival, while partially an entertainment event, was strongly suffused with unsubtle lessons for Mexicans regarding how to become responsible and productive members of the community. This paternalistic tone also highlighted a palpable sense of superiority on the part of the English-speaking population toward the new settlers. By using the festival to "educate" the Mexican settlers it also suggests tension on the part of the festival organizers toward the changes that Mexican settlement is bringing to the community. Thus the festival communicates acceptance conditioned on the Mexican settlers' acculturation to customs and values of the established community.

I would not, however, characterize this festival as a mere hegemonic expression. True, the organizers were rigid in their interpretation of a "celebration of Mexican culture," but there are implicit risks when access to public space is opened, particularly to those who have lived on the margins of the community and whose access to that space has been limited. Even festivals where the events are strictly prescribed can have unintended consequences and at a minimum provide a venue for a temporary social inversion. Historically, authorities have used festivals intentionally to channel the ambitions of the disenfranchised to prevent social unrest by ceding power, for a brief time, to the disenfranchised (Cantwell 1993; Brandes 1988). Kennett Square's Cinco de Mayo serves a similar political purpose in that it provides a token welcome. Although Mexicans were not given access to the public life of the community on their own terms, the festival provided a means of civic engagement that approached cultural familiarity. State Street was previously the exclusive domain of the citizen population; for three consecutive years it was also the site used to celebrate Mexican cultural and national heritage.

The Cinco de Mayo allowed Mexicans symbolically to be in possession of the heart of the town, albeit temporarily. Once this access was granted, no matter how brief or partial, the majority population's ability to control the public space was changed. The festival organizers could set a time for the festival to end, but they could not enforce it; they could host an Americanized festival, but Mexican participants were nevertheless free use the event to display their commitment to their Mexican identity and to poke fun of the cultural stereotypes paraded by the English-speaking majority. Thus the festival became an example of "the traditional and temporary conquest of official society by the . . . [sub]culture that lives within it" (Cantwell 1993, 97).

Yet is it accurate to characterize the Cinco de Mayo, or any regulated public festival, as an opportunity to shift the balance of power in a multi-ethnic community? And if so, is such a "conquest" necessarily temporary? Public display events bring diverse groups together to share public space, and they have a variety of intended and unintended consequences. Thus festivals can create lasting changes, regardless of whether or not they were planned to do so.

In the United States, public spaces are presumed to be open to all, yet access to the public sphere is often regulated. The means to limit access are not always visible: some are formal, such as legislation that limits the times and number of people who can congregate; some are informal behavioral mores, the unwritten rules that govern the use of space. Whenever a large crowd is allowed to congregate in a public arena, its very presence legitimizes the people's right to that place. It is no coincidence that groups "take to the streets" to protest racial or economic injustices. Thus, the transformation of commonplace activities in the public arena is significant, especially opening the space to large numbers of people who are not typically visible in that public space. The significance is even greater when sacrifices are made to enact the transformation, such as interruptions in commerce, decreased convenience for those who typically control public space, or disruption when a major thoroughfare is blocked off.

The infusion of Mexican settlers into Kennett Square's town center not only legitimized their presence in the community but also introduced the possibility that Mexicans could begin to shape the community, and therefore transform Kennett Square's place identity. Place identity includes the perceptible distinctions that are used to describe the difference between one place and another and are used to situate or symbolize interpretations of individual or group identity (Cuba and Hummon 1993). It is based on a variety of factors, including the natural landscape (seaside or mountain), the built environment (historic structures or modern development), and, most important, the people who dwell in the place. Edward Casey (1996) argues that local sense of place and place identity correspond directly to the people who dwell there, and argues that the very idea of place is only understood in the context of somebody having resided there. He writes, "Bodies and places are connatural terms. They interanimate one another" (Casey 1993, 24; see also Basso 1996). Thus the identity of a particular place is directly related to the people who inhabit it, and as people bring particular places into existence, so, too, do places shape the people who inhabit them. I would add that the qualitative differences that one experiences in different places, the actual attributes that distinguish one place from another, will vary according to who is given access to the place, and under what conditions.

Until the first Cinco de Mayo, the English-speaking population had assumed de facto ownership of Kennett Square's centrally located public spaces. Kennett Square's downtown property is held in common, of course, but in cases where the ownership is collective or ambiguous it is typical for the social group that has the longest history in the area to assume proprietary ownership of the public space (Fried 2000). For many years Kennett Square's majority population was the only population, therefore it isn't surprising that they would claim the town center as their own. As the longstanding (predominantly Anglo-European) identity of Kennett Square was slowly challenged by Mexican settlement, it could no longer be assumed they would continue to have preeminence over the public space. This was demonstrated in the ways Mexicans were routinely excluded from festivals and public events until 2001. Thus, placing a festival celebrating Mexican cultural heritage into the heart of Kennett Square's downtown was a dramatic shift in the public face of the community. Consequently this seemingly small step in local ethnic relations made way for a shift in the place identity of Kennett Square.

Festivals like the Cinco de Mayo, as well as the 16 de Septiembre before it, offer opportunities for settlers to develop a sense of themselves as a distinct group. Although the majority of Mexican settlers in Kennett Square are from the same home community, the pueblo of Textitlán, this hometown is large enough so that settlers do not necessarily know one another or have friendships and social networks that draw upon their experiences in Mexico. Even when settlers do know one another, they may not live in proximity of their former friends and neighbors, and their new day-to-day and work routines in Pennsylvania can limit social contact with old friends. The settler population is very much a nascent community trying to find its place in a new home. Collective experiences lead to shared memories in place, and as a result work to construct a new local group identity.

The development of shared experience and memory in place is significant. Festivals and other common experiences provide a break from day-to-day routines and enable participants to engage one another. Such experiences connect people to the place in significant ways. Just as humans live their lives someplace, memories are always rooted to particular places so that the places in return hold memories and facilitate what Anthony D. Smith (1996, 25) has termed the "territorialization of memory." After the festival, the location of the event will be associated with memories of what was experienced that day, and the connections made during the festival are likely to be recalled whenever the participant passes through the festival site at other times. A similar process occurs in the creation of historic sites as the location of particular significant collective memories. Vacationers journey to historic places in order to connect with the events associated with the site; the sites in turn cultivate the recollection of significant past events.

Some of the changes brought about by the Cinco de Mayo festival were quite obvious. It made the Mexican community's visibility more acceptable. Since the first festival in 2001, Mexican businesses and agencies have been moving into space on State Street, something that was unthinkable just a decade earlier. The first was La Comunidad Hispana, a social-service agency for migrants, which moved its offices from an obscure space behind a heating oil company on the far edge of town to central offices on State Street. Two additional Mexican-owned businesses have opened in the center of town. For a few years it appeared that things were changing in Kennett Square and that the Mexican population was on its way to being incorporated as full members of the community. In addition, the festival continued to grow and was successfully celebrated on State Street through 2003. The following year local support for the event apparently began to moderate.

I arrived in Kennett Square in the early afternoon of May 2, 2004, with my sister Susan to conduct participant-observation research on the 2004 Cinco de Mayo.[15] I was surprised to find State Street open to traffic and no indication of a festival in progress. It had rained that morning; at first I thought the event had been canceled. We decided to head to Mi Casa Su Casa, a gift shop specializing in Latin American arts and crafts.[16] When I asked the shop manager, Betty Haag, about the festival, she told me it had been moved into the parking lots and alleys behind State Street. She explained, "The merchants didn't want the street closed. They think it's bad for business." As we talked, I found that this decision not to close State Street was not part of an overall policy change and that the street would be closed for the Mushroom Festival in the fall. When I inquired why the merchants would allow the street closed for one festival and not the other, Haag said that the crowds would be bigger for the Mushroom Festival and thus would not affect business.

This change had a significant effect on the 2004 Cinco de Mayo. Tucked away in the parking lots and alleys, it was much less impressive than the 2002 event had been (see figure 11.4). Gone also were the booths promoting public health issues; in their place were vendors, many Mexican, selling arts and crafts. There were also more refreshment options. The same Mexican-owned restaurants that were present in 2002 were back, and joining them were a vendor from a Mexican-style restaurant owned by a local Anglo and an ice cream vendor, Paleteria La Michoacana, a locally owned franchise of a company that is based in Mexico.

FIGURE 11.4   Cinco de Mayo 2004, a View of the Alley from State Street

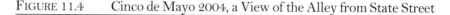

Source: Photograph by Debra Lattanzi Shutika.

The alleys were too narrow for a parade, so instead there was a walking procession. The Mexican folk dance troupe returned to perform, and once again there was a parade of flags, but these flags did not represent English-speaking Kennett Square's heritage but were from each of the Mexican states. They were carried by Anglo and Mexican teenage girls wearing regional Mexican costumes. There was also a procession of Anglo school-age children carrying masks that they had made in preparation for the festival. Festival organizers had asked two local elementary schools to have the children create masks that represent what they thought about Mexican culture. The masks were bright and colorful, in some cases bearing skeletal images that resembled those of Jose Guadalupe Posada, which are associated with the Days of the Dead. However, most of the masks bore no resemblance to any Mexican cultural icon (see figure 11.5).

The masks were followed by the "March of the Sombreros." Papier-mâché hats had been crafted and were worn by English speakers and were disproportionately large—their brims up to three feet in diameter—and decorated in a variety of ways, almost all brightly colored, in a style that was clearly stereotypical of a common Mexican symbol. There was no explanation of the purpose of the sombreros, nor was it obvious what constructive messages those wearing the hats might be trying to communi-

FIGURE 11.5   Student Masks Representing Mexican Culture,
                Cinco de Mayo, 2004

Source: Photograph by Debra Lattanzi Shutika.

cate to or about their Mexican neighbors. I call masks and sombreros used in these ways "pseudosymbols," that is, material objects that are used to represent a misunderstood aspect of Mexican culture. Later Ghione explained that the sombreros and masks were included to represent Mexican cultural heritage and because "that is what they do in Mexico." Here Ghione was referring to the Mexican custom of parading giant puppets during fiestas. The masks created by the Kennett Square children were flat and were carried on poles during the procession. Although they bore little resemblance to the Mexican puppets, I found the connection that Ghione made to Mexican festival masks intriguing. Festival masks, such as the ones carried by the Kennett Square children and the sombreros worn by English-speaking revelers, are often used in festivals and signify transformation (Napier 1987).[17] Masks hide the identity of the wearer, but in the process they also reveal other cultural personae. In masking their Anglo-European identity, the English-speaking festival participants where symbolically adopting a Mexican persona in the form of a common Mexican stereotype (see figure 11.6).

The transformation in the Cinco de Mayo in this two-year period articulates the ambivalence that the English-speaking community has had toward the Mexicans who are settling in Kennett Square. Having shed its

FIGURE 11.6   March of the Sombreros, Cinco de Mayo 2004

Source: Photograph by Debra Lattanzi Shutika.

paternalistic impulse, the Cinco de Mayo was more festive than educational and, therefore more analogous to other Kennett festivals. The change in the parade of flags indicates that there is recognition of Mexico as a diverse nation, just as the parade of Kennett Square flags at the 2002 festival represented the town's English-speaking "diversity." Nevertheless, the mixing of the Mexican folk traditions with the pseudosymbols is indicative of how little the English-speaking community understands about their Mexican neighbors' culture. In this sense, the Cinco de Mayo is a true instance of what Cantwell (1993) termed ethnomimesis: a point of convergence where the majority engages the minority and for a moment imagines itself as part of the minority culture. This is temporary for the majority culture, which in this case can just as easily set the Mexican aspect of their community aside. As there is no consistent basis of association between the two groups, the festival provides a false sense of understanding, one that comes from the dominant culture's projecting, or perhaps looking for, itself in the other.

The most revealing attribute of the 2004 festival was the choice of location. By moving the event to less visible alleys and parking lots, locations that would be unthinkable for any other community event, the festival represents how Mexicans are "placed" in the broader community. The statement of the shop manager Betty Haag suggests that there was a bias on the part of the merchants when it came to closing the street. Later,

Vince Ghione acknowledged that the State Street merchants do not see Mexicans as potential customers. He explained that moving the festival "was my idea from the start. The conflict, and it's really not a conflict, but the merchants just howl when you close that street. And, you know if you close the street and you bring enough people in, they still complain. Even the Mushroom Festival, it's like, you put the wrong thing in front of me and no one can get to my store. So I decided to try this, this other area."

While taking responsibility for this decision, Ghione also points out that his prior experience with the State Street merchants had influenced his decision to avoid the potential conflict of closing the street in 2004. He also insisted that he prefers the new location, as did other residents. He continued, "You being familiar with Mexico should understand this. Someone, I can't remember right now who, came up to me and said, 'This is just like Mexico, all the little plazas.' Now with everything, we have different plazas [parking lots]." Of course, when Mexican villages host their festivals they typically take place in central plazas, not side streets, alleys, and parking lots.

When the mayor of Kennett Square got up to make his customary remarks to the crowd, he emphasized, "All are welcome here." Standing beside me my sister whispered, "That's right, you Mexicans can come use this parking lot any time you want." Her appraisal echoes Cantwell (1993) in that this festival is a type of "street theater that makes a major statement of cultural identity" (99). Mexicans are welcome, but should remain barely visible on the fringe of the community.

These changes I believe resulted from the English-speaking community's discomfort with the experience of opening up the center of town to the Mexicans and realizing that they had set a precedent for the Mexicans to associate their own memories with the locus of the English-speaker's own traditional memories. This could be termed the territorialization of memory. Shared memory is linked to a particular place for all participants, not only Mexican settlers. The festival brought these two normally isolated groups together, but what the organizers did not anticipate is that the English-speaking community would not experience "Mexican culture" in the abstract, distilled version advertised for the festival and caricatured through masks and sombreros. Instead they were experiencing Mexicans, the live flesh and blood people who are now part of Kennett Square and whom the festival publicly acknowledged as such.

Moving Mexicans from the fringe of the community for the first three festivals emplaced them and facilitated the process of locality for Mexicans and their English-speaking neighbors. Once this process began to take hold, the reciprocal nature of locality became apparent, and in this context moving the festival to the alley was an attempt to reposition Mexicans vis-à-vis others in the community.

The process of integration involves more than setting aside one day to acknowledge the existence of the marginalized. It must also incorporate the development of meaningful relationships and social networks from all parts of the community. Mexicans have assumed ownership of the community symbolically and materially, through communal participation in the festival and ownership of homes and businesses. As newcomers, Mexican in Kennett Square are no longer seen as transients, but they are not yet "people who belong."

I see the shift in the content and location of the festival as an indication that the first years of the Cinco de Mayo were successful in creating a point of convergence between Kennett Square's English speakers and Mexicans. Perhaps the festival was too successful in the sense that it may have required the English-speaking community to engage the Mexican population to the point of discomfort. This would explain the decision to withdraw the event from its central location and include stereotypical representations of Mexican culture. Both actions restructure ethnic relations. They increase the English speaker's control over public space and interpret local Mexican culture in ways that conform to American sensibilities.

Other changes are also revealing. The move away from a social services and health education event to an entertainment event, and the parade of Mexican state flags are both significant transformations. These changes suggest that local Mexicans are beginning to shape the festival, albeit slowly. They are changing the margins of the event while the main authority rests with the English-speaking majority. These changes suggest that the Cinco de Mayo is a representation of Kennett Square as the English-speaking community would like it to be: a rural American town with a Mexican flavor, but one that is not too noticeable.

NOTES

1. Before Mexicans arrived to pick mushrooms in Kennett Square these jobs were filled by Puerto Rican laborers. There is a small population of Puerto Rican families in Kennett Square, but the majority of these workers never settled there permanently.

2. For details of these narratives see Debra Lattanzi Shutika (forthcoming).

3. Fictive kin networks refer to persons who assume the status of supplementary or replacement kin, but are not consanguineal relatives.

4. Kennett Square's longer-term residents often expressed this sentiment when they spoke of their community vis-à-vis other neighboring towns. At the time of this writing, Kennett Square was the only town in this corner of

Chester County that regularly held community festivals and parades. The exception was Chadds Ford, a small suburban community some five miles to the north that regularly held Chadds Ford Days, a festival celebrating local history and identity. In 1999 the Mushroom Festival was scaled back significantly, with no parade and only a modest street fair. It was rumored then that it would soon be canceled, but it was not.

5. Dorothy Noyes's (2003) examination of the Patum of Berga, a festival to celebrate Corpus Christi in Catalonia, is an example of how cultural performance is used to construct identity.

6. The first permanent Mexican settlers were those who were legalized under the Immigration Reform and Control Act of 1986. Subsequent settlement has been driven by job growth that resulted from Chester County's rapid suburban development in the early years of the 2000s.

7. For example, there has been considerable dispute in the community regarding proper property management, the number and types of persons who should be allowed to live in a single-family home, and aesthetic preferences for exterior home decoration. For a complete account of these issues, see Shutika (forthcoming).

8. Textitlán is a pseudonym.

9. It should be noted that the Latino Cultural Alliance was a well-organized group, and was registered as a 501C3 nonprofit organization.

10. In California, the campaign called Cinco de Mayo con Orgullo: Nuestra Cultura no se Vende (Cinco de Mayo with Pride: Our Culture Is Not for Sale) is a statewide effort (Staples 2001, 1).

11. The parade of flags did not begin with the Cinco de Mayo, but is also a regular event in Kennett Unity Day, a festival created a decade ago to highlight community diversity and to promote unity among the town's population.

12. The Democratic Party also had a booth at the event, but its materials were available only in English.

13. This is not to say that information presented at the festival is not necessary or useful. Public health education is an essential part of all communities. I do take issue with the choice of venue in which it was presented, however, and the fact that these types of displays are not common at other Kennett Square festivals. Furthermore, these organizations have other opportunities to reach this population. Every April local social-service organizations host an Expo Latino, where they present similar information about local services.

14. Ghione's concern here is that the attendance has to reach certain levels to maintain sponsorship support, and thus Anglos will have to attend in order to reach this goal.

15. The Cinco de Mayo takes place on the Saturday that falls closest to May 5.

16. Mi Casa Su Casa is owned and operated by La Comunidad Hispana. The shop sells Latin American items and is used to generate income for the agency.

17. A mask need not completely cover one's face to create its desired effect. Partial masks, such as those worn at masquerade balls, achieve similar effects.

REFERENCES

Alamillo, José M. 2003. "More than a Fiesta: Ethnic Identity, Cultural Politics, and Cinco de Mayo Festivals in Corona, California, 1930–1950." *Aztlán* 28(2): 57–86.

Appadurai, Arjun. 1996. *Modernity at Large: Cultural Dimensions of Globalization.* Minneapolis, Minn.: University of Minnesota Press.

Basso, Keith H. 1996. "Wisdom Sits in Places: Notes on a Western Apache Landscape." In *Senses of Place,* edited by Steven Feld and Keith H. Basso. Santa Fe, N.M.: School of American Research.

Brandes, Stanley H. 1998. *Power and Persuasion: Fiestas and Social Control in Rural Mexico.* Philadelphia, Penn.: University of Pennsylvania Press.

Cantwell, Robert. 1993. *Ethnomimesis: Folklife and the Representation of Culture.* Chapel Hill, N.C.: University of North Carolina Press.

Casey, Edward. 1993. *Getting Back Into Place: Toward a Renewed Understanding of the Place-World.* Bloomington, Ind.: Indiana University Press.

———. 1996. "How to Get from Space to Place in a Fairly Short Stretch of Time: Phenomenological Prolegomena." In *Senses of Place,* edited by Steven Feld and Keith H. Basso. Santa Fe, N.M.: School of American Research.

Cohen, Abner. 1993. *Masquerade Politics: Explorations in the Structure of Urban Cultural Movements.* Berkeley, Calif.: University of California Press.

Cuba, Lee, and David Hummon. 1993. "Constructing a Sense of Home: Place Affiliation and Migration Across the Life Cycle." *Sociological Forum* 8(4): 547–72.

Fried, Marc. 2000. "Continuities and Discontinuities of Place." *Journal of Environmental Psychology* 20(3): 193–205.

Kashatus, William C. 2002. *Just Over the Line: Chester County and the Underground Railroad.* State College, Penn.: Penn State University Press.

Koch, Philip J. 1987. "Emotional Ambivalence." *Philosophy and Phenomenological Research* 48(2): 257–79.

MacAloon, John J., editor. 1984. *Rite, Drama, Festival, Spectacle: Rehearsals Toward a Theory of Cultural Performance.* Philadelphia, Penn.: Institute for the Study of Human Issues.

Mexican Migration Project. 2004. Database: MMP107. Accessed at http://mmp.opr.princeton.edu.

Napier, David. 1987. "Festival Masks." In *In Time Out of Time: Essays on Festival,* edited by Alessandro Falassi. Albuquerque, N.M.: University of New Mexico Press.

Noyes, Dorothy. 2003. *Fire in the Plaça: Catalan Festival Politics After Franco.* Philadelphia, Penn.: University of Pennsylvania Press.

Saxton, Lisa. 1992. "Cinco de Mayo Promos Hit 'Gringos.' " *Supermarket News* 42: 126.

Schechner, Richard. 1985. *Between Theater and Anthropology.* Philadelphia, Penn.: University of Pennsylvania Press.

Shore, Bradd. 1990. "Human Ambivalence and the Structuring of Moral Values." *Ethos* 18(2): 165–79.

Shutika, Debra Lattanzi. 2005. "Bridging the Community: Nativism, Activism and the Politics of Inclusion in a Pennsylvania Mexican Settlement Community." In *New Destinations of Mexican Immigration to the United States: Community Formation, Local Responses and Inter-Group Relations*, edited by Rúben Hérnandez-Léon and Víctor Zúñiga. New York: Russell Sage Foundation.

———. Forthcoming. *Beyond the Borderlands: Mexican Transnational Lives, New Destinations, and the Sense of Place*. Berkeley, Calif.: University of California Press.

Smith, Anthony D. 1996. "Culture, Community and Territory: The Politics of Ethnicity and Nationalism." *International Affairs* 72(3): 445–58.

Sommers, Laurie Kay. 1991. "Inventing Latinismo: The Creation of 'Hispanic' Panethnicity in the United States." *Journal of American Folklore* 104(411): 32–53.

Staples, Kathy. 2001. "Taking Back Cinco de Mayo." *Prevention File Ventura County*, Spring 2001, 1.

Taylor, Frances Cloud. 1976/1998. *The Trackless Trail: The Story of the Underground Railroad in Kennett Square, Chester County, Pennsylvania and the Surrounding Community*. Kennett Square, Penn.: Graphics Standard Printing.

———. 1995/1999. *The Trackless Trail Leads On: An Exploration of Conductors and their Stations*. Kennett Square, Penn.: Graphics Standard Printing.

Turcsik, Richard. 1996. "Retailers Brew Cinco de Mayo Beer Events." *Supermarket News* 46: 2A.

Turner, Victor W. 1969. *The Ritual Process*. Chicago, Ill.: Aldine.

———, editor. 1982. *Celebration: Studies in Festivity and Ritual*. Washington: Smithsonian Institution Press.

U.S. Census Bureau. 2000. Census 2000, Summary File 1, generated by Debra Lattanzi Shutika using American FactFinder. Accessed January 15, 2004 at http://factfinder.census.gov.

CHAPTER 12

⅄

RACE TO THE TOP? THE POLITICS OF IMMIGRANT EDUCATION IN SUBURBIA

MICHAEL JONES-CORREA

In 2000, 52 percent of America's immigrants lived in suburbs (U.S. Census Bureau 2001), up from 48 percent in 1999 (Schmidley and Gibson 1999). Thanks in part to the suburbanization of immigrant populations, the percentage of minorities in suburbs has also increased dramatically. In 2000, 33 percent of blacks, 45 percent of Latinos, and 51 percent of Asian Americans lived in suburbs (Humes and McKinnon 2000; McKinnon and Humes 2000; U.S. Census Bureau 2001).[1] The suburbanization of immigrants and minorities is beginning to approach that of the population as a whole. Nonetheless, suburbs, like the nation as a whole, are still largely white, whites making up 75 percent of the total suburban population (where 54 percent of them live).[2] Thus, immigrants currently moving to suburbia enter a context where they are for the most part clearly minorities.

The question asked in this chapter is how suburban institutions react to increasing ethnic and racial diversity (much of it driven by immigration) in the context of white domination of these institutions. Using the Washington, D.C., suburbs of Fairfax County, Virginia, and Montgomery County, Maryland, as case studies, the chapter focuses on a key policy arena, education, to examine how demographic changes work through intermediary internal, external, and contextual variables to change bureaucratic policies and structures. The analysis seeks to untangle which variables explain why change occurs, and when and what kind of change takes place in local policies and structures in response to demographic shifts.

The evidence for the argument is drawn from a variety of sources, including local media as well as governmental and nongovernmental reports, but comes primarily from 114 interviews conducted in the Washington metropolitan area with actors in the public and private sector from 2003 to 2004.[3] Twenty-seven of these interviews were with school administrators, school board officials, PTA leaders, and other actors in the education field. The argument presented here is based on these interviews, though for the sake of clarity of presentation, illustrations are drawn largely from interviews with the superintendents of public schools in Fairfax and Montgomery counties, Jerry Weast and Daniel Domenech, both men clearly key players in the politics of education in their respective areas.

The puzzle that emerges from the evidence is that the usual language of competing interests does not easily explain the policies that schools in the Washington metropolitan area chose to pursue. In an era of stagnant budgets, schools chose to redistribute funding in order to accommodate the needs of newly arriving students, many of whom are racially and ethnically diverse, potentially alienating politically engaged white middle class constituents. The question of why school administrators chose this politically perilous path, rather than simply follow the status quo, lies at the heart of the issues discussed in this chapter.

ETHNIC AND RACIAL CHANGE IN METROPOLITAN WASHINGTON

All metropolitan areas are not alike. According to William Frey (2001), the 102 metropolitan areas in the United States with more than 500,000 residents in 2000 (which accounted for 62 percent of the United States population) fell into three distinct categories:

- White-dominant metros, where whites made up a large majority of the total population. Fifty such areas contain 51 million people and represent 18 percent of the United States population.

- Black-white metros where African Americans and whites together make up a large majority of the population. Twenty-five such areas contain 39.8 million people and account for 14 percent of the United States population.

- Melting-pot metros, which containing substantial numbers of racial and ethnic minorities besides blacks and in which nonwhite groups together sometimes outnumber whites. There are thirty-five such metropolitan areas, accounting for 30 percent of the United States population; in this category are some of the nation's largest cities, which are often major immigrant gateways.

Much of suburbia's growing racial and ethnic diversity has occurred in the thirty-five melting-pot metros, where interregional and international migration combine to produce new multi-ethnic neighborhoods, schools, and workplaces. Metropolitan Washington, D.C., is one such area; like other urban centers in this category, over the twenty years from 1986 to 2006 it has experienced rapid demographic change. Its population grew by 16 percent in the decade from 1996 to 2006, more rapidly than the populations of comparable metropolitan areas such as Los Angeles, New York, and Chicago. In 2000, the D.C. metropolitan area contained 5.4 million people, up from 4.7 million in 1990, making it among the dozen largest in the United States, though not nearly as large as the behemoths New York and Los Angeles. The Washington metropolitan area is overwhelmingly suburban, and the District of Columbia itself accounts for just 10 percent of the region's population. Although the D.C. population shrank by 6 percent between 1990 and 2000, over the same period the suburbs of northern Virginia grew by 25 percent and those in Maryland increased by 17 percent.

Much of this growth was attributable to immigration. The Washington metropolitan region has ranked among the top ten immigrant-receiving areas of the country since the early 1980s, and its suburbs have long ranked high in the residential preferences of the area's burgeoning black middle class. African Americans are the largest minority group in the metro area with 22 percent of the total, and Asian and Latin American immigrants and their descendants each make up approximately 15 percent of the population. Salvadorans (from El Salvador) are the single largest immigrant group, but by themselves they constitute only 10.5 percent of all foreigners. After El Salvador, the other nations in the top ten for immigration are Vietnam, India, China, the Philippines, South Korea, Ethiopia, Iran, Pakistan, and Peru. Even combined, however, these ten nations only account for half of all immigrants to the area (Price et al. 2005). The immigrant population in the Washington metropolitan area is thus more diverse than other major metropolitan areas, and more diverse than the migration to towns and cities in the other new receiving areas discussed in this volume, though it is not atypical of suburban immigrant populations along the Eastern Seaboard (Singer 2003).

Ethnic and racial minorities now make up more then 75 percent of the population in Prince George's County, Maryland, and around 40 percent in neighboring Montgomery County. In northern Virginia, minorities constitute almost half of the population of Arlington and Alexandria (44 percent and 46 percent, respectively) and a third of Fairfax County (32 percent). The number of minority individuals varies considerably by municipality, but minorities are present in substantial numbers even in outlying suburbs such as Virginia's Loudoun County (17 percent).

The Washington metropolitan region can be divided into three distinct demographic zones: the slow-growth "urban core," taking in the District of Columbia, Arlington County, Virginia, and the city of Alexandria, Virginia; the "inner suburbs," with modestly increasing populations, of Montgomery and Prince George's counties in Maryland and Fairfax County in Virginia; and the fast-growing "outer counties" to the west, including Virginia's Loudoun and Maryland's Frederick counties. Though growth is most evident on the margins of the metropolitan area, the largest employment sectors, and hence populations, are in the inner suburbs. The Washington metropolitan area's two largest inner suburbs, Fairfax County in Virginia and Montgomery County in Maryland, are the setting for the analyses presented here.

RESPONSE TO DEMOGRAPHIC CHANGE

As the demography of suburbia has changed, both nationally and around Washington, it has led to other changes. Demographic shifts inevitably trigger responses in bureaucratic policies and structures. As an area's population changes, local policies and structures presumably shift in response, as indicated by changes in organizational funding, staffing, services, and accountability structures. For instance, with population growth and rising racial and ethnic diversity, budget priorities may shift so that funding is reallocated from one line item in the budget to another; funding may also be increased in some categories relative to others; or certain streams of funding may be protected from budget cuts. Population change may also lead to the creation of new, staffed programs or the redefinition of existing staff lines, or the provision or expansion of services. New accountability structures may be developed that cross or link various administrative departments.

A compelling question is why there should be any institutional response at all to demographic change, as long as there is a dominant majority governing coalition in place that is capable of blocking changes in the distribution of resources and spending. And if change does occur, what are the intermediate variables that explain when and what kind of change takes place in local structures and policies in response to demographic shifts? Among political scientists, the usual explanatory narrative for policy change in response to demographic shifts privileges the role of electoral representation. Consider, for example, Robert Dahl's classic book *Who Governs?* (1961), in which he traces policy and structural change to the political system and argues that change occurs only as newcomers shift from their corporate loyalties to partisan mobilization in which ethnicity plays at most a symbolic role. The double lesson of the book is that political

FIGURE 12.1   Factors of Change in Local Bureaucratic Structures and Policies

	Internal	External	Contextual	
Demographic shifts ⟶	Governmental system Institutional interests Professional norms	Political representation State and federal mandates Court decisions	SES Prior immigration Native minorities	Change in bureaucratic structures and policies

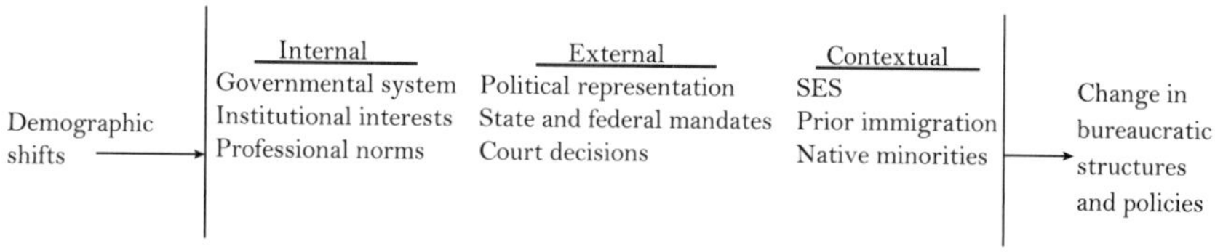

Source: Author's compilation.

representation precedes substantive changes in policy, and that political representation for newcomers comes to fruition only over the generations, and then only through the mobilization of interests.

This view seems to close off the possibility that local contexts might vary, for instance, if a locality has a history of immigration and therefore an institutional infrastructure of immigrant-service organizations, or if there is already a native-born ethnic or racial minority in place when immigrants arrive. It assumes that the electoral sphere is the primary (and perhaps the only) arena for policy change, while ignoring other avenues for change outside electoral politics that might be used by immigrants and their advocates as they seek to advance their interests. An alternative and, I would argue, better way to model the causes of change in local structures and policies is to view policy change not only as a function of demographic shifts, or of demographic shifts arbitrated through the electoral sphere, but also of demographic shifts mediated through an intermediary set of internal, external, and contextual variables. These relationships are represented in figure 12.1.

Internal variables include characteristics intrinsic to local governments and bureaucracies: the design of the governing system (such as council-manager versus a mayoral systems), the institutional interests of bureaucrats (to increase their power or maintain their jobs), and the professional norms that define the culture of bureaucratic agencies. External variables include forces that place pressure on bureaucracies to change, or present constraints on change. Among these are political representation in all its forms (electoral representation, campaign contributions, and so on), county budgets, court decisions, or external state and federal rules and mandates. Contextual variables are factors such as the socioeconomic characteristics of an area's inhabitants, the history of immigration, and the residence of native-born minorities that might shape the contemporary reception of ethnic and racial minorities to an area. This chapter examines this model's application to a single, central policy arena, education, in Fairfax and Montgomery counties in the Washington, D.C., area.

EDUCATION IN WASHINGTON'S SUBURBS

Education has always been at the center of suburban politics. From the development of the first suburbs in the late nineteenth century, the quality of schools in suburbia has been one of the principal selling points to new residents. As Jerry Weast, the Montgomery County school superintendent at the time of this study (2003), put it, "The unwritten compact, if you will, is that you come here . . . [and] your child gets a good education and in return for that good education [you] will contribute to keep the system strong and viable."

This compact has been held to particularly strongly in the Washington, D.C., area, where three suburban counties (Fairfax, Loudoun, and Montgomery) rank among the ten wealthiest counties in the United States, in terms of income per capita. In many other metropolitan areas, school governance is fragmented among multiple school systems, which may selectively include or exclude municipalities or unincorporated areas of counties. Washington, D.C., area school systems, however, are by and large organized at the county level. The population of the surrounding suburban counties now significantly exceeds the population of the region's central city, which has fewer than half a million residents. Fairfax County, in northern Virginia, alone has more than one million residents and Montgomery County in Maryland has almost as many.

The area's suburban school systems reflect their counties' wealth and populations. Montgomery and Fairfax counties' public schools rank among the top twenty largest school systems in the United States, with Fairfax County being twelfth largest and Montgomery County ranking eighteenth. Fairfax public schools, with 166,601 students in 2004, had a budget of $1.67 billion for 234 schools. Of this amount, some $1.24 billion, or 74.5 percent, was allocated by the county from local tax revenue (mainly property taxes) with the rest coming equally from state and federal sources. In FY 2005, Montgomery County's public schools had a budget of $1.59 billion for 139,203 students, with 75.3 percent of these funds coming from the county, 17 percent from the state, and 6.8 percent from federal sources.

The influx of a more multiracial (and sometimes non-English-speaking) population has posed complications for the area's schools systems. In Montgomery County in 2000, foreign-born residents accounted for 27 percent of the total population, and 31 percent of all households did not speak

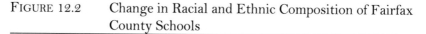

FIGURE 12.2   Change in Racial and Ethnic Composition of Fairfax
County Schools

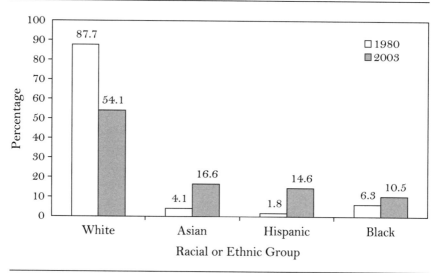

Source: Fairfax County Public Schools (2003).

English at home. The county's public school population hailed from 163 countries and spoke 123 languages. Eight percent of the county's students (12,000 children) were English learners taking special courses for English Speakers of Other Languages (ESOL). In 2003, the county's public schools were for the first time, majority minority, with a student body that was 45 percent white, 22 percent African American, 19 percent Latino, and 14 percent Asian American.

The figures for Fairfax County's schools tell a similar story—over the last twenty-five years, the public schools have become increasingly ethnically and racially diverse. Figure 12.2 shows the remarkable degree of change over a twenty-three-year period. As can be seen, from 1980 to 2003 the proportion of Asian American students in the public schools quadrupled, the percentage of Latino children increased sevenfold, and the percentage of blacks almost doubled. As in Montgomery County, in Fairfax over 120 languages are spoken in households around the county and 13 percent of students were in ESOL programs, an indication of the effect that immigration has had locally.

The influx of minority children—black, Asian, and Latino, many of them immigrant and poor—threatened to disrupt the unwritten compact described by Weast. For one thing, the new students generally had lower test scores than their white native-born counterparts, which could potentially lower average results for the county school system as a whole and thus damage its national reputations and standing. Paradoxically, Weast noted, scores for the school system's traditional middle class white students might be going up even as average scores were being dragged down by worse-performing immigrants and minorities. In Montgomery County in 2002, for example, whites taking the SATs scored an average of 1159, whereas blacks' scores averaged 906. The average scores for Latinos, many of whom speak English as a second language, actually declined from previous years (Nancy Trejos, "Area's Students Did the Math, SAT Scores Show," *Washington Post*, August 28, 2002, B01).

VARIATION ACROSS COUNTIES?

One might expect that the degree and mode of response to these demographic shifts would vary substantially across school systems. After all, Virginia and Maryland are, politically, quite different states. At the institutional level, Virginia is a "Dillon's Rule" state, one where authority for taxation and hence spending is kept in the hands of the state legislature. Maryland, on the other hand, has delegated substantial powers to its localities. At the level of political culture, Maryland is a much more liberal state. Politics tend to be dominated by the Democratic Party, and the views of the liberal wing of the party usually are the starting point for discussions of ethnic and racial diversity. Montgomery County also has more experience than Fairfax County in handling ethnic diversity: as early as 1970, the county was receiving almost a third of all immigration to the area, not that different from the percentage it receives today.

Virginia is also, of course, a southern state, with the history that such a legacy entails, including a recent history of segregated public schooling and resistance to integrated schools. The state generally has a more conservative political culture than Maryland's. For example, it recently passed laws to require public schools to "prominently post" placards informing passers-by "In God We Trust" (Rosalind Helderman and Christina Samuels, "Virginia Schools Forge Ahead with National Motto," *Washington Post*, June 28, 2002, B01) and requiring students to recite the Pledge of Allegiance every day in class (Craig Timberg, "House Weakens Pledge Measure," *Washington Post*, February 22, 2001, B01). The state legislature also passed a bill in 2002 to prohibit undocumented immigrants from attending state universities and paying in-state tuition—illegal aliens were not to be considered residents of the state (Tom Steinfeldt, "Activists, Officials Urge Delay on Immigrant Legislation," *Fairfax Journal*, January 24, 2003, A1). This law, however, was vetoed by the governor (R. H. Melton, "Warner Vetoes Tuition Curbs," *Washington Post*, May 1, 2003, A01).

In this kind of environment, as Daniel Domenech, then Fairfax County school superintendent, pointed out, immigrants and their children are unlikely to get involved in, much less challenge, the school system:

> Many of them are undocumented and they are afraid of what might happen. Again, particularly in a very conservative community like here where the General Assembly in Virginia just a year ago was threatening to pass laws that would require the school system to report these kids to immigration and denying them access to state colleges and universities unless they could prove residency.

"That kind of stuff really makes you feel welcome," he noted sardonically. Domenech noted that Jerry Weast, his counterpart in Montgomery County "acknowledges that he does have a more liberal element than I do and so that it does make it easier for him to do some of the things that he does. I think [the] Potomac [River] . . . does create a significant division in cultures between the two places. It may be just a river [separating us], but we are like worlds apart."

Despite this seeming contrast, one surprising finding in this study is how little these differences seemed to matter in determining how schools responded to changes in racial and ethnic diversity. Despite Fairfax County being a more conservative county in a more conservative state, its school administrators accomplished much of what they wanted to do, in some cases by simply calling what they wished to do by a different name. As Domenech, Fairfax County's school superintendent, recalled:

> The word "bilingual education" is still not utterable in Fairfax County. So I said, fine. But I learned that we had some outstanding language emerging programs, which are bilingual education, except that unlike the traditional bilingual education program that's geared to the language-minority child, the language emerging program is seen as an enrichment program, almost a GT [gifted and talented] program, for American kids who want to speak a second language, will be taught in that language and, in this case, it's French, it's German, it's Japanese and it's Spanish.
>
> Well, we use that opportunity to take the Spanish component of that and create dual-language programs where we've provided many of our Spanish-speaking students the opportunity to learn in Spanish with their American counterparts who were learning Spanish while

they continued to learn English. We extended that program to the kindergarten level and we have a number of dual-language kindergartens in the district, which are doing very well, and we're still not calling it a bilingual education.

Thus, despite significant differences in regional political cultures and institutions, administrators in both counties' schools implemented remarkably similar programs to address the challenges brought about by changing demographics, thus providing the first indication that we may not be seeing politics as usual —at least as political scientists see it. In Montgomery County, the school system's response took the form of commitments to schools in what administrators called the "red zone"—schools containing the great majority of the county's racial and ethnic diversity and many immigrant-origin children receiving federally subsidized lunches—to provide additional funds for all-day kindergarten, smaller class sizes, and teacher benefits.[4] In Fairfax County, school administrators went out of their way to design programs to meet the needs of schools coping with diversity, poverty, and English-language learning. Schools falling into this category became "Project Excel" schools and received additional funds to reduce class sizes, offer all-day kindergarten, and more. In both cases, these programs required millions of dollars in extra funding: $67 million in Montgomery County over a four-year period and $68 million in Fairfax—not an insignificant share of these school systems' discretionary funds.

FACTORS EXPLAINING POLICY AND STRUCTURAL CHANGES

Why did these changes take place? It seems unlikely that demographic shifts automatically translated into policy changes. As Jerry Weast, superintendent of Montgomery County's public schools, noted, the easier path was for the county to do nothing:

What's really interesting is that while the community knew [this demographic change] was happening, but they weren't gearing up for it. . . . What we were doing when we put our administration together five years ago was forcing people to bring to the forefront the issue. The issue had been there and had been evolving over a period of time, but there was a fear, in my opinion, of it being brought here right on the table. The fear was that we'll promulgate flight, it will . . . have a negative effect on property values and won't have any laudable effect on improving anything but just makes things more confusing.

Not only was the path of least resistance to do nothing, but it was certainly choosing a path of greater resistance to implement policies that would entail the redistribution of resources in the school budget to less well-off schools in Fairfax and Montgomery counties. So what explains the schools' response? What were the critical intervening variables?

There are several different variables that singly or together could explain when and why changes in education policy occurred. The first four are external to the public schools: electoral politics, federal and state mandates, court decisions, and the budgetary constraints. The last two are internal to the public school system: the interests of professionals such as ESOL teachers, and the role of professional norms. I explore each of these briefly.

Electoral Politics

Political scientists tend to look to politics as the explanation for policy change, focusing particularly on electoral politics. And certainly electoral politics play a role, as representatives push for changes in policies and programs. Electoral politics are particularly important for schools; after all, local politicians control the purse strings and provide the bulk of the funding for local schools. More than half of all county tax dollars in Fairfax and Montgomery counties go to public school funding, and schools receive three quarters of their funding from the counties. Certainly school administrators are aware of the importance of electoral politics: as Weast emphasized to us, "You're got to remember that at the bottom of most political equations is the ballot box."

However, neither he nor his counterpart in Fairfax County saw the new racial or ethnic minorities moving to the county as major political actors. In fact, in neither Montgomery nor Fairfax counties does the descriptive representation of racial or ethnic minorities—the election of representatives who look like their constituents—approach their proportional numbers in the population as a whole. For instance, although racial and ethnic minorities make up approximately 40 percent of Montgomery County's total population, in 2003 there was only one minority representative out of nine on the county's board of supervisors. Given national patterns of voting for minority candidates, whereby minority candidates are more likely to be elected in single-member districts than in at-large districts, the board's composition of four at-large seats and five district-based seats likely lower the odds of greater minority representation. In 2003, Fairfax County had ten members on its board of supervisors; nine were elected by their districts, whereas the tenth, the chair of the board, was elected at-large. However, no racial or ethnic minorities had ever served on the county's board.

Racial and ethnic minorities fared better on boards of education in the two counties. In Montgomery County, ethnic and racial minorities had been represented for more than a decade. In 2003, two of the seven members of the board of education in Montgomery County were black, one was Asian, and one was Latino, together well over half the board's membership. Note that these members were elected from the board's five single-member districts and that the two at-large members of the board were both white. Fairfax County's Board of Education only began electing its members in 1996, with six elected by district and three at-large, for a total of nine. In the early 1990s its first minority members were appointed to the board, but by 2001 the board had three elected minority members (two black, one Latino) out of nine; in 2003 the board had only one minority member on it, a Korean-American. Note again that the at-large members of the board have been white, while representatives of ethnic and racial minorities have either been appointed or elected from single-member districts.

The direction in both counties has been toward greater representation of ethnic and racial minorities, but in neither Montgomery nor Fairfax County has this representation been very significant. In the case of the school board, the presence of minority representatives has been much more substantial and consistent, if still very recent. In both counties, these representatives have been important backers of policies to implement programs targeting "schools in need"—schools with greater percentages of minority students, of students in ESOL programs, and of students receiving federally provided lunches. In Fairfax County, minority representatives have also been crucial actors in keeping admissions to gifted and talented (GT) programs on the agenda, and in pushing for the development of alternative admissions procedures for the county's most selective high school. Thus, the presence of minority representatives on the school boards in Fairfax and Montgomery counties matters—they have helped nudge the education debate toward addressing the gap between whites, Asian Americans, and other racial and ethnic groups. But given their numbers, their role is not, and cannot be, decisive.

Federal and State Mandates

State and National politics have a hand in shaping educational policy as well. In 2001, for example, Congress passed the No Child Left Behind Act (NCLB), which set federal standards for schools nationwide, requiring testing to provide benchmarks by which every school, as well as key subsets of students in each school, would have to show progress every year. In addition, the law promised to hold schools accountable if they did not meet these standards, by sanctioning schools that failed to meet achievement targets on standardized tests. Though it may well be the case that the legislation was insufficiently funded, according to the Center on Education Policy the law did succeed in focusing attention on the achievement gap between disadvantaged and mainstreamed students, since schools are marked as failing if any subset of students failed to make progress (Sam Dillon, "One in Four Schools Fall Short Under Bush Law," *New York Times*, January 27, 2004, A1).

In 2002 Maryland passed similar legislation at the state level, the Bridge to Excellence in Public Schools Act, which like federal legislation set standards and penalties for schools and focused particular attention on the achievement gap between different racial and ethnic groups.[5] In 2002 Maryland first administered its High School Assessment Tests to all graduating seniors, as Virginia had with its Standards of Learning Exams in 1998.

The cumulative effect of these various school standards and student exams is hard to measure. Neither Weast nor Domenech saw these federal and state accountability measures as being crucial, and in some ways they saw them as detrimental or at least annoying. Weast said of No Child Left Behind:

> No Child Left Behind is visionary, but when you talk about operationalizing things, the farther you get away from the schoolhouse the more difficult it is to operationalize [anything]. Laws are very difficult to operationalize. If they weren't, we could legislate morality and we could legislate all kinds of things. But we have not been successful. There, at the local level, you've got to attack the real systemic issues and they may not all be the same. In fact, one size doesn't fit all. So, [Congress] got it down to not the federal unit, but to the state unit, which is better, but not a whole lot, because states, one, don't have any money, small departments of education tend to be extremely bureaucratic, tend to measure things rather than deal with building capacity of people and tend to want to do short-term turnarounds rather than long-term kind[s] of things.

The standards and penalties set at the federal and state levels could conceivably affect a school's—or a school system's—reputation. But neither the federal nor state laws had the funding behind them to compel or persuade schools to really change course. For example, in Montgomery public schools, federal dollars accounted for less than 7 percent of the schools' total budgets; state funding was more significant at 17 percent. In both

Fairfax and Montgomery counties, the most likely effect of NCLB was to provide additional ammunition to school administrators who were already advocating programs to reduce the gap in test scores and other measures of educational outcomes between white and minority students. The programs themselves, and their funding by the counties (particularly since NCLB offered little in the way of additional funding), preceded these state and federal mandates.

Court Decisions

Two court cases, both decided by the United States Court of Appeals for the Fourth Circuit, in Richmond, Virginia, had a direct influence on school policies toward racial and ethnic minorities in the Washington, D.C., area. In both cases, not coincidentally, the plaintiffs and defendants were drawn from the Washington metropolitan area. In Eisenberg v. Montgomery County Public Schools et al., a white non-Hispanic first grade student was denied admission to Rosemary Hills Elementary, a magnet school in Montgomery County, Maryland.[6] The denial was based upon the negative impact the student's departure would have had on the "diversity profile" of the school he was leaving. The district court had upheld the school's decision, but this was then overturned on appeal. The court of appeals left "unresolved" the question of whether diversity is a compelling state interest, but it concluded that even so, the school's policy was not sufficiently narrowly tailored because it explicitly compared the diversity in the school to that of the population. Montgomery County filed a petition for certiorari to the Supreme Court, which was denied on March 21, 2000.

In April 1998, the Court for the Eastern District of Virginia, ruling on the case Tuttle v. Arlington County School Board, struck down the admissions program to Arlington Traditional School, an alternative public elementary school in Arlington County, Virginia, a suburb of Washington D.C.[7] The admissions program compared the pool of applicants to the district's overall student population with respect to family income, race and ethnicity, and the question of whether English was a student's first language. Depending on how different the composition of the pool was from that of the population, the admissions lottery would be weighted for those characteristics. The Fourth Circuit Court of Appeals ruled, "Even if the court accepts defendants' contention that diverse student enrollments are educationally preferable, the court cannot conclude that the goal of diversity excuses racial discrimination." In short, the circuit court found that the school's admissions policy was not narrowly tailored to the government's interest in racial diversity. The school board filed a petition for a writ of certiorari to the Supreme Court, which was denied on March 28, 2000.

Together these two cases prompted the wholesale dismantling across the Southeast of programs and admissions processes taking explicit account of race and ethnicity, and in particular, any policies that compared percentages of racial and ethnic minorities in the student body with those same percentages in a larger population, say, of a city, county, or state. If anything, the overall effect of these court cases was to make government officials and school administrators think twice before attempting to implement race-conscious programs. They were a potential stumbling block to proposals to reallocate funding among the schools to benefit schools with more racial and ethnic minority children.[8]

Budgetary Constraints

In the early part of the decade, states and counties across the country underwent the most wrenching deficits and budget cuts since the Depression. Fairfax and Montgomery counties, though among the wealthiest counties in the United States, were not immune to these pressures.[9] The budget, then, was potentially a key constraint on the implementation of new programs, particularly ones that created zero-sum gains and losses—in which a gain by one program would require a loss by another—by shifting funding in an era of tight budgets. However, although both Weast, the Montgomery superintendent of schools, and Domenech, the Fairfax superintendent, talked about the constraints in the budgets they had to work with, neither of them saw the county or school budgets as the main obstacles to their proposals to shift money to schools in need. As Weast stated:

> The budget becomes a secondary [consideration]. . . . At the board level, we like to think . . . first let's talk about the problem and see if we can really fully identify it. . . . Can you look at it? Can you map it out? Really [have] a thorough discussion of truly what the issues are? And then what does the potential research say about the best way to solve those issues? How does that feel to the folk[s] who are going to be embarking on this, the citizens themselves, the kids themselves? And then, what is the plan, after we've put [it] together, and then what does it cost? And then what is the cost-benefit ratio and how much time does it take?

A little later in the interview he added:

> If this is just something you want to do, or you'd like to do, you're not going to get anywhere. . . . [But if] this is something that you've

got to do in order to maintain those average 1,100 SATs for a district where 81 percent of the kids take the SAT, [and] then to find yourself on the front of the *Wall Street Journal* or on *Newsweek*, this is what you've got to do to maintain that quality. Then it becomes "got to," and when you have put the "got to" label on it, then it becomes "how" and "under what conditions" can you do that.

Of course, one should recall the setting for these remarks: Fairfax and Montgomery counties are among the wealthiest in the United States, and so perhaps school administrators in these counties are relatively free of budgetary constraints. But even in the lean years from 2001 to 2003, when area budgets were under severe strain, school administrators were still able to go forward with their plans to redistribute funds to the neediest schools (see Matthew Mosk, "Shortfall of $23 Million Looms in Montgomery," *Washington Post*, November 23, 2003, C07; Lisa Rein and Tom Jackman, "Fairfax Official Lays Out Plan to Cut Budget," *Washington Post*, April 11, 2002, B01).

Professional Interests

It is possible that if county-level programs had shifted resources to schools with greater numbers of minorities, immigrants, and poorer students, it might have been advocated by bureaucrats whose professional interests would benefit from such a shift. One can also imagine that ESOL administrators might like to see ESOL programs expanded, not only because they believed this was the right policy but also because it would lead to larger budgets and more resources under their control. This scenario might be doubly plausible if funding for the expansion of ESOL and other programs came from the state or federal government rather than the county. In this case, the county might have seen the expansion of ESOL as a free public good, benefiting them at little or no cost. However, both these suppositions are wrong.

Weast pointed out that some of the strongest resistance to his efforts to redirect funding to less well-off schools came from teachers and administrators in those very schools. The resistance from within these schools came because, Weast opined, teaching staff thought "this looks like work—it looks like hard work." It took convincing a cadre of teachers—in this case, the kindergarten teachers where the new funding and accountability were going to be focused—for the program to gain a constituency within the schools. Until then, and until the teachers saw the new program work, there was a preference for letting things continue as they had been going.

In addition, the proposals to reallocate funding among the schools brought in no additional funding from the federal or local. Even having additional ESOL students was not a net gain for the school system. In Virginia, 90 percent of the costs of an ESOL student in these school districts is locally funded, with 9 percent coming from the state and 1 percent from the federal government under the Federal Emergency Immigration Act. Title III of the No Child Left Behind Act requires that the federal government fund ESOL. But funding for the program has not increased in two years and President Bush's proposed fiscal 2004 budget offered no additional funding for ESOL.

The average cost of educating each student in Fairfax Count public schools—dividing the overall budget by the number of students—is about $10,000 per year, and each ESOL student costs Fairfax County an additional $3,000. If the county is contributing 90 percent of an ESOL student's funding, then each ESOL student costs the county an additional $2,700. Immigrants are not cost-free to localities, so it's unlikely that ESOL or other administrators could make the argument that these students brought in additional funding.

Professional Norms and Bureaucratic Ethos

Every bureaucratic agency has a set of norms that express its raison d'être, its mission; less formally, bureaucrats may share an ethos—a way of looking at the world that shapes their policies. Montgomery County Public school system's strategic plan for 2003 to 2008 begins not with a balance sheet or a set of objectives, but with a statement titled "Beliefs" that consists of eighteen bulleted points, including the following:

- All people have equal worth.
- All children are society's highest priority.
- Progress requires openness to change.
- The right to opportunity is nonnegotiable.
- People have the obligation to help one another
- Education for all is a prerequisite for a strong society (Montgomery County Public Schools 2002, 1)

These points illustrate a set of starting principles for policymakers that makes crafting some response to demographic change seem unavoidable—it has already been defined as part of the bureaucracy's mission. Weast expressed these same norms more forcefully. At one point in his interview he described educators as having a covenant with society, and the terms of that covenant required educators to strive to provide the best education they possibly could: "The covenant is not about high quality for some. The covenant is [about] the highest quality for all. Since we are getting more kids who have these needs, then we've got to create new conditions to get them to the [highest] level. You can't lower the level. That breaks the covenant."

Inherent in the view of education as a "covenant" with the community to provide high-quality education is the idea that children with greater needs will receive greater resources, and this redistribution of resources is a public good. Weast also indicated, "We've got to do a better job of reestablishing an egalitarian society because this is a fundamental tenet of democracy. Democracy spins from an educated electorate. Well, if most of your electorate is going to be growing by immigrants or children who have historically been deprived of educational opportunities, then you've got to do something about it."

Again, Weast is describing education as a public good, one fundamental to the workings of a democracy. If one subscribes to Weast's view, leaving immigrant and minority kids behind is not an option. Similarly, Domenech, the Fairfax superintendent, talked at length about how his own immigrant background gave him the perspective to deal with issues of inequity in education, and justified policies redistributing resources as simply the "right thing to do."

Principles, whether formally stated as norms or shared informally as an ethos, fundamentally shape the way bureaucrats think about their policy options and implement change. In the case of Fairfax and Montgomery school administrators, shared norms about equity in education and the opportunity for education for all led to the vigorous implementation of plans to redistribute funding to schools handling the brunt of the racial and ethnic demographic changes to the region.

The Factors Behind Change Reconsidered

Each of the variables discussed—county politics, federal and state mandates, court cases, budget constraints, professional interests, and bureaucratic ethos—together with the very different state contexts for Virginia and Maryland shaped the decisionmaking landscape for the redistributive educational policies pursued in Fairfax and Montgomery County public schools. But the variables' influences were not equal, nor were they even always in the same direction (see compilation of summary data in table 12.1).

As can be seen, educational policies to address racial and ethnic performance gaps generally went against the grain of suburban politics as usual. A combination of factors—demographic shifts, minority representation on

TABLE 12.1   Direction of Variables' Effects on Redistributive
Educational Policies

Variable	Direction	Comments
Electoral politics	Mixed	Minority representation insufficient to determine policy
Federal and state mandates	Positive	Set guidelines favoring attention to minority achievement gap
Court decisions	Negative	Limited race-conscious policies
Budget	Negative	Set constraints on spending; created zero-sum budget politics
Professional interests	Mixed	Professional interests offset by inertia
Bureaucratic norms	Positive	Lens for decisionmaking by key administrators

Source: Author's compilation.

the counties' school boards, federal and state mandates—persuaded administrators that they needed to take significant steps to address the issues brought up by racial and ethnic diversity in the schools. But given the obstacles—the effort required to persuade non-Hispanic white majority lawmakers holding the power of the purse; court cases curtailing race-conscious policies; a period of budget cutbacks; and professional inertia—none of these changes would have been possible without adherence to the norms underlying what many school administrators felt was their educational mission. Without the active intervention of these administrators to implement changes in Montgomery and Fairfax counties' school systems, change would not have happened.

THE PROACTIVE RESPONSE OF EDUCATIONAL BUREAUCRATS

By the early 1990s, administrators in the public school systems of Montgomery and Fairfax counties were fully aware of the unprecedented demographic transformation they were experiencing. Consequently, when both counties found themselves looking for a new school superintendent in the mid-1990s, they sought a particular kind of candidate. Daniel Domenech, Fairfax school superintendent until the spring of 2004, had a background dealing with the complexities of ethnic and racial diversity as a school superintendent in Long Island, New York. He recalled the circumstances of his hiring: "The [Fairfax school] board was very aware, at that time, that this was a school system that was about to undergo some significant demographic changes, and they wanted somebody with my background and experience here in hopes that the system would be able to effectively deal with those significant demographic shifts."

The challenges of ethnic and racial diversity meant that resources had to be found to address the needs of students who were poorer than what the counties had become accustomed to—a native-born, upper-middle class, overwhelmingly white student body. This meant that new policies would have to be crafted not only to allocate resources to the new immigrant and minority students but also probably to redistribute them away from the counties' middle class students. As Domenech noted:

> The strategy for implementing those programs was a carefully crafted one because it meant that we had to divert resources within the school system. We weren't getting any more money from state, federal or county sources. So to do these things, we in essence had to reallocate resources to take it from one area to put it where they were needed. For example, my Project Excel Schools each received, on the average, a million dollars more, for full-day kindergarten, for reduced class size, for the technology and programs that are used in those schools. Our ESOL program has expanded dramatically, as has dual language and full-day K[indergarten]. To do all of these things we had to convince the community that in order for Fairfax County to remain as a world-class organization and to have the average student perform in that we were so proud of, we . . . had to bring the bottom up.

The argument that the bottom had to be brought up for the good of everyone in the school system was brought to bear in Montgomery County as well. Superintendent Weast played out a conversation with an imaginary detractor:

> If you came into me and said, "Look, I'm a big-time taxpayer, my kid is [in a class with a ratio of] 1 to 23 in a kindergarten and you don't pay much taxes and you just got off the boat and your kids are going [to a kindergarten class with a ratio of] 1 to 15 all day . . . Don't you get it? Who votes and who doesn't, here, Jerry?" My answer would be back, yes, I get who votes and who doesn't and I know you do, but, let me tell you, do you get what your property value is based on? It is based on MCPS's [the Montgomery County public school system's] quality, not just your individual child's quality.

This argument was both an appeal to principles, that redistributing funds was the right thing to do, and an appeal to self-interest, that bringing up the scores of the kids on the bottom would ultimately benefit everyone, particularly homeowners, by protecting their investment in their homes and the community.

This combination of appeals to both principles and interests worked. Administrators were able to convince their internal and external constituents—the voters and county councils that approved their budgets, the principals and teachers who would actually be putting the programs into effect and parents with children in the schools. In Fairfax, Domenech claimed opposition to spending on schools with needs was never truly coordinated or organized. There was not much resistance to the proposals:

> Beyond just the grumbling, [it was] never organized. It was always the occasional remark at [school] board meetings or letters to the papers, etc., that, well, here at Great Falls [a wealthy area of Fairfax County] while we are paying all of these taxes . . . and we don't have . . . all these wonderful things . . . [they have in] those other schools. They were right. . . .
>
> And, so, yes, we are diverting resources from your kids and from your schools, but, you know, when the quality of education in Fairfax County starts to slide, the first ones that are going to put their homes up for sale to get out is going to be you folks because these other kids have no place to go. They are here. They don't have much choice. So the quality of the education that everyone is getting and the quality of these schools is dependent on our ability to do what we [have to] do. And, so, that [argument] worked.

Domenech went on to note, "[Detractors] could be angry over what they saw was a reallocation of resources, but, on the other hand, how could they attack me effectively as long as the performance of everyone in the school system kept going up, the performance of their children, as well as the performance of the minority kids."

Again, the superintendent's argument was not only that a reallocation of resources was "the right thing to do" but was also in everyone's interests: spending those resources meant that average test scores continued their upward climb, enhancing the reputation of the school system and, indirectly, keeping property values in the county high. While this section reinforces points highlighted earlier, two items merit further attention. The first is that both Weast and Domenech carefully calibrated their arguments to their audiences. They were aware of the kinds of arguments that would work with different audiences. But it doesn't seem as though these interest-based appeals were what was driving their own decisions. As Superintendent Weast put it, "I'll appeal, I'll use any lever I can and try to figure out any way I need to explain it to get people interested in reengaging in a more egalitarian society, either as an individual reaching out to somebody, or as a contributor. Or, in the worst case, my worst-case scenario, is [that at least they] not get in the way."

The second point is that, whatever the arguments used, proposals to deal with the demographic shifts taking place in schools preceded any external pressures or outside politics. School administrators were the initiators of these policy changes. Political scientists have written about the incorporation of newcomers as taking place only as newcomers accumulate resources and are able to mobilize (or be mobilized) effectively in the political arena. What we see in the suburban counties in the D.C. metropolitan area is something else entirely: bureaucratic actors—in this case, those in the educational system—taking action to incorporate racial and ethnic minorities, well before these administrators are under any political pressure to do so. The timing of the proposals suggests, as does the other evidence presented so far, that the driving force behind these decisions is coming from the schools themselves, and particularly from the administrators making decisions about school policy. What we see, in short, is bureaucratic incorporation.

The Limits of Bureaucratic Incorporation?

The success of the school systems and particularly of their top administrators in formulating a rationale for being proactive in response to growing ethnic and racial diversity, and their ability to sell this rationale to their constituents, shouldn't obscure some of the real constraints on their capacities to respond. The success of Washington's suburban school systems rested on these systems' ability to attract and keep the allegiance of the upper middle class. To capture this constituency, school systems constructed extensive special programs for bright students. Some of these, such as the gifted and talented (GT) programs, are virtual schools within schools: students in these programs can take advanced-placement courses and have little contact with the broader curriculum or student body. Some schools are "magnet schools" emphasizing special subjects, designed to attract students from across the county school system; for instance, Jefferson High School in Fairfax County has an emphasis on science and technology.

Entry into these accelerated programs is exam-based, with student testing as early as first grade for placement in GT classrooms and courses. For instance, members of the entering class of Jefferson High School are largely chosen by means of selecting the top test scorers for the county. These advanced-placement and magnet school programs have a substantial constituency among the county's well-educated upper middle class, who see them as the edge their children need for entrance into elite colleges. In Montgomery County, two thirds of seniors are enrolled in AP courses, and half take AP exams (see Montgomery County Public Schools 2002).

As suburban counties have become more ethnically and racially diverse, some critics have noted that these programs do not mirror the diversity of the student body. Although blacks and Latinos make up 25 percent of students in Fairfax County in the academic year 1999–2001, they made up only 8 percent of those in gifted programs (Liz Seymour, "Too Few Make Cut as Fairfax's Gifted," *Washington Post*, April 28, 2002, C01). The problem, critics said, was that testing worked to the disadvantage of minority kids. "The odds are really stacked against kids who don't come from the most mainstream backgrounds and kids who aren't white," said James H. Borland, a professor and the coordinator of programs in gifted education at Teachers College, Columbia University. "If tests are the gatekeepers . . . they will systematically screen out poorer kids and children of color from their pool," he noted. "If schools are serious enough about identifying gifted kids beyond what's found in white middle class and upper-middle class [neighborhoods], then they have to find other ways to identify those children" (Liz Seymour, "Too Few Make Cut as Fairfax's Gifted," *Washington Post*, April 28, 2002, C01).

Criticism that Fairfax County's classes for the gifted and talented were filled mostly with wealthy white students created pressures for reform, originating in the school board's minority members and its Minority Oversight Board. In 2001, the county's school superintendent announced that the county would change its entry criteria for the program. Beginning that year, students were given an ability test that focused on problem solving and patterns and relationships, in hopes of identifying gifted children who did not speak English and poorer students who didn't score as high on traditional tests.

In addition, the test normally given in first grade to all gifted-program applicants was moved to second grade, thus allowing students another year of school before they were tested. Administrators also allowed students to be considered for GT programs if their parents referred them, even if their test scores didn't immediately qualify them. The result was an increase of nearly 1,000 children in the semifinalist pool, from 2,616 in 2001 to 3,588 in 2002. School officials said that 563 of the additional students in the pool were added due to testing changes and 409 originated from parent and private-school referrals.

Finalists were selected on the basis of a packet of information on each student, including test scores, progress reports, other information from teachers and parents, and samples of the student's work. The changes seem to have had real effects: in 2002 there were 168 percent more Hispanics, 41 percent more African Americans, and 53 percent more Asian Americans in the GT program across the county. Overall, minority students in 2002 made up 36 percent of the GT program, up from 32 percent the previous year (Liz Seymour, "Minorities Swell Pool of Gifted in Fairfax," *Washington Post*, July 3, 2002, B01).

A good example of how these political pressures played out is Thomas Jefferson High School, a magnet that opened in the Fairfax County public school system in 1985. "The concept of the high school was for it to be a school for science and technology, not necessarily a school for GT kids," Domenech said.

> The [school] board's intent was for Jefferson to reflect the diversity in the community. The admissions process into Jefferson had an affirmative action component, which meant that after you went through the typical selection process of the best four hundred kids the selection committee then went into the pool and selected fifty minority candidates that had not made the original group and brought them into that pool and about thirty to forty of them would get into Jefferson on an annual basis. That affirmative action component stopped [in 1998] because of the changing mood of the country on the issue of affirmative action.

As recounted earlier, in 1998 the United States Fourth Circuit Court had ruled in two separate cases that although taking racial and ethnic diversity into account was not necessarily unconstitutional, it had to be both a pressing state need and narrowly tailored as a remedy. Thomas Jefferson High School's admissions process, the school district's lawyers informed Domenech, met neither of these criteria, so the school's admissions committee dropped race as a factor in the intensely competitive admissions process to the school and dismantled a much-lauded preparation program for disadvantaged students.

"The minute that happened," Domenech said, "not surprisingly, minority admissions at Jefferson, just based on the testing process, just dropped to the point of a handful of African American and Hispanic kids." In the academic year 2001–2002, Thomas Jefferson's entering class had only two black students and seven Latinos. Domenech recalled:

> So the [school] board was very concerned and they turned to me and they said, we've got to change this. . . . I talked to the attorneys and the attorneys said, well, you can do anything you want, but you can't do affirmative action. So you can't do what they were doing before and you can't say that you're doing it because of race. So, I looked at the pattern of the middle schools and the number of youngsters that fed into Jefferson from those middle schools and then obviously there was a huge disparity there. There were at least ten to twelve middle schools that never sent anybody to Jefferson, and not surprisingly, those ten to twelve middle schools were those schools that had the greatest percentage of minority and language minority and poor kids. So I came up then with a notion of just geographic representation, that every middle school, based on their enrollment, would have a percentage of the Jefferson population. So the kids that applied to Jefferson from that school, let's say if Whitman Middle School had ten slots and twenty kids applied to Jefferson, well, ten of them would get in to Jefferson and then we would have geographic equity.

It was clear that six of the district's twenty-four middle schools, located in affluent neighborhoods where children were coached years in advance for their entry into Thomas Jefferson High School, accounted for as much as half of each entering class. As Domenech noted, another half dozen schools, located in lower-income neighborhoods with larger black, Hispanic, and immigrant populations, sent few if any students to Jefferson. To fix this imbalance, Domenech proposed a system based on both testing and geographic distribution.

The first phase of applying for the school would remain the same: students would take an entrance exam and the eight hundred or so with the highest scores would become semifinalists. The change would be that these semifinalists would be sorted by school, and the number of slots for each school would be determined proportionally by its eighth-grade enrollment. The greater the number of students in the school, the greater the number of slots the school would be allotted at Jefferson High. The selection committees reviewing the applications would give first preference in each school to students eligible for free or reduced lunch. Then additional students would be given the remaining seats (Liz Seymour, "Parents Decry Minority Plan: Proposal Would Alter Admissions at Jefferson," *Washington Post*, October 1, 2001, B01). By allocating entry slots by school and then within each school to economically disadvantaged students, the proposal would most likely result in significantly higher minority enrollment at Jefferson High School.[10]

As might have been expected, parental opposition, particularly from schools whose entries to the magnet high school were likely to be cut, was ferocious. Domenech:

> Well, when that hit the GT community, they very quickly realized that middle schools like Longfellow, who now send maybe sixty to seventy students to Jefferson, would be restricted to maybe ten or twelve, and that would not do. That community stormed the palace gates and basically scared the hell out of the school board, and the school board retreated and basically shelved the proposal.

The school board received hundreds of emails from aggrieved parents, most of them from the half dozen "feeder schools" that provided the bulk of Thomas Jefferson's entering class—that is, students from the disproportionately white, upper-middle class northeast quadrant of Fairfax County. As Domenech noted, the school board quickly withdrew its plan for a geographical distribution of entry slots into the elite high school.

In response, Bob Frye, the one African American school board representative, proposed an alternative: to create thirty additional places for the September 2002 entering class that would be allocated to middle schools that had been underrepresented in Thomas Jefferson's entering classes. The expectation was that these thirty slots would be drawn from schools with greater percentages of black and Latino students. This expectation was not met. "Unfortunately," Domenech commented, "the way that has worked is that the kids going to Jefferson from those middle schools tend to be the few white middle class kids who live in those communities as opposed to minority kids or language-minority kids or poor kids." Despite these extra thirty students, in academic year 2003–2004 Thomas Jefferson had a student body that was 65 percent white, 28 percent Asian American, 2 percent Latino, and only 1 percent black (the remaining portion of the student body either identified as multiracial, or chose no racial identification).[11]

In his interview in March of 2003, shortly before he stepped down as superintendent, Domenech noted:

> The problem at Jefferson today continues and will continue. I have a lot of issues with that because for me Jefferson should not be a private academy funded with public dollars. Jefferson should be a

school that's available to all of the students in the county and equity should override the strict academic performance. We are not Harvard or Yale or the Potomac Academy. We are a public school system. If we have something good, then every section of the county should have the opportunity to avail themselves of that good thing because it is a county school, it's not just a school for Great Falls or McLean or Oakton or any of those [more well-to-do] areas of the county. But, until such time as there is a willingness on the part of our school board to rethink their philosophy on Jefferson, it will remain predominantly a GT school [oriented] toward primarily white middle class [students], and the Asian community.

This is not the end of the story, however. The Fairfax Board of Education's two minority members sponsored a resolution, passed by the board, for the appointment of an independent blue-ribbon commission to reexamine Thomas Jefferson's admissions procedures and to recommend changes if any were warranted.[12] The panel presented its report in June of 2004 (Fairfax County School Board 2004a), and the school administration, accepting the thrust of the panel's recommendations, proposed changes to the admissions procedure to the magnet school that fall (Fairfax County School Board 2004b).

The successful expansion of GT programs in the lower grades of the Fairfax County public schools stands in contrast to the attempt to adjust the pool of those admitted to Thomas Jefferson High School, indicating both the possibilities and limitations of bureaucratic action. In the first case, GT slots across the county were expanded to allow more children access to GT programs. In the second case, the initial proposal was to reallocate admissions to Thomas Jefferson while the pool of students admitted was essentially capped. The schools' white middle class constituents agreed to the first, but rejected the zero-sum calculations of the second. Domenech acknowledged as much:

I think the key has been to expand and open the doors. In other words, rather than being exclusive as to the GT standards and the GT school-based programs, we have expanded those programs and thereby created more opportunity for minority kids to be in those programs. At the same time there are more white kids because we just expanded it as opposed to restricting it. That's the problem with Jefferson. I don't think anyone would object if we expanded Jefferson so that it would include more schools, as Mr. Frye [the African

American representative to the school board⏋ did, as long as you're not restricting the number of white middle class kids that can go to that school. So expansion will always be a much more agreeable solution than talking necessarily about increasing the percentages ⏌of underrepresented groups⏋.

The Fairfax superintendent was quite aware of realities of politics: in the calculus of politics it's always easier to sell change under conditions of expanding resources than it is to sell change when resources are capped or constrained. The politics of the latter scenario of course becomes zero-sum, and the best-organized groups are likely to mobilize to protect their interests at the expense of groups that have fewer resources to bring to bear in the political process.

This is precisely what happened with Jefferson High School. The most vocal parents—those whose children were attending schools that had historically been overrepresented at Thomas Jefferson, children who would have had a more difficult time getting in under the proposed system of geographic distribution—were also those with the most resources in terms of socioeconomic clout. These were the parents who sent angry emails, attended protest meetings, and applied whatever pressure they could to see that the rules didn't change. Minority parents were much less vocal and active. Given the imbalance of resources, Domenech commented:

> I think if it's a matter of pressure, the status quo will prevail. It's a matter of doing the right thing or it won't get done. Because when you talk about pressure, the minority community is not going to put pressure on the board because the minority community tends to be more concerned with the needs of their lower-achieving students than necessarily the high-achieving students that would be going to Jefferson. There aren't that many of them, or they're not in sufficient number to come out in hordes as the GT ⏌parents⏋ will, and do, and have. So, you're just not going to get the pressure from the minority community.

Domenech was thus well aware of the politics surrounding GT programs such as Thomas Jefferson High School, but he still couched his response in terms of "doing the right thing." The ethos of administrators like Domenech was what kept the admissions issue at Thomas Jefferson alive. Without it, the status quo would have prevailed, and the issue would simply have faded away.

Conclusions

The central puzzle of this chapter is why the suburban schools systems in Fairfax and Montgomery counties chose to implement policies shifting resources to schools with greater numbers of racial and ethnic minorities at a time of shrinking budgets, when in all likelihood this would alienate their middle class constituencies. Why did they choose these policies when they were not under any political pressure to do so? The choice of policy seems to run counter to interest-based theories of politics. The answer, I have suggested in this paper, is that organizations have their own internal norms or professional ethos that may lead bureaucrats to espouse policy change preceding any external political pressure; indeed, these bureaucrats may try to mobilize pressure for policy change themselves.

In the case of educational policy in suburban Washington, D.C., there were a number of other variables also shaping the decisionmaking landscape, but the evidence points to bureaucratic norms and administrators' own ethos as being the key factors behind redistributive policy change. To summarize:

- Despite the fact that Maryland and Virginia have very different political contexts and histories, the policies implemented in Montgomery and Fairfax counties are substantially the same.

- None of the other possible variables—electoral politics, federal and state mandates, court decisions, budgetary issues or professional interests— are sufficient to explain the direction of policy change. Some of these (politics, mandates and professional interests) may have helped to reinforce the direction of educational policy change (while some, court decisions and budget concerns, likely hindered it), but none of these was enough to drive educational policy on their own.

- Federal and state mandates followed, rather than preceded, the redistributive policies that had already been put into effect in the counties, and professional interests were divided, and only coalesced in favor of the policies once it seemed they would be successful. Some elected representatives had raised issues of gaps in the performances of different racial and ethnic groups, but although these groups were key allies for educators, their representatives could not, and did not, drive policy on their own.

- Despite the fact that administrators tailored their arguments for different audiences, the language they use to describe their own positions in favor of redistribution are purely normative.

- Even when redistributive educational policies reach their limits—that is, when they hit the realities of zero-sum politics—the fact that the issues of educational equity and the incorporation of racial and ethnic minorities refuse to go away suggests that something else is at work rather than simply interests.

Taken as a whole, the evidence all points in the direction of a process of bureaucratic incorporation of ethnic and racial newcomers against the interests of many of their core constituents, driven by a professional ethos shared by actors in the educational bureaucracy. Political science has focused on the expression of interests through electoral politics as the engine of policy change and the incorporation of racial and ethnic newcomers. This chapter suggests instead that a kind of "bureaucratic incorporation" can take place, driven by a professional ethos and bureaucratic norms. Change is certainly abetted through electoral access and representation, but bureaucratic action can precede and anticipate electoral pressures. Not all bureaucracies share similar norms and a similar ethos; the preliminary research in the D.C. area suggests that they do not, and that bureaucracies are divided in their orientations by those that are client-driven and those that are primarily regulatory in nature, and that these differences matter substantially in determining the responses of these bureaucracies to immigrants in suburbia.

One should keep in mind, however, that Fairfax and Montgomery counties are among the best-case scenarios for immigrants and minorities in suburbia. They are among the wealthiest counties in the United States and their schools have resources almost unmatched by other school districts around the country. Their graduation rates for minority students are the highest among the fifty largest American school districts: Fairfax ranks first and Montgomery second, according to a study by the Manhattan Institute for Policy Research (Jay Matthews, "Area Schools Rank High in Graduating Minorities," *Washington Post*, November 14, 2001, A01). If school administrators in these counties are driven by a distinct educational ethos to propose redistributive policies, they also generally have the resources to make these policies happen. That may not be true at all times elsewhere. Other case studies of Latino immigrants in school systems in the southern United States—Edmund Harmann's (2003) ethnography of the responsiveness of the Dalton, Georgia, schools and Andrew Wainer's (2004) of schools in the Atlanta, Georgia, suburbs, Research Triangle Park in North Carolina, and northwestern Arkansas—find that administrators are aware of and usually willing to try and tackle issues around the integration of new immigrant students, which supports the bureaucratic-incorporation thesis. However, the studies also suggest that the absence of resources imposes real limits on the ability of schools to deal with demographic change (from the hiring of bilingual personnel to the adoption of new programs to the adaptation of school space), no matter how great their willingness to address the changes taking place. Thus, although the possibility that bureaucratic norms can drive policy merit further exploration, the limits of bureaucratic incorporation must be kept in mind as well.

Finally, the conclusions reached here merit further investigation because they have quite concrete policy implications. Not least of these is that the best advice to new political actors, such as immigrants and other racial and ethnic minorities in suburbia, might be to search out and lobby sympathetic bureaucrats for responsive policy changes, rather than concentrating their energies in trying to tackle the problem of representation in the more impenetrable and sometimes hostile electoral sphere. The response of sympathetic bureaucrats suggests there is more than one avenue to incorporation.

NOTES

1. Throughout this chapter, "whites" refers to non-Hispanic whites, "blacks" refers to non-Hispanic blacks, and "Asians" refers non-Hispanic Asians.

2. Seventy-five percent is greater than the 69 percent of the general population that is white, so whites are somewhat overrepresented in suburbia.

3. The interviews were conducted by the author, together with Lorrie Frasure of the University of Maryland and Junsik Yoon of George Washington University.

4. Around 75 percent of all racial- or ethnic-minority children in elementary schools (79 percent of blacks, 75 percent of Hispanics, and 48 percent of Asians), almost 85 percent of all children whose first language at home is not English (and 74 percent of kids in ESOL classes), and 81 percent of all children receiving federally subsidized school lunches.

5. The legislation is MD SB-856.

6. See Eisenberg v. Montgomery County Public Schools et al., 197 F. 3d 123 (4th Cir. 1999), 19 F. Supp. 2d 449 (D. Md. 1999).

7. See Tuttle v. Arlington County School Board, 195 F. 3d 698 (4th Cir. 1999).

8. Note, however, that the 2003 Supreme Court decision in Grutter v. Bollinger probably had the opposite effect, that of reopening the question of race-conscious admissions policies, particularly in the case of Fairfax County, in connection with the magnet program at Thomas Jefferson High School.

9. In addition, in 1990 Montgomery County amended its county charter to restrict increases in the property tax, which further hobbled its budgetary freedom. The charter amendment limits the growth of annual property tax revenue to the rate of increase in the metropolitan consumer price index

from the previous fiscal year plus the value of new construction. This limit may be exceeded only if seven of nine members of the county council agree to a higher increase.

10. The proposal's strategy is similar in some ways to the alternatives to affirmative action adopted in Texas and Florida, which guarantee entry to the state's publicly financed universities to the top 10 percent of each high school's student body. Because the racial makeup of schools' student bodies reflect their neighborhoods, and because neighborhoods themselves tend to be racially segregated, guaranteeing entry to the best students of every school in essence acts much like the affirmative action programs they replaced.

11. In 1998, the ethnic-racial breakdown at Thomas Jefferson was 70 percent white, 21 percent Asian American, 4 percent Latino and 3 percent African American.

12. In 2003 the board also amended the entrance procedure to allow students to take the Naglieri Nonverbal Ability Test, so that students for whom English might not be their first language would have a greater opportunity to be admitted.

REFERENCES

Dahl, Robert. 1961. *Who Governs? Democracy and Power in the American City.* New Haven, Conn.: Yale University Press.

Fairfax County School Board. "Report of Student Membership by Ethnic Group and Gender." Fairfax, Va.: Fairfax County School Board. Accessed at http://www.fcps.edu/Reporting/historical.index.html.

———. 2004a. "Report of Fairfax County School Board Blue Ribbon Committee on Admissions." Fairfax, Va.: Fairfax County Public Schools, Office of the Superintendent. Accessed at http://www.fcps.edu/schlbd/ws06-07-04/blueribbon.pdf.

———. 2004b. "Fairfax County Public Schools Memorandum to School Board from Brad Draeger." Fairfax, Va.: Fairfax County Public Schools, Office of the Superintendent. Accessed at http://www.fcps.edu/schlbd/ws7-12-04/TJHSST.pdf

Frey, William. 2001. *Melting Pot Metros: A Census 2000 Study of Suburban Diversity.* Washington: Brookings Institution, Center for Urban and Metropolitan Policy, June 2001. Accessed at http://www.brookings.edu/es.urban/census/frey.pdf.

Harmann, Edmund. 2003. *The Educational Welcome of Latinos in the New South.* Westport, Conn.: Praeger.

Humes, Karen, and Jesse McKinnon. 2000. "Asian and Pacific Islander Population in the United States, March 1999." Current Population Reports. Washington: U.S. Government Printing Office.

McKinnon, Jesse, and Karen Humes. 2000. "Black Population in the United States, March 1999." Current Population Reports. Washington: U.S. Government Printing Office.

Montgomery County Public Schools. 2002. "2003–2008 Strategic Plan: A Successful Tomorrow Begins Today." Report. Rockville, Md.: Montgomery County Public Schools.

Price, Marie, Ivan Cheung, Samantha Friedman, and Audrey Singer. 2005. "The World settles In: Washington, D.C. as an Immigrant Gateway." *Urban Geography* 26(1): 61–83.

Schmidley, A. Dianne, and Campbell Gibson. 1999. "Profile of the Foreign Born Population in the United States." Current Population Reports. Washington: U.S. Government Printing Office.

Singer, Audrey. 2003. *The Rise of the New Immigrant Gateways.* Washington: Brookings Institution, Center for Urban and Metropolitan Policy.

U.S. Census Bureau. 2001. *2000 Summary File 1, 100 Percent Data.* Washington: U.S. Census Bureau.

Wainer, Andrew. 2004. *The New Latino South and the Challenge to Public Education: Strategies for Educators and Policymakers in Emerging Immigrant Communities.* Los Angeles, Calif.: University of Southern California, School of Policy, Planning and Development, Tomás Rivera Policy Institute.

PART III

$\diagdown\!\!\!\!\diagup$

CONCLUSION

CHAPTER 13

ASSIMILATION IN A NEW GEOGRAPHY

DOUGLAS S. MASSEY

The foregoing chapters have clearly documented the remarkable transformation of immigration to the United States that began during the 1990s and continued into the early years of the twenty-first century. During this time, immigration shifted from being a regional phenomenon affecting a handful of states and a few metropolitan areas to a national phenomenon affecting communities of all sizes throughout all fifty states. Although this geographic diversification of destinations was experienced by all immigrant groups, it was most evident among Mexicans and, to a lesser extent, other Latin Americans. Among major immigrant groups, the diversification of destination was least evident for Asians. As a result of this unprecedented geographic transformation, millions of native white and black Americans found themselves directly exposed to the Spanish language and to Latin American culture for the very first time.

CAUSES OF GEOGRAPHIC DIVERSIFICATION

The fact that the geographic diversification was most significant among Mexicans suggests the relevance of United States border policies to the transformation. The 1990s were characterized by the selective hardening of the border in two sectors—the Tijuana–San Diego and Juarez–El Paso border crossings in California and Texas, respectively, which earlier had been the two busiest border-crossing points, where more than 80 percent of undocumented migrants had entered the United States (Massey, Durand, and Malone 2002). The placement of steel walls and metal fences in these sectors was accompanied by the deployment of newly hired U.S. Border Patrol officers and newly purchased detection equipment on the American side, and together these measures raised the odds of apprehension to the point where the likelihood of capture became quite high (Durand and Massey 2003). In response, migrants quite rationally sought out new crossing points that lacked such concentrations of enforcement resources, notably the desert between Sonora State and Arizona, thereby deflecting migratory flows away from historical pathways and toward new destinations outside traditional gateway cities in California, Texas, and Illinois (Orrenius 2004).

Although the diversification of destinations was most pronounced among Mexicans, it was not confined to them, and its emergence among other immigrant groups, especially Latinos from Central and South America, suggests that other forces besides border enforcement were also at work in effecting the transformation. Judging from the chapters in this volume, foremost among these forces is the restructuring of manufacturing, particularly nondurables manufacturing, and food processing that occurred in the final decades of the twentieth century. Producers of apparel, meat, poultry, and other agricultural products came under intense competitive pressure during the 1990s as the economy globalized and foreign producers gained access to American markets. In order to keep plants in the United States and prevent their relocation overseas, American firms responded by consolidating ownership to achieve administrative efficiencies and economies of scale. Then, in factory after factory, the consolidated corporate owners undertook a massive deskilling of the productive process, a deunionization of the workforce, and the subcontracting of labor. These actions often required closing unionized factories with skilled workers in metropolitan areas and opening new, larger, and more efficient factories with unskilled workers in nonmetropolitan areas. In some cases, plants in smaller communities that were unionized were simply closed and reopened under a new production regime and new terms of employment; in the process the workforce in such factories shifted from predominantly native to predominantly foreign.

This restructuring of production may have been taken to ensure survival in a global market and preserve American jobs, but it made the jobs that remained in this country much less attractive to native-born workers. In addition, the relocation of plants to nonmetropolitan areas may have worked to escape the areas where unions were centered, but it placed the plants in a demographic setting characterized by a declining, aging population and few young people, thereby necessitating the recruitment of workers from elsewhere. The only people really interested in moving to nonunionized plants located in small towns in out-of-the-way states were foreigners, mainly workers from poorer nations in Latin America, particularly Mexico.

In most cases, immigration to new destinations in the South and Midwest did not simply erupt spontaneously, but was jump-started by private recruitment efforts. Companies took out ads in Mexican newspapers and broadcast the availability of jobs on Mexican radio and then sent down subcontractors to recruit workers directly, at times under the auspices of the program of temporary H-visas, but more often outside of official channels. As Mark Leach and Frank D. Bean note (see chapter 3), however the flows began, once started they continued to perpetuate themselves through network-based processes of cumulative causation. In a few short years, places that had no experience of immigration within living memory suddenly came to house large pluralities, and sometimes even majorities, of foreign-born residents, overwhelming local schools, clinics, hospitals, and other social services that were ill equipped to handle a rapid increase in clients, much less the sudden appearance of immigrants speaking different languages and bearing unfamiliar cultures.

THE PROSPECTS FOR ASSIMILATION

As several chapters chronicle, within the new receiving communities, native-born Americans occupying administrative, professional, and other privileged positions generally expressed openness and tolerance with respect to the newcomers, whereas working class natives, especially in nonmetropolitan areas that had never before experienced immigration, at best expressed ambivalence and often expressed outright hostility toward the Spanish-speaking arrivals. As several authors in this book have shown, tensions were particularly acute in the South, where the arrival of large numbers of brown-skinned people upset a traditional system of race relations that historically had revolved around a black-white color line and a one-drop rule of racial identification, whereby just "one drop" of black blood meant that one's social identity was that of a black person. Moreover, given the legacy of Jim Crow and the imperfect realization of civil rights after the 1960s, African Americans often felt more threatened than whites and generally expressed greater animosity toward the new immigrants, though the degree of hostility varied depending on the relative size of the black population and whether one considers the political or economic realm.

Despite acknowledging these emerging indications of nativism, xenophobia, and anti-immigrant hostility, most of the authors remain mostly cautiously optimistic about the prospects for assimilation, suggesting that today's immigrants will follow in the path of those in the past and integrate into American society by learning English, forming relationships with native-born Americans, moving up the economic ladder, and eventually intermarrying with native-born European Americans. Although they recognize that United States labor markets may be more segmented now than in the past, and that immigrants today have relatively less education than in earlier times, they take comfort in the fact that, culturally and socially, American society is much more open and tolerant than it was before the 1960s. In general, strict norms of Anglo conformity no longer prevail and unilateral assimilation to the "American way of life" is not demanded in the way it once was.

As evidence for their sanguine view, the authors point to immigrants' low rates of retention of their original languages, significant socioeconomic progress among immigrants who spend significant time in the United States, clear evidence of intergenerational mobility, and relatively high rates of intermarriage between European whites and both Hispanics and Asians in the second and third generations. Against this optimistic scenario, however, I see at least five reasons to believe that the path of immigrant adaptation may be more difficult than in the past and that worry about the future of assimilation is not entirely misplaced. The features of contemporary American society that give me pause are the changed nature of the United States' opportunity structure; the stagnation of educational achievement beyond the second generation; the perpetual nature of contemporary immigration; the rapid growth of the undocumented population; and remarkable revival of immigrant baiting and ethnic demonization currently being undertaken by demagogues in politics, the media, and even academia.

After World War II, the postwar economic boom was a major engine driving the assimilation of the children and grandchildren of immigrants from Southern and Eastern Europe (Alba and Nee 2003), which steadily increased earnings throughout the income distribution and offered unprecedented opportunities for social mobility as the service sector expanded while the manufacturing sector remained strong (Levy 1998). From 1945 to 1975, average incomes rose, poverty rates dropped, and millions of Americans entered the middle class, purchasing homes, cars, and a new panoply of consumer goods. In such an economy, it was possible for working class Americans with no more than a high school degree to advance economically, thanks to strong unions and generous contracts. Millions of working class parents were able to use this firm economic base to purchase a college education for their children, many of whom went on to become a part of the white collar world. The end result was a "diamond shaped" socioeconomic distribution that was wide in the middle and narrow at the top and bottom and that provided numerous avenues for mobility and material improvement, many of which did not rely on educational achievement (Massey 2007).

After 1975, however, this fluid socioeconomic structure which was so conducive to intergenerational mobility and integration came under increasing attack both internally and externally—internationally from rising competition in the global marketplace that was exacerbated by an oil crisis and domestically from the collapse of the economically progressive New Deal coalition over the issue of race (Massey 2005). From 1975 to 2005, median incomes stagnated, real wages fell, income inequality increased, wealth distributions polarized, and both poverty and affluence became more concentrated geographically (Massey 2007). Instead of a diamond-shape structure, the socioeconomic distribution increasingly resembled an "hourglass," with large strata at the top and bottom and a small stratum in between, a configuration offering few opportunities for mobility for those without a college education (Massey and Hirst 1998).

In the new political economy, workers faced bleak economic prospects as levels of unionization declined to record lows, strikes became a rarity, wages fell in real terms, benefits steadily eroded, and federal safety nets that had been erected in the New Deal and Lyndon Johnson's Great Society were steadily cut back (Massey 2007). The only reliable way to advance in the new postindustrial economy was through the acquisition of education, and increasingly not simply a college degree but postgraduate education was needed (Massey 2000). The economic returns to education skyrocketed during the 1980s and 1990s (Autor, Katz, and Kearny 2006). Those who possessed high levels of education were able to earn high salaries and to translate their material security into education for their children, thus passing on their advantaged class position (Massey 2007).

Unfortunately, access to education is not equally distributed and as the income distribution polarized over time, so did the distribution of schools offering high-quality education (Phillips and Chin 2004). Given the very low levels of schooling possessed by most Mexican immigrants to the United States (an average of eight years), educational achievement has been particularly problematic for their children and grandchildren. Although studies generally confirm a substantial upgrading of educational attainment from the first to the second generation, this improvement reflects the very low educational level of parents as much as the attainments of their children, and a particularly troubling pattern is the apparent stagnation of attainment in the third and fourth generations, with the result that the average level of schooling of native-born is just twelve years (Smith 2003; Tienda and Mitchell 2006; Telles and Ortiz forthcoming). Clearly this offers a poor prognosis for these citizens' economic future in the United

States, as high school education is no longer sufficient to ensure membership in the middle class, much less to gain access to the higher reaches of the hourglass economy.

In addition to the favorable opportunity structure of the postwar political economy and the mobility it provided to those with little more than a high school education, another factor in the assimilation of the children and grandchildren of European immigrants was the long hiatus in immigration that occurred between 1925 and 1965 (Massey 1995). The passage of restrictive immigration quotas in the early 1920s and the economic depression that began in 1929 effectively ended immigration from Southern and Eastern Europe—indeed, it ended virtually all immigration for several decades.

As a result of this hiatus, processes of adaptation, integration, and mobility played out within just one or two generations at a time. Ethnic identity, which was dominated by the experience of first and second generation immigrants before the 1940s, came to be defined by the experiences of second generation immigrants from 1945 to 1975 and by third and fourth generation immigrants thereafter—with no renewal of the first generation by arriving immigrants. The absence of new immigrants—who would have lacked English and would have brought with them the cultures of their sending countries—thus facilitated assimilation of the earlier wave of European immigrants.

Immigration since 1965 has seen no hiatus, even for a short period, much less for decades. Mexican immigration has been constant since it was revived by the Bracero program in the 1940s, and additions to the Mexican-origin population have been steady. Similar trends are observed for other Latin American groups beginning in the 1970s. As a consequence, Latin American immigrant populations in general and Mexicans in particular are characterized by a multigenerational complexity that never prevailed for Italians, Poles, or Russian Jews. Rather than being defined by steady advance of generation cohorts without experiencing "dilution" from newcomers, Mexican identity is constantly renewed by large numbers of new immigrants. Now, the Mexican American population comprises people who have just arrived from Mexico, long-settled immigrants, native-born children and grandchildren, and even significant numbers in the fourth and fifth generations (Telles and Ortiz forthcoming). In sum, since the 1940s the Mexican-origin population has steadily been renewed linguistically and culturally by a constant stream of new arrivals from south of the border.

If anything, in recent years there has been a dramatic increase in the rate of growth and thus of the proportion of the foreign-born Mexican origin population (Massey, Durand, and Malone 2002) as the rate of return migration has fallen, in response to America's militarization of the Mexico-United States border. Unlike earlier cohorts of European immigrants, moreover, these most recent arrivals from Mexico and Latin America generally have undocumented status, especially those going to new destination areas. Never before has such a large share of immigrants—those with illegal status—lacked even the most elemental economic, social, and political rights (Massey and Bartley 2005). At present at least half of all foreign-born Mexicans in the United States—and a fifth of all persons of Mexican origin—are undocumented (Massey 2007). The growing share of undocumented Mexican migrants is far more exploitable and patently much less assimilable than earlier immigrants.

Consequently, in my view predictions that today's Mexican and Latino immigrants will follow the path to assimilation established by earlier cohorts of immigrants are hardly assured, despite the prevailing optimism. In contrast to European immigrants earlier in the twentieth century, and even Latino immigrants arriving before 1980, the latest arrivals face a remarkably unfavorable context for adaptation, integration, and assimilation. Mexicans, in particular, are arriving and settling in growing numbers with no sign of a hiatus to facilitate the process of assimilation. Most of these newcomers arrive without legal documents and possess low levels of education, and once in the United States they face a polarized hourglass economy that offers few avenues of upward mobility without a college education. Moreover, despite educational progress between the first and second generations, the gains are insufficient to assure middle class status in a postindustrial economy and even these modest educational gains are not sustained into the third generation and beyond.

In sum, Mexicans are poorly equipped to compete in an economy where the returns to education are sharply rising and a college degree has become a prerequisite of middle class status. And if these conditions are not daunting enough, public discourse has taken a sharp turn toward nativism and xenophobia in recent decades and anti-Mexican hostility has risen to new heights. Leo R. Chavez (2001) examined magazine covers relating to articles about immigration in American publications between 1965 and 2000 and coded them as "affirmative" (with text and images celebrating immigration), "alarmist" (with text and images conveying problems, fears, and dangers associated with immigration), or "neutral" (text and images in articles that offered balanced and factual coverage of immigration). He found that nearly three quarters of the covers were alarmist and the prevalence of alarmist covers steadily increase through the 1970s, 1980s, and 1990s.

Chavez (2001) found that the most common metaphorical device used to frame alarmist covers was martial in nature, portraying the border as a "battleground" that was "under attack" from "alien invaders" and where Border Patrol agents were "outgunned" "defenders" trying to "hold the line" against attacking "hoards." Within the United States, illegal aliens constituted a "ticking time bomb" waiting to explode and destroy American culture and values. Whatever the framing device, however, immigration from Latin America was always portrayed as a "crisis."

Although anti-immigrant sentiments may have been visible before 2001, after the events of September 11 they have became more public and strident. In academia, Professor Samuel P. Huntington (2004, 30–32) of Harvard warned Americans of the "Hispanic Challenge," which threatened "to divide the United States into two peoples, two cultures, and two languages": "Unlike past immigrant groups, Mexicans and other Latinos have not assimilated into mainstream U.S. culture, forming instead their own political and linguistic enclaves—from Los Angeles to Miami—and rejecting the Anglo-Protestant values that built the American dream. . . . The United States ignores this challenge at its peril."

In similar vein, the former presidential candidate and political pundit Patrick Buchanan (2006) sees a "state of emergency" brought about by the "third world invasion and conquest of America." In his recent book, aptly titled *State of Emergency* (2006), he revealed to Americans the existence of an "Aztlán Plot" hatched by Mexican elites to "reconquer" lands lost in 1848, when the United States annexed the northern third of Mexico in the wake of the Mexican-American War. In an interview with *Time* magazine (August 28, 2006, 6), Buchanan warned, "If we do not get control of our borders and stop this greatest invasion in history, I see the dissolution of the U.S. and the loss of the American Southwest—culturally and linguistically, if not politically—to Mexico."

This alarmist attitude is perhaps given its maximum expression in the nightly commentaries of Lou Dobbs, the anchor and managing editor of CNN's popular *Lou Dobbs Tonight*, which has a viewing audience of about 800,000. At the beginning of his March 21, 2007, broadcast, for example, he announced a series devoted to the "broken border" and the "illegal alien invasion" it caused. Calling on viewers to "feel violated," he argued that "a common front in our illegal-alien crisis [is] the war on drugs and the global war on terror. That front line is easily defined as our nation's borders, airports, and seaports. And Arizonans know only too well the pain and problems of living and working on the front line of our border with Mexico."

It is perhaps too early to tell what effect these blatant appeals to nativism and xenophobia might have on American public opinion or on the acceptance of immigrants within American society. Recent work by Tiane L. Lee and Susan T. Fiske (2006) suggests that undocumented migrants have moved into the perceptual space of American social cognition usually reserved for despised out-groups such as drug dealers and the homeless Whatever the ultimate influence of these anti-immigrant tirades, they represent a level of ethnic demonization not seen since the 1920s (see Higham 1955); whatever their intent, they clearly serve to harden the lines of categorical inequality between immigrants and the native-born population (Massey 2007).

NEW PLACES, NEW ASSIMILATION?

This troubling societal context prevails for immigrants in traditional as well as new destination areas, and can be expected to undermine the prospects for assimilation throughout the United States. But in many ways traditional immigrant gateways such as New York, Chicago, Los Angeles, Miami, and Houston are quite different from the new, nonmetropolitan destinations that emerged in the 1990s. Natives in traditional immigrant-receiving cities have considerable experience interacting with immigrants on a daily basis and often have immigrant roots themselves, making them quite tolerant of the newcomers. In addition, native inhabitants of gateway metropolitan areas are among the most educated of all Americans, and pro-immigrant attitudes generally rise with schooling (Haubert and Fussell 2006).

Gateway areas are also home to well-developed institutions within and outside the immigrant community to facilitate integration and advancement. Government institutions generally have multilingual specialists so that immigrants seeking public services can communicate in their native language. Bilingual classrooms, ballots, and written instructions are commonplace, and people in positions of public responsibility are often second- or third-generation immigrants themselves, who if they do not speak the language will at least share many cultural affinities with the newcomers. At the same time, in gateway cities numerous civil organizations such as the ACLU (American Civil Liberties Union), the National Council of La Raza, the Mexican American Legal Defense Fund, the League of Latin American Citizens, and the National Council of Churches generally are on hand to provide assistance and defend the interests of immigrants and their children. Private welfare and social-service agencies are also prevalent to provide material assistance, not to mention immigrants' own hometown associations and other civic organizations.

In a very real way, gateway cities have historically served as "assimilation machines" for the nation, incorporating immigrants, helping them to adjust to American society, and turning their children into Americans who then move outward to encounter native whites and blacks in the rest of the country. Gateway cities thus served as buffers between the masses of immigrants and the rest of American society, easing their entry so that most natives never encountered relatively unassimilated, monolingual, and culturally foreign immigrants, only their English-speaking children and grandchildren who had grown up in the United States, attended American schools, and were substantially Americanized.

The geographic dispersion of immigrants away from urban gateways into smaller communities throughout the country means that for the first time in living memory, millions of natives lacking any experience with foreigners are now having and will continue to have direct and sustained contact with unassimilated immigrants. In the new destinations, moreover, immigrants will have few institutional resources to rely on to bridge the social and cultural gap. How this experiment in intergroup relations will play out is, of course, an open question, but whatever happens, low levels of immigrant education and the rising tide of xenophobia cannot help the situation. One thing is crystal clear: undocumented status constitutes an unprecedented barrier to immigrant integration. Removing this barrier is an essential first step in giving the new immigrants a fighting chance of realizing the American dream.

REFERENCES

Alba, Richard D., and Victor Nee. 2003. *Remaking the American Mainstream: Assimilation and Contemporary Immigration*. Cambridge, Mass.: Harvard University Press.

Autor, David H., Lawrence F. Katz, and Melissa S. Kearney. 2006. "The Polarization of the U.S. Labor Market." *American Economic Review* 96(1): 189–94.

Buchanan, Patrick J. 2006. *State of Emergency: The Third World Invasion and Conquest of America*. New York: Thomas Dunne Books.

Chavez, Leo R. 2001. *Covering Immigration: Population Images and the Politics of the Nation*. Berkeley, Calif.: University of California Press.

Durand, Jorge, and Douglas S. Massey. 2003. "The Costs of Contradiction: U.S. Immigration Policy 1986–1996." *Latino Studies* 1(2): 233–52.

Haubert, Jeannie, and Elizabeth Fussell. 2006. "Explaining Pro-Immigrant Sentiment in the U.S." *International Migration Review* 40(3): 489–507.

Higham, John. 1955. *Strangers in the Land: Patterns of American Nativism, 1860–1925*. New Brunswick, N.J.: Rutgers University Press.

Huntington, Samuel P. 2004. "The Hispanic Challenge." *Foreign Policy* March–April(141): 1–12. Accessed at http://www.foreignpolicy.com/story/cms.php?story_id=2495.

Lee, Tiane L., and Susan T. Fiske. 2006. "Not an Outgroup, Not Yet an Ingroup: Immigrants in the Stereotype Content Model." *International Journal of Intercultural Relations* 30(6): 751–68.

Levy, Frank. 1998. *The New Dollars and Dreams: American Incomes and Economic Change.* New York: Russell Sage Foundation.

Massey, Douglas S. 1995. "The New Immigration and the Meaning of Ethnicity in the United States." *Population and Development Review* 21(3): 631–52.

———. 2000. "Higher Education and Social Mobility in the United States, 1940–1998." In *America's Research Universities: Quality, Innovation, Partnership,* edited by Ann Leigh Speicher. Washington: Association of American Universities.

———. 2005. *Return of the L-Word: A Liberal Vision for the New Century.* Princeton, N.J.: Princeton University Press.

———. 2007. *Categorically Unequal: The American Stratification System.* New York: Russell Sage Foundation.

Massey, Douglas S., and Katherine Bartley. 2005. "The Changing Legal Status Distribution of Immigrants: A Caution." *International Migration Review* 39(2): 469–84.

Massey, Douglas S., and Deborah Hirst. 1998. "From Escalator to Hourglass: Changes in the U.S. Occupational Wage Structure: 1949–1989." *Social Science Research* 27(1): 51–71.

Massey, Douglas S., Jorge Durand, and Nolan J. Malone. 2002. *Beyond Smoke and Mirrors: Mexican Immigration in an Age of Economic Integration.* New York: Russell Sage Foundation.

Orrenius, Pia. 2004. "The Effect of U.S. Border Enforcement on the Crossing Behavior of Mexican Migrants." In *Crossing the Border: Research from the Mexican Migration Project,* edited by Jorge Durand and Douglas S. Massey. New York: Russell Sage Foundation.

Phillips, Meredith, and Tiffani Chin. 2004. "School Inequality: What Do We Know?" In *Social Inequality,* edited by Kathryn Neckerman. New York: Russell Sage Foundation.

Smith, James P. 2003. "Assimilation Across the Latino Generations." *American Economic Review* 93(2): 315–19.

Telles, Edward E., and Vilma Ortiz. Forthcoming. *Generations of Exclusion: Racialization, Assimilation, and Mexican Americans.* New York: Russell Sage Foundation.

Tienda, Marta, and Faith Mitchell. 2006. *Multiple Origins, Uncertain Destinies: Hispanics and the American Future.* Washington: National Academies Press.

INDEX

⋎